SITTING BULL, CRAZY HORSE, GOLD, AND GUNS

The 1874 Yellowstone Wagon Road and Prospecting Expedition

AND THE BATTLE OF LODGE GRASS CREEK

COL. FRENCH L. MACLEAN, US ARMY (Ret.)

Schiffer Publishing Ltd

4880 Lower Valley Road • Atglen, PA 19310

Library of Congress Control Number: 2016940136

Designed by Molly Shields
Type set in Aachen BT/Times New Roman
ISBN: 978-0-7643-5151-8
Printed in China

Published by Schiffer Publishing, Ltd.
4880 Lower Valley Road
Atglen, PA 19310
Phone: (610) 593-1777; Fax: (610) 593-2002
E-mail: Info@schifferbooks.com
Web: www.schifferbooks.com

Other Schiffer Books by the Author:
The Fifth Field (978-0-7643-4577-7)
Dönitz's Crews (978-0-7643-3356-9)
Custer's Best (978-0-7643-3757-4)

Other Schiffer Books on Related Subjects:
The Officer Corps of Custer's Seventh Cavalry by James B. Klockner (978-0-7643-2660-8)
Fort Abraham Lincoln by Lee Chambers (978-0-7643-3026-1)
No Greater Calling by Eric S. Johnson (978-0-7643-4255-4)

For our complete selection of fine books on this and related subjects, please visit our website at www.schifferbooks.com. You may also write for a free catalog.

Schiffer Publishing's titles are available at special discounts for bulk purchases for sales promotions or premiums. Special editions, including personalized covers, corporate imprints, and excerpts, can be created in large quantities for special needs. For more information, contact the publisher.

We are always looking for people to write books on new and related subjects. If you have an idea for a book, please contact us at proposals@schifferbooks.com.

Contents

Foreword

In Memory – Boot Hill and Crazy Horse

In Memory

of those who blazed the trail
and showed to us our west
in boots and spurs they lie
and on the hill find rest.

The stream flows on, but it matters not
to the sleepers here by the world forgot.
The heroes of many a tale unsung,
they lived and died when the west was young.

This monument marks a historic spot
where thirty-five lie buried.
They played the drama called life for fortune
and fame.
Lost their lives; lost their game.

Upon this rugged hill
the long trail past,
these men of restless will
find rest at last.

The stream flows on, but it matters not
to the sleepers here by the world forgot.
The heroes of many a tale unsung,
they lived and died when the west was young.

— Boot Hill Cemetery memorial inscription, Billings, Montana

"My lands are where my dead lie buried."

— Reported statement by Crazy Horse

Voices from the Past

"It's the Big Horn country, an' someday some feller with book larnin' will write it up."

— Ben Walker, 1874 Yellowstone Wagon Road and Prospecting Expedition, buried in Boot Hill Cemetery

"A bunch of us was called the 'sooner mess' because we were strangers and of doubtful character. Some of this gang had been run out of Texas, Nevada and other states and were tough as well could be. Of us, it was said, that they would have to kick us out from under the wagons to get us to fight, but they never did. In my opinion there never were as tough a band of men together in the mountains. We were always ready for trouble and quit a friend in need."

— Charles Avery, 1874 Yellowstone Wagon Road and Prospecting Expedition

"This was the expedition which brought on the war of 1876 that was so disastrous to General Custer and his command."

— William T. "Uncle Billy" Hamilton, 1874 Yellowstone Wagon Road and Prospecting Expedition

"That is about all the information I can give you because at that time I was so badly scared

that I didn't know whether I was in Montana or Idaho."

— Tom Allen, 1874 Yellowstone Wagon Road and Prospecting Expedition

THE STORY OF THE KILLING OF SITTING BULL'S SON

Which was Accomplished by John ANDERSON, colored, of Bozeman, one of Gallatin County's Most Respected Citizens—Rare Bravery Displayed—Amid a Rainstorm of Bullets he Goes Into The Very Jaws of Death and Takes the Scalp of Sitting Bull Jr.

No story of bravery and of courting death at the hands of the pesky redskins by the pioneer scouts have excelled the record of John Anderson of Bozeman. He is a natural born fighter, and even unto today he holds the record in the Gallatin Valley for his prowess as a hunter of the wild game that abounds so plentifully in the mountains adjacent to the fertile valley of the Gallatin. The publisher of THE PLAINDEALER heard the confirmation of this story from Mr. Anderson's own lips, and the scalp of Sitting Bull, Jr., which is at the apartments of Mr. Bogart is still a silent witness to the hair-raising encounter on this occasion.

Mr. Anderson informed us that he disposed of the shirt and cap of the Indian Chief some years ago for $300, and had been offered $1,000 for the scalp, but that he would never need money badly enough to sell it.

This encounter was along about '74 in the Rosebud and Tongue River Country, which was a perilous time in Montana's history.

The following is the story told by an eyewitness of the killing of the son of the famous Sioux Chief, Sitting Bull:

"It was a beautiful day, and our party had planned a trip into the hills where we thought gold could be found. We had been surveying the country in a roundabout way of fix our position relative to what we had reason to believe was held by the enemy, the Sioux. It was midday, and the sun shone in tropical splendor, still it was not hot—travel was not tedious or inconvenient.

"But there is nothing certain in times like those, and while we exulted over the glorious possibilities which lay before us, a cloud of dust arose in the distance over the brow of a hill, and we guessed the cause of it. Before an expression could be put into words, a swarm of Indians appeared on the brow of the low hill. The leader exercised a wonderful influence over his men, and by a mere wave of his hand the entire division of Sitting Bull's Army halted. One by one, and in pairs, and in fours and squads the full strength of the army gradually presented itself to our view. There were less than one hundred and fifty in our party, and what to do and how but a moment's thought. We must retreat, and go it in a hurry.

"All but twelve hacked into a kind of draw or gully, out of sight of the red devils, who still held the top of the hill in magnificent alignment. The Chief drew away from his men and rode the war circle in our front, bearing to the right and nearing our squad of twelve. Defiantly he galloped to the left and cut in directly towards us, shouting that demoniacal shout so common then.

"The rest of our men retreated down the draw, and as they disappeared they continued to call to us to follow. Why we did not follow is a mystery explainable only, perhaps, by that dominant desire to kill an Indian.

"There was no command—it was as if the invisible hand had signaled for action, and simultaneously twelve shots rang out. The Indian Chief fell.

"Still, the army, budged not a foot, it was resting upon the crest of the hill. Probably ignorance of our position and strength held the Indians in check, for they did not essay to take up the war cry. Our men had disappeared down the draw, but were still within earshot range of our action. As we fired, we sank back into a coulee and expected an attack momentarily from the overwhelming numbers.

We were in a tight place, and after the shots we realized our utterly defenseless position.

"But now that we had disabled the Indian Chief (we thought at first he had been killed,) it was our desire and determination at all hazards to take his scalp away with us. He lay motionless upon the ground. His horse was nearby eating good bunch grass. Anderson was first to notice his first move—the Chief raised his head slightly as if trying to signal an order to his men. Anderson raised his head over the top of the little mound behind which we lay, and a terrific shower of bullets literally harrowed the ground directly in front of us.

"We consulted hastily and agreed to run the gauntlet, and escape if possible. But Anderson declared that he would take that Indian's scalp if he died in the attempt, and with a bound he sprang towards the dying Chief who lay but a few paces ahead of us, he ran like a demon, and the bullets pecked the earth all round about him. He shouted to the Chief, who raised his arm, and dropped it in to his pistol holster; in a flash he whipped out the gun and we could hear the clicking of the hammer as it was brought up for action. But before he could bring it into play, Anderson had driven his dirk into the breast of Sitting Bull's son. He ripped the front of that red Chief from his heart clear down to his abdomen.

"The bullets continued to hail about him, and we continued to shout at the now almost insane Anderson to retreat and follow us out of range of what looked like sure death.

"No retreat for Anderson. He crouched behind the bleeding corpse, and the bullets peppered the ground like shot from a tower. He tugged and hauled and shouted like mad and swore defiance at the bloodthirsty reds, who by the way retained their positions, not advancing a foot, but continued to fire in rapidly recurring volley.

"For a hundred feet Anderson carried the limp corpse, backing down towards us holding his dead enemy in front as a sort of shield for his own unpunctured hide. When he reached the draw he was as bloody as the man he had disemboweled. He was a terrible looking sight, but he smiled and seemed to enjoy it to the limit.

"Finally he dropped the burden at our feet. Each member of the party took a cut of the scalp, and old Sitting Bull's son was duly and scientifically scalped. The head piece was cut into bits and each man retained a piece as a souvenir of the day's sport. But Anderson insisted on keeping the war bonnet and shirt. It was a magnificent bonnet, a fine piece of Indian workmanship: a veritable war bonnet, one like you read about. He had indeed earned the prize.

"With the trophies in our saddle bags we disappeared down the draw and were soon with our main party. A mile down the depression we saw the chief's army, but we did not wait to learn which trail they took, for we hastened down the river, and thus another escape was effected."

— "The Story of the Killing of Sitting Bull's Son," *The Montana Plaindealer*, July 13, 1906, Helena, Montana.

Acknowledgments

"Did I ever tell you about the battle that took place here back in the old days?" That question, from Montana rancher Ron Wald as we sat on his porch one glorious June morning, piqued my interest and set this entire project in motion. Ron—who easily could pass as a reincarnated "Marlboro Man"—later explained what had happened on the valley floor now under irrigation and on the rising slopes next to his son's ranch; he later graciously allowed me to drive around the battlefield with his Gator and was enthusiastic about the plan to re-create the famous rifle shot by Jack Bean. So first and foremost, my thanks go to Ron, his wife Donna and their two sons who live nearby for their wonderful hospitality at their bed & breakfast outside Lodge Grass.

Next in line is Emory Y. "Hank" Adams, of Bozeman, Montana. Hank and I go way back to army service together at Fort Ben-ning, Georgia, now twenty years ago. Hailing from a family of distinguished army officers and soldiers—his father was Col. James Yeates Adams, commander of the US 23rd Infantry Regiment, when that unit captured a previously little-known Hill 1211 that became famous as Heartbreak Ridge in the Korean War. Hanks' grandfather, Emory S. Adams, was the adjutant general of the United States Army at the beginning of World War II after receiving the Distinguished Service Cross in World War I. Another grandfather, Robert O. Van Horn, was the military aide de camp to President Theodore Roosevelt. A great-grandfather, James Judson Van Horne, graduated from West Point in 1858, fought at Antietam and Cold Harbor in the Civil War and served on the 1872 and 1873 Yellowstone expeditions that are described in this book.

Two old guys trying to recapture their youth! Hank Adams (left) spotting for the author who is holding a Shiloh Sharps .45-70 with telescopic sight similar to the one used by 1st Sgt. John Ryan of Company M of the US 7th Cavalry at the Little Bighorn (see *Custer's Best*.) The weapon is extraordinary; but the author fired so high that the bullet is probably still in orbit. *Courtesy Olga MacLean, June 2015*

Hank is also a firearms aficionado and when I explained the project to him, he jumped on board to organize the Bean re-creation found in the epilogue of the book. However, Hank did even more and when it proved too difficult for the author to find several of the more obscure laager sites of the 1874 expedition, Hank came to the rescue in the middle of a cold Montana winter with his jeep and in miserable weather, he and the author found many of these forgotten locations. Equally important, Hank was one of the "Wild Bunch" that participated in my retirement ceremony from the United States Army on Last Stand Hill at the Little Bighorn battlefield in August 2004. Hank's attitude to the challenges of the West is the same as that of William T. Sherman who once wrote: "Better a camp on the Missouri, than a palace on the Potomac."

Wes Pietsch, of Decatur, Illinois, was an outstanding researcher, going above and beyond the call of duty by reading every page of this manuscript and offering his sage advice on the storyline. Wes is also an avid gun historian and assisted in numerous sessions of determining what weapons could have been present at the fighting, and the important characteristics of each one.

Dennis Hagen, archivist, 10th Mountain Division Resource Center, the Denver Public Library came to the fore as he did during the preparation of *Custer's Best*. Dennis located several important letters from William Cable Barkley to famed researcher Walter Camp that contained unpublished information on the expedition. Then Dennis retired, and fortunately Ms. Coi E. Drummond-Gehrig, digital image collection administrator at the Denver Public Library picked up the baton and saved my bacon on numerous photographs in the book.

Donovin A. Sprague Hump of Black Hills State University was a last minute treasure trove for the warrior side of the story. A great-great-grandson of Hump, he provided significant information on the relationships of the various warrior leaders and made this a much better study than it would have been had I not met

him purely by chance—proving that it's better to be lucky than good.

Mr. John Bean, grandson of Jack Bean, helped me immensely with information about his grandfather. John was born in March 1923, some four months before his grandfather died. An experienced firearms expert himself, John served as a flight engineer/top turret gunner on a B-25 Mitchell in the 7th Air Force in the Pacific theater. On one mission to bomb Eniwetok, his B-25 was severely damaged by enemy ground machine-gun fire. After dropping their bomb load, as one of the two engines was inoperative, the crew nursed the plane back to base by jettisoning the machine guns and other weighty equipment. The captain told the crew to bail out over the landing field, which two did. John remained with the aircraft, occupying the co-pilot seat. The ensuing belly-landing was the "longest ride of my life," he recalled. Mr. Bean is a true gentleman.

Rachel Phillips, the Research Coordinator of the Gallatin History Museum at Bozeman, was a "gold nugget" herself and helped me navigate through their extensive archives. As the Gallatin Historical Society has more than 18,000 photographs dealing with the history of Gallatin County and southwest Montana, as well as extensive narrative holdings, I never could have made it through this treasure trove without her help. Equally as important, Rachel's analysis of freight transportation times to Gallatin County from the East Coast in the early 1870s put into serious doubt the accepted theory concerning the type of weapon Jack Bean used in his famous long-range shot at Lodge Grass Creek.

Zoe Ann Stoltz, reference historian at the Montana Historical Society Research Center in Helena, Montana, deserves praise as well. She provided many participant recollections including Charles Avery and George Herendeen, as well as copies of numerous articles from 1873 and 1874 of the Bozeman *Avant Courier*. Matthew Peck of the society also was a major asset. Penny Redli, executive director of the Museum of the Beartooths in Columbus,

Montana deserves my thanks as well; she researched several expedition participants that later resided in that area; on a last-minute visit to the museum, she graciously opened her extensive files on "Uncle Billy" Hamilton, as well as provide an original photograph believed to be of "Muggins" Taylor—perhaps the only one known to be in existence; Lorrie Koski helped with his effort as well. Becki Plunkett, special collections archivist, State Historical Library & Archives of Iowa, also did fabulous work concerning the photograph of warrior chief Inkpaduta. Paul Shea worked diligently to find photographs at the Yellowstone Gateway Museum in Livingston, Montana. Glen Heitz of the Prairie County Museum in Terry, Montana, spent the bulk of a Sunday afternoon guiding the author to a very difficult-to-find grave marker of one of the participants in the expedition; thanks Glen.

During a research trip to Bozeman, I visited Montana State University and its excellent archives. Professor Kim Allen Scott, university archivist, and his assistant Gary Barnhart patiently listened to my description of the project and quickly guided me to numerous key documents that greatly facilitated my research. Steven Jackson, curator of art and photography at the Museum of the Rockies, assisted me greatly in locating numerous essential photographs.

David K. Frasier, Colleen Barrett, Isabel Planton and Laura Thompson of the Lilly Library at Indiana University at Bloomington helped me immensely. My visit there to see the manuscripts of Walter M. Camp concerning the 1874 Expedition was the easiest I have ever had at an archive due to their excellent organization and prior planning. Camp's notes proved crucial in identifying the life story of Eli B. Way of the expedition, as well as many other crucial items.

Patricia Adkins-Rochette of Duncan, Oklahoma, saved the day in my research on Frank Grounds, the trail boss of the expedition. Her extensive files on Texas in the Civil War finally proved where Grounds had been during that conflict, dispelling previous notions of

his past with her meticulous collection of detailed facts and sources.

Dorman Nelson has been researching John "Liver-Eating" Johnston for almost fifty years, has created a comprehensive website on the subject, is in the midst of writing "a tome" on Johnston, and is regarded by many to be the most knowledgeable person in the country on this fascinating Wild West figure. He helped cut through the legend surrounding Johnston and showed me that I was not chasing my tale on determining Johnston's participation in the expedition.

My thanks also go to Lead Park Ranger Bob Hall at Pompeys Pillar National Monument for showing me the database of signatures that saved me at least one full day of searching on my own.

Mike Venturino proved to be a font of knowledge on Sharps Model 1874 black powder rifles. Not only does he know the history of such weapons, he is also an accomplished black powder marksman. I read his excellent book, *Shooting Buffalo Rifles of the Old West*, night after night to get a good feel of what these rifles could do, especially in the hands of such legendary shots as Jack Bean, Oliver Hanna, and George Herendeen. Without Mike, the re-creation of Jack Bean's shot would not have happened.

Dr. Richard J. Labowski of Philadelphia, Pennsylvania, provided outstanding help concerning the Sharps rifle that could have been used by Jack Bean. Dr. Labowski is the current owner of the surviving production and shipment records for the Sharps Rifle Manufacturing Company/Sharps Rifle Company and through a thorough review of the records he determined that two calibers previously thought to have been delivered to Bozeman, Montana Territory, in 1873 were not.

While I feel comfortable with my knowledge of weapons, military-style tactics, and general analytical ability, understanding Lakota and Northern Cheyenne warrior tactics, tribal structure, and the life histories of many of these men are not my forte. I therefore relied on several individuals for assistance.

The first is my personal friend Ken Real Bird at Crow Agency, Montana. His guidance for me as I wrote about the Little Bighorn and now about the 1874 Expedition has been that for me to fully understand what happened, I had to see the terrain while riding a horse. My second thanks go to Paul N. Beck, professor of history for Wisconsin Lutheran College in Milwaukee and author of *Inkpaduta: Dakota Leader*. In addition to authoring this excellent book, he took the time to answer many questions via emails.

A special thanks go to Mike Clark and his excellent store, *Collectors Firearms of Houston Texas* for their gracious consent for the book to use pictures of many of the period firearms they have for sale. Mike is truly an expert in the field.

I would be remiss if I did not give a special thanks to Mr. Don Weibert, whose book *The 1874 Invasion of Montana: A Prelude to the Custer Disaster*, written over twenty years ago, brought the story into our modern historical consciousness. He had a much greater task than I, having far fewer resources to consult and at a time in the infancy of the Internet that has enabled even greater searches, often quite quickly, of distant archives and books. Don, I hope this book passes your muster as you ride the great range in the sky.

Another special thanks must go to the Montana State government. Their *Montana Cadastral* program, a public domain software program easily accessible on the Internet, allows for topographic maps and aerial photograph maps to be made of the entire state. Once a base map is made using this program, it is easy to overlay text and symbols on top of it; every map showing laager locations and phases of the three major battles was constructed in this manner, by your author, who by everyone's admission, is not especially computer savvy!

Numerous gracious individuals opened their personal photograph libraries for inclusion in the book. These generous folks include: Pat Armstrong, John Bean (grandson of Jack Bean,) Janet Davis, Bob Dollenmeyer, Thomas J. Fisher, Steve Florman (great-great-grandson of Bill Officer), Dorman Nelson, Barbara Sell, Norb Sonen, Allen Sorensen, and Mike Parr.

A recent godsend is Dr. Kevin McVary, professor and chair, Division of Urology, Southern Illinois University School of Medicine in Springfield, Illinois. He made the key diagnosis that I had cancer and personally conducted the da Vinci robotic prostate surgery that saved my life.

And finally, a special word of thanks goes to my best friend and wife of thirty-five

In search of history in southeastern Montana in June 2015; writing a book is always a team effort. *Courtesy Hank Adams, June 2015*

years Olga. After she helped find this story in the first place in June 2013, she drove with me to Montana in the fall of that year to research the route of the wagon train (each of the two roundtrips to Montana was 4,500 miles,) take photos of old graves in garden spots such as "Boot Hill" and walk the Lodge Grass battlefield. She spent the next eleven months helping me pull through prostate cancer and then made sure I finished the project instead of sitting around and feeling sorry for myself.

Disclaimer

Latitude and longitude locations were recorded by my *TomTom* Global Positioning System. The number of triangulation GPS sources varied with atmospheric conditions and thus could contain small errors.

Additionally, many of the laager sites of the expedition, as well as the entire location of the Battle of Lodge Grass Creek, are on private property. This work requests that any reader visiting these locations first check with the property owner before walking the terrain. Eastern Montana is home to many, many rattlesnakes, so walking on any of the terrain discussed in this book should be undertaken very carefully.

Finally, any tests or re-creation with firearms should include an inspection of the weapons to be used by qualified gunsmiths, especially if period firearms are used. Never load more than the recommended amount of powder, and ensure that when shooting long range that there are no people or livestock downrange as buffalo gun type rifles can shoot and kill at more than one mile—as Jack Bean proved in 1874!

Courtesy Mike Venturino, 2015

Introduction

They called themselves "The Boys," and they numbered about 150 of the most adventurous—and cantankerous—*hombres* to ever ride a wagon train in the Old West. Eminent researcher Walter Mason Camp said that they were men without fear and that only men who had been tried and proven were accepted on the expedition.[1] Scouts, gold prospectors, possibly a former Texas ranger, buffalo hunters, and Civil War veterans of both sides—men who had counted coup at Antietam, Seven Pines, Fredericksburg, Chancellorsville, the Wilderness, Petersburg, Stones River, Nashville, Missionary Ridge, Vicksburg, Kennesaw Mountain and Atlanta—they may have been the deadliest collection of shooters to ever hit the trail west of the Mississippi River.

Now, however, they were not trying to corral Confederate raider John H. Morgan or hunting the trail of "Reb" cavalry commander Jeb Stuart. "The Boys" were now up on the Great Plains, along the mighty Yellowstone River and her tributaries—waterways with fabled names of Powder, Tongue, Rosebud, Big Horn, Lodge Grass, and Little Horn. And their adversaries now were the Lakota and Northern Cheyenne—some of the greatest light cavalry to ever gallop over the North American continent. The Lakota were no strangers to fighting, having engaged in protracted raids and counter-raids for decades against their traditional enemies Chippewa, Shoshone, Crow, Arikara, and Pawnee. In fact, fighting the Crow (*Apsaàlooke*) had been such an integral part of Lakota life that no one could remember there not being a state of war between the two tribes. This time, it was the warriors, not the frontiersmen, doing

Yellowstone River Watershed.
Courtesy of DEMIS Mapserver,
Public Domain

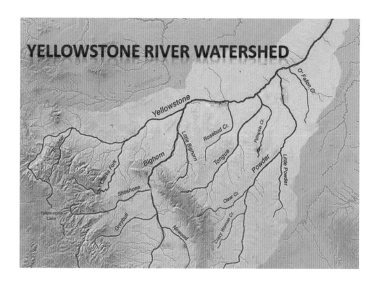

YELLOWSTONE RIVER WATERSHED

the hunting and they were led by the formidable chieftains Hump and Inkpaduta, with Sitting Bull waiting in the wings. The experienced warriors, who learned how to ride almost before they could walk, knew the terrain and what waited around every corner.

What the warriors did not know—but soon found out—was that "The Boys" were armed with two cannons, for which they had devised ingenious canister rounds—as well as dozens and dozens of Springfield "Big Fifty" rifles and powerful Sharps buffalo guns, and that with these weapons "The Boys" could drop anything on two or four legs a long, long way away. What both sides had in common was suffering through three months of a brutal Montana winter, where temperatures plummeted to thirty degrees below zero and where only the strongest survived; on some nights the expedition herders had to keep the livestock walking around all night to avoid freezing to death. Meanwhile, the men huddled under buffalo robes, some trying to fortify themselves with "Snake-bite Medicine" (whiskey.)[2] Additionally, the area was experiencing the aftermath of the Great Epizootic of 1873 [equine influenza] that weakened—and often killed in conjunction with extreme weather— the hardiest of horses on both sides.

Despite its obscure place in our history— much of which was caused by the expedition not being associated with the United States Army, and thus overlooked by strictly military historians—we are blessed with over one-hundred years of sources, if only we will search for them. Unlike the demise of George Custer some two years later at the Little Bighorn—only a few miles from where "The Boys" had fought—there were plenty of survivors to tell the tale, and what a tale it was:

"It was in '74, and I don't think there was ever a march made into the heart of a hostile Indian country that ever equaled it. The country was alive with Sioux Indians and yet we made that march, losing only one man out of 146. We were in search of gold. In one fight, we had the best warriors

of the Sioux nation pitted against us … The prime object of the movement was to open up the Wolf Creek country, where, as the party then supposed, rich placers [alluvial deposits] could be found."[3]

These were the words of James A. Gourley, years after participating in the Yellowstone Wagon Road and Prospecting Expedition; what he did not write was that in that last battle, there may have been upwards of 1,400 warriors riding in to attack—long odds for any defense. The warriors understood this, and perhaps out of respect, "The Boys'" opponents, certainly led by Hump and Inkpaduta—and likely in the presence of the great Sitting Bull—called them *Wan-tan-yeya-pelo* (straight-shooters) and *Maka-ti-oti* (dug-out dwellers) because the frontiersmen dug rifle pits from which they poured out round after round of accurate fire when attacked. And the warriors soon nicknamed these huge rifles the "shoot today, kill tomorrow" guns.[4]

The written history of the events you are about to read is as such: In February 1874, the Yellowstone Wagon Road and Prospecting Expedition, a quasi-military operation, departed Bozeman in the Montana Territory, and proceeded along the Yellowstone River for the purpose of determining the furthest point west on that waterway that riverboats could navigate, and then scouting a wagon road that would link the Gallatin Valley to the river at that point. Equally as important—at least to the members of the expedition—it was a search for gold, possibly even the mystical Lost Cabin Mine. This expedition, headed by veteran Indian-fighter Frank Grounds, was supposed to travel down the Yellowstone River to the mouth of the Tongue River, but began changing course short of that goal, near Armells Creek, in part to search for gold, but also because bison had eaten most of the grass in this area earlier in the year—and more importantly because Grounds realized the Lakota and Northern Cheyenne would not stop their attacks against the expedition until the last man in the wagon train went down.

Yellowstone Expedition Route. *Courtesy of DEMIS Mapserver, Public Domain*

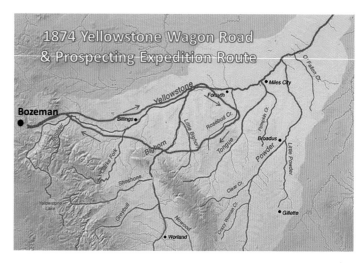

Key Laager Positions. *Author-made map using Montana Cadastral program, Montana State Government*

And so, the expedition survived and at least nine key participants of this 1874 trek played prominent roles with the United States Army at the Little Bighorn campaign two years later. Behind the scenes is another story. The territorial governor of Montana played a significant role in the formation of the expedition, but his motivation—at least in part—may have been less than noble. And what role did the United States Army play in equipping the expedition through a cavalry major at Fort Ellis, who was a Civil War hero and West Point classmate of Lt. Gen. Philip Sheridan, the commander of the Military Division of the Missouri?

But, as Napoleon once said, "What is history but a fable agreed upon?" That question has never been more prescient than with the 1874 Yellowstone Wagon Road and Prospecting Expedition, which entered the legend of the Wild West almost before the prospectors made it back to Bozeman. This book seeks to cut through that lore, with a result that what really happened is actually much more incredible than what—until now—we like to believe happened. Equipped with two mysterious artillery pieces, the men of the wagon train had in their midst some of the greatest buffalo hunters of the era. One of them, Jack Bean, would fire a long-range shot at the expedition's climactic Battle of Lodge Grass Creek that would vie for the title of the longest-range recorded successful rifle-shot against a single opponent in the history of frontier America.

And who would ever believe that a former slave—who escaped and became a sergeant in an elite all-black Union unit in the Civil War, the only combat element of the war to serve under exclusive leadership of black officers—went hand-to-hand, with knife versus tomahawk in a Herculean struggle against a Lakota warrior, vanquishing a foe that some believe may have been a son of Sitting Bull? That momentous *mano-a-mano* event occurred during the expedition at what this study refers to as the "Battle of Great Medicine Dance Creek"—an event that truly needs to enter the historical lexicon of Wild West history.

One could make the argument that every frontiersman on the expedition, and all of their Lakota and Northern Cheyenne opponents as well, were also heroes, who defied the odds by simply surviving. Warfare between frontiersmen and warriors was brutal, with no quarter given or asked. Oliver Perry Hanna, a famed frontier hunter, summed up many of the harshest aspects of this conflict:[5]

"Those old Indian fighters always scalped every Indian they could get hold of, so many were busy scalping the Indians. They claimed it was the right thing to do for the Indians think their dead will not go to the 'Happy Hunting Ground' if they are minus their scalps … some of the men jumped on the stolen ponies and began to ride in a war circle, shaking the Indian scalps at the Indians, shooting off their guns and shouting to them to come on and have another fight. The experienced Indian fighters in the party insisted on doing these things because Indians admire bravery and would think there was a much larger number in our party…others who had cut off Indian ears and fingers were drying them in the hot ashes. This may sound inhuman, but the men of our expedition were experienced in war, and especially Indian warfare, and said we had to be 'daredevils' and put the fear into them."

Such conduct was not confined to one side. The battle between white and red could get ugly. The only reason that the warriors did not torture and mutilate the prisoners of the expedition was that they did not take any. Two years later, any differences in the way each side treated captives or dead of the other would be indistinguishable.

Whether they were saints or sinners, most of the expedition's members were previously just listed as non-descript names, often misspelled, in the occasional old book found only in specialized archives; with today's resources, we can now determine exactly who many of them were, how they shaped history before and after the fight and what happened to them in their twilight years of harmlessly telling old stories—exaggerated to a degree as old men will—to their grandchildren around the hearth.

Perhaps an understanding of the 1874 Yellowstone Wagon Road and Prospecting Expedition may also shed light on one of the West's greatest mysteries that will never be solved—the defeat of George Armstrong Custer at the Little Bighorn on June 25, 1876. Just thirty years after the expedition, Jorge Ruiz de Santayana y Borrás, better known as George Santayana, wrote his oft-quoted line that, "Those who cannot remember the past are condemned to repeat it," but what about those participants in history who remember events incorrectly or take the wrong lessons of the past and try to apply them to different circumstances in the future? The warrior chiefs fighting the 1874 expedition, younger warriors such as Red Hawk, and several frontiersmen on the wagon train, would later play prominent roles in the Great Sioux War of 1876. How these men saw the conduct of the 1874 fighting and how they correctly or incorrectly interpreted this information to adapt to the fighting in 1876 would significantly affect the outcome of that latter conflict for better or worse.

In our collective history, the 1874 Yellowstone Wagon Road and Prospecting Expedition has remained an obscure forgotten sidelight, never to be much more than a small footnote in the settling of the West. Even the great historian Dr. Walter S. Campbell (born Walter Stanley Vestal) wrote in 1956 to another historian that he was generally not informed about the expedition. To date, there have been only one book and one lengthy magazine article about the expedition and both are now dated with respect to the ability to use new research tools and to reach new sources of information. It is the intent of this study to answer as many questions concerning the expedition as possible. More importantly it raises additional questions for others to answer, whether that is in an archive, out on the trail of the expedition, or at one of the three battlefields that still exist—using the many maps as a guide. So turn the page, you are breaking a new trail.

Notes

1. Walter Camp Manuscripts, Box 2: Folder 2, Bozeman Expedition of 1874, University of Indiana, Lilly Library.

2. All period slang terms come from the *Glossary of Indian Wars Slang*, http://www.abuffalosoldier.com/slang.htm, The New Buffalo Soldiers Website.

3. "The Story of a March," *The Northwest Illustrated Monthly Magazine*, St. Paul, Minnesota, Volume VII—No. 8, August 1890, 12.

4. Frank Sellers, *Sharps Firearms*, Maricopa, Arizona: Karen S. Sellers, 2011, 315.

5. Charles Hanna Carter (editor), *An Oldtimer's Story of the Old Wild West; The Recollections of Oliver Perry Hanna, Pioneer, Indian Fighter, Frontiersman and First Settler in Sheridan County*, Wyoming, compiled June 1926, 34-35.

CHAPTER ONE

Sitting Bull and the Lakota/ Cheyenne Situation in Eastern Montana

Synonymous with the efforts of the Lakota (Lakóta) to maintain their autonomous lifestyle during the second half of the nineteenth century is the name Sitting Bull. Probably born along the Yellowstone River, southwest of present-day Miles City, Montana (other sources believe it was along the Grand River in the Dakotas,) he received the name Jumping Badger at birth. Due to a later leadership role in a fight between the Lakota and the Crow, he was bestowed with one of his father's names, Tataŋka Iyotaŋka, translated as "Sitting Bull."

Although his name is also synonymous with constant fighting and strife, such was not always the case. Joe Cook was an experienced frontiersman and a member of the expedition and later recalled the relationship between the Lakota and the white men:[1]

It may be of some interest to a great many to know that the Sioux Indians were not hostile to the whites at that time until the fall of 1864. In the fall of 1863 we visited their tepees that were strung all along the Platte Valley from Fort Kearny [Nebraska] to the mouth of the Cache La Powdre River [Cache La Poudre River in Colorado.] In August, 1864, eleven four-mule teams loaded with freight for Denver were quietly driving up the Platte Valley, and when within three miles of Plum Creek station they noticed a band of Indians coming from the south in a leisurely way on horseback, and when the Indians got within 250 yards of the train they set up their blood curdling yell and whipping

Sitting Bull in a studio portrait taken between 1895 and 1900. He is believed to have fought against the expedition. *Courtesy of Denver Public Library Digital Collections, Call Number X-33214*

their ponies they surrounded the wagons and began shooting the drivers. I never heard what caused them to turn hostile.

In the spring of 1865, when I went to Montana, all that was left of the stage stations was the metal that would not burn, such as heating and cooking stoves, the irons off wagons and other metal. They cut open sacks of flour and poured the flour on the prairie. Two feather beds that were a part of family's freight, which had gone to Denver on the stage coach, were cut open for the ticks. In the spring of 1865 when I again went over the road the feathers were still hanging to the sage brush.

Sitting Bull was no stranger to this later combat. In 1864, along with Gall and Inkpaduta, he fought in a group of skirmishing Lakota against Brig. Gen. Alfred Sully (an 1841 graduate of West Point) and two brigades of US Army troops. In September 1864, Sitting Bull led about one hundred Hunkpapa Lakota near what is now Marmarth, North Dakota, against elements of a wagon train and was shot in the left hip by a soldier. The bullet exited through the small of Sitting Bull's back, but the wound did not prove fatal.[2]

From 1865 through 1868, Sitting Bull led other numerous Lakota attacks against Fort Berthold, Fort Stevenson, and Fort Buford (all in the Dakota Territory,) as well as raids on emigrant parties. By early 1868, the US government had had enough and desired a peaceful settlement to the overall Indian operations in the area that were known as Red Cloud's War. The Treaty of Fort Laramie on July 2, 1868, signed in the Wyoming Territory agreed to Red Cloud's demands that Fort Phil Kearny and Fort C.F. Smith be abandoned. However, Sitting Bull did not agree to the treaty and never signed, continuing his hit-and-run attacks on forts in the upper Missouri area throughout the early 1870s. Historian Dr. Walter S. Campbell concluded in 1930 that Sitting Bull became what was in effect the "Supreme Chief of the whole Sioux Nation," although the Lakota would not have used this terminology. Later historians have disagreed with this assertion, though.[3]

In 1871 and 1872, the Northern Pacific Railroad surveyed for a route across the northern plains. Sitting Bull attacked the expedition in both years, finally forcing them to turn back.[4] However, in the summer of 1873, another Northern Pacific Railroad expedition began. Gen. David S. Stanley, who graduated from West Point in 1852, took 2,000 men (including George A. Custer and the US 7th Cavalry Regiment) starting from Fort Rice, Dakota Territory, and surveyed west, while Col. Eugene M. Baker (West Point, 1836) with 800 men, started from Tacoma, Washington, and surveyed east. They met at a point they called Pompey's Pillar on a small island in the Yellowstone River.[5]

Once again, the Lakota—very likely with Sitting Bull, Crazy Horse, Gall, and Rain in the Face, with approximately 1,000 warriors monitored the progress of the white column. Finally, on August 4, 1873, the warriors struck a 7th Cavalry advance detachment ahead of Stanley's column near Sunday Creek; the skirmish lasted about three hours. On August 11, the forces skirmished again near the mouth of the Bighorn River. While the total casualties on both sides numbered only one to two dozen, warrior resistance against the cavalry showed that if the Lakota and Cheyenne detected an incursion into the Yellowstone River region, they would tenaciously fight it.

That lesson had been learned by the government, if perhaps not by George Custer. In the annual report of the commissioner of Indian affairs to the secretary of the interior for 1874, there is a section by William W. Alderson, agent at the Milk River Agency, Fort Peck, dated September 1, 1874. In it, he discusses the Lakota and Sitting Bull:[6]

The Uncpapa Sioux constitutes the third class [concerning their progress toward civilization.] They are extremely difficult to manage, perhaps as much so as any Indians in the country. They are wild, demonstrative, and ungrateful for favors. There is still a formidable force of hostile Indians occupying the Yellowstone and Powder River country. Among them are many relatives, former friends, and associates of these Uncpapa Sioux. On this account I find it almost impossible to keep them under proper subjection, or retain them within the reservation limits. They claim some right or interest in the country through which the Northern Pacific

Railroad is projected, and do not propose to relinquish their claim without remuneration; consequently many of them come and go when they please. I have no doubt that some of the best disposed of these Uncpapa Indians go there with no worse intentions than to visit and hunt; but once there, they are restrained and overawed by Sitting Bull, his associate chiefs, and his formidable soldier lodge; so that they cannot return to the agency when they wish.

Some two months before this report, on July 2, 1874, George Armstrong Custer led a military expedition from Fort Abraham Lincoln to the Black Hills to ostensibly determine a suitable location for a future military fort in that area, but in reality to explore the Black Hills for gold. Sitting Bull did not attack Custer's expedition, which was a departure from his previous tendencies. The Black Hills Expedition commenced about a month and a half after the 1874 Yellowstone Wagon Road and Prospecting Expedition ended in May. The last month of the wagon train saw the prospectors heading west toward Bozeman, although the warriors had no idea at this point concerning its destination. This westward direction pulled the warriors farther and farther away from the Black Hills. Could it have been that the reason the Lakota and Northern Cheyenne did not attack Custer at the Black Hills was that the warriors had been 250 miles west of the Black Hills following and fighting the Yellowstone Expedition just months before?

Furthermore, could Sitting Bull have been with these warriors in the Montana Territory? Famed army scout George B. Herendeen, who participated on the expedition and who was one of George Custer's scouts two years later, always maintained that Sitting Bull had been present in the fighting against the wagon train.[7] So did Charles Avery in his own recollections of the expedition.[8] On September 12, 1956, James S. Hutchins typed a seven-page letter to Dr. Walter S. Campbell at the University of Oklahoma, describing what he knew of the wagon train fighting and asking if the distinguished historian knew what the "Indian side" of the battle was. Professor Campbell replied that he was generally not informed about the expedition. He stated that in the summer of 1874, four tribes of the Lakota were camped together near the Powder River and Big Bottom: Hunkpapa, Oglala, Minneconjou, and Sans Arc. Campbell added that when he interviewed White Bull, the warrior made no mention of the fight. One Bull, Sitting Bull's nephew, also never mentioned any fighting with white men during the time of the expedition in late winter/early spring of 1874. Campbell finally concluded:[9]

> It is not impossible that a Brule chief would be visiting up there and take part, but on the other hand, I cannot believe that that tribe was there in force on the Yellowstone. Had that been so, White Bull would have mentioned it.

James Hutchins wrote a detailed article, "Poison in the Pemmican: The Yellowstone Wagon-Road & Prospecting Expedition of 1874," for *Montana: The Magazine of Western History*, just two years after his correspondence with Campbell. Hutchins did not write that Sitting Bull was present at any of the fights during the expedition—nor did he write that he was not there. Hutchins did add some interesting information: present at the fighting in 1874 was the Two Kettle Lakota tribe—with Red-End-of-Horn—and the Minneconjou under their chief Hump or High Backbone.[10] None of the participants had ever mentioned either of these names and Hutchins' revelation added a new dimension to the subject. Hutchins had deduced this information from a statement that he obtained from Spotted Bear of the Hunkpapa that was made to Judge Frank B. Zahn[11] at Fort Yates, North Dakota in October 1956:[12]

> Two years before Long Hair was killed (1874) I heard from Indians who were there say that a large group of men with wagons, horses and mules, came up the

valley of the Rosebud River looking for maza-ska-zo (gold.) Two Kettle band of Sioux Indians under their chief, High-back-bone or Hump and the Minne-con-jou band under their Chief, Red End of Horn were camped there. It was the warriors from these two bands who fought the gold-hunters. I do not recall where I was at that time, but I heard that it was quite a fight.

Stands-With-Horns-In-Sight, born in 1866 and a small boy during the events in question, also made a statement to Judge Zahn that Hutchins was able to analyze:[13]

Two years before Long Hair was killed, we were camped in the valley of the Rosebud River, in southeastern Montana … Some time during the spring of that year (1874) a lot of white men with wagons, horses, mules and dogs, came up the Rosebud River and we heard afterwards that these (Wasicu) white men were looking for yellow-metal (gold.) Two divisions of the Teton were camped there; they were the Owohe-numpa (Two Kettle) band under their chief High-Back-Bone or Hump (I meant to say Chief Red End of Horn, He-inkpa-luta) and the Minne-con-jou band, under their chief

Hump the younger (Etokeah), a Minneconjou of the Lakota, fought the 1874 Yellowstone Wagon Road and Prospecting Expedition and two years later at the Little Bighorn, with two wives. Photo was taken close to 1900. *Courtesy of Denver Public Library Digital Collections, Laton Alton Huffman photograph, Call Number X-31816*

High-Back-Bone or Hump. It was the warriors from these bands who fought the gold-hunters.

Hump, or High Backbone, Etokeah, was born in 1848, possibly in what is now Montana. According to some oral tradition, Hump's mother was a Cheyenne. A fighter by heritage, his father saw combat in Red Cloud's War, and Hump the son fought at the Rosebud battle against Gen. George Crook on June 17, 1876, and at the Little Bighorn a week later, where he reportedly killed one cavalryman and captured four enemy weapons, before he was wounded above the knee (the

This is believed to be the only known photograph of Inkpaduta in his late middle age or old age. He is believed to have fought against the expedition.
Courtesy of Frank I. Herriott Papers, State Historical Society of Iowa, Des Moines

round tumbling inside his leg to his hip,) while charging Company L of the 7th Cavalry on Calhoun Hill. In March 1877, Hump finally surrendered to Gen. Nelson A. Miles at the Tongue River Cantonment.[14]

The presence of Red-End-of-Horn, or Iŋkpáduta, along the route of the wagon train is even more intriguing. Inkpaduta was probably born in present-day southern Minnesota in about 1805 (sources put his birth between 1797 and 1815) a member of the Wahpekute Santee; his father, Wamdesapa, was the chief of the small tribe that numbered about 550 people. When Inkpaduta was a young man, white whiskey-sellers and horse thieves murdered his blood brother's family. Descriptions of Inkpaduta indicate that he may have stood as tall as 6'6" (although one source lists him at 5'10") had a large forehead, severe facial pockmarks from smallpox and had long incisor teeth that gave him a fearsome appearance; he possibly suffered from acromegaly.[15] In the 1830s and 1840s, Inkpaduta and a small band of followers hunted and foraged in present-day southern Minnesota, northwestern Iowa, and southeastern South Dakota. In 1840, Inkpaduta and a small band of Wahpekutes were expelled from the main tribe, following the murder of a chief (Tasagi). Inkpaduta's role in the murder has remained unclear to this day, although it is believed that his father, who died about 1848, was a major perpetrator.[16]

It was likely the murder of Inkpaduta's blood-brother, "Old Chief Three Fingers" Sintomniduta, in Iowa by two white men would lead to what happened next. The perpetrators were Sintomniduta's elk hunting companions, John Henry Lott and Lott's stepson. John Henry had been born in 1808 in Pennsylvania, subsequently moving to Geauga County, Ohio. There, he married Sally White Huntington and the couple moved west to Kentucky and then southern Missouri. About 1840, Lott moved to present-day Worth County, Missouri and began trading with the Sac and Fox tribes; the business proved so successful that the family moved to Red Rock, Marion County in Iowa to expand the enterprise.

In 1845, Lott moved his family to Fort Des Moines and opened a trading post. Apparently, John Henry began to specialize in stealing horses from both Indians and whites and selling the animals to new owners. This did not endear him to the United States Army and soldiers at the fort attempted to arrest him. Lott escaped to Boone Forks in Webster County, Iowa. In 1846, he began trading with Sioux Indians, but the tribe soon felt cheated and Sintomniduta ordered him to leave. When Lott did not, in 1847 warriors attacked his log cabin and Lott's twelve-year-old son Milton died in the encounter. His wife Sally died a few days later of the effects of exposure. John Henry Lott vowed revenge as he stood over the makeshift grave of his son.[17]

Lott moved south to Dallas County, Iowa, re-married and had three children. He returned north in 1853 and possibly stole five ponies from Sintomniduta, then the chief of the Red Top Band. The two apparently then patched up their rocky relationship, but John Henry Lott was biding his time and knew that revenge was a dish best served cold. In January 1854, Lott invited the unsuspecting Sintomniduta to join him on an elk hunt. According to an eyewitness, when Sintomniduta stood to shoot the first animal, the two white men shot him in the back and decapitated him. The two murderers then slunk back to Sintomniduta's camp, slaughtered the fallen warrior's mother, wife, and five children and rode away. After hearing of the incident, Inkpaduta naturally became infuriated. Authorities attempted to defuse the situation, promising to arrest and punish the murderers. However, the inquiry never resulted in justice. At Fort Dodge, the nearest law enforcement site, peace officer William Wilson quickly concluded that Henry Lott was the murderer and a grand jury indicted him *in absentia*. The prosecuting attorney of Hamilton County, Granville Berkley, appeared less than interested. Berkley decided not to try the case and did not even bother to return Sintomniduta's remains to the tribe, instead nailing Sintomniduta's skull to a pole over the attorney's house.[18]

Inkpaduta subsequently sought justice from the United States Army at Fort Ridgely along the Minnesota River (south of present-day Fairfax, Minnesota.) After a short patrol to find the fugitive, the army announced that John Henry Lott could not be located and dropped the issue. It was believed at the time that Henry Lott supposedly fled to Missouri and then across the plains to California, where he may have been killed in a quarrel. One researcher, however, believes that Lott fled southwest to northeast Kansas, and sought refuge with his old friends the Sac and Fox tribes. A document from Doniphan County, Kansas, later listed a Henry Lott as the postmaster of Lafayette Landing. Three years later, white settlers approached Inkpaduta's small band and demanded they turn over their weapons, which was the proximate cause for Inkpaduta and his dozen warriors killing twenty-six white settlers and abducted four women between West Okoboji Lake and East Okoboji Lake, Iowa, on March 8, 1857. The event was later widely publicized as the *Spirit Lake Massacre*. Inkpaduta took his band north to Springfield, Minnesota, where he was joined by a band of Sisseton Sioux. On March 26, 1857, the combined group of warriors murdered eight settlers.[19]

The government pursued Inkpaduta farther into Minnesota—telling the Santees at the agencies there that they would not receive their annuities until Inkpaduta had been caught—which added to the already poor situation that led to the Dakota War of 1862, in which some 450-800 settlers were killed; 150 Lakota were killed; and the US Army hanged thirty-eight prisoners in a mass execution on December 26, 1862, in Mankato, Minnesota. When the army expanded operations by sending several thousand troops into the Dakota Territory, Inkpaduta and his band were living with the Yanktonai, a branch of the Nakota/Assiniboine. Inkpaduta led Lakota warriors in the fights at Big Mound (Tappen, North Dakota) on July 24, 1863, against Brig. Gen. Henry Sibley and at Whitestone Hill (Merricourt, North Dakota) on September 3-5, 1863, when Brig. Gen. Alfred Sully attacked the Yanktonai, Santee, Hunkpapa, and Blackfoot villages at this location. It is possible that Sitting Bull was also present at Big Mound and Whitestone Hill.

On July 28, 1864, Gen. Sully was on the march again and engaged the Yanktonai, Santee, Blackfeet, Sans Arc, and Minneconjou at Killdeer Mountain in the Badlands near present-day Killdeer, Dunn County, North Dakota. Reportedly, Inkpaduta, Gall, and Sitting Bull were together at this engagement.[20] In the late 1860s and early 1870s, Inkpaduta and his small group roamed along the Powder River and the Upper Missouri River.[21] Prof. Paul N. Beck, author of the acclaimed *Inkpaduta: Dakota Leader*, stated in response to an inquiry by this study:[22]

Thus, I would find it possible that Inkpaduta would have been there [against the 1874 Yellowstone Wagon Road and Prospecting Expedition.] Especially when you do have sources from witnesses that say he was. However, by this time, Inkpaduta would have been an old man and likely going blind so he would not have participated in any actions against the military. His sons would have been more likely involved as two of them did fight at the Little Big Horn.

Prof. Beck's comments open the door that Inkpaduta's sons, Gray Earth Tracking (also known as Sounds-the-Ground-When-He-Walks, and Noisy Walking) and White Earth Tracking may have been present at the fighting against

Flying By (Keya Heyi), a Minneconjou of the Lakota, fought the 1874 Yellowstone Wagon Road and Prospecting Expedition and two years later at the Little Bighorn. *Courtesy of Denver Public Library Digital Collections, D.F. Barry Cabinet Card, Call Number B-497*

Three-quarter length photo of a studio portrait of Dakota Chief Gall, taken about 1881. He is believed to have fought against the expedition. *Courtesy of Denver Public Library Digital Collections, D.F. Barry Cabinet Card, Call Number B-917*

the wagon train that April 1874 as well as their father—who would have served in an advisory role.

Historian Robert M. Utley posited that several other Lakota chiefs were present at some point during the expedition's journey, to include Makes Room (Musselshell band of the Minneconjou) and Flying By (Minneconjou.)[23] Flying By, Keya Heyi, son of Lame Deer, was born in 1850.[24] Makes Room, Kiyukanpi, was born in about 1825; he was the father of White Bull, Pte San Hunka, who was born in 1850, and One Bull, Tatanka Winjila, who was born in 1853. Given the presence of their father, it makes it possible that White Bull and One

Bull fought against the expedition, although Dr. Walter S. Campbell thought that was unlikely. In 1892, Little Bighorn survivor Edward S. Godfrey—then a brevet major—wrote a detailed account of the Custer battle; he slightly revised the account in 1908; both mentioned Gall. Gall was born in the Dakota Territory near the Moreau or Grand River about 1840. His mother first named him Matohinshda, Bear Shedding His Hair, but this was later changed to *Pizi*. Standing over six feet tall, he fought at the Fetterman and Fort Buford fights in 1866. At the beginning of his narrative, Maj. Godfrey described the major warrior participants and concerning Gall wrote:[25]

He [Gall] it was who followed the "Bozeman Expedition" about 1874, for days, when they were searching for gold, compelling them at all times to be in readiness for battle. One of their entrenchments may yet be seen on the divide between the Rosebud and the Little Big Horn at the head of Thompson Creek.

Initially, this study was uncertain about Sitting Bull's whereabouts in 1874 or his exact influence over the Lakota warriors fighting against the expedition. Dr. Thomas Marquis asserted that Sitting Bull was not present at the fights against the Yellowstone wagon train in 1874, but that the warriors were almost all Northern Cheyenne and led by Braided Locks.[26] On the other hand, we have the work done by 1st Lt. James H. Bradley, US 7th Infantry Regiment, who was stationed at Fort Shaw and Fort Benton in the Montana Territory. Bradley was also a historian, who chronicled the events of Montana and the Northwest, as well as his own military career, keeping a detailed journal of his findings. Unfortunately, Lt. Bradley was killed fighting the Nez Perce at the Battle of the Big Hole (Wisdom, Montana) on August 9, 1877, before he could publish these accounts. However, all was not lost and in 1917, much of this research appeared as the "Bradley Manuscript," in the *Contributions to the Historical Society of Montana, Volume Eight*. He based his observations on interviews with participants of the expedition and warriors he interviewed later. Concerning warrior participation and leadership present in fighting the wagon train, Bradley wrote:[27]

The number of Indians who participated in the battle was variously estimated at from 1,000 to 1,500. They afterward admitted at Fort Peck that it was the combined force of three large camps under the leadership of the famous Sitting Bull.

Minneconjou Lakota warrior Red Hawk, in an interview with researcher Walter M. Camp in 1915, stated that Sitting Bull was at the first

fighting on the Rosebud (April 4) and that he had led 500 to 700 warriors there.[28] Additionally, eminent historian Robert Utley in his groundbreaking work, *Sitting Bull: The Life and Times of an American Patriot*, concluded that

Northern Cheyenne Chief Braided Locks (later known as Arthur Brady) and his wife Ellen Brady in 1925. He is believed to have fought against the expedition. *Courtesy of Native American Encyclopedia*

Sitting Bull. *Courtesy of PBS, "The West"*

Red Hawk, (Cetan Luta), an Oglala of the Lakota, fought the 1874 Yellowstone Wagon Road and Prospecting Expedition, sits on horseback at a watering hole in the Badlands. *Courtesy of Denver Public Library Digital Collections, Edward S. Curtis, Call Number X-34083*

not only was Sitting Bull present with the Lakota facing the expedition along its route, but that he actually led the attack at the 1874 Battle of Rosebud Creek:[29]

> Before daybreak on April 4, about thirty-two miles upstream from the mouth of the Rosebud, Sitting Bull led several hundred men to the attack.

The study believes that Sitting Bull, as well as Gall, was present in the area of the 1874 expedition, most likely beginning with the Battle of Rosebud Creek, continuing at the Battle of Great Medicine Dance Creek and perhaps remaining through the Battle of Lodge Grass Creek.

And what of Crazy Horse; was he at the fighting along the Rosebud in 1874 as well? Acclaimed author Kingsley M. Bray states in his book, *Crazy Horse: A Lakota Life* that in the spring of 1874, in addition to Hump and Sitting Bull who fought the wagon train, Crazy Horse did as well as his village "was in the district between the Rosebud and the Little Bighorn." This is precisely where the expedition traveled that spring.[30] Robert Marshall Utley, in his *The Lance and the Shield: The Life and Times of Sitting Bull* wrote that Sitting Bull was present and led his men in one of the attacks against the wagon train. He also stated that Crazy Horse and Hump were present.[31] Unless we can find evidence that Sitting Bull

The question of whether or not a photograph of Crazy Horse was ever taken will probably never be resolved for certain. Some experts believe that this is an actual image of the warrior chief; other historians do not believe this individual is the famous Crazy Horse. The photo has had many owners and many to whom it was loaned; it apparently first surfaced in about 1952, although the source at that time maintained that no photograph of Crazy Horse ever existed, so who is this? The study believes that he fought against the expedition. *Numerous websites and retail outlets, none presenting proof that they have rights to the image.*

An 1872 oil painting called *American Progress* by John Gast, which can be described as an allegorical representation of "Manifest Destiny." The female figure of Columbia, a personification of the United States of America, leads westward expansion of settlers and technology. *Public Domain*

spent that spring away from his own village, we should assume that he was in the area of the expedition and fought the frontiersmen. There is another piece of tantalizing history that supports the presence of Crazy Horse in the fight against the wagon train.[32]

During the last stages of research, Donovin A. Sprague Hump of Black Hills State University—and the great-great-grandson of Hump the younger, reviewed the list of warriors believed to have been opposing the expedition (see appendix 1.) The oral history of the Lakota expert then stated:[33]

> All of these warriors and chiefs shown could well have been present along the Rosebud in the winter of 1874 as it was very close to their traditional Tongue River encampments.

These encampments were not only rich in wild game, but also served as a shield against the Lakota traditional ancient enemy—the Crow—and made it more difficult for the Crow to move east into Lakota sacred ground. He then added some additional names, not found in white sources: Little Wolf and Dull Knife, of the Northern Cheyenne, and the Minneconjou Lakota warrior Touch the Clouds.

Regardless of what leaders and warriors were at the major fighting with the 1874 Yellowstone Wagon Road and Prospecting Expedition, the Lakota and Northern Cheyenne situation in eastern Montana in 1874 was precarious. The juggernaut of American frontier expansion was hurtling directly at the Lakota and Northern Cheyenne from both east and west. Outnumbered, outgunned, and out-resourced, the warriors could either surrender to the inevitable tidal wave of "Manifest Destiny" or fight—and in 1874, surrender was not in their vocabulary.

Notes

1. Jesse Brown and A.M. Willard, *The Black Hills Trails: A History of the Struggles of the Pioneers in the Winning of the Black Hills*, edited by John T. Milek, Rapid City,

South Dakota: Rapid City Journal Company, 1924, 557-558.

2. Stanley Vestal, *Sitting Bull, Champion of the Sioux: A Biography*, Norman, Oklahoma: University of Oklahoma Press, 1989, 63; and Robert Utley, *Sitting Bull: The Life and Times of an American Patriot*, New York: Holt Paperbacks, 2008, 80-82.

3. Utley, *Sitting Bull*, 22, 66-73.

4. John W. Bailey, *Pacifying the Plains: General Alfred Terry and the Decline of the Sioux, 1866–1890*, Westport, Connecticut: Greenwood Press, 1979, 84-85.

5. Pompey's Pillar is a 150-foot-high sandstone butte along the Yellowstone River. Captain William Clark (Lewis and Clark Expedition) named the butte "Pompeys Tower" in 1806, in honor of Sacagawea's son Jean Baptiste Charbonneau, whom Clark had nicknamed "Pomp." Nicholas Biddle, the first editor of Lewis and Clark's journals, changed the name to "Pompey's Pillar."

6. Letter from James S. Hutchins to Dr. Walter S. Campbell dated October 4, 1956, Western History Collections, University of Oklahoma, Norman, Oklahoma, as found in http://digital.libraries.ou.edu/utils/getfile/collection/CampbellWS/id/5792/filename/5774.pdfpage/page/75.

7. Montana Historical Society Research Center, Helena, Montana, General Correspondence and Transcripts; Oral History Transcripts, George B. Herendeen Papers, SC 16, 3.

8. Ibid, Charles Avery Reminiscence, SC 372, 1.

9. Letter from James S. Hutchins to Dr. Walter S. Campbell dated September 12, 1956, and letter from Dr. Walter S. Campbell to James S. Hutchins, dated September 18, 1956, Western History Collections, University of Oklahoma, Norman, Oklahoma, as found in http://digital.libraries.ou.edu/whc/nam/manuscripts/Campbell_WS_109_3.pdf.

10. James S. Hutchins, "Poison in the Pemmican: The Yellowstone Wagon-Road & Prospecting Expedition of 1874," *Montana: The Magazine of Western History*, Volume 8, Number 3, Summer 1958, 15.

11. Born in 1891, the son of William P. Zahn and a Hunkpapa mother, Frank Zahn attended the Riggs Institute (Flandreau Indian School) in Flandreau, South Dakota, and the Carlisle Indian School in Carlisle, Pennsylvania. Fluent in Teton and Yanktonai Lakota dialects, he also spoke German, as well as English. Frank Zahn was an author, a senior judge on the Court of Indian Offenses at Standing Rock Indian Reservation, and an interpreter. He died in 1966.

12. Statement from Spotted Bear of the Hunkpapa made to Judge Frank B. Zahn, Fort Yates, North Dakota, in October 1956, as found in http://digital.libraries.ou.edu/utils/getfile/collection/CampbellWS/id/5792/filename/5774.pdfpage/page/81.

13. Statement from Stands-With-Horns-In-Sight made to Judge Frank B. Zahn, Fort Yates, North Dakota, in October 1956, as found in http://digital.libraries.ou.edu/utils/getfile/collection/CampbellWS/id/5792/filename/5774.pdfpage/page/82

14. Jerome A. Greene, *Lakota and Cheyenne: Indian Views of the Great Sioux War, 1876–1877*, Norman, Oklahoma: University of Oklahoma Press, 1994, 145.

15. Acromegaly is a long-term condition in which there is too much growth hormone and the body tissues get larger over time.

16. Maxwell Van Nuys, *Inkpaduta—The Scarlet Point: Terror of the Dakota Frontier and Secret Hero of the Sioux*, Denver, Colorado: Maxwell Van Nuys, 1998, 5-7.

17. Mabel Nair Brown, "The Tragedy of Milton Lott," *The Ogden Reporter* (Ogden, Iowa,) July 8, 1970, 17.

18. Mark Fode, "Inkpaduta's bloody path in 1856 went through quarries," *The Pipestone County Star*, April 10, 1997; Mary Lethert Wingerd, *North Country: The Making of Minnesota*, Minneapolis, Minnesota: University of Minnesota Press, 2009, 260-261; and A. Baker, *Statement on Henry Lott at Worth County, Missouri, Genealogy and History*, http://www.predinkle.com/history/lott.htm.

19. Bruce E. Johansen and Donald A. Grinde Jr., *The Encyclopedia of Native*

American Biography, New York: Henry Holt and Company, 1997, 177-178; and Gregory F. Michno, *Encyclopedia of Indian Wars: Western Battles and Skirmishes 1850–1890*, Missoula, Montana: Mountain Press Publishing Company, 2003, 52.

20. Michno, *Encyclopedia of Indian Wars*, 120, 124, 125, 144-146.

21. Paul N. Beck, *Inkpaduta: Dakota Leader*, Norman, Oklahoma: University of Oklahoma Press, 2008, 132.

22. Email discussion with Professor Paul N. Beck, author of *Inkpaduta: Dakota Leader*, August 23, 2013.

23. Utley, *Sitting Bull*, 118.

24. Richard G. Hardorff, *Lakota Recollections of the Custer Fight*, Lincoln, Nebraska: University of Nebraska Press, 1997, 87, 107, 109 and 119.

25. Colonel W.A. Graham, *The Custer Myth: A Source Book of Custeriana*, Mechanicsburg, Pennsylvania: Stackpole Books, 2000, 131; and Donovin Arleigh Sprague, *Images of America: Standing Rock Sioux*, Charleston, South Carolina: Arcadia Publishing, 2004, 18.

26. Dr. Thomas B. Marquis, "Bozeman Men Located Highway, Sought Gold and Fought Indians on Yellowstone in '74," *The Billings Gazette* (Billings, Montana,) February 10, 1935.

27. James H. Bradley, "Bradley Manuscript," Contributions to the Historical Society of Montana, Volume Eight, Helena, Montana: Montana Historical and Miscellaneous Library, 1917, 124.

28. Camp Manuscripts, Box 3: Folder 8, Rosebud, Battle of, 1874.

29. Utley, *Sitting Bull*, 118.

30. Kingsley M. Bray, *Crazy Horse: A Lakota Life*, Norman, Oklahoma: University of Oklahoma Press, 2006, 432.

31. Robert Marshall Utley, *The Lance and the Shield: The Life and Times of Sitting Bull*, New York: The Random House Publishing Group (Ballantine Book,) 1993, 118-119.

32. Cleve Walstrom, *Search for the Lost Trail of Crazy Horse*, Crete, Nebraska: Dageforde Publishing, 2003, 35.

33. Multiple discussions with Donovin A. Sprague concerning the oral history of the Lakota, June 2015.

CHAPTER TWO

The Bait

The Situation in the Montana Territory

Prior to 1864, the ground now known as Montana was part of the Idaho Territory. That was about to change and the reason was gold. A fur trapper known as Francois Finlay (also called Benetsee) discovered gold in the Deer Lodge Valley. A few years later, brothers Granville and James Stuart staked a claim on a location they named Gold Creek. In July 1862, John White and William Eads found gold along a small tributary of the Beaverhead River that was so thick with grasshoppers that they named it Grasshopper Creek. The town of Bannack sprang up and trouble started. In May 1863, two prospectors left Bannack, in the far southwest of Montana, and traveled down the Yellowstone River—right into the heart of Crow territory. The Crow were not amused; they disarmed the prospectors and sent them back west. Another gold-seeking party made a successful strike at Adler Gulch, along a stream in the Ruby River Valley. However, it was the gold strike on July 14, 1864, in the Prickly Pear Valley that changed everything. Nicknamed Last Chance Gulch— because the four prospectors had determined that they would return home if this last attempt failed—the location would produce $19,000,000 worth of gold nuggets—over a quarter of a billion dollars in today's currency.[1]

Frontiersmen, prospectors, businessmen, soldiers of fortune, farmers, and anyone else with a dream or an ability to take advantage of the newly rich, flocked into Montana by the hundreds and thousands on foot, horse, wagon, or steamboat along five major avenues. From the east ran the Northern Overland Route from present-day North Dakota, and paralleling the Missouri River to Fort Union near the confluence of the Missouri River and the Yellowstone River. The route continued west to Fort Benton in north-central Montana. From due west, in Walla Walla, Washington, meandered a 624-mile long dirt trace, known as the Mullan Road. Inside Montana, it passed through Deer Lodge Valley, before also ending at Fort Benton. From the southwest ran the Corinne Road, a dirt trail leading from Corrine, Utah, to Virginia City, Montana—a twenty-five-day journey.[2]

However, the most dangerous route—at least from the standpoint of the Crow, Lakota, and Cheyenne—was the 500-mile long Bozeman Trail that ran northwest from Fort Laramie, then in the Dakota Territory— branching off the Oregon Tail—across the Powder River, across the Tongue River, into the southern Montana Territory, across the Little Bighorn River and the Bighorn River, then paralleling the Yellowstone River westward past Bozeman and then southwest to Virginia City. Prior to its establishment, the most direct way from the East to Montana was the Northern Overland Route, but its end point at Fort Benton still left a hefty journey to be made south if one wished to arrive at Virginia City or Gallatin County.

Capt. William Raynolds, an 1843 graduate of West Point and classmate of Ulysses Grant, of the Army Corps of Topographic Engineers led an expedition that covered much of the later Bozeman Trail in 1859–1860, mapping many of the features of the area. Then, in 1863, John Bozeman and John Jacobs scouted the route from Virginia City southeast to what would become central Wyoming that would connect with the major east-west passage to the Pacific—the Oregon Trail. Bozeman and Jacobs ensured that the route, which was wide enough for wagons, was shorter and had better water resources than some of the terrain Captain Raynolds had traversed. The establishment of the Bozeman Trail led to a flood of travelers from the East—and the tribes in the area did not like what they saw. From 1863 to 1866, some 3,500 settlers used the trail, which soon led to warfare between the United States Army and the Northern Plains Indians that erupted along the route in 1865–1866.[3]

Red Cloud's War (also known as the Bozeman War, or the Powder River War) was named for Red Cloud, a prominent Lakota Oglala chief, who allied the Lakota with the Northern Cheyenne and Northern Arapaho to fight the United States in the Wyoming and Montana territories from 1866 to 1868. The conflict really got underway in 1865, when Maj. Gen. Grenville M. Dodge—a graduate of Norwich University and the commander of the Department of the Missouri—ordered that a soiree—that became known as the Powder River Expedition—be made against the Lakota, Cheyenne, and Arapaho. Brig. Gen. Patrick E. Connor took command and promptly moved into the Powder River country with three columns of troopers, led by one of the foremost scouts in America—Jim "Old Gabe" Bridger. Old Gabe knew the area

Red Cloud in approximately 1891 taken at the Pine Ridge Agency. *Courtesy of Denver Public Library Digital Collections, Call Number X-31722*

Jim Bridger, greatest of Plainsmen, Scouts, Guides and Trappers.

intimately; a year before he had blazed what became known as the Bridger Trail that went through the Big Horn Basin west of the Bozeman Trail and thus avoided most of the tribal areas and potential trouble for settlers passing through.

The operation later was described as beginning ostensibly in response to the Lakota attack on July 26, 1865 near Casper, Wyoming, that became known as the "Battle of Platte Bridge," a large fight that included 1,000 warriors, although the expedition had actually started three weeks before that fight! Three columns:

one, under Col. Nelson Cole with the 12th Missouri Volunteer Cavalry Regiment; the second, under Lt. Col. Samuel Walker and the 16th Kansas Volunteer Cavalry Regiment; and the third, under Col. James H. Kidd and the 6th Michigan Volunteer Cavalry Regiment, remained in the field for several months. The 2,650 soldiers fought several skirmishes, destroying an Arapaho village near present-day, Ranchester, Wyoming, on August 29, 1865—known in some circles as the "Battle of the Tongue River" or the "Connor Battle"—but the army force did not defeat the tribes in any significant fight.[4]

After the Powder River Expedition, the United States government realized the difficulty in fighting the combined tribes in such a remote territory and attempted to obtain safe passage through Indian Territory. The government negotiated several treaties with Lakota, Cheyenne, and Arapaho leaders in the remainder of the year that provided monetary compensation for the Indians in exchange for their agreement to withdraw from the overland routes (current and those to be established) in the Powder River country. The rub was that none of the Indians, who lived near Fort Laramie, and who were prepared to sign the agreements, were respected leaders of the warriors that had fought the army. Red Cloud, Hump the elder, Crazy Horse (Tašúŋke Witkó) and Young-Man-Afraid-of-His-Horses (Tašúŋke Kokípapi) were nowhere to be found when it was time to put pen to paper. These last three men were not yet familiar to the United States Army, but they soon would be.[5]

Finally, on March 12, 1866, Red Cloud, Young-Man-Afraid-of-His-Horses and several other warrior leaders proudly rode into Fort Laramie to begin extended talks with government agents. The negotiations lasted until June 13, when Col. Henry B. Carrington, a graduate of Yale University and commander of the US 18th Infantry Regiment, rode into Fort Laramie and announced that he had orders to construct several army forts in Powder River country. In response to this abrupt slap in the face, Red Cloud and several other tribal leaders stormed out of the discussions. Those warriors that remained at the fort signed an agreement and on June 17, 1866, Col. Carrington rode out of Fort Laramie for the Powder River, with Jim Bridger again in the lead, to begin establishing additional forts.[6]

Carrington's column reached Fort Reno on June 28, 1866, and exchanged two companies with the existing garrison. Col. Carrington then established Fort Philip Kearny on July 14, 1866, near present-day Buffalo, Montana. The column moved into Montana and on August 13, 1866, founded Fort C.F. Smith—named for Maj. Gen. Charles Ferguson Smith (an 1825 graduate of West Point) who served in the Mexican War and the Civil War—on the Bighorn River. However, all was not well. Combat with various tribes had already commenced on July 16; between that day and September 27, there were no less than fifteen warrior attacks near Fort Kearny alone, the most noted being a vicious fight at Crazy Woman Creek east of present-day Buffalo, Wyoming.[7]

In December 1866, Red Cloud, encouraged by success against the army in the area, decided to undertake a large raiding operation against Fort Phil Kearny, before winter snows forced the tribes to disperse their large village on the Tongue River. His warriors, possibly more than 1,000, gathered ten miles north of the fort and decided to set a trap along the Bozeman Trail—out of sight, but only four miles from the stockade. The plan was to lure a group of soldiers from the fort and to destroy this group of soldiers sent to chase them. The Cheyenne and Arapaho took up positions on the west side of the trail and the Lakota on the east. Among the warriors chosen to decoy the soldiers into advancing precipitously (and perilously as it would turn out) included Crazy Horse. At 10:00 a.m. on December 21, 1866, Col. Carrington dispatched a wagon train from the fort to cut construction timber and firewood. Guarding the wagon train were approximately ninety soldiers.[8]

A short time later, army pickets on Pilot Hill signaled that warriors were attacking the wagon train. Col. Carrington dutifully sent Capt. William J. Fetterman, Capt. Frederick H. Brown and Lt. George W. Grummond, with forty-nine infantrymen and twenty-seven cavalrymen from detachments belonging to Companies A, C, E, and H of the US 18th Infantry Regiment and Company C of the US 2nd Cavalry Regiment respectively (three civilians also joined the party.) Confusion exists to this day concerning any limit of advance order that Carrington gave or did not give Fetterman as the troopers prepared to depart. None of the eighty-three men would return.

Eighty-three men, predominantly from the US 18th Infantry Regiment and US 2nd Cavalry Regiment went down this ridge, before they were surrounded and attacked by warriors in the gullies to the left and right. None of the eighty-three survived. *Author photograph, June 2015*

Here was Red Cloud's plan: two large groups of warriors would be concealed north of Lodge Trail Ridge on both the west and east sides of the Bozeman Trail. The Northern Cheyenne, Arapaho, and Oglala selected the gullies on the west side of the trail, while the Minneconjou took up positions on the east side. At the same time, forty warriors would launch a fake attack on the wood cutters' train, which would lure a relief party out of the fort. Ten hand-picked "decoy" warriors—including Little Wolf, Wolf Left Hand, Big Nose, American Horse, Sword, and very likely Crazy Horse—would lure this relief force over Lodge Trail Ridge and out of sight (and support) of the fort, where the waiting warriors would

pounce on them from either side of the trail. The weather was miserably cold; the relief force, under Capt. Fetterman, left the fort about 11:00 a.m., followed the decoys, crossed Lodge Trail Ridge, and ran straight into the trap. Although it would not have made much difference, Lt. Grummond and his cavalrymen raced ahead of the slower infantrymen, which meant that the two groups could not support each other. The infantrymen were armed with obsolete Springfield muzzle-loading rifles that had a slow rate of fire, although the cavalrymen carried Spencer repeaters. The fighting probably lasted no more than forty minutes—twenty minutes to dispatch the infantry, which had holed up among some large rocks on a snowy

Capt. William J. Fetterman, US 18th Infantry Regiment, killed at the Fetterman Fight also known as the Fetterman Massacre. He is buried at the military cemetery at the Little Bighorn. *Author photograph, June 2015*

Capt. Frederick H. Brown, Regimental Quartermaster for the US 18th Infantry, was also killed at the Fetterman Fight. He is buried at the military cemetery at the Little Bighorn. Lt. George W. Grummond, the other officer killed, is buried at Franklin, Tennessee. *Author photograph, June 2015*

field, and another twenty minutes to kill the cavalry that was attempting to fight dismounted on a flat plain about 400 yards from the infantry. The incident later became widely known as the Fetterman Massacre.[9] Most importantly, the willingness of Crazy Horse to serve as a decoy then would mirror the behavior of an un-named warrior on April 16, 1874, at the Battle of Lodge Grass Creek.

After the Fetterman fight, the tribes dispersed into small bands to better survive the upcoming winter. That spring, the tribes re-united and in July 1867, the Lakota held their annual Sun Dance along the Tongue and Powder Rivers. Tribal leaders discussed a continuing strategy to defeat the army, but it

appears that they came to an impasse concerning the massing of forces. On August 1, 1867, about 800 Cheyenne and Arapaho warriors attacked a wood-cutting party three miles from Fort C.F. Smith. The party survived the fight, losing two men; warrior dead were probably about eight. The battle, near present-day Yellowtail, Montana—was termed the Hayfield Fight.[10]

The following day—August 2, 1867—nearly 1,000 Oglala, Minneconjou, and Sans Arc Lakota warriors, under Red Cloud and Hump the elder, struck a woodcutters' camp along Piney Creek, some five miles northwest of Fort Phil Kearny (near present-day Story, Wyoming.) The detail had placed heavy

Until the Battle of the Little Bighorn in 1876, the Fetterman battle in December 1866 was the United States Army's most significant defeat against the Plains tribes. Crazy Horse fought in this battle. *Author photograph, June 2015*

wooden boxes off fourteen wagons on the ground in an oval corral near the main cutting site; most of the soldiers and civilians were able to take refuge behind the wagons and boxes when hundreds of Indian warriors on horseback suddenly appeared. The defenders repelled at least eight charges during the day in what would become known as the Wagon Box Fight. The woodcutters and soldiers lost seven men killed; warrior losses that day have been estimated at six to sixty.[11]

Although over the next several months there were no major engagements with the Lakota or Cheyenne, the army realized that a peaceful solution might be preferable to garrisoning the Powder River country amidst unfriendly bands looking to attack here and

there, with no end in sight. And when some estimates indicated that it might take 20,000 troopers to actually subdue the Northern Plains Indians, the army gagged—given that the service's authorized end-strength in 1866 was just 54,000 men and this number was heading downward.[12]

Washington sent peace commissioners to Fort Laramie in the spring of 1868. However, Red Cloud refused to meet with them until the army abandoned its Powder River outposts— Fort Phil Kearny, Fort C.F. Smith, and Fort Reno. The government acquiesced and in August 1868, the United States Army abandoned the three forts and withdrew to Fort Laramie far to the south (some 230 miles from Fort Phil Kearny.) This decision effectively closed

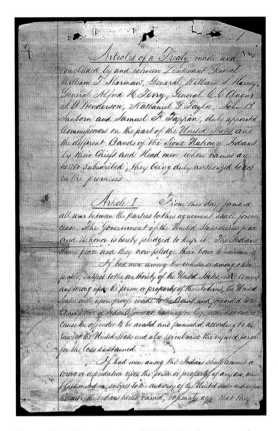

Page of the Sioux Treaty of 1868, also known as the Fort Laramie Treaty, 1868. The wagon train would violate this treaty in 1874. *Courtesy of National Archives*

territory, and also stipulates and agrees that no white person or persons shall be permitted to settle upon or occupy any portion of the same; or without the consent of the Indians, first had and obtained, to pass through the same; and it is further agreed by the United States, that within ninety days after the conclusion of peace with all the bands of the Sioux nation, the military posts now established in the territory in this article named shall be abandoned, and that the road leading to them and by them to the settlements in the Territory of Montana shall be closed.

In practical terms, this meant that the Powder River country was to be a reserve for the Indians who chose not to live on the new Great Sioux Reservation, and to serve as a hunting reserve for the Lakota, Cheyenne, and Arapaho. Thus, no white person or persons would ever be permitted to settle upon or occupy any portion of the Powder River country or without the consent of the Indians to pass through the Powder River country. Six years later, passing through Powder River country is precisely what warriors believed the wagon train was attempting to do.

Enter Governor Benjamin F. Potts

In 1863, knowing that some of the gold from the Montana area was making its way to the Confederacy and understanding that the federal government needed gold to fund the Civil War, President Abraham Lincoln sent Sidney Edgerton to the Idaho Territory to be the Chief Justice of the Idaho Territorial Supreme Court. A shrewd politician (he had been in the US House of Representatives for four years from Ohio's Eighteenth District,) as well as an experienced jurist, Edgerton immediately saw that the gold fields would be of immense benefit to the Union and that efficient administration of such fields would require its own territorial government. In the Idaho Territory, Edgerton found there was no administrator to swear him in to his formal

the Bozeman Trail, as the safety of travelers along this route would be in jeopardy almost every day without army presence. Twenty-four hours after the soldiers left the forts, warriors burned the structures to the ground.

When Red Cloud signed the Treaty of Fort Laramie in 1868, creating the Great Sioux Reservation—including the Black Hills and all of South Dakota territory west of the Missouri River, as it flowed from north to south before turning eastward—the treaty specified:[13]

> The United States hereby agrees and stipulates that the country north of the North Platte river and east of the summits of the Big Horn mountains shall be held and considered to be unceded. Indian

Sidney Edgerton, first Territorial Governor of Montana, in his later years. *Courtesy of Wikipedia*

Sidney Edgerton in his prime years. *Courtesy of Wikipedia*

Gov. Edgerton remained in office for over one year, during which time—disgusted that there was no assistance from a non-existent court system—he helped form what would be called the Montana Vigilantes to bring order to what was becoming a lawless community. That order started on December 21, 1863. George Ives, a bushwhacker, was on trial for murdering and robbing a German immigrant named Nicholas "Dutchman" Tbalt. Twenty-three of the twenty-four jurors found the defendant guilty, which was enough for prosecutor Wilbur Fisk Sanders. Ives requested time to write his mother and sister and it appeared his request would be granted. Suddenly, John X. Beidler, known often as "X" or "Vigilante X," who was serving as a guard at the trial yelled out, "Sanders! Ask him how much time he gave the 'Dutchman!'" Ives was hanged a few minutes later and the race was on for the vigilantes. Starting as a small secret institution in Virginia City, with an established set of regulations and bylaws, the movement soon spread, recruiting members throughout the territory. The group hanged many suspected road agents (bushwhackers that ambushed, robbed, and sometimes killed miners and the freighters who transported both gold and supplies.) Among those they sentenced and hanged was Sheriff Henry Plummer of Bannack, suspected by many of

position and so he never assumed the role of chief justice. He became what would be termed today a "lobbyist" and was chosen to return to the nation's capital to seek a positive decision for Montana to become a separate territory.

Realizing that his silver tongue may need some golden collateral, Edgerton lined his pockets with $2,500 to $5,000 (the exact amount has never been truly determined) worth of gold nuggets. Back in the nation's capital, he doled out nuggets to key members of Congress, as well as President Lincoln in a private meeting, just to show these decision-makers that there was, indeed, "gold in them thar hills" and that this gold would be extremely useful to the Union cause, which at this time was balanced on a razor's edge. It worked. On June 22, 1864, after Edgerton had returned to the Idaho Territory, President Abraham Lincoln appointed him the first governor of the Montana Territory.

A good-sized crowd attends a hanging by Montana Vigilantes in the 1870s. *Courtesy of Legendsofamerica.com*

being the ringleader of the road agents. Sheriff Plummer took the drop on January 10, 1864—three days before fellow gang member George "Clubfoot George" Lane. The vigilantes hanged men using the testimony of other men, who faced imminent execution unless they divulged their associates, as the sole evidence; out West, justice often had had no time for legal niceties common east of the Mississippi River.[14] The Montana Territory was, in many respects, a wild land until it formally became a state in 1889—many would say that it retained its rough edges long after that.

Gov. Edgerton returned to Ohio in late 1865 to attend to personal business and never assumed the territory's chief executive position again. However, his participation in the Montana Vigilantes—whatever that level was in respect to meting out justice—became a watchword for Montana territorial governors in the future for doing what it took to get the job done, whether that was cutting the occasional corner or stepping on a few toes. That attitude would be seen in spades six governors later, when big Ben Potts assumed the governorship on July 13, 1870.

Benjamin F. Potts had been born on a farm in Fox Township, Carroll County, Ohio, on January 29, 1836. After working as a clerk in a dry goods store in nearby Wattsville, he attended Westminster College in 1854–55, until he ran out of money. He then taught school and read law starting in September

Benjamin F. Potts, governor of the Montana Territory. He helped set the expedition in motion. *Courtesy of Wikipedia*

1857 under Ephraim R. Eckley, later a US congressman. Potts was an active supporter of President James Buchanan and joined the Democratic Party. After passing his bar exam in Canton, Ohio, and establishing a successful law practice in Carrollton, he served on the Ohio delegation to the 1860 Democratic National Convention in Charleston, South Carolina, supporting the candidacy of Stephen A. "The Little Giant" Douglas.[15]

Although Douglas received the nomination, he lost in the general election to Republican Abraham Lincoln, an event that sent the country on the path to conflict. With the outbreak of the Civil War, Potts served as a captain in the 32nd Ohio Volunteer Infantry Regiment in western Virginia and was present at the Battle of Cheat Mountain and the Battle of Greenbrier River. In 1862, he fought at the Battle of McDowell. In July 1862, Potts was temporarily detached from his infantry company and assigned command of an artillery battery in Winchester, Virginia. He soon found himself at Harpers Ferry, where Confederate forces captured his unit, following the Battle of Harpers Ferry. Capt. Potts was later paroled and sent north to Camp Douglas, Illinois, until exchanged.[16]

Potts then returned to the regiment as commander and then led the unit in numerous campaigns with the Army of the Tennessee in the western theater, including the Siege of Vicksburg and the Atlanta Campaign. In January 1865, Potts was promoted to brigadier general of volunteers. He led his brigade during the Carolinas campaign and in the Grand Review of the Armies in Washington, DC. Following the end of hostilities, the army bestowed the grade of brevet major general on the distinguished colonel. Before Potts left the service, a rumor circulated about Washington among foreign diplomats that during the final Union march through the South, Maj. Gen. William T. "Uncle Billy" Sherman, an 1840 graduate of West Point, had starved his own army to conserve supplies and to stoke the fires of meanness and resentment, as they burned their way through Georgia and South

Carolina. During a review of troops marching past the White House, at which were assembled several foreign ministers, as Gen. Potts rode by—all six feet and one inch, and weighing 230 pounds—Gen. Sherman pointed out to these dignitaries that Potts was one of his "Sample Vandals" and clearly had not been deprived of food![17]

Benjamin Potts was mustered out of the army in January 1866 and returned to Carroll County, Ohio, resuming his legal and political careers. Changing political parties and joining the Republicans, he won a seat in the Ohio State Senate in 1867. Three years later, he accepted an appointment from fellow Ohioan and former general, President Ulysses S. Grant to be the governor of the Montana Territory, a position that would pay him $2,300 per year.[18]

When Potts arrived in the Montana Territory, the gold rush had peaked and some of the western areas were experiencing an economic slowdown. However, Gov. Potts was impressed with the territory, recognizing that cattle and non-gold mineral resources could make Montana an economic powerhouse. Having seen the effect of railroads in unleashing the industrial engine in states in the East, such as Ohio, Potts realized that only a railroad tying his region to the East would do the same for his territory; Montana's trading future lay eastward and not westward. Just two months after arriving in the territory in August 1870, Potts began contemplating energizing the Northern Pacific Railroad, even writing to famed financier Jay Cooke, who had become interested in the venture a few months earlier.[19]

Congress had originally chartered the company on July 2, 1864, to connect the Great Lakes in the Midwest with Puget Sound, Washington—the goal being the opening and development of thousands of square miles in between for ranching, mining, and lumbering. The land devoted for use by the company was forty million acres. However, the backers of the venture struggled to obtain private financial support. In 1870, Jay Cooke—who by this time held national financial and political power second only to President Grant—entered the

Jay Cooke, financier behind the expansion of the railroads. *Courtesy of National Park Service, Public Domain*

picture; money started to flow and after groundbreaking took place at Thompson Junction, Minnesota—just west of Duluth—the rail line gathered momentum. By the end of 1871, workers had laid track to Morehead, Minnesota. The next year, the company advanced the track 164 miles across North Dakota—as well as constructing an impressive railroad bridge over the Mississippi River at St. Cloud—and by June 4, 1873, they had reached the Missouri River.[20]

During this time an important event occurred that would shape the situation in 1874. Knowing that the Plains Indians would resist the building of the Northern Pacific Railroad west of the Missouri River, on June 29, 1872, Lt. Gen. Phil Sheridan ordered that two armed, near-simultaneous survey parties be dispatched to conduct a thorough reconnaissance of the projected route. The first, under Col. David Stanley (West Point Class of 1852) with 600 men of the US 22nd Infantry Regiment, was ordered to depart Fort Rice (south of present-day Bismarck, North Dakota,) head west along the Missouri River, and proceed down the Yellowstone River to roughly the mouth of the Powder River, before returning. Stanley reached his objective on August 18, 1872, after numerous skirmishes and returned to Fort Rice. The second reconnaissance, led by Col. Eugene M. Baker (West Point Class of 1859) had 400 men, including 182 troopers from the US 2nd Cavalry Regiment. It departed Fort Ellis on July 27, 1872, heading east, and fought a significant battle with warriors at the mouth of Pryor's Creek on the Yellowstone (near present-day Huntley, Montana) on August 14. Although he repulsed the warriors, Maj. Baker sensed that his force was outnumbered and he traveled only to Pompey's Pillar—not the mouth of the Powder River as ordered—before turning north toward the Musselshell River and from there southwest to Fort Ellis.[21] Baker failed in his mission of reaching the Powder River, but several men on the expedition—including George Herendeen and Oliver Perry Hanna— gained valuable experience on this trek that they would put to good use two years hence.

A year later, disaster struck. Jay Cooke was financially overextended and went bankrupt on September 18, 1873. This contributed the Panic of 1873 that swept the United States and severely curtailed new railroads—in existence or planned. Northern Pacific leaders established austerity measures; combined with last-minute loans, the business survived, but by 1874, the company was on life support.

Historian and expert on the 1874 expedition Don Weibert asserted that at this time Gov. Ben Potts took a personal interest in the progress of the railroad, believing that if he had advance warning of inside information, he could legitimately profit by it—the insider trading rules of today not being established then. Regardless of the personal profit that may have gone Potts' way, the governor knew that for Montana to prosper, the railroad must get through.[22]

The problem in late 1873 was that in addition to a shaky economic situation, the railroad would soon be confronted by the **Indian tribes along the Yellowstone** watershed—a direct obstacle to the planned route across North Dakota and Montana that came directly down the Yellowstone Valley. To succeed, this Yellowstone Valley needed to be civilized to facilitate coaling and water stations for the railroad—and to this point, the valley was only home to small numbers of

hunters and trappers, and these men could make do with trails instead of the roads necessary to truly develop the area. The drumbeat for new roads began softly, as many harbingers do. On December 12, 1873, the Bozeman *Avant Courier* newspaper printed this small article on page two, which read in part:[23]

Now that it is intended to make an effort to get goods into Montana in the direction of Musselshell and the Yellowstone, it is highly important that good roads should be made to both these rivers. They are in our own Territory, and all done in that direction will be developing in our own borders. The first Legislature met in Montana in 1864, nine years ago, and it does not occur to us at this writing that a dollar was devoted to a road, or to a public edifice; the people having paid taxes to support the territory and there is nothing to show for it, except a Territorial debt of $150,000 created mostly to pay extra compensation. We do not care to discuss which of the controlling parties are responsible for this, but it is a crying shame and reflects no credit on past Legislatures.

While we may never fully know the exact details of Gov. Potts' involvement in the decision to launch the 1874 Yellowstone Wagon Road and Prospecting Expedition, circumstantial evidence indicates that he may have been up to his eyeballs in the plan. In an August 1, 1873, letter he wrote to the Northern Pacific Railroad, Potts attempted to dissuade the company leadership from establishing its route through Montana along the Missouri River to the Musselshell River in the north of the territory, but instead to pursue a southern route. Potts wrote that the Musselshell area (over one hundred miles north of the Yellowstone) was entirely through "Indian country" and that it was "rough, hilly and rocky and soldiers will be necessary to keep it open." On the other hand, the southern route would be much easier:[24]

If the Yellowstone can be navigated to the mouth of the Big Horn, a Wagon Road will be built from Bozeman to that point by our people and kept open without expense to your company.

The *Avant Courier* newspaper had articles about the upcoming expedition on at least six different days. Other newspapers chimed in as well. The January 22, 1874, issue of *The Montanian*, published in Virginia City, noted that Gov. Potts had made available 10,000 rounds of rifle ammunition for any expedition that might be formed.[25] Potts appears to have also directed the regular army garrison at Fort Ellis to provide the expedition with a mountain howitzer and upwards of 150 Model 1870 Springfield .50-70 "Needle Guns," although one source wrote that the weapons came from the territorial arsenal.[26] Permission to provide these arms would have had to be approved by the Fort Ellis post commander, Maj. Nelson B. Sweitzer.[27]

Nelson Bowman Sweitzer was no ordinary frontier major—not by a long shot. Hailing from Brownsville, Pennsylvania, he graduated twenty-fourth of fifty-two cadets from West Point in the class of 1853, along with such future luminaries as James B. McPherson, Joshua W. Sill, John A. Schofield, John Bell Hood, and Philip H. "Little Phil" Sheridan. After graduation, he served in the US 1st Regiment of Dragoons, which was renamed the US 1st Cavalry Regiment; the regiment was headquartered in 1856 at Fort Tejon, California. During the Civil War, Sweitzer was brevetted for promotion five times (finishing the war as a brevet brigadier general,) fighting at Winchester, the Peninsula Campaign and Yellow Tavern and served as the aide-de-camp to Gen. George B. "Little Mac" McClellan, an 1846 graduate of West Point. Perhaps his most noteworthy accomplishment from a historical standpoint was his appointment on November 12, 1864, to command the 16th New York Volunteer Cavalry Regiment. After the assassination of President Abraham Lincoln in April 1865, a detachment of this unit discovered, cornered, and killed Lincoln's murderer, John Wilkes Booth, in a tobacco barn near Port Royal, Virginia.

By 1874, Sweitzer was a major in the US 2nd Cavalry Regiment. With Gov. Potts' Civil

Gen. George B. McClellan and staff in the Civil War. Nelson Sweitzer is fourth from the right. Sweitzer assisted the expedition obtain a mountain howitzer on the eve of its departure. *Courtesy of National Archives and Records Administration; Catalogue Number 111-B-498*

Photograph from the main eastern theater of the war, Battle of Antietam, September-October 1862; from left, Col. Delos B. Sacket, I.G., Capt. George Monteith, Lt. Col. Nelson B. Sweitzer, Gen. George W. Morell, Col. Alexander S. Webb, chief of staff, 5th Corps, Gen. George B. McClellan, Scout Adams, Dr. Jonathan Letterman, Army Medical Director, Unknown, President Abraham Lincoln, Gen. Henry J. Hunt, Gen. Fitz-John Porter, Unknown, Col. Frederick T. Locke, A.A.G., Gen. Andrew A. Humphreys, and Capt. George Armstrong Custer. *Courtesy of Library of Congress.*

War record, he could have certainly talked as military equals with Maj. Sweitzer, and he knew better than to send a subordinate to request the howitzer and the rifles.[28] What happened next was detailed later by Oliver Perry Hanna, an expedition member, and sounded like a classic case of a "midnight requisition" (theft under cover of darkness.):[29]

Of course, Army officers had no authority to give civilians government property, so, through the influence of the [expedition] committee [and perhaps General Sheridan,] the officers decided that the

Fort needed "extra protection" and they placed two cannons and two wagon loads of ammunition out on a hill near the fort. That night they were taken to the camp and hooked on to the wagons. <u>There was no search for the missing cannons.</u> (Author's underline)

Classmates Sweitzer and Sheridan had previously been in close communication concerning several Yellowstone expeditions. In the summer of 1873, Paul McCormick—who would also go on this expedition—organized his own prospecting excursion to Yellowstone country.

Lt. Gen. Philip Sheridan, the commander of the Division of the Missouri. Maj. Sweitzer was his West Point classmate years before. *Reproduction cabinet card in author's collection.*

Maj. Sweitzer most likely reported the event through higher channels, for on August 2, 1873, he received this telegram from Lt. Gen. Philip Sheridan, commanding general of the Military Division of the Missouri:[30]

> You can notify the members of McCormick's party that they will not be permitted to invade the Crow Indian Reservation to hunt gold, <u>but I do not consider we have any authority over the party outside the Reservation</u>. (Author's underline)

Maj. Sweitzer relayed Sheridan's instructions to the McCormick party, which, in turn, promised they would stay out of forbidden territory. Less than a year later, an even larger expedition would be heading eastward.[31]

Merely sending an expedition through the Yellowstone River valley and through tribal lands to the south along the Rosebud, Powder, and Tongue Rivers would not keep the land free for the Northern Pacific Railroad to continue laying track westward. The warriors would simply ambush the trains and attack the coaling and water stations, unless these facilities were heavily guarded all the time. No, what was needed to sweep the Yellowstone River watershed was the commitment of large portions of the United States Army. To accomplish this, the wagon train had to complete its journey (to show that it could be done) by the skin of its teeth (to convince Washington that civilians could not subjugate the Yellowstone River watershed on their own.) Gov. Potts also needed the Lakota and Cheyenne to conduct reprisal raids after the incursion; that might force the army to take the field, regardless of what the treaty said. Over the years, Gov. Potts would send a stream of letters to General of the Army William T. Sherman, Phil Sheridan's superior, describing the deadly Indian problem that the Montana Territory faced. In fact, Potts once suggested that Montana be organized into its own military department with Nelson A. Miles in command.[32]

Gov. Ben Potts had his motive, and with funds coming in from private citizens and weapons and ammunition from the United States Army at Fort Ellis for the expedition, only two things remained: an executive committee to organize the expedition and tough men to actually ride the trail. Twelve prominent citizens stepped forward to do their civic duty on the committee and the *Avant Courier* solemnly announced the new organization, not including the men's occupations, which are annotated here:

Maj. James P. Bruce, President—resident and veteran Indian fighter
John V. Bogert, Treasurer and Secretary—correspondent, *Avant Courier*
Horatio Nelson Maguire—Probate Judge for Gallatin County and Bozeman City Commissioner and editor of *The Pick and Plow* newspaper.
L.L. Perkins—resident
Walter Cooper—owner Walter Cooper's Armory and Gun Manufactory at Bozeman

General of the Army William T. Sherman. *Courtesy of the National Archives and Records Administration*

T.C. Burns—rancher and logger (he would go on the expedition)
C.L. Clark—Sheriff and commissioner for the new town of Bozeman
Nelson Story—banker and former Montana Vigilante
Charles Rich—partner of Willson & Rich freighting company
D.H. Carpenter—rancher whose land was raided by Lakota warriors in 1872
S.W. Longhorn—Druggist and probate judge for Gallatin County
S.B. Bowen—Gallatin County Treasurer

The following men would also assist the executive committee in its duties:

Daniel Rouse—businessman (he would go on the expedition)
Lester Willson—former Civil War general and businessman; owner of Tuller, Rich and Willson General Store

Perry W. McAdow—miller and owner of a general store

Gov. Potts now had his organization. The only facet left to be chiseled into this endeavor was a motivation that would attract tough, capable men to actually sign up and ride into the unknown. As the governor was finding, this was proving to be more difficult than originally thought. Addison M. Quivey wrote two years after the expedition about finding men for the venture:[33]

About the 1st of January, 1874, it was determined by citizens of Bozeman and the surrounding country, to send an expedition down the Yellowstone river for the purpose of opening a wagon-road to the head of navigation on the Yellowstone, and thus open the most direct route connecting with the present terminus of the Northern Pacific Railroad, and it was

John V. Bogert. *Courtesy of Museum of the Rockies Photo Archives, Catalog Number: x85.3.127*

Horatio Nelson Maguire, probate judge for Gallatin County, Bozeman city commissioner, and editor of *The Pick and Plow* newspaper. *Courtesy of Find-A-Grave, Horatio Nelson Maguire*

Nelson Story Sr. about 1900. *Photograph by Hamilton, courtesy of Museum of the Rockies Photo Archives, Catalog Number: x65.3.27*

also expected that the expedition would build a stockade and form a settlement for the purpose of holding the country and road against hostile Indians, etc.

For the purpose of effecting the above object, a meeting was held in the town of Bozeman, and an association formed, styled "The Yellowstone Wagon-road Association;" officers elected for the same; also an executive committee, who canvassed the town and surrounding country for subscriptions of money and materials with which to equip the proposed expedition. But slow progress was made, as many were of the opinion that it would be quite impossible to keep a road open in that country, unless large settlements could be formed along the line of same more rapidly than could usually be done by the inducements of trade and agriculture.

As can be seen, the county of Gallatin had an enormous stake in the expedition. With the Northern Pacific's current railhead no closer

Main Street in Bozeman. It was a wild and wooly place in 1874. *Courtesy of Gallatin History Museum*

than Bismarck—approximately 556 miles to the east—the businessmen of Gallatin needed to create a town along the Yellowstone River where the water was navigable for steamboats, similar to Fort Benton to the north on the Missouri River. Then steamboat traffic could go back and forth between this new settlement and Bismarck, until the railroad finally made its way west. Since the Yellowstone was not navigable by steamboat all the way to Bozeman, the settlers would build a road from Bozeman paralleling the river to the location of this new river town, wherever that site might be. That last mission was clearly indicated in the name Yellowstone Wagon-road Association. The expedition itself would not build the road, but merely identify the last navigable position west on the Yellowstone River and a ground route from that location west to Bozeman. Based on the west-to-east movement of the wagon train,

Stereograph of Walter Cooper's firearms workshop and store on Main Street in Bozeman. If you wanted a Sharps buffalo rifle, he had one to fit your every specification. *Courtesy of Gallatin History Museum*

Main Street in Bozeman; on the left is a rifle used as part of a sign; this is the store of Walter Cooper.
Courtesy of Gallatin History Museum

the men would be accomplishing those missions in reverse order, which was not an issue as long as both tasks were accomplished.[34]

There was only one problem: how many men would sign up for the purpose of locating a suitable wagon trail through unknown, but certainly dangerous, territory in eastern Montana, into the heartland of the Lakota and Northern Cheyenne, in the middle of a bleak Great Plains' winter, when there was nothing really in it for them? A salary could be offered, but it definitely would not compensate them for the anticipated hardship. Certainly there would be adventure, but there was no tangible reward in mapping the land for the surveyors, only potential earnings for the men who financed the operation—older, wealthier men who faced no personal hardship or danger, as is so often the case throughout history.

There was only one word needed to lure more than enough men to action—that word was *gold*.

Enter J.L. Vernon

According to legend, in 1284, the Lower Saxon town of Hamelin was suffering from a rat infestation. A man dressed in a long cloak—half red and half yellow—and carrying a flute appeared, claiming to be a rat-catcher.

The man promised the mayor a fool-proof solution for Hamelin's problem. The mayor, in turn, promised to pay the man in the cloak for the removal of the vermin. The man accepted, and played his musical pipe to lure the rats into the nearby Weser River with a magical song, and all but one of the pests drowned. Despite this success, the mayor failed to keep his promise and refused to pay the rat-catcher the full amount of money. The strange man left the town but vowed to return some time later. Later was on Saint John and Paul's Day (June 26) while the inhabitants of Hamelin were in church. The man, this time dressed as a hunter in green, played his flute once again, this time not charming the rats but rather attracting the children of Hamelin. One hundred and thirty boys and girls followed him out of the town, where they were lured into a mysterious cave and never seen again.

The Brothers Grimm, Johann Wolfgang von Goethe, and Robert Browning, authors and poets that addressed this tale, never mentioned the name of this mysterious pied piper in their works, but the good people of Montana may have believed they knew him—one J.L. Vernon. Expedition member Joe Cook later recalled the charlatan:[35]

A straggler by the name of Vernon came up the Yellowstone with [General] Stanley [in 1873.] He claimed to be a prospector and that he washed out one dollar and twenty-five cents to the pan and that he drove an iron picket pin into a cedar tree at the mouth of the gulch, and that he could take us right to the spot. This created quite a furor over Montana, and in the early spring of 1874 one hundred and forty-eight of us went down into that country to get a gold mine, Vernon agreeing to pilot us to the El Dorado on Goose Creek.

Vernon's "piping" came in the form of an advertisement on December 26, 1873, in the *Avant Courier* that read:[36]

Wanted

Twenty-five able bodied men, who are able and willing to outfit themselves for six months, to prospect in the Yellowstone country. Apply to or address.
J.L. Vernon, Bozeman

Vernon also appeared in and wrote an article for *The Pick and Plow*, a Bozeman newspaper. He claimed that he was a miner and had been on the Yellowstone expedition of 1873 (some sources stated he was a surveyor for the Northern Pacific Railroad) with Gen. David S. Stanley and George Custer and that he had found gold in streams flowing from the Wolf Mountains. In one unnamed location, Vernon claimed that he found gold nuggets and had driven an old iron pick into the trunk of a tree to mark the spot for future prospecting.[37]

However, a *Montana Standard* newspaper article in 1942, using source material provided by Charles Avery, who had been on the expedition—to his brother Bert, who in turn provided it to the newspaper—stated that Vernon had been the founder of Butte, Montana's Mount Vernon Hotel, later re-named the Paragon Hotel and finally the Library Hotel, near the terminus of the old stage coach line from Corinne, Utah. In addition to operating a hotel, the newspaper stated, he had also served as a mail carrier and general messenger between the mining camps in the area. The article further stated that Vernon once rode from Butte to Fort Bridger in Wyoming.[38] Prof. John S. Gray's notes indicate that in 1872 J.L. Vernon went north from Denver to the Montana Territory and subsequently taught school in Bozeman.[39]

For the next three weeks, Vernon received inquiries about his expedition, some serious and some not. On January 9, 1874, the *Avant Courier* reported that James Gemmell of Madison County had departed with eight men on his own prospecting expedition. Gemmell was a widely known name; he had been active in the gold-mining trade a decade before. He was a peculiar figure. Born in South Ayrshire, Scotland, on February 4, 1814, he traveled to the United States as a youngster, living in New York City. When he became an adult, Gemmell promptly went to Canada, where he participated in the Canadian Rebellion in 1837.

British authorities captured Gemmell and sentenced him to death for treason. He returned to England for execution, before Daniel Webster intervened on behalf of the US government and secured a commutation to life imprisonment. A prison ship transported James Gemmell to Australia, but he escaped his prison there after two years. Fleeing to Michigan, he married for the first time. After his wife's death, James Gemmell traveled to Salt Lake City and the Mormon settlement. He married again, and again, and again, becoming a polygamist. James Gemmell rode to Texas and organized a group of Texas Mormons, assisting them to head to Salt Lake. In November 1858, Brigham Young of the Mormon Church excommunicated Gemmell—reportedly over a mysterious linkage to the "Mountain Meadow Massacre"— and Gemmell moved, with just one of his wives, to what would become the Montana Territory.[40] On January 9, the *Avant Courier* published a second article:[41]

Just now there is a good deal of excitement among parties in regard to expeditions to the Yellowstone river, and which have for their object the development of the resources of that section. There is a strong belief that rich minerals abound there, and parties are now organized, who mean to start in a few days in that direction. There is a pretty fair road to the mouth of the Powder river, and the road will be traveled and marked out, and bridges will be built this spring wherever it may be necessary to bring freights that may come up the Yellowstone for Montana. Arrangements are being made with the Northern Pacific with a view to have them send boats up that river this season. The Company is anxious to use that stream on account of their work at Yellowstone Crossing.

The exploration of Eastern Montana this season is now a fixed fact, and we look for large and extensive settlements on the Yellowstone river from the railroad crossing to its head. It is bound to be a flourishing region, filled with a teeming population. Those who are fortunate enough to get a foothold there early will be largely repaid for their enterprise.

It was a masterful understatement and each reader could only hope that he would be the first to jump on this opportunity before everyone else. The floodgates burst open a week later, on January 16, 1874, and once again the *Avant Courier* was the agent provocateur, with a simple article entitled "Yellowstone Wagon Road":[42]

The citizens of Gallatin County are at last aroused to the necessity of opening up a wagon road to the head of navigation on the Yellowstone and having an EASTERN CONNECTION extending to Bismarck. They have become convinced that such a route will prove highly advantageous to them in a variety of aspects. Experience has taught them that if emigration is to come, it must be from this direction. Heretofore the travel has been to Corinne and the West and no advantage has resulted from pursuing so circuitous a route. What is needed and demanded is a *direct* connection East not West, if we are to derive substantial advantages. Open up connections by good roads with the Yellowstone, Bismarck, Cheyenne and Point of Rocks on the Union Pacific and this will be a country. The people of Cheyenne are alive to the importance of connection with Montana and her enterprising citizens are working with vigor to accomplish this desirable result. The military, under the auspices of General Ord, will make a road this year from Point of Rocks on the U.P.R.R. to Fort Ellis. From information of a reliable character, we are advised that there are large parties, who mean to avail themselves of the road traveled last summer by General Stanley's large expedition to reach the Yellowstone, believing that there is an abundance of placer diggings in that direction.

There exists a determination on the part of thousands in the East to reach the Yellowstone the coming season with a view of prospecting for gold and silver, and also to secure good homes in advance of the railroad. In view of all this, the citizens of Bozeman and Gallatin county have been for several weeks earnestly engaged in getting up an expedition to be fully equipped and provisioned for SIX MONTHS to open up a good wagon road to the head of navigation on the Yellowstone and to establish a connection with Bismarck, the present terminus of the *Northern Pacific Railroad*. Very little has been said in regard to this action in this paper, as it was desired by the prospectors of this great enterprise that certain success should be assured before publicity was given to the object. Public meetings have been held during the last two weeks in Bozeman, Gallatin City, Hamilton, Central Park, Reece Creek and on East Gallatin, where the citizens have been addressed on the question, and committees appointed in each locality, the scheme meeting with unexampled success and unanimity in all parts of the county as to the success and usefulness of the proposed expedition, and all are willing to aid it according to their ability.

They see in it a measure calculated to afford relief from the present embarrassed condition of affairs, and have an abiding faith in its advantages. This *Eastern* connection is what has been required to bring emigration to Montana. Had travel to our territory been uninterrupted on the Powder River route, we should have had double the population now living here, and when good roads are opened up from the terminal points on the Northern and Union Pacific railroads East of us, we will see prosperous times again, and not before. The *front door* to Montana is on the *East side, and it must be opened* and invitations extended to all to enter therein. The mode of coming into the Territory by the *back door* has not paid heretofore, and when emigration has a chance to come *directly* from the *East* it will pour in on us, thereby creating a demand and outlet for our products.

The article continued but the die had been cast—the Powder River and eastern Montana must be made free from Lakota control in order for the Montana Territory to grow and prosper, and this expedition was to be the first nail in the coffin for the land ceded by treaty to the Lakota five years earlier. What was not said in the article was as important as what was actually printed. Who would get to the gold first, the existing prospectors of Montana or a flood of "thousands in the East"? Both James Gemmell and J.L. Vernon were believed to be the only men who knew exactly the location of the gold. Addison M. Quivey later explained after the expedition:[43]

In the fall of 1873, one J.L. Vernon arrived in Bozeman, having traveled from the Missouri River with the expedition of that year engaged in surveying the *Northern Pacific Railroad* from the crossing of the Missouri River, connecting with the survey of 1872 near the landmark known as Pompey's Pillar, on the bank of the Yellowstone. Vernon claimed to have found rich gold mines on the south side of the Yellowstone, somewhere between the Rosebud and Powder rivers, and proposed to lead a party to the same. Some progress was made in its organization, when it was proposed to unite both the expeditions in one, as they were both going to the same country and their interests could be made identical, and many men could be obtained for a prospecting expedition who could not be induced to have anything to do with a wagon-road

enterprise. But all efforts to consolidate seemed likely to fail, when Mr. Vernon, without consulting any of his party or informing them of his purpose, gave notice through the press that he had abandoned his expedition, and advising all who had signed his articles of agreement to join the wagon road expedition, the style of which became the "Yellowstone Wagon-road and Prospecting Expedition.

It appears that Gov. Benjamin Potts had intervened in the shadows. What do you do when a competitor has an advantage over you in business? You buy him out. Vernon, without consulting the ten or so men who had signed on with him, gave notice through the *Avant Courier* that he had abandoned his expedition. He advised everyone who had signed his articles of agreement to join this new venture, which became known as the Yellowstone Wagon-road and Prospecting Expedition. Vernon informed his supporters that once this larger expedition started, "that he would meet them at some point below, and guide them to his discoveries; and he soon left Bozeman, accompanied by three men."[44] What the price was to "encourage" Mr. Vernon to drop his own trek and guide this new one has never been recorded. However, whatever the amount, J.L. Vernon had the last laugh. As Addison M. Quivey recalled two years after the expedition:[45]

… it being generally understood that he intended to join the main party on the road … J.L. Vernon joined our party on the road, as expected, but gave us the slip a few days after, and was heard of next at Ft. Benton, where he and his companion stole a skiff, and went down the Missouri River. He was a fraud.

However, J.L. Vernon had fulfilled the role that Gov. Potts needed and had stoked the fires of gold mania. Momentum continued and the following article appeared in the *Avant Courier* on January 23, 1874:[46]

YELLOWSTONE WAGON ROAD
AND PROSPECTING EXPEDITION.
A LARGE EXPEDITION WILL LEAVE
BOZEMAN, MONTANA
On or about February 10th

To locate a Free Wagon Road to Tongue River, and generally survey and prospect the country between Bozeman and that point. It will go well outfitted. Good men are invited to join it, and contributions of supplies are solicited. Men should come provided with transportation, arms, ammunition and supplies for a term of six months. Cattle, horse and mule teams will accompany it, and saddle outfits will be admitted.

Rich mineral deposits are believed to exist in the region referred to, and the best men of the Gallatin Valley are interested in, and have contributed $5,000 toward, the movement, which is endorsed by Messers Gemmell and Sharp of Madison county, who have decided to move with this Expedition, which will be provided with 25,000 rounds of extra ammunition and three pieces of artillery.

All who intended joining the late Vernon Expedition are invited to join the Wagon Road and Prospecting expedition with their outfits. All that would have resulted from that movement will be obtained under this, and the attention is hereby called to the reports published in Bozeman and Virginia City papers this week.

All who wish to join the Wagon Road and Prospecting Expedition are requested to correspond with the Secretary IMMEDIATELY. Letters should state the amount of outfit the writer can supply and the date he can report at Bozeman. As the Expedition will start by February 10th at latest, it is necessary that the suggested correspondence be attended to without delay. Those intending to contribute toward it must advise the Secretary fully immediately. Contributions should be sent to the Bozeman Depot without delay, and at the latest by February 1st, and all men and material MUST report at Bozeman before February 10th.

As this enterprise will do much to develop various resources of the lower country, induce immigration and encourage railroad and steamboat approaches, the interest of every citizen will be consulted by assisting by men and material.

Executive Committee.

J.P. BRUCE,	N. STORY,	L.L. PERKINS,
L.L. WILLSON,	H.N. MAGUIRE,	CHARLES RICH,
J.V. BOGERT,	D.H. CARPENTER,	W. COOPER,
T.C. BURNS.	C.L. CLARK,	S.B. BOWEN.
	S.W. LANGHORNE.	
	J.V. BOGERT, TREASURER AND SECRETARY	

And so, men started signing up for this new expedition in droves, much to the chagrin of Charles Avery who thought that the original name—without the addition of "Prospecting"— might serve as camouflage to prevent the federals from finding out the true purpose of the wagon train. As Avery later wrote:[47]

> We did not care to have our old Uncle Sam take too much interest in our trip, as we had very sure knowledge that the boys with the brass buttons at Fort Ellis would take us in before we got started.

Of course, everyone knew, or thought he knew, what the word "Prospecting" meant in the name of the expedition; it meant that they could suspend farming, or buffalo hunting, or trapping, or logging or ranching for a while. Here was a much bigger fish to fry and its potential rewards could last them a lifetime. They may have later called themselves "The Boys," but the men that joined the expedition were a long way from being mere babes in the woods.

Notes

1. Krys Holmes, *Montana: Stories of the Land, Helena, Montana*: Montana Historical Society Press, 2008, 101-104, 112. Amount is in US dollars in 2013 equivalent.

2. Ibid, 105-106.

3. Fort Phil Kearny State Historic Site Pamphlet.

4. Michno, *Encyclopedia of Indian Wars*, 179, 184, 185.

5. Charles J. Kappler, *Indian Affairs: Laws and Treaties*, Volume II, Treaties, Washington, DC: Government Printing Office, 1904, 885 showing Article 4 of the treaty.

6. James C. Olson, *Red Cloud and the Sioux Problem*, Lincoln, Nebraska: University of Nebraska Press, 1965, 29-40.

7. Michno, *Encyclopedia of Indian Wars*, 189-190

8. Ibid, 192-193.

9. Michno, *Encyclopedia of Indian Wars*, 192-193; John M. Monnett, *Where a Hundred Soldiers Were Killed: The Struggle for the Powder River Country in 1866 and the Making of the Fetterman Myth*, Albuquerque, New Mexico: University of New Mexico Press, 2008, 122.

10. Ibid, 204-205.

11. Ibid, 206-207.

12. French L. MacLean, *Custer's Best: The Story of Company M, 7th Cavalry at the Little Bighorn*, Atglen, Pennsylvania: Schiffer Publishing, 2011, 21.

13. "Fort Laramie Treaty, 1868," *Archives of The West*, Episode Four (1856 to 1868,) PBS, as found at http://www.pbs.org/weta/thewest/resources/archives/four/.

14. Richard W. Slatta, *The Mythical West: An Encyclopedia of Legend: Lore and Popular Culture*, Santa Barbara, California: ABC-CLIO Inc., 2001, 273; Thomas J. Dimsdale, *The Vigilantes of Montana*, Norman Oklahoma: University of Oklahoma Press 1953; and Dave Walter, et al., *Speaking Ill of the Dead: Jerks in Montana History*, Guilford, Connecticut: Morris Book Publishing, 2011, 42.

15. Whitelaw Reid, *History of Ohio during the War, Her Statesmen, Generals and Soldiers, Volume 1: The History of Ohio during the War and the Lives of Her Generals*, Cincinnati, Ohio: The Robert Clarke Company, 1895, 898-900.

16. Ibid.

17. Ibid.

18. Mocavo Genealogy Website: 1873 Official Register of the United States at http://www.mocavo.com/Official-Register-of-the-United-States-1873/228899/355#358.

19. Don L. Weibert, *The 1874 Invasion of Montana: A Prelude to the Custer Disaster*, Self-Published: D. L. Weibert, 1993, 129-131.

20. Ralph W. Hidy, et al., *The Great Northern Railway: A History*, Minneapolis, Minnesota: University of Minnesota Press, 2004, 22, 56-61.

21. Eugene Virgil Smalley, *History of the Northern Pacific Railway*, New York: G. P. Putnam's Sons, 1883, 435.

22. Weibert, *The 1874 Invasion*, 131-132.

23. "Improvement and Opening of New Roads," *Avant Courier* (Bozeman,) December 12, 1873, 2.

24. Weibert, *The 1874 Invasion*, 131.

25. "Ten Thousand Rounds of Ammunition," *The Montanian* (Virginia City,) January 16, 1874, 7.

26. Utley, *Sitting Bull*, 118,

27. Fort Ellis, named for Col. F. Augustus Ellis, who was killed at the Battle of Gettysburg in 1863, was established in 1867 by Capt. Robert S. La Motte and three companies of the US 13th Infantry Regiment. Designed to protect the residents of Gallatin County from Indian raids, it was a log stockade measuring 390 feet by 458 feet, with a ten-foot-high outer wall. The army closed the fort in 1889.

28. *Register of Graduates, and Former Cadets of the United States Military Academy, West Point, New York*, West Point, New York: Association of Graduates, 2000, 4-33, 4-34.

29. Carter, 31.

30. Mark H. Brown, *The Plainsmen of the Yellowstone: A History of the Yellowstone Basin*, Lincoln, Nebraska: Bison Books, University of Nebraska Press, 1969, 212.

31. Ibid, 213.

32. Michael A. Leeson, editor, *History of Montana, 1739–1885*, Chicago: Warner, Beers & Company, 1885, 161; and Weibert, *The 1874 Invasion of Montana*, 132-133. Weibert used an article in the *Billings Gazette* of February 5, 1891, and Muriel Sibell Wolle's *Montana Pay Dirt* to develop his assertion.

33. Addison M. Quivey, "The Yellowstone Expedition of 1874," *Contributions to the Historical Society of Montana*, Volume One, Helena, Montana: Rocky Mountain Publishing Company, 1876, 268.

34. Brown, *The Plainsmen of the Yellowstone*, 212.

35. Brown and Willard, 558-559.

36. Weibert, *The 1874 Invasion*, 2-3.

37. Carter, 30.

38. M.G. O'Malley, "Thrilling Frontier Experiences in Montana," Part 2, *Montana Standard*, Butte, Montana, October 4, 1942, 25.

39. John S. Gray Research Papers, 1942–1991, Box 16, Folder 136, Scouts, Newberry Research Library.

40. Ancestry.com and Find-A-Grave, James Gemmell.

41. "Expeditions to Yellowstone," *Avant Courier* (Bozeman,) January 9, 1874, 2.

42. "Yellowstone Wagon Road," *Avant Courier* (Bozeman,) January 16, 1874, 2.

43. Quivey, 268-269, 283.

44. Ibid.

45. Ibid.

46. *Avant Courier* (Bozeman,) January 23, 1874.

47. Avery Reminiscence, SC 372, 1.

CHAPTER THREE

The Yellowstone Wagon Road and Prospecting Expedition

"Young Hanna swears it beat anything he ever read in *Beadle's Dime Novels*."

The Men

The Yellowstone Wagon Road and Prospecting Expedition started with approximately 125 men, but soon swelled to 147 participants by the time it reached the mouth of the Bighorn River. It was truly a cross-section of frontier America. At least seven men had been born in Scotland, six in Germany, three in Canada, one in Denmark, one in Wales, one in Sweden, one in England, and three in Ireland. For the men born in the United States, at least fourteen hailed from New York, seven from Ohio, six from Pennsylvania, four from Iowa, two each from Indiana, Illinois, and Maine, one each from Connecticut, Michigan, Vermont, Minnesota, and possibly New Jersey. The south was represented as well with three men from Tennessee, two from Kentucky, one from Arkansas, one from North Carolina, and eleven from the border state of Missouri. It is not unusual that so little is known about the men's birthplaces; many people traveled west to start completely new lives, whether that was for adventure, economic fortune, or running away from some problem in their previous existence, such as desertion from the army, and for many a frontiersman, the less people knew about his past, the better—even the wagon train boss may have been in this category of someone who had something to hide.

Many of the men had humble backgrounds. Before one participant made his name as an accomplished scout, he worked as a shoe salesman. Another appears to have run away from home rather than follow in his father's footsteps as a florist. Numerous men had been hard-scrabble farmers; others cut lumber for a living. Those who had military service were almost all from the enlisted ranks.

At least sixteen men have documented service in the Union Army, while six men are definitely known to have served with Confederate forces. The veteran rebels had fought at Wilson's Creek, Stones River, Pea Ridge, Lexington and Vicksburg, with one riding with Confederate raider John H. "Thunderbolt" Morgan, while the Yankees had battled at Shiloh, Island Mound, Poison Spring, Westport, Perryville, Stones River, Hoover's Gap, Second Bull Run, Seven Pines, Fredericksburg, Chancellorsville, the Wilderness, Petersburg, Chickamauga, Lookout Mountain, Missionary Ridge, Kennesaw Mountain, Atlanta, Jonesboro, Bentonville, Nashville, Antietam, Savannah, the pursuit of Confederate raider Morgan, counter-guerilla operations against Quantrill's Raiders, and the Shenandoah Valley Campaign. Expedition member Oliver Hanna stressed the importance of this wartime experience:[1]

The close of the Civil War threw many soldiers out of employment and, with a spirit of restlessness, they gathered their possessions, with a few teams, joined a party and made their way Westward. There were many of these men in our party, both Federal and Confederate, well-trained, disciplined men. Had it not been for them and their previous experience, we never would have escaped with our lives.

Almost all of the men were white; two were black, of which, one—John Anderson—played a documented heroic role in the fighting.[2] Jim Gourley, a member of the expedition, later said the following about the group:[3]

> The outfit … was composed of ranchmen from the Gallatin Valley, citizens of Bozeman, hunters and trappers from the Yellowstone, and prospectors and miners from various portions of the Territory. There were twenty-five or thirty quite young men who had never seen any Indian fighting, and after the first two fights we had lots of trouble to keep them from charging on the Indians at all times. In fact, they had no more fear of a band of Indians than of a band of antelope; they didn't seem to know that an Indian could hurt them. There was also about fifty or sixty men who could fight Indians; men who knew Indians and all their methods, and who even knew their habits of thought.

The fact that many of the men were professional hunters should not be under-estimated; at least thirteen of the men fell in this category, which is certainly an undercount. Veteran firearms writer Elmer Keith wrote of this caliber of marksman long ago:[4]

> The old buffalo hunters knew what was needed far better than any hunters of today and as a class were probably the most skilled game shots of all time.

1st Lt. James H. Bradley—a Civil War veteran and frontier officer of the US 17th and 7th Infantry Regiments—who understood the value of marksmanship and combat experience, later interviewed many of the participants and concluded the following: [5]

> A great majority of the members of the expedition had been soldiers on one side or the other during the Civil War or life-long frontiersmen, so that the personnel was [were] all that could be desired.

The following participants have been identified by name as part of the expedition. Those **103** names highlighted in **bold** are supported by multiple citations and/or extremely reliable sources placing them on the wagon train. Those names not highlighted have less sourcing; some of these names may be slight variations of other names or even names of men who were not on the expedition at all, although dozens must have been, given that the overall strength of the expedition was about 150. The one name *italicized* has the least support showing participation in the expedition. The information in the biographical sketches in this chapter covers only their lives before the expedition. Post-expedition material is found in the "Fading Away" chapter.

Tom Allen (William Cable Barkley.) Tom Allen was born about 1844 in Ohio as William Cable Barkley, but changed his name after the Civil War. Allen is believed to have served as a private in Company I of the 52nd Ohio Volunteer Infantry Regiment in the conflict, enlisting on July 19, 1862 and receiving his discharge on June 3, 1865. The regiment saw heavy fighting at Chickamauga, Missionary Ridge, Atlanta, Kennesaw Mountain, Jonesboro, and Bentonville. After the conflict, Allen served with the Army Quartermaster Corps (possibly as a teamster) with the US 3rd Infantry Regiment at Fort Larned on the Arkansas River, along the Santa Fe Trail. Shortly afterward, in 1866, when entrepreneur Nelson Story traveled to Texas to organize a drive of cattle to Montana, Tom Allen helped herd the 1,000 head along the 2,000 mile trail from the Lone Star state to the Big Bend of the Yellowstone in the Montana Territory, an event that years later served as the inspiration for Larry McMurtry's Pulitzer Prize winning novel *Lonesome Dove* that was later made into a popular television movie. Allen subsequently met renowned frontier guides Jim Bridger and James "Jim" Baker in 1872 at Fort Bridger in the Wyoming Territory.[6]

Harry Anderson

John "Uncle John" Anderson. John Anderson was born to a black slave mother and a Cherokee slave father (both who had been born in Georgia) belonging to Lewis Hildebrand, an assistant wagon master, who led a large group of Cherokee Indians to Indian Territory (in present day Oklahoma) along the Trail of Tears. Anderson's exact date of birth was unknown, but was probably about 1836; he believed that he had been born in the Indian Territory. In 1861, he escaped to Kansas and freedom. In 1862, Anderson joined the First Kansas Volunteer Colored Infantry Regiment— the first black regiment to be organized in a northern state and the first black unit to see combat during the Civil War—at Fort Scott, Kansas; he later served with the Independent Battery (Douglas' Battery,) US Colored Light Artillery, one of the few Union units to serve under exclusive leadership of black officers. He fought at Westport, Missouri, in October 1864 and was discharged in 1865, after being shot in the right lung. Earlier, he had probably fought at the Battle of Poison Spring, where the regiment lost half its number and the Confederates refused to take any black soldiers prisoner—killing them instead. After the war, Anderson traveled to Salt Lake City before arriving at Virginia City, Montana Territory, on December 5, 1865. He moved to Helena and then to Bozeman in 1872. On the expedition, John Anderson served as one of the cooks.[7]

Union veterans of the Grand Army of the Republic, William English Montana Post No.10 pose on Main Street on Memorial Day, 1900; John Anderson (far right) holds US flag. *Courtesy of Gallatin History Museum*

Robert Anderson

Henry "Hank" Ashmead. Henry Ashmead was a woodcutter living in Bozeman City, Gallatin County, Montana Territory in 1870. He was born in 1827 in Pennsylvania.[8] The Records of Enlistment for the US Army indicates that a Henry Ashmead from Washington County, Pennsylvania, age thirty-five, enlisted on November 18, 1861, at Carlisle, Pennsylvania, in the infantry and that he deserted on October 1, 1862. A second source confirms that this Henry Ashmead was assigned to Company E of the US 16th Infantry Regiment, a regular army formation.

This information would indicate that Henry participated in the march to Nashville, Tennessee, February 14-25, 1862 and the occupation of Nashville on February 25, 1862. From there, Ashmead would have seen service in the advance to Duck River on March 16-21, 1862, and to Savannah, Tennessee, from March 31 – April 6, 1862. The regiment then fought at Shiloh on April 6-7, 1862. Pvt. Ashmead would have had no respite in his service, as his regiment then advanced to and laid siege of Corinth, Mississippi, from April 29 – May 30, 1862. From June to August 1862, the regiment marched with Gen. Don Carlos Buell's campaign in Alabama and Tennessee. From August 21 to September 26, the US 16th Infantry Regiment turned north in pursuit of Confederate Gen. Braxton Bragg's invasion of Kentucky, an attempt to arouse supporters of the Confederate cause in that border state and to draw the Union's Army of the Ohio north out of Confederate territory. Shortly after this event, it appears that Ashmead deserted.[9]

Charles E. Avery. Charles Avery was born on March 2, 1850, in Fallsburg, Sullivan County, New York, the son of Amos and Maria (Wakeman) Avery; he had four brothers and three sisters. He came to the Montana Territory in 1873, living in the Gallatin Valley.[10]

William H. Awbrey. William Awbrey was born in St. Charles, St. Charles County, Missouri, on April 18, 1828, the son of Joseph Awbrey and Mary Prewitt. He married Francis Thorp in Linn County, Missouri, on February 27, 1851; the couple would have six children; one was John, born in 1860, while another son was named William and was born in 1858. Awbrey arrived in the Montana Territory sometime between 1859 and 1864. In 1870, he lived in Gallatin City, Gallatin County and was a farmer.[11]

William H. Babcock. William Babcock was born in Onondaga County, New York, on June 10, 1837, the son of Godfrey Babcock and Amelia Diffin. In 1844, he moved to Dodge County, Wisconsin, but soon ran away from home. Babcock remained in Wisconsin until 1855, when he moved to Winona County, Minnesota. He spent part of 1858 in Chelsea, Michigan. In 1859, Babcock headed west to San Francisco and from there to the Bitter Root Mountains in May 1862. He then came to Bannack in the fall of 1862; in 1864, Babcock settled in Gallatin County. In 1871, William Babcock made a quick trip to Faribault, Minnesota, and married Sarah D. Macy.[12]

William D. Bassett. William D. Bassett appears to have been born in Blue Clay County, Minnesota, on October 25, 1851, the son of Phillip G. and Hannah M. Basset, both from New Hampshire—from which the family left in 1848; his father was a laborer. William had three brothers and a sister. He lived in the town of Hastings, in Dakota County, Minnesota, in 1860.[13]

William D. Bassett and his wife in Stillwater County, Montana, about 1910. *Jim Annin, courtesy of the Museum of the Beartooths, Columbus, Montana.*

John Barker "Jack" Bean. Jack Bean was born in 1844 on a small farm near Dover, Maine. His parents, Rueben and Rhoda, moved the family to Wisconsin when Jack was a small boy; they later moved to Minnesota. In 1860, Jack headed southwest to try his hand in the gold mines of Colorado, but spent his first summer there cutting hay between Denver and Pikes Peak instead. He then headed fuarther west and spent a short time hauling lumber in Carson City, Nevada. Bean later resided in Portland, Oregon, and Boise, Idaho, before heading to the Montana Territory in about 1864. Over the next several years, Bean trapped for beaver along the Jefferson, Gallatin, and Madison Rivers. He also became an accomplished rifle hunter. Prior to joining the expedition, Bean and Stewart Buchanan had established a hunting base in the Crazy Mountains, twenty miles northwest of today's Big Timber, Montana. Jack Bean was armed with a Sharps Model 1874 buffalo rifle.[14]

Jack Bean with hunting client at Jackson Hole, Wyoming, in August-September 1889. Photograph was taken by Bean's brother-in-law Charles D. Loughrey. Hunting was Bean's life in his early days. *Courtesy of John Bean, grandson of Jack Bean*

Jack Bean, left, guiding an English hunter that has just shot an elk at Jackson Hole, Wyoming, in August-September 1889. Photograph was taken by Bean's brother-in-law Charles D. Loughrey. *Courtesy of John Bean, grandson of Jack Bean*

Jack Bean hunting party in 1880s in Wyoming; Bean is sitting right front. *Courtesy of Gallatin Pioneer Museum*

Joe Carter Black[15]

Charles Preston Blakeley. Charles P. Blakeley was born at Platte City in Daviess County, Missouri, on June 6, 1834, the son of Nathaniel H. Blakeley and Frances Creekmore. He married Elizabeth Downing in 1856 in Doniphan County, Kansas. At the beginning of the Civil War, Blakeley enlisted in the Missouri State Guard—under his uncle Capt. Felix Blakeley in Slayback's Regiment (commanded by Col. Alonzo W. Slayback)— initially not a formal part of the Confederate Army, but an auxiliary force under the command of Gen. Sterling "Old Pap" Price. He probably fought at Wilson's Creek. Discharged in December 1862, he intended to serve in the regular Confederate Army, but Union forces arrested him and held him prisoner until he escaped confinement at St. Joseph, Missouri. Blakeley fled west and arrived in Denver in 1863 and from there traveled to Virginia City,

Charlie P. Blakeley.
Courtesy of Ancestry. com, Charles P. Blakeley

Montana Territory, arriving on May 16, 1864. He bought farmland that he called the Farmington Ranch. Living in Bozeman, he was a miner and stock raiser. Blakeley was a Member of the Montana House of Representatives (Third Session) in 1866. In 1870, he opened a gold mine at Deer Lodge named the Gold Hill Mine. From 1871–1874, Charles Blakeley served as Under Sheriff in Gallatin County.[16]

Green Berry Blakeley. Green Blakeley was the younger brother of Charles Blakeley and was born in Daviess County, Missouri on

September 19, 1842. After serving in the Missouri State Guard in Slayback's Regiment, along with his brother, he probably served with Company C of the 1st Regiment, Missouri Cavalry in the Confederate Army. The unit fought at the Battle of Pea Ridge, the Battle of Helena, (Arkansas) and the Siege of Vicksburg. After the war, Green Blakeley went with his brother to Montana and was a partner in 1870 at Deer Lodge in the Gold Hill Mine.[17]

Anton Blank. Anton Blank was born in Württemberg, Germany about 1835. In 1870, he lived at the Cedar Creek Mines in Missoula County, Montana Territory. His occupation was listed as a brewer.[18]

Taylor Blevin. Taylor Blevin was born in New York in about 1848, possibly the son of Ashbel Andrew Blevin and Adelia V. Brisbain. His father, who was a butcher, died in 1855, when the family lived in Sarasota Springs. A year after her husband's death, Adelia remarried Ransom Varney. In 1860, the census showed that Taylor Blevin was working as a laborer on Varney farm in the town of Wilton, Saratoga County, New York. Taylor later went west and was hired in the Wyoming Territory to work for the Office of Indian Affairs. Blevin worked as a laborer at the Crow Indian Agency from September 24, 1873 to February 12, 1874.[19] His compensation as a laborer at the agency in 1873 was listed as $1,800 per year.[20]

Henry S./W.A. Bostwick. Bostwick was armed with a Winchester on the expedition. He reportedly lived in Deer Lodge. There is some confusion about the identification of this man. 1st Lt. James Bradley referred to him as W.A. Bostwick, while several others referred to him as Henry. Henry S. Bostwick, once described as a "long-haired mountaineer" was born, possibly in New York, on November 12, 1830, the son of Orasmus Ferdinand Bostwick and Sarah Bardwell. Orasmus and Sarah later moved the family to St. Louis, Missouri. An experienced interpreter, he reportedly guided the hunting party of Sir George Gore (the Eighth Baronet of Manor Gore near Sligo in northwest Ireland) in 1854 and 1855 in the company of famed frontiersmen Jim Bridger and Mitch Bouyer. Bostwick was married and had a son.[21] A Henry S. Bostwick was a private in Company G of the 21st Missouri Volunteer Infantry Regiment in the Civil War; this Union Army unit fought at Shiloh, Corinth, Fort Blakely, and Pleasant Hill. It is not known with certainty if this Civil War soldier was the Henry S. Bostwick of the expedition.

Edwin R. Bradley. Edwin Bradley was born in Missouri in 1846 and was a harness maker. His parents had both been born in Kentucky. It appears that Edwin returned to Kentucky as a youngster and became a saddler's apprentice in Georgetown in Scott County in 1860. He was single and reportedly understood the Lakota language.[22]

Wesley "Yank" Brockmeyer. Wesley Brockmeyer was a buffalo hunter. He had paid $300 for his horse. He is also listed as "William" in James Willert, *After Little Bighorn: 1876 Campaign Rosters*.[23]

Joseph "Uncle Joe" Brown. Joseph Brown was born in Baden-Baden, Germany, on October 1, 1833, the son of Joseph Brown and Laterna Myer. He immigrated to the United

States in 1849 and first lived in Long Island, New York, where he worked as a gardener. Brown then moved to western New York and worked at a hotel, before moving to Oil City, New York, where he worked in an oil field. In 1859, Brown headed west to the iron mines at Marquette near Lake Superior, but after a few years moved east to Pennsylvania. But the lure of the frontier was now in his blood and heading west once again, he arrived at Adler Gulch in 1864, becoming a miner and prospector. Brown later recalled the vigilante period, stating he was present at the hanging on March 10, 1864, of Joseph Alfred "Jack" Slade, a man who reportedly kept a string of ears of the men he had killed (it was only two ears that he had on his watch chain.) Slade, born in Carlyle, Illinois, had helped form the *Pony Express*, before gaining a reputation as a vicious killer—although most of the killings are disputed. No matter; it was the drop for Jack. Slade was hanged from the beam of a corral gate; his body would later be preserved in alcohol. Joseph then moved to Helena, where he worked at placer (stream bed or open pit) mining in Grizzly Gulch, before moving to the Gallatin Valley.[24]

Stewart "Buck" Buchanan. Born in Scotland in October 1833, Stewart Buchanan emigrated from Scotland in 1849; he came to Bannack in 1862, when gold was first discovered. He later traveled to the Bozeman area in 1864. In 1866, Stewart ventured into Indian country in Wyoming and southeast Montana, spending the winter at Fort Phil Kearny. In the fall of 1867, Stewart Buchanan wintered at Fort C.F. Smith; he later set up a hunting camp with Jack Bean in the Crazy Mountains, where the pair hunted elk.[25]

William "Bill" Buchanan. Born in Scotland in November 1831, William Buchanan emigrated from Scotland in 1849 and came with his younger brother Stewart to Bannack in 1862. He also traveled to the Bozeman area in 1864. In 1866, still with his brother, he ventured into Indian country in Wyoming and

Joseph "Jack" Slade, who's hanging by Montana Vigilantes was witnessed by Joseph "Uncle Joe" Brown on March 10, 1864, ten years before Brown went on the expedition. *Courtesy of Original oil painting hangs in the Bale of Hay Saloon in Virginia City, Montana.*

southeast Montana, also spending the winter at Fort Phil Kearny. In the fall of 1867, he wintered at Fort C.F. Smith with his brother.[26]

T.C. Burns. T.C. Burns was born in Iowa on November 27, 1837, the son of a wheel-wright. Burns married Ellen Wright, also a native of Iowa, on December 25, 1863. He traveled to Montana in May 1864, settling initially in Emigrant Gulch and subsequently at Helena, where he remained until about 1869. He then returned east until the spring of 1872, when he returned to the territory and settled in Bozeman. On the expedition, he carried either a small telescope or a pair of field glasses.[27]

James "Joe" Burrill. James Burrill was born in Canada about June 1839. He came to Montana no later than 1866. In 1870, he lived in Gallatin City, Gallatin County, and worked as a farmer; it appears that a brother lived with the family. Joe Burrill married Lena in 1864 and had a daughter and two sons.[28]

Henry Bird Calfee. Henry Bird Calfee was born January 3, 1848, in Fayetteville in Washington County, Arkansas, the son of Henry Roy Calfee and Margaret Elizabeth Cannon. He moved west to Montana in 1867, following his older brother White Calfee, and settled in the Bozeman area. Calfee initially made his living as an artist and later as a prospector. In the early

Henry Bird Calfee about 1875. *Courtesy of Henry Bird Calfee, Museum of the Rockies Photo Archives x64.6.29*

1870s, he opened a photography business with partner Nelson Catlin. Henry Calfee reportedly owned a Colt Peacemaker .45 revolver on the expedition, one of the few to be so armed.[29]

William D. "Billy" Cameron. William Cameron was born in Edinburgh, Scotland, on October 25, 1832, the son of James A. Cameron and Annie E. McGregor. Billy Cameron immigrated to the United States in about 1849 and lived in New York City. He had been a Union artilleryman in the Civil War, serving in Company H and Company I of the 50th New York Volunteer Engineer Regiment, which specialized in building pontoon bridges for the Union's Army of the Potomac; it was at Seven Pines, Fredericksburg, Chancellorsville, the Wilderness and Petersburg. In Gallatin, he was a practicing lawyer. Cameron was in charge of the Big Horn Gun.[30]

Archie Campbell. Archie Campbell appears to have been born in Scotland in about 1848–49. He was a miner in Radersburg in Jefferson County, Montana Territory, in 1870.[31]

Elias "Blacky" Carter

John Carter. A John Carter lived in Middle Creek Valley in 1880. He was born in 1831 in Ohio. His twenty-two-year old son had been born in Missouri (1858); an eighteen-year-old daughter had been born in Colorado (1862.)[32]

Nelson "Nelse" Catlin. Nelson Catlin operated a photography store with his partner Henry Bird Calfee in Bozeman. Nelse Catlin was born in 1849 in New York, the son of William and Sarah Catlin. It is believed by some that he is one of the people shown in the stereopticon *No. 226, Tourist Camp, near Castle Geyser*, but it remains unknown as to which person he may be. [33]

George Chadbourne[34]

Charley. Charley was described as a young black man. Early on the expedition he suffered frostbite of his toes.[35]

B. Clark

L. Conners

A. Connery

Joseph Ethelbert "Joe" Cook. Joseph Cook was born on October 20, 1844, in Holt, Missouri. In 1870, he lived in Gallatin County and was a farmer.[36] During the expedition he carried a Springfield Trapdoor Single-Shot Rifle, Model 1870, in caliber .50-70. Years later, he explained how he came to the territory:[37]

> We arrived in Virginia City, Montana, on the 25th of August, 1865. From there I went to the Gallatin Valley and farmed it for ten years. The Indians (Lakota) made raids into the Gallatin Valley nearly every fall, always driving off a lot of horses and killing one or two men that they would catch on the outskirts of the valley.

James H. Cooper. James Cooper was born in about 1846 in Missouri. In 1870, he lived in Noble in Gallatin County and worked as a farm laborer.[38]

Andrew "Andy" Cowan. Andrew Cowan was born on March 17, 1834, in Pulaski County, Kentucky. He was probably a cousin of Doctor F. Cowan. Raised on a farm, he traveled to Missouri in about 1854. Early in the Civil War, he served with Gen. Sterling "Old Pap" Price and fought for the Confederates at Wilson's Creek, Pea Ridge, and the First Battle of Lexington. In 1863, he rode by stage coach to Salt Lake City and from there to Virginia City. Andrew Cowan engaged in freighting for one year, after which he bought a farm of 480 acres in the Gallatin Valley, where he raised cattle and horses. In 1870, he lived in Gallatin County, Montana Territory. Andrew married Rachel C. Tribble in 1872. On the expedition, Cowan carried a Springfield Model 1870 .50-70 caliber rifle.[39] He may have also carried a Springfield muzzle-loading shotgun for close-in protection and for hunting game birds for food during the expedition.[40]

Doctor F. Cowan. Doctor F. Cowan was born in Somerset, Pulaski County, Kentucky, on August 12, 1843, the son of a former sheriff. In 1862, he lived in Stanford, Kentucky, and with the outbreak of the Civil War, he enlisted as a private in September that year in Company B, 6th Regiment of Cavalry, Kentucky Volunteers (Confederate Army); he later transferred to Company H. The regiment skirmished in Kentucky, attached to Buford's Brigade, and then fought with Gen. John Hunt Morgan. On July 13, 1863, during Morgan's

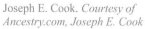

Joseph E. Cook. *Courtesy of Ancestry.com, Joseph E. Cook*

Andy Cowan. Cowan carried a Springfield Model 1870 .50-70 caliber rifle on the expedition; he may have also carried a Springfield muzzle-loading shotgun for close-in protection. *Courtesy of Gallatin History Museum*

Raid into Kentucky, Indiana, and Ohio, his marauders crossed into Ohio at Harrison, pursued by several columns of Union cavalry under Brig. Gen. Edward H. Hobson. On July 19, two of Hobson's brigades attacked Morgan near Buffington Island. During the night, Morgan and about 400 men escaped encirclement by following a narrow woods path. The rest of his force surrendered. On July 26, 1863, Morgan's survivors surrendered at New Lisbon. Apparently, Cowan was wounded in one of these battles, captured, and spent the rest of the conflict as a prisoner of war at Camp Douglas, Illinois. After the war, he briefly lived in Georgia. In 1870, Cowan was a farmer in East Gallatin, along with his brother William.[41]

James S. "Old Man" Crain/Crane. James Crain, sometimes spelled Crane, was a veteran frontiersman. He was born in New York in about 1825. One of the first settlers of the Lower Yellowstone, he had previously lived in Illinois, before moving to Placer County, California, where he was a miner in 1852. Crain had also resided in Wyoming.[42]

William "Bill" Cudney

Zadok H. "Zed" Daniels. Zadok H. Daniels was born on February 3, 1849, in Tioga County, Pennsylvania, the son of D.L. and Patience Daniels; it appears that he had four sisters and two brothers. The family had moved there from New York a year earlier. He probably resided in Bruce Township in Macomb County, Michigan, in 1870, where he worked in a boot and shoe store.[43] After moving to the Montana Territory, Daniels was a superintendent of farming at the Crow Indian Agency at Fort Parker through the fall of 1873. He participated in the Doane-Pease Expedition from December 16, 1873, to January 30, 1874. This outing, led by Gustavus C. Doane and Fellows D. Pease, with fewer than a dozen troopers from the US 2nd Cavalry Regiment, explored the area near Big Spring Creek and Little Casino Creek (near present day Lewiston).[44]

David Davis. David Davis was born in Wales on August 19, 1843. He arrived in the Montana Territory in 1864. In 1870, Davis lived in Gallatin County and was a farmer.[45]

David Davis was born in Wales. *Courtesy of Gallatin History Museum*

James Delaney

A. Detsson

Benjamin R. Dexter. Benjamin Dexter is believed to have been born on December 4, 1842, in Granville, Nova Scotia, Canada; his family had emigrated there from Wales. From Nova Scotia, he later moved to Illinois and to the Montana Territory in about 1872. Dexter was a lumberman. He was married to his wife Caroline (also born in Nova Scotia) and had five children.[46]

Black Dick.[47]

John H. Dillabaugh. This may be the John Dillabaugh who was born in Canada in about 1839. He later lived in Pontiac, Michigan. In the census of 1870, he lived in the Wyoming Territory, but the 1880 census shows him in Madison County, Montana Territory. John Dillabaugh was a shoemaker. Later in life, in Montana, he applied for a pension, stating that he had served in Company A of the 22nd Michigan Volunteer Infantry Regiment and Company A of the 29th Michigan Volunteer Infantry Regiment. The 22nd fought at the Defense of Cincinnati, Chickamauga, Kennesaw Mountain, Siege of Atlanta, and the Battle of Jonesboro; Dillabaugh enlisted on January 30, 1863.[48]

John H. Dillabaugh had served in the Union's 22nd Michigan Volunteer Infantry Regiment that fought at the Defense of Cincinnati, Battle of Chickamauga, Battle of Kennesaw Mountain, Siege of Atlanta and the Battle of Jonesboro. *Courtesy of glendalemt.com*

C.J. Doyle. This could be Charles J. Doyle, a miner born about 1843 in Massachusetts. In the federal census of 1870, he was listed as a miner at the Cedar Creek Mines in Missoula County, Montana Territory.[49]

James Driskle

Charles W. "Bishop" Dryden. Charles Dryden was born about 1842 in Scott County, Indiana. It is likely that he served in the Civil War in Company C of the 38th Indiana Volunteer Infantry Regiment; the unit saw heavy combat at Perryville, Stones River, Hoover's Gap, Chickamauga, Lookout Mountain, Jonesboro, and Savannah. He was mustered in on September 18, 1861. He acquired the nickname of "Bishop"—others called him "Charlie"— because he had lived in Utah before coming

to Montana. Dryden then lived in Bozeman, Gallatin County, Montana Territory, in 1870 and listed his occupation as a farmer.[50]

Hugh Early. Hugh Early was born in New York on August 9, 1849, the son of Hugh and Celia Early. His parents were both from Ireland. Hugh Early departed St. Louis, Missouri, for the Montana Territory, serving as a boat-hand traveling up the Missouri River and arriving at Fort Benton on July 4, 1867.[51]

James Edwards. James Edwards hailed from Atchison County in northwest Missouri. He arrived in the Montana Territory about 1869 and initially lived near Virginia City.[52]

John Engesser. John Engesser was born in Baden, Germany, about 1820. Engesser served as a sergeant in Company E of the 5th Regiment, Missouri State Militia Cavalry; the unit fought mounted guerillas—such as Quantrill's Raiders—in the state during the Civil War. In 1870 he lived in Bozeman, Gallatin County, Montana Territory, with his wife Rosena and son Adolph; he ran a small restaurant. Given this occupation, Engesser may have served as the chief cook on the expedition.[53]

J. Eppler

Robert Henry Evans. Robert Evans was born in Sligo, Ireland, on January 3, 1839, the son of James Evans and Ellen Boyle. He came to the United States when he was only one and the family moved to Ottawa, Illinois. In 1851 he began moving west, first to Omaha, Nebraska,

Robert Henry Evans, left rear, and family in Spearfish Creek, South Dakota. He was born in Sligo, Ireland. *Courtesy of Ancestry.com, Robert Henry Evans*

and then California, before arriving in Bannack on July 27, 1864. In 1870, Robert Evans was a gold miner in Prickly Pear Valley, Lewis and Clark County in the Montana Territory.[54]

Edward K. "Yank" Everett/Everetts/Evarts. An Edward Everett lived in Bozeman City in 1870. He was born about 1832 in New York. Everett worked in a blacksmith's shop.[55] "Yank" reportedly rode on the 1870 Washburne and Doane Expedition from Helena to the Yellowstone country. He became separated from the rest of the party and nearly died on Sheep Mountain but was rescued.[56] In the National Park Service, *The Civil War, Soldiers and Sailors Database*, there is one man from New York, Edward K. Everetts, who also went by the name Edward K. Evarts. He was assigned to Company K in the 98th New York Volunteer Infantry Regiment. This unit was recruited in the Franklin and Wayne County areas of the state. Part of the Union IV Corps, it fought in the Peninsula Campaign in 1862, including Seven Pines. This Edward K. Everetts joined the regiment on January 14, 1862 and was discharged for disability on October 27, 1862. Service in the Union Army could have resulted in the nickname of "Yank," but it could be a different man.

P. Farley

Edward J. Farnum. Edward Farnum would chisel his name in a sandstone cliff along the route of the expedition.[57]

Enoch Douglass "Doug" Ferguson. Enoch Douglass Ferguson was born on March 1, 1844, in Spring City, Tennessee, the son of a planter. At the beginning of the Civil War, he enlisted in the 1st Tennessee Cavalry Regiment in the Confederate Army and later fought at Mill Spring, Kentucky, and at Stones River in Tennessee. Ferguson was later captured by the Union Army and subsequently paroled. After the war, he moved to Indiana, where he went to school and taught. In 1869, Ferguson went to Fort Benton in the Montana Territory. Soon after, Enoch Ferguson bought 640 acres of land in the Gallatin Valley and later started the Rocky Ford Coal Mine; in 1870, he lived at Noble in the same county.[58]

Charles Fisher

George Fisher. This may have been the George Fischer who was born about 1849 in Germany and who was a miner.[59]

Joseph Fisher

James Fleming. James Fleming was born in Ireland in about 1838. He immigrated to New York. Fleming served in the Civil War in Company H of the 35th New York Volunteer Infantry Regiment. The unit fought at the Second Battle of Bull Run, Antietam, and Fredericksburg. In 1870, he lived in Deer Lodge County and worked as a miner.[60]

E.S. Flint

Robert Forbes

A.B. Ford. A.B. Ford was born in Missouri about 1835. In 1870, he was a miner in Jefferson County, Montana Territory.[61]

John French

Charles Gale. Charles Gale was born in Pennsylvania about 1853. He participated in the 1873 expedition up the Yellowstone River with Gen. David Stanley. He had reportedly been a trooper in the US 7th Cavalry Regiment, but had deserted, winding up in Bozeman sometime before the 1874 expedition; a review of US Army enlistments for the period does not support this assertion. Don Weibert's study of the expedition concluded that Gale was a partner of J.L. Vernon, but that also does not appear to be the case.[62]

George Gibson

Neil Gillis. Neil Gillis was a long-time resident of Livingston, Montana Territory.[63]

James A. "Jim" Gourley. Jim Gourley was born on May 4, 1840, in Diveruagh, County Armagh, Ireland, the son of John and Mary (Cleland) Gourley. He immigrated to America in 1859, subsequently moving to Galena, Illinois; he later traveled up the Missouri River on the steamer *Emilie*, arriving at Fort Benton on June 17, 1862. The same year he lived in Bannack. In 1869–1870, with four other men, he prospected for gold—in their newly formed Prickly Pear Gold and Silver Mining Company—in the Beartooth Mountains—near present day Cooke City—as well as in present-day Yellowstone; the group named several features in Yellowstone, including the Hoodoo Basin, and observed Grasshopper Glacier in the Beartooth Mountains. They subsequently viewed Pilot Peak and discovered gold in Fisher Creek, in the Cooke City area. Jim Gourley was a miner and a merchant.[64]

Benjamin Franklin "Frank" Grounds. On the expedition, the men selected Frank Grounds to be in command. He was born in Madison County, Missouri, in 1833. Don Weibert believed that Frank fought in the mid-1850s in the Rogue River Wars in southern Oregon against the Rogue River Indians, and that after serving in the Civil War in the Union Army, he moved to the Texas Panhandle, where he reportedly served in the Texas Rangers with his brother William A. "Doc" Grounds (born in 1845 in Missouri) and his nephew William Franklin "Bud" Grounds (born in 1851 in Arkansas.)[65]

More recent sources, however, provide other details and indicate that Frank was the son of Peter Grounds and Rebecca Ann Johnson (born in Missouri); Peter had been born in North Carolina. The federal census of 1850 showed that the family lived in Fulton County in northern Arkansas; the family probably had moved there in 1849. The Grounds family subsequently moved to Palo Pinto County, Texas, and Frank did not serve in the Union Army, but instead fought for the Confederacy with Col. James G. Bourland's Texas Border Cavalry, a unit that hanged forty-one Union

sympathizers in what became known as the Great Hanging in Gainesville in Cooke County, Texas, in October 1862.[66]

Texas had been significantly divided about secession and this was nowhere more apparent than in North Texas along the Red River. By 1862, sentiment for leaving the Union had waned under the pressure of an unpopular military draft and martial law. Undisciplined troops led by Brig. Gen. Paul Octave Hébert—the despised state military commander—contributed to autocratic control, especial on the North Texas plains northeast of Dallas. This was not the heart of Dixie; 90% of white males owned no slaves, the Sherman, Texas, *Patriot* newspaper called for the secession of North Texas from Texas and a branch of the Peace Party remained active in the region.[67]

Matters took a turn for the worse when the Confederacy's Conscription Act went into effect; it required military service for all non-slaveholders, but exempted slaveholders. After infiltrating Unionist and draft-dodger circles, Confederate spies reported the "guilty" parties to the local provost marshal (he was the provost marshal of the Twenty-first Militia Brigade stationed in the area) Col. James Bourland, who began arresting the Northern sympathizers on October 1, 1862. Some 200 would ultimately be incarcerated. Trials for treason began the next day. As in Montana—during the vigilante days—justice did not move swiftly enough for the mob and on October 12 a large group of men stormed the courtroom and left with fourteen detainees, whom they hanged the following day. The court retried nineteen other men with a new vigor—the initial proceedings having been headed for numerous acquittals—and all of these defendants were duly convicted and hanged. Bourland's men hanged five more draft dodgers in Decatur, Texas.[68]

There is no evidence that Frank Grounds participated in any of the lynchings. Research does indicate that he joined Company A—commanded by Maj. Charles L. Roff—of Col. James G. Bourland's Texas Border Cavalry, a unit that was also called; Bourland's

Confederate Border Regiment; Border Regiment; and Bourland's Regiment, Texas Cavalry. James Bourland formed the regiment in the early spring of 1863, placing his units along the Red River. On August 23, 1863, orders attached the Texas Border Cavalry to the Northern Sub-District in the District of Texas, New Mexico, and Arizona in the Trans-Mississippi Department, having a mission to guard the northern border of Texas. Texas militia cards show that Frank Grounds was assigned to the 21st Brigade, under Brig. Gen. William Hudson, fighting Indians in Palo Pinto County—in Brazos River country—west of Fort Worth in 1863. Fresh orders on December 26, 1863, attached Bourland's Border Regiment to Col. Richard Montgomery Gano's Brigade in the District of Indian Territory of the Trans-Mississippi Department.[69]

The following day, the brigade fought at Waldron, Arkansas. The regiment confronted the Federals in the Indian Territory and Texas, but fought more extensively against Comanche and Kiowa raiders along both sides of the Red River and as far north as Fort Arbuckle. On March 1, 1864, the unit was officially accepted into the Confederate Army, having previously been a Texas militia unit. The regiment reported four officers and 564 men fit for duty on January 1, 1865. Bourland's Regiment did not surrender until June 2, 1865. Historian Robert M. Utley wrote in his work *Lone Star Justice: The First Century of The Texas Rangers* that Bourland was a "combative old Ranger" and this description could be the reason that Don Weibert believed that Grounds had served with the Texas Rangers.[70]

It is not clear what Frank Grounds did for the next five years; his brother and nephew lived in Coleman County, Texas (southeast of Abilene), during this time. By 1870, Frank Grounds was at the Cedar Creek Mines in Missoula, Montana Territory; his occupation was that of a miner. He later bought a ranch in the Gallatin Valley and started a sawmill. On January 1, 1874, Frank Grounds mortgaged his land and sold most of his possessions to invest in supplies for the upcoming expedition.

One veteran of the wagon train recalled Frank Grounds in the following manner:[71]

Not a man in the party ever questioned his authority. I think it is probable that no man ever lived who excelled him in the qualities that he possessed as a leader of men; his every action showed his absolute control over every man. No matter how difficult the duty that was to be done, when Grounds gave the order, the work was done without flinching and done cheerfully. In several instances it seemed to be inevitable death for those who were commanded to perform some duty, but the men never hesitated, simply going ahead as ordered.

Eugene S. Topping was equally as effusive in his praise concerning the expedition's leader:[72]

… he was the guiding spirit. He was quick to decide where haste was necessary, and his judgment was always sound. Probably there was not another man in the expedition who could have controlled so well these turbulent and independent spirits. His tact made all his friends, and their courage and dash, tempered by his caution and prudence, gave them the victory in every conflict had.

Charles Grove

E./F. Grunbacher

W. Guitzer

John Gundorf

John Hall

William T. "Uncle Billy" Hamilton. A protégé of William S. "Old Bill" Williams, Old Gabe Bridger and John Bozeman, William T. Hamilton was born in the Cheviot Hills on the Scottish border on December 6, 1822—the son of Alexander and Margaret Hamilton—and

Uncle Billy Hamilton; he was friends with numerous Wild West characters in the Montana Territory including "Liver-Eatin" Johnston. *Courtesy of the Museum of the Beartooths, Columbus, Montana*

William T. "Uncle Billy" Hamilton in later years. Hamilton had fought in the Medoc War as a member of the Buckskin Rangers, a group of mountain men recruited for their tracking skills; he also fought in the Rogue River War and the Coeur d'Alene War. *Courtesy of Billings Public Library*

arrived in New Orleans as an infant. He grew up in St. Louis, suffering from asthma, prior to becoming a Hudson Bay Fur Company trapper with Old Bill Williams. Known as "Uncle Billy" or by his Indian name of "Crooked Nose," he went to California in 1849 during the gold rush, where he married; unfortunately, his wife and infant died in 1851 as he prospected for gold near Yuba. Hamilton fought in the Medoc War as a member of the Buckskin Rangers, a group of mountain men recruited for their tracking skills; he also fought in the Rogue River War and the Coeur d'Alene War. Hamilton was one of the first settlers to build a cabin in Missoula, Montana, after seeing the area first in September in 1858 as an army scout from Fort Walla Walla. In 1862, he lived in Bannack. In 1864, Hamilton moved to Fort Benton, where he was elected sheriff and later was appointed Deputy United States Marshal. The next year, Hamilton fought against the

Gros Ventres, using a twelve-pound brass cannon and rifle pits similar to the tactics that would be used on the 1874 expedition. In 1869, while trapping for furs on Bouvais Creek in the Montana Territory with Ben Walker and Oliver Hanna, he got into a fight with Indian warriors. Prior to the expedition, William Hamilton worked with George Herendeen at the Crow Agency. Known by some warriors as "Sign Man" and by other frontiersmen as "Wild Cat," Hamilton was considered by many to be the best-versed scout in Indian sign language in the West. Among his many weapons on the expedition, Hamilton reportedly carried a cap and ball pistol.[73] He was supposedly a friend of John "Liver-Eatin" Johnston.

Green Alexander Hampton. Green Hampton was born on March 27, 1830, in Georgia. He married Susan Ford in 1858 in Linn Creek, Missouri. In 1863 he was listed as having twelve months of previous military service as a quartermaster sergeant in Company G of the Third Provisional Enrolled Missouri Militia Infantry (Union) and that he was a boatman in Camden County. The unit fought at St. Joseph and in Henry and St. Clair Counties in Missouri against Confederate bushwhackers. In 1873, the family lived in Diamond City, Montana Territory. Two of their three daughters died in childhood.[74]

James Hancock

Oliver Perry "Big Spit" Hanna. Oliver Hanna was born on May 10, 1851, in Metamora, Illinois, to James Harvey Hanna and Nancy Taylor. His mother died when Oliver was five years old and his father remarried a year later. However, in 1860, Oliver's father died and soon after his four older brothers joined the Union Army for the Civil War. Hanna started west from Illinois on August 11, 1869. Later that year, while trapping for furs on Bouvais Creek in the Montana Territory with Ben Walker and Bill Hamilton, Hanna was engaged in a tough fight with a group of warriors. As Oliver later wrote:[75]

Oliver Perry Hanna in his younger years. A buffalo hunter, his later descriptions hint that he carried a Sharps Model 1874 .50-70 on the expedition. *Courtesy of Ancestry.com, Oliver Perry Hanna*

Oliver Perry Hanna in midlife. Hanna was born on May 10, 1851, in Metamora, Illinois. *Public Domain*

Oliver Perry Hanna and Grace Raymond Hebard in Sheridan County, Wyoming, on August 8, 1926. Partial caption on the rear states that he is holding his "buffalo gun." The weapon has the double trigger option, in which one trigger sets the primary trigger for lesser pull to improve accuracy. It also has a buckhorn rear sight. It is possible that he carried this rifle on the expedition. *Courtesy of Oliver P. Hanna Photofile, American Heritage Center, University of Wyoming*

In a short while I could handle a gun with any of them, and at the end of our hunting and trapping expedition I could show as fine a lot of furs as any of them.

Hanna also wrote that he served as a scout on the Baker expedition along the Yellowstone River in 1872 and took part in that expedition's fight near present-day Billings. He also inferred that he was on the Yellowstone Expedition of 1873 under Col. David S. Stanley in which the 7th Cavalry participated (Hanna wrote, "I was with Gen. Custer on one of his expeditions in the Yellowstone country.") Just before or after this 1873 scout, Hanna prospected for gold at Porcupine Stream in the Montana Territory. Hanna was living in Old Gallatin City when he joined the expedition in early 1874, having also notified Hugo Hoppe, at Benson's Landing, of the upcoming adventure.[76] A buffalo hunter, his later descriptions hint that he carried a Sharps Model 1874 .50-70.

He received his nickname because of his fondness for chewing tobacco.

John Hanson

H. Harbaugh

A. E. F. Heinze

A. Heloick

J.C. Henry

George B. Herendeen. George Herendeen was born in Parkman in Geauga County, Ohio, on November 28, 1846, the youngest of three children. His parents, Ann (born in New York) and Frederick (born in Massachusetts) died—probably in an epidemic—when he was thirteen. In late 1864, Herendeen joined the Union Army and was stationed at the Johnson Island, Ohio, prisoner of war camp for captured Confederate soldiers. He was very likely assigned to the 128th Ohio Volunteer Infantry Regiment. After the war, he briefly lived with his uncle, George A. Herendeen, at Green in Noble County, Indiana. In 1868, he moved to Denver, Colorado, where he worked briefly in the mines, but this did not suit him and George traveled to New Mexico. There he became a cowhand. Herendeen helped drive a herd of cattle from New Mexico to Montana in 1869, during which the drive wintered at Cherry Creek, north of Denver. The following spring, the drive continued, narrowly avoiding Red Cloud and 800 warriors. George Herendeen spent the following winter at Three Forks of the Missouri. In the spring of 1870, Herendeen traveled to Bozeman. In 1872, he served as a guide on the Yellowstone River during the Baker Expedition. Prior to the 1874 expedition, George Herendeen was working at the Crow Indian Agency, making $600 a year.[77] He served as the personal escort for the commissioner of Indian affairs and was involved in the successful treaty signing with Crazy Head of the Crow tribe. During George Herendeen's upbringing, his family situation led to a haphazard education, as shown in the following letter, dated February 13, 1874, at the beginning of the expedition, to his brother and sister:[78]

Dear brother and sister,
I wrote you the 8 of this month and I was working here [Crow Agency.] I have changed my minde. I am going down the River with the waggon Road expedition there is about 150 men now and well armed. we take six month grub and we air going right in the Soux Country. we will not be near any setelment for the time. You need not write any more ontile you here from mee. Wee air agoing to look for Gold. you must look at the papers and see how we get along.

GEORGE HERENDEEN.
The last of the Great Scouts.

George Herendeen in his later years. Herendeen had been in the Union Army and was stationed at the Johnson Island, Ohio, prisoner of war camp for captured Confederate soldiers. He was very likely assigned to the 128th Ohio Volunteer Infantry Regiment. *Courtesy of Al J. Noyes, In the Land of Chinook, or the Story of Blaine County, 1917 (Not in Copyright)*

This letter, so early in the expedition, is revealing. Herendeen confirms the number of men taking part, that they have supplies for a six-month trek, that they are looking for gold and that they are well-armed. More importantly, the veteran scout confirms, in so many words, that the expedition will go south of the Yellowstone River and that this will be directly through Lakota territory, a direct violation of the 1868 treaty.

William Cornelius "Bill" Hickey. Bill Hickey was born October 1, 1846, in Massena in St. Lawrence County, New York, to Irish parents Thomas Hickey and Catherine Curran, who had emigrated in 1828. He was the youngest of four girls and four boys. Hickey left home in 1865 and initially went to Wisconsin, but returned to New York soon thereafter. Following his older brother Michael—a Civil War veteran, who had been wounded four times—William

William C. "Bill" Hickey at his wedding in 1888. *Courtesy of Find-A-Grave, provided by Alison Fuchs*

came to Montana in 1868 and initially settled in Butte. In 1870, Hickey lived in Deer Lodge, Montana Territory, working as a miner, along with Michael and another brother Edward.[79]

William "Bill" Hindman. Bill Hindman was born in Brown County, Ohio, in about 1843. During the Civil War, he served as a private in Company K of the 12th Ohio Volunteer Infantry Regiment. The unit mustered out in 1864 and Hindman transferred to Company C of the 23rd Ohio Volunteer Infantry Regiment (future Presidents Rutherford B. Hayes and William McKinley served in this unit as well.) Hindman probably fought at Second Bull Run, bloody Antietam, the pursuit of Confederate raider Gen. John Hunt Morgan, and later in the Shenandoah Valley Campaign. In 1870, he lived in East Gallatin, Gallatin, Montana Territory, and worked as a farm laborer.[80]

Fred Hollins/Hoelin/Harlan/Harland. Fred Hollins served on the crew of the six-pound cannon. He reportedly fought in the Civil War.

Irvin (Irving) B. Hopkins. Irving Hopkins was born about 1852 in Fairview, Erie County, Pennsylvania, the son of George C. and Eliza Ann Salisbury, both of whom hailed from New York. In 1870, he lived in West Gallatin, Montana Territory, working on a farm.[81]

Joseph R. Hopkins

Hugo John "Hugh" Hoppe. Hugo Hoppe was born Hugo Johann Leopold von der Gabelenz in Grenzhausen Nassau, Germany (northeast of Koblenz), on February 4, 1836. Seeking to avoid the anarchy following the Revolution of 1848, Hugo's parents Justus and Wilhelmine immigrated with the family to the United States in 1849, residing initially in Belleville, Illinois. Changing his name to his mother's last name of Hoppe, he traveled west from St. Louis to California in 1851 and to Utah in 1856 before moving to Virginia City in the Montana Territory in 1863 as part of the first gold seekers. He joined the Montana

Hugo Hoppe was born Hugo Johann Leopold von der Gabelenz in Grenzhausen Nassau, Germany (northeast of Koblenz), on February 4, 1836. *Photo #2006.044.2411, Whithorn Collection, courtesy of Yellowstone Gateway Museum, Livingston, Montana*

Vigilantes and helped hang Sheriff Henry Plummer among others. Just prior to this move, he served in the 2nd California Volunteer Cavalry Regiment in the Union Army from April 1861 to 1862; he was mustered out of the service for ill health at Camp Douglas, Utah. He married Mary Gee James in Salt Lake City in 1863, also adopting her six-year-old daughter. One story about Hoppe said that Mary's estranged first husband was later killed while serving with "Bloody Bill" Anderson's Raiders, but this tale appears to have been false. From 1866 to 1869 Hoppe lived mostly in Helena, starting several breweries. The following year—and through 1872—he bought several farms in the Bozeman area. In Montana, he was a close friend of scout Frank Grouard. Hoppe's 1870 occupation in Bozeman, Gallatin County, was that of freighter. He built a small hotel and trading post at Benson's Land-

ing in 1873, where he became friends with Oliver Hanna.[82]

George Hurbert

Charles Jamieson

Charles "Charley" Johnson. Charles Johnson was born about 1843 in Pennsylvania. In 1870, he was living in Bozeman, Gallatin County, Montana Territory, and worked as a woodcutter. He joined the expedition with his big Newfoundland dog.[83]

G.W. Johnson. A gold miner named George W. Johnson worked in Deer Lodge County, Montana Territory, in 1870. He had been born in 1839 in Tennessee. However, given the commonality of the name, we do not know if this man was the G.W. Johnson on the expedition.

John "Liver-Eatin" Johnston. Near the end of research, I found "Happenings and Remembrances of the Officer Family, as Written and Told by Guy C. Officer," September 1964. This remarkable unpublished document was dictated by the son of expedition member William C. Officer and sheds valuable insights on this frontiersman. Although no documents were found to corroborate this claim that follows, no other sources provided an air-tight alibi location for John Johnston in early 1874. Guy's account reads:

Another one they [William Officer and William T. Hamilton in 1903] talked about was how Liver-Eating Johnson earned his nick name. I believe this and not all of the bunk I have read about it. Just when and where this happened I don't remember but I think it was on the foretold [1874 Yellowstone] expedition. Two mules were loaded each with a mountain howitzer and the guns were loaded with nails bolts and scrap iron. [author's underline] In one engagement the howitzers were used with terrible effect. Afterwards, as was the custom, some of the men went out to kill any wounded Indians that could be found. Johnson and some others came up to an Indian that had been struck with a piece of metal, just below the breast bone, tearing the whole stomach area open. Johnson had a chew of tobacco in his mouth. The Indian's liver was exposed, Johnson said, "I wonder how Indian liver tastes?" He cut a piece of the liver off, picked it up with the point of his knife, threw it over his shoulder and chomped down on the tobacco as though he was chewing the liver. I saw Johnson as a boy. (I was the boy.) Wilbur [another son of William Officer] and I went swimming with him [at Hunter's Hot Springs] and counted twenty-seven knife and bullet scars on his body. Johnson was a big man, standing six foot four or five inches tall and I know he must have weighed two hundred and fifty pounds at least.

Here is the gist of the Liver-Eating legend courtesy of Dorman Nelson: Liver-Eating Johnston's real name was probably William Garrison. He was born in Little York, Hunterdon County, New Jersey (near Bethlehem, Pennsylvania), in about 1831 to Isaac Garrison and Eliza Mettler. During his life, he was known as John Johnson, Jack Johnson, John Johnston, Liver-Eating Johnston, Slippery Dick, and the Liver-eater. He was

John "Liver-Eatin" Johnston about 1877. The photo was probably taken by John H. Fouch in his studio at Fort Keogh, Montana. *Courtesy of Dorman Nelson*

also known as "*Dapiek Absaroka*" ("Crow-Killer") by the Crow. As a youngster, he was sent by his father to work on various local farms; the boy tired of the work and left home to work on a coastal schooner, hunting whales. He remained in this trade for about a dozen years, before reportedly joining the United States Navy; it is possible that he had been impressed by the Navy from the schooner. After an incident in which he probably struck his superior officer on the ship, he deserted. Fearing capture, he changed his name to John Johnston and headed west.

Over the next several decades, the legend continues, Johnston joined the gold rush in California, as well as trapped, hunted, and pedaled whiskey in Colorado and the Montana Territory. He reportedly served in Company H of the 2nd Colorado Cavalry Regiment in the Civil War. The unit was initially stationed at Fort Lyons in the Colorado Territory and then moved east to fight Confederate guerillas in Missouri; he apparently was wounded during this service. It is likely that he fought at the Second Battle of Newtonia on October 28, 1864. His brother John was killed in action in the Union Army at Cold Harbor on June 1, 1862. After the war, he returned to the Montana Territory and owned a wood yard that provided cord-wood to river boats (known as wood-hawking) including John Marsh over the years in the *Nile*, the *North Alabama* and the *Far West*, with his partner John X. Beidler, who had been a Montana Vigilante during the war. Johnston later pedaled whiskey along the Missouri River to Indians and also sold the spirits across the border in Canada.

John "Johnny" Jones. John Jones was born in about 1855. In addition to a rifle, he carried a large butcher knife.

William Jones

Charles E. King. Charles King was born in Saxony, Germany in about 1835. He was a brewer by trade. King was only associated with the expedition for five days, as he rode back from Hunter's Hot Springs with a report for the executive committee in Bozeman on February 16, 1874.[84]

Hans Peter Gyllembourg Koch. Peter Koch was born in South Church Town on the Island of Falster in Denmark on October 8, 1844, the son of a Lutheran clergyman. He immigrated to the United States in 1865; in 1870, he traveled to the Montana settlements, nearly freezing in a snow storm. Koch arrived in Bozeman on December 31, 1870. He began working as a woodcutter and a clerk at Fort Ellis and later worked as a clerk for Lester Willson's store. In this position, he refused to sell a rope on January 31, 1873, to a group of men, as he thought it would be used in a vigilante lynching; the lynching of two men—Z.A. Triplett who had knifed and killed a man and John "Steamboat Bill" St. Cloud, who had killed a Chinese prostitute—occurred anyway. A bookkeeper and surveyor by profession, Peter Koch served as the latter for the expedition.[85]

C. Langmade

William C. "Billy" Langston

P. Leon

William Lindsey

James Males

Olaf Malmborg. Olaf Malmborg was born on June 6, 1840, in Sweden. He immigrated to the United States in 1869. He was married (to Nellie, who was also from Sweden) and a farmer. He sported a red beard.[86]

John Mann

Aime J. Malin. Aime Malin was born about 1849 in Jefferson Township in Switzerland County, Indiana, the son of Ira N. and Elizabeth J. Malin. He is shown living at this location through 1860.[87]

Stereoscopic card showing lynching of Z.A. Triplett and John "Steamboat Bill" St. Cloud at Bozeman on January 31, 1873. Peter Koch refused to sell the lynch mob the rope, but it was to no avail. *Joshua Crissman, courtesy of Museum of the Rockies Photo Archives, Catalog Number: x85.3.1032*

Charles Mate

Tyler McClees. Tyler McClees was born in New York City about 1854. By 1865, he was living with an aunt and uncle—along with his brother James—in Middleton, New York. He was a farm worker in 1870 in Bozeman and was not living with his family.[88]

Paul McCormick. Paul McCormick was born in Greenwood, Steuben County, New York, on June 14, 1845, the son of Irish immigrants James and Margaret McCormick. He attended the Alfred Academy in New York until 1862. In 1866, he moved to Middle Creek in the Gallatin Valley and began farming and freighting, living with two brothers that had arrived in the territory two years previously. He began fighting Indians in 1870, operating the supply wagons on a small expedition by the US Army 13th Infantry Regiment out of Fort Shaw, during the expedition of Col. Eugene M. Baker against the Piegan Indians. In the summer of 1873, he organized an expedition to head into Yellowstone country to prospect.[89]

Paul McCormick in later years, as shown in a book sketch. *Courtesy of Find-A-Grave, Paul McCormick*

Paul McCormick in later years. He began fighting Indians in 1870, operating the supply wagons on a small expedition by the US Army 13th Infantry Regiment out of Fort Shaw, during the expedition of Col. Eugene M. Baker against the Piegan Indians. *Courtesy of Find-A-Grave, Paul McCormick*

Neil McCrea

Archie McDonald. Archie McDonald was born in 1842 in Argyllshire, Scotland, the son of Laughlin McDonald and Anna McFarland. The family immigrated to Port Elgin, Ontario, Canada; Archie departed this location on May 1, 1865, and made his way to New York City. From there he took a ship to Panama, traveled across that country by land and took another ship from Panama to San Francisco. From California, he traveled by land to Boise, arriving at Adler Gulch in the Montana Territory in June 1865. He became a naturalized citizen in 1870. On the expedition Archie had a yellow dog.[90]

William McDuff. William McDuff was born in Scotland about 1834. In 1870, he was a farmer in East Gallatin, Gallatin County.[91]

Duncan McRae

George H. "Doc" Miller. Doc Miller was responsible for providing medical support for any man on the expedition who became sick, injured, or wounded.

B. Mitchell

Jacob "James" Morngester. Jacob Morngester was born in Ohio about 1833. He lived in Gallatin County in 1870 and was a hunter.[92]

F. Mosbacher

Hugh O'Donovan. Hugh O'Donovan served as the Signal Officer for the expedition.

William Carroll "Bill" Officer. William C. Officer was born in White County, Tennessee, on May 13, 1846 to Alexander Officer and Lucinda Bohannon. The family moved to Andrew County (north of St. Joseph), Missouri, in 1848. By 1860, he had three younger brothers and a younger sister. In July 1863, Union elements killed Alexander Officer in Missouri; oral family history indicates that William witnessed his father's death. William came to Montana in 1872.[93]

Archie McDonald in later years (top row, second from left.) Archie McDonald was born in 1842 in Scotland, the son of Laughlin McDonald and Anna McFarland. *Courtesy of Gallatin History Museum*

William Carroll Officer, probably about 1880. *Courtesy of Steve Florman and Barbara Sell*

Addison M. Quivey, top row on the left, who was with a Crow delegation in Washington, DC, in 1880. Quivey was fluent in the Crow language. *Catalogue number P03423, courtesy of National Museum of the American Indian*

W. Olenger. "Jack" Olenger lived in Basin Precinct, Jefferson County in 1870. He was a miner, who had been born in Illinois in about 1840. Unlike most of the other miners in his immediate area that were not wealthy, he listed his personal property value at $3,000.[94]

William Omcer

Frank Overman

French Pete

F. Phillips

Charles Pietsch. Charles Pietsch was born in June 1842 in Germany. He immigrated to the United States in 1869.[95]

A.O. Piper

William Polfer

Addison M. Quivey. Addison Quivey was born in Ohio on February 20, 1832, the son of John William Quivey and Sophronia V. Story. The family lived in Greenfield in Dane County, Wisconsin, in 1850. Originally a blacksmith by trade, he was reportedly a favorite scout of Gen. Nelson A. Miles (this must have been after 1876.) Quivey was fluent in the Crow language. On the expedition, he served as the wagon master for a prairie schooner wagon—drawn by five pair of oxen—that had been donated to the expedition by Nelson Story, his cousin.[96]

Joseph A. Ramsdell. Joseph Ramsdell was born in Essex County, New York, on February 15, 1836, the son of Joseph Randall and Sarah Cutler; he had at least three brothers and a sister. By 1858, he lived in Dodge County in the Minnesota Territory.[97]

Thomas E. Rea. On the expedition, he cut his name on a sandstone formation near the Yellowstone River.

Herbert Fernando Richardson. Herbert F. Richardson was born in February 1854 in Waitsfield, Washington County, Vermont, the son of Eli Baker Richardson and Sylvia A. Sweat. He had five sisters and seven brothers. Richardson was a butcher in Bozeman. He may have served as one of the cooks on the expedition, given his profession.[98]

M. Ritchie

William D. "Dick" Robinson. Dick Robinson served as a herder on the expedition.[99]

James "Rocky" Rockfellow.[100]

G. Rookman[101]

Daniel Elliott Rouse. Daniel Rouse was born on September 30, 1834, in Washtenaw County, Michigan. In 1852, he moved to Minnesota and then to Iowa. Rouse traveled to Colorado in 1862 and from there went to Bozeman, where he became a freighter and farmer in 1864. After Col. John M. Bozeman was killed on April 20, 1867, Daniel Rouse was one of the men who recovered his body. In 1870, he was a farmer in Bozeman in Gallatin County. Daniel Rouse was married twice and had three children.[102]

W.F. Rowe

Bannock Smith

Charles Smith. Charles Smith was a farm laborer who was born in Connecticut in about 1845. He lived in Gallatin City, Gallatin County, in 1870.[103]

Conger "Con" Smith. Conger Smith was born in New York City on September 19, 1851, the son of Philip and Nancy Smith, both born in Ireland. In 1861, the family moved to Denver, Colorado; three years later, the Smiths continued their journey, arriving at Alder Gulch, Montana Territory. A year later, the family moved to the Boulder Valley.[104]

John M. Bozeman blazed the Bozeman Trail in 1863, founding Bozeman, Montana Territory, the following year. He was killed in 1867; the death was blamed on Indians and pressured the army to establish Fort Ellis to protect settlers of the area. This painting of his death was done by artist Edgar S. Paxson in 1898. *Source: catalog number: x89.89.1, courtesy of Museum of the Rockies Photo Archives*

Daniel Rouse in 1893. After Col. John M. Bozeman was killed on April 20, 1867, Daniel Rouse was one of the men who recovered his body. *Courtesy of Gallatin History Museum*

John B. Smith. John Smith was born in Württemberg, Germany, in 1837. He lived in Gallatin County in 1870 and worked as a farm laborer.[105]

J.C. Smith

W.H. Smith

George M. Southard. George M. Southard was born in Ohio about 1846. His father was Irish. He lived in Logan in Dearborn County, Indiana, in 1860. He probably served in the 52nd Indiana Volunteer Infantry Regiment in the Union Army as a private in Company B and Company G; given his age, he would have only fought late in the war at Nashville.[106]

Christian Speigle. Christian Speigle was born in Saxony, Germany, about 1825. In 1870, he lived in Diamond City, Meagher County, with his two daughters; he was a miner.[107]

John Henry Stevens. John Stevens was born in Iowa on March 30, 1847. In 1870, he was a farm laborer living in Gallatin City, Gallatin County.[108]

Patrick "Pat" Sweeney. Pat Sweeney was armed with a .50-caliber Springfield rifle.[109]

H.M. "Muggins" Taylor. Muggins Taylor was born about 1830, by one report in Mexico, but was raised in Mississippi. His nickname came from his favorite card game, "Muggins." Taylor claimed that he had been a high roller gambler and race horse owner in his youth; he also said that he had seriously wounded a man in an argument over a woman in Salt Lake City, and jumped a $20,000 bail, escaping to Montana in about 1870. Another source links him with Civil War service in the 17th Virginia Infantry Regiment and the Regular Army 8th Infantry Regiment, although serving in both Union and Confederate armies seems incompatible. Prior to the expedition, Taylor hunted wolves.[110]

Elisha Terrill. An E.S. Terrill was a deputy in Gallatin County in 1867 and was a judge by June 1874. This could also possibly be the E.S. Terrill, who was a miner at Radersburg in Jefferson County in 1870. This Terrill was born about 1818 in Kentucky.[111]

John Tobin

J.L. Vernon. Vernon served as a school teacher in Bozeman before absconding with the school library fund. He then reportedly participated in the 1873 expedition up the Yellowstone River with Gen. David Stanley. One source states that he had been a trooper in the 7th Cavalry Regiment but had deserted. Enlistment records show a John J. Vernon, born in New York about 1838, enlisted in New York on December 3, 1860, in Company B of the US 1st Artillery Regiment but deserted on August 8, 1863.[112]

Ira Vincent. Ira Vincent was born about 1848 in Iowa. In 1870, he lived in West Gallatin.[113]

Benjamin J. "Honest Ben" Walker. "Honest Ben" Walker appears to have been born in England about 1835. He had previously been a Hudson Bay Fur Company trapper. In 1869, while trapping for furs on Bouvais Creek in the Montana Territory with Oliver Hanna and Bill Hamilton, he got into a fight with Indian warriors.[114]

P. Walters

Timothy C. "T.C." Ward. T.C. Ward was born in Maine on December 30, 1828.

I. Warmling

Eli Britton Way. Eli B. Way fulfilled the duties of adjutant during the expedition, which involved posting guards and as a tactical battle commander, who often quickly organized counterattacks and charges during fights with the warriors. He was born at Trenton, Henry County, Iowa, on May 29, 1845. On July 18, 1861, he lied

"Muggins" Taylor in a small boat on the Yellowstone River at Coulson in 1882. Photograph in the book source, *Horace Countryman – Unsung Hero,* written by Jim Annin, identifies Taylor as being in the boat. Taylor is standing in the front, in dark clothes and a white shirt. His deputy sheriff star is clearly visible. This is the original photo that was used for the book and is of much higher quality. *Courtesy of Penny Redli and the Museum of the Beartooths, Columbus, Montana*

about his age and enlisted in Company K of the 6th Iowa Volunteer Infantry Regiment. During the Civil War, he rose to the grade of corporal on January 1, 1864, and to second lieutenant on January 1, 1865. Eli Way was mustered out of the service at Louisville, Kentucky, on July 21, 1865. He probably fought at Shiloh, Jackson, Missionary Ridge, Resaca, Dalton, Kennesaw Mountain, Atlanta, and Benton. It appears that he was a saloon keeper in Humboldt County, Nevada, in 1870.[115]

Dr. B.P. "Doc" Wickersham. Doc Wickersham filled the position of secretary for the expedition.[116] An individual with the same last name and initials, was born in Pennsylvania in 1851 and a druggist in 1872 in Madelia, Watonwan County, Minnesota. One man on the expedition said that Wickersham was a druggist in Bozeman so this is probably the same man.

Edward C. "Charlie" Wilson. Charlie Wilson had been in the Union Army in the Civil War. He would serve as the commander of the Big Horn gun on numerous occasions during the expedition.[117]

Fred B. Wilson

Harry J. Wilson

Henry A. Willson. Henry A. Willson was born in January 1841, probably in Niagara County, New York. A farmer, he married Mary J. Casper (born in 1851) on June 25, 1871 in Gallatin County in the Montana Territory. They had a son George in July 1871 and another son Edwin in December 1872. On the expedition, Willson took a dog with him that was later killed by warriors.[118]

Dr. A. Witty/Witby/Whitby

Thomas "Tom" Woodward. Tom Woodward was born in North Carolina about 1845. He was a farmer in East Gallatin, Gallatin County, in 1870.[119] During the expedition, he would be slightly wounded.

William M. "Bill" Wright. Bill Wright served as the "wagon boss" on the expedition. He was born at Humphrey, Cattaraugus County, New York, on September 8, 1831, the son of Richard and Polly Wright. He went west in 1855 to Denver and finally arrived in Bannack on June 6, 1862. Wright then went to Adler Gulch and later to Gallatin City. In 1865, Wright served as clerk and recorder of Gallatin

County. He was a miner, farmer, and stock raiser, and had a ranch on the Shields River.[120]

George Anderson "Andy" Yates. George Anderson Yates lived in Lower Boulder Township in Jefferson County in the Montana Territory in 1870. He was born in July 1832 in Missouri. On his farm were a daughter, age seventeen and a son, age fifteen. Andy was the son of Solomon Yates and Rachel Wells who died a year later.[121]

Hezekiah "Ki" Yates. Hezekiah "Ki" Yates, a son of George Anderson Yates and Mary Holt, was born on March 16, 1855 in Andrew, Missouri.

Zachariah F. "Zack" Yates. Zack Yates was born in Missouri on November 22, 1853. In 1870, he was a farm hand in Radersburg, Montana Territory, possibly on his mother's farm. Just before the expedition, he lived in Boulder Valley. He was the son of Solomon Yates and Mary "Polly" Wells (half sister of Rachel), which made him a half brother to George Anderson Yates, and an uncle to Ki Yates.[122]

J.M. Young

Weapons and Equipment

The 1874 Yellowstone Wagon Road and Prospecting Expedition was a self-contained, self-sufficient entity, designed to get all of its men over a journey of hundreds of miles, during several months, in winter weather, through hostile territory, and home again in one piece. To do this, a robust organization was required—as Addison M. Quivey recalled two years after the expedition:[123]

> … before we arrived at the mouth of the Big Horn, the number had increased to one hundred and forty-seven men, with over two hundred horses and mules, twenty-eight yoke of oxen, and twenty-two wagons, with supplies of provisions for four months.

One veteran of the expedition later recalled that "our outfit" consisted of twenty wagons, with nearly all of our provisions donated by the citizens of Montana. Nelson Story, a wealthy man of Bozeman, donated a big Murphy wagon and six yoke of oxen to haul it.[124]

Another veteran, Oliver Hanna, later wrote that there were nineteen wagons that carried bedding, tents, and provisions; he also recalled yokes of oxen and four and six-mule teams.[125]

The most important single element on the expedition was the livestock: oxen, horses, and mules. James Gourley later estimated the number of horses on the expedition:[126]

> The outfit consisted of about twenty wagons and I should judge about 100 pack horses, and almost everyone in the party had a saddle-horse.

That would put the total number of horses at 250, a large number for which to care. Jack Bean later wrote that he, and presumably other men, would tie the bridle or lead of a pack horse to a wagon; this would keep the animal from straying away from the wagon train. As strange as it may seem, the wagon train was designed to "shrink" over the route. The expedition started with twenty-eight yoke of oxen, pulling the heaviest of wagons. As the provisions in these wagons, pulled by oxen, were expended, the men would abandon (sometimes burning) the wagon, slaughter the oxen and eat them.[127] From his interviews with expedition participants, researcher Walter M. Camp concluded that there were fifty-six oxen, as well as mules and the 250 horses.[128]

Having said that, what would be remembered most about the expedition was the wide variety of legendary weapons employed—from powerful buffalo rifles to ingenious cannons. The 1874 Yellowstone Wagon Road and Prospecting Expedition fielded several types of weapons among the civilian miners, trappers, buffalo hunters, scouts and general adventurers. From a logistics standpoint, this was a cumbersome situation, as many types of ammunition were required to be on hand. However, from a tactical standpoint, these varied weapons gave the expedition a wide-variety of capabilities—from massed, short range, rapid fire, to phenomenal long range accuracy of some of the buffalo guns that had the potential to hit a man-sized target at over 1,000 yards in the hands of an expert marksman. As Addison M. Quivey recalled two years after the expedition:[129]

"…and two pieces of artillery, with about one hundred and fifty rounds of shell and canister. All the men were armed with the best breech-loading rifles, and were supplied with over forty thousand rounds of metallic cartridges for the same. A large portion of the materials, such as provisions, teams, etc., was furnished by the citizens of Bozeman and vicinity. Governor Potts gave great assistance in the way of arms, ammunition, etc."

The following weapons formed the backbone of the arms carried by the men of the expedition.

Firearms

Firearms used in 1874 had significant differences than those used today; the custom of the time was to name big-bore black powder cartridges by their nominal bullet diameter (caliber) and the typical maximum powder charge (in grains) that propelled them. Many times the descriptions included the bullet weight (in grains.) Thus the ".45-70" was a black powder cartridge that used a .45 caliber bullet (actually .458 inches in diameter) propelled by 70 grains of black powder. Therefore, the designation ".45-70-405" would indicate the .45-70 cartridge loaded with a 405 grain bullet. This could sometimes get confusing, as Sharps' weapons featured a marking indicating caliber, but then had the length of the cartridge case stamped on the barrel of the weapon instead of its powder capacity.

The development of reliable, controlled expansion jacketed bullets was far in the future, with bullets of all calibers in the 1870s' West generally made of cast lead. Additionally, velocity had pretty much hit its upper limit with black powder. The only way to increase shock power (the killing energy a bullet delivers to the target) then was to increase bullet diameter. Additionally, the sole way to increase penetration was to increase bullet weight (and thus sectional density.) In 1874, terminal ballistics was generally pretty simple—the bigger and heavier the bullet, the greater the killing power—whether that was against game animals or human beings.

Henry Repeating Rifle

The Henry Repeating Rifle, sometimes known as the Golden Boy for its shiny brass frame, was first introduced in 1861 as an improved version of the Volcanic Repeating Rifle. With the aforementioned brass frame, a hardwood butt, and an octagonal barrel, the lever-action weapon weighed in at close to ten pounds unloaded. Its twenty-four-inch barrel had six grooves that helped make it accurate to an effective range of 200 yards; experts could achieve good results at 400 yards. The Henry fired a .44 rimfire cartridge and by 1865 some 8,000 weapons were in the service of the Union Army; two regiments armed with the Henry played a major role at the Battle of Franklin. These cartridges were loaded with 25 grains of black powder and propelled the .44-caliber bullet weighing 210-215 grains. Muzzle velocity was 1,125 feet per second; muzzle energy was 568 foot-pounds. Although the tubular magazine under the barrel, which could hold fifteen rounds, had some potential structural deficiencies, most firers could send about twenty rounds a minute toward their targets. At close range, this rapid rate of fire could be devastating—at 400 yards this would generally only be a nuisance. An estimated 13,500 Henrys came out of the workshops. William T. Hamilton supposedly had the first Henry rifle that came into the Montana Territory.[130]

Top rifle is standard model of Henry .44 Rimfire. Bottom weapon is Winchester Model 1866 in saddle ring carbine configuration. Caliber is also .44 Henry Rimfire. *Courtesy of Mike Venturino*

Receiver of Henry Rifle in .44-caliber. The Henry Repeating Rifle was sometimes known as the Golden Boy for its shiny brass frame. *Courtesy of Collectors Firearms of Houston Texas*

Winchester Repeating Rifles

The Winchester Model 1866 was basically an improved Henry; it was also often called a Golden Boy because of its bronze alloy receiver. Its hinged King's Patent loading gate on the right side allowed the firer to insert cartridges without taking his eyes off the target; it also fired the .44 rimfire cartridge; seventeen rounds could be held in the magazine. The lever-action handle was pulled down and forward, which cleared the chamber of any spent shell casing, while introducing a fresh round and cocking the hammer. A carbine when it came with a twenty-inch barrel (127,000 made) and a magazine capacity of thirteen rounds, the rifle version had a twenty-four-inch barrel— sometimes round and sometimes octagonal; it had a smaller production run of 28,000.

Given that only eighteen Winchester Model 1873s were produced in 1873, and the expedition left Bozeman in mid-February 1874, the odds are that no one in the wagon train carried this newer model firearm. The Winchester Model 1873 fired the .44-40 round, now propelled by 40 grains of black powder, which developed quite a following. It was said that the round "killed more game, large and small, and more people, good and bad, than any other commercial cartridge ever developed." Muzzle velocity for this round was 1,245 feet per second, while the muzzle energy was now 688 foot-pounds.

The Winchester Model 1866 was basically an improved Henry; it is also often called a Golden Boy because of its bronze alloy receiver. It also fired the .44 rimfire cartridge; seventeen rounds could be held in the magazine of the rifle version. *Courtesy of a private collector*

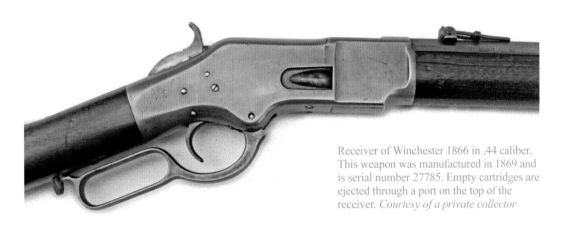

Receiver of Winchester 1866 in .44 caliber. This weapon was manufactured in 1869 and is serial number 27785. Empty cartridges are ejected through a port on the top of the receiver. *Courtesy of a private collector*

View of receiver of Winchester 1866 in .44 caliber. Rear sight has been elevated. *Courtesy of a private collector*

Winchester Model 1873 captured and used by Lakota warriors. This model, in .44-40 Winchester, was first made in 1873 and this study found none of these were present in the wagon train. However, captured weapons were often decorated in this manner. *Courtesy of a private collector*

Close-up view of the Indian-used Winchester Model 1873. Note the use of brass tacks for decoration, often found in captured weapons on the frontier. This weapon was manufactured in 1874 and is serial number 2317. It was captured by Capt. Alexander Moore and his Company F of the US 3rd Cavalry Regiment, commanded by Col. Joseph J. Reynolds, on March 17, 1876. This attack was on a village of about 700, led by Northern Cheyenne Chief Old Bear and Lakota Chief He Dog; it occurred on the Powder River just south of present-day Moorehead, Montana, under freezing conditions. It is not known how the warriors acquired the weapon in the first place. *Courtesy of a private collector*

The bullet could penetrate 4.9 inches of white pine at one hundred yards. Loaded, the rifle weighed 9.27 pounds; while the carbine weighed 7.5 pounds.[131]

Spencer Repeating Rifle/Carbine

The Spencer Repeating Rifle, designed by Christopher Spencer and patented in 1860, came into service about the same time as the Henry, but was much different in construction. It had a seven-shot magazine, but one that was inside the butt stock, making it more robust in design than the Golden Boy. While

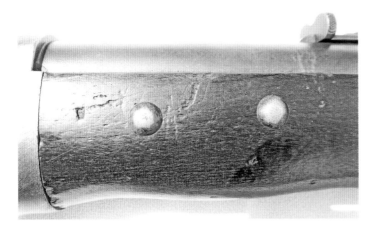

Close-up view of the lower portion of the front hand-guard of the stock. The uneven wear on the lower edge of the wood is often caused by the warrior resting that part of the weapon. Note the use of brass tacks for decoration, often found in captured weapons on the frontier. *Courtesy of a private collector*

Repeater cartridges: (left) .44 Henry rimfire, (middle) .44 Winchester centerfire (also known as .44 WCF or .44-40) and (right) 56-50 Spencer rimfire. *Courtesy of Mike Venturino*

The weapon became famous after Col. John T. Wilder's "Lightning Brigade" attacked Confederate forces at Hoover's Gap. According to legend, one Confederate soldier said concerning the Spencer, "the Yankees could load on Sunday and shoot all the rest of the week." *Courtesy of Rock Island Auction Company*

it was also operated by lever action, the caliber of the weapon was .56 and the bullet weighed 362 grains. Propelled by 34 grains of black powder, the muzzle velocity of the Spencer was about 931 feet per second. Eight times as many Spencers were fielded by the Union Army as Henrys during the Civil War.

The weapon became famous after Col. John T. Wilder's "Lightning Brigade" attacked Confederate forces at Hoover's Gap, Tennessee. According to legend, one Confederate soldier said concerning the Spencer, "the Yankees could load on Sunday and shoot all the rest of the week." Accuracy was similar to the Henry. In 1864, a special device—known as the "Stabler Cut Off"—could be fitted to the weapon, which prevented the rounds in the tubular magazine from cycling through the receiver, turning the weapon into a single shot weapon in which the operator manually inserted each round. The device could be disengaged when fast firepower was needed. Later models were in caliber .50; a Spencer carbine of this caliber could drive a bullet through 6.95 inches

of white pine at one hundred yards. The Spencer's rate of fire was generally fourteen rounds per minute. Barrel length was 20, 22, or 30 inches. The weapon weighed ten pounds with a thirty-inch barrel. The production run of the Spencer was approximately 145,000.[132]

Springfield Trapdoor Single-Shot Rifle Model 1870

By 1864, Union Chief of Ordnance Brig. Gen. Alexander Dyer had concluded that breech-loading firearms were the wave of the future for the military and that the use of these weapons should not be confined to the cavalry, but extended to the infantry as well—of course in the form of a longer rifle instead of the shorter and lighter carbine. Several manufacturers began developing prototypes, including Springfield, where the Master Armorer Erskine Allin (with apparent disregard for potential patent infringements) converted the standard .58-caliber muzzle loader in 1865 by cutting away the breech and inserting a breech block

The Springfield Model 1870 Rifle was manufactured by Springfield Armory as part of a cost effective method for the government that took leftover muzzle loaders and converted them into single shot metallic breech loaders. The weapon is in caliber .50 (also known as .50-70) It was often nicknamed a "Long Tom." *Courtesy of Mike Venturino*

The big and the small: (left) .44 Henry rimfire and (right) .50-70. *Courtesy of Mike Venturino*

hinged at the front end that could be swung upward to expose the chamber and permit loading and then swung down and locked before firing. Overall length was 51.75 inches.

The following year, Master Armorer Allin modified the weapon to chamber a .50-70 copper cartridge—a .50-caliber bullet powered by 70 grains of black powder. The weight of the conical bullet was 450 grains, traveling through the 32 5/8 inch barrel at 1,250 feet per second. This combination would later be nicknamed the "Big Fifty" and the "Long Tom." The first model came out in 1868; another model with modifications came out in 1868 and a third in 1870. Some 11,000 weapons were produced from 1870 to 1873, initially mostly issued to the army. The rifles could deliver accurate fire to 500 yards and kill at 1,000 yards. At thirty yards, the bullet would penetrate 17-19 one-inch white pine boards. After the introduction of the Model 1873, more and more Model 1870s made their way into the civilian market. James Butler "Wild Bill" Hickok used a variant of Model 1870.[133] Hundreds of expended .50-70 cartridges have been found at the 1874 expedition sites.

Springfield Model 1865 Joslyn Rifle

The 1865 Joslyn was the first breech-loading rifle made by Springfield. Expedition archaeological finds indicate that at least one was present. Using the Joslyn Company-supplied actions, but otherwise resembling Model 1863 rifle muskets, the weapon used a special rimfire .50-caliber cartridge that was slightly more powerful than the .56-50 Spencer. It was thus the first breech-loader made at the Springfield Armory. The bullet weight was 450 grains. The Springfield Armory produced 3,007 weapons in 1865.[134]

Buffalo Rifles

American Bison/Buffalo were (and are) exceptionally rugged creatures with heavy bones and thick hides. The rifles used to hunt them had to be of a large caliber and power

to be effective. The big-bore buffalo cartridges, like the other cartridges of the day, were loaded with black powder, as smokeless powder had not yet been introduced. Because black powder is an inefficient propellant by volume, big cases with large powder charges were necessary, but even so, muzzle velocities were typically limited to around 1,250-1,500 feet per second.

Remington Rolling Block

Along with the Sharps rifle, the Remington Rolling Block was one of two rifles used more than any other by the buffalo hunters in the 1870s and 1880s. With an extremely strong breech, it came in numerous calibers from its first use in the 1860s.

Model 1874 Sharps

At the apex of bison hunting (1870–1884,) the Sharps rifle was a favorite among many buffalo hunters because of its accuracy at long range. Other rifles were available, such as the Ballard, the Springfield 1873 and the Remington Rolling Block, but the vast majority of frontiersmen who needed a large caliber rifle opted for the Sharps. The company itself—the

The action of the Remington Rolling Block, shown in part here, could easily withstand the increased pressure of the new smokeless powders coming into use by the late 1880s. *Author photograph, June 2015*

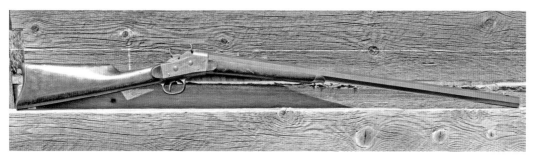

Early Remington Rolling Block rifle in .44-77 caliber. This weapon is a prized possession of black powder expert Mike Venturino. *Author photograph, June 2015*

Sharps Rifle Manufacturing Company of Hartford, Connecticut—called the rifle, "Old Reliable." Buffalo hunters called it the "poison slinger." Historians have come to call it, "The gun that shaped American destiny." The original Sharps Model 1874 was actually introduced in 1871, but the model number was changed in 1874, when new owners purchased the company. In 1876, reorganized as the Sharps Rifle Company, the business moved to Bridgeport, Connecticut. The change may have been intended to show prospective purchasers of Sharps rifles that the company had something new to offer.

What set the Sharps apart from other large-caliber rifles was the ammunition for which it was chambered. The Sharps rifle action was inherently strong and could withstand chamber pressures that would seriously damage other rifles. One of the largest of these buffalo calibers was the .50-170-700 (.50 caliber, 170 grains of powder, 700-grain bullet.) The most widely used caliber for the buffalo hunters probably was the .50-90, basically a lengthened .50-70. Another extremely popular cartridge (some would say as popular as the .50-90) was the .44-90, in essence a necked down .50-90 firing a 520 grain bullet. Some hunters believed that with properly adjusted telescopic sights they could hit anything they aimed at up to 1,000 yards,

although experienced hunters generally fired at far shorter ranges. At longer ranges, some experts believed the .45-125-550 was the ideal load. As most plains buffalo hunters reloaded their ammunition with varying amounts of black powder to save money, cartridges like the .50-90 were not always loaded with a maximum powder load.

For this reason, Sharps (and ammunition-makers) referred to the standard cartridges by caliber and case length with most Sharps rifles marked as such. The .50-90, for example, was designated .50-2½. Many cartridges for Sharps rifles were bottlenecked; ones that were not included the .45-70, the .50-70 and the .50-90. Before the expedition in 1874, Sharps Model 1874 rifles were chambered for the following cartridges and thus it would have been possible for these caliber Sharps to have been present with the wagon train: the .40-90 Bottleneck (2⅝") using 265 to 370 grain bullets, the .44-77 Bottleneck (2¼") with 380 or 405 grain bullets, the .44-90 Sharps Bottleneck (2⅝") with 450 or 500 grain bullets, the .50-70 Government (1¾") with 425 to 500 grain bullets and the .50-90 Sharps (2½") firing 425 or 473 grain bullets.[135]

Many .50-70 government cartridges were found by Don Weibert during his lengthy research on the positions along the expedition's route (and Ron Wald on his land where the

Sharps Model 1874 Sporting Rifle in .45 caliber, with thirty-inch octagonal barrel and double trigger. *Courtesy of a private collector*

Close-up of the same rifle. Small screw between triggers can be used to set trigger pull. *Courtesy of a private collector*

Business end of the same rifle. And business was booming. *Courtesy of a private collector*

Breach mechanism of the same rifle. It was one of the strongest of all firearms. This weapon was manufactured in 1878 and is serial number 161057. *Courtesy of a private collector*

Sharps Model 1874 Sporting Rifle in .50 Caliber. Case length is unknown; the weapon has a thirty-inch octagonal barrel and a single trigger. *Courtesy of Collectors Firearms of Houston Texas*

Receiver of the same Sharps Model 1874 Sporting Rifle in .50-caliber. Case length is unknown; the weapon has a thirty-inch octagonal barrel and a single trigger. It weighs ten pounds. *Courtesy of Collectors Firearms of Houston Texas*

third battle was fought.) However, this does not mean the other caliber Sharps Model 1874s were not there, as almost all buffalo hunters reloaded their ammunition and would have saved as many expended cartridges as possible. The following testimony is from a letter that described buffalo hunting on the Texas plains near San Angelo in 1876:[136]

Another Sharps Model 1874 Sporting Rifle. The rifle is marked Walter Cooper of Bozeman, Montana. The rifle has a twenty-seven-inch heavy, octagonal barrel chambered for the Sharps .50, 2½" cartridge. The top of the barrel is roll-stamped with the first style legend: "SHARP'S RIFLE/MANUFG. CO./ HARTFORD, CONN." used from 1871–1873. The top barrel flat behind the rear sight is stamped with "FROM", "W.COOPER" and "BOZEMAN M.T." in separate oval cartouches. "CALIBER 50" is stamped behind the dealer markings and "30" is stamped on the rounded portion of the barrel just ahead of the receiver. The barrel is fitted with a dovetail mounted knife blade front sight with brass blade and an R.S. Lawrence patent high notch folding rear sight. The receiver is fitted with factory double set triggers. The left side of the receiver is stamped; "C. SHARPS' PAT./SEPT. 12th 1848" in two lines. The serial number, C53505 is on the upper receiver tang, on the underside of the barrel beneath the forearm and on the inside of the forearm. The rifle has a walnut pistol grip stock with army rifle style butt plate and a Schnabel forearm with metal tip. The butt plate and the forearm both have checkered panels. The barrel is blued and the receiver, hammer, lever, and butt plate have a casehardened finish. The weapon sold at auction in 2011 for $14,000. *Courtesy of Rock Island Auction Company*

> The gun they swear by is Sharps .44 caliber just like yours; they shoot 90 grains powder, some use the .50-caliber and 120 grains. The best gun in this part of the country is a Sharps .40 caliber with 90 grains of powder, the ball weighs 420 grains. The hunter who has it says he can hit and kill a bull as far as he can see it. It holds up wonderfully. The .44 caliber

Walter Cooper received about 10% of all Sharps Model 1874s produced. Some he sold without modifications; others he modified to fit the customer's wishes. Some, but not all, of these modified rifles had his name stamped on them. There are at least four variants of this stamp. This picture is of the same weapon above. *Courtesy of Rock Island Auction Company*

day before yesterday loaded with 85 grains of powder, 420 grains of lead, shot through several bulls in succession at 500 yards.

Model 1874 Sharps rifles weighed from ten to sixteen pounds and were referred to by their weight. Twelve pounds was about average for the rifle in its early days, although 16-pound models were described from time to time. Later models increased in average weight to about fourteen pounds, although Sharps was truly a custom shop and would build a rifle to whatever specifications the purchaser desired. Options included barrel length (often 26 to 36 inches) and barrel outside form, such as full octagon barrel, half octagon barrel or round barrel. Double set triggers were an option, as were globe and peep iron sights. A Malcolm telescopic sight would cost the Sharps customer an additional $40—more than the cost of the rifle alone in some cases, although accounts of several hundred dollars paid in the era are not unusual. Another excellent optic was the 20-power telescopic sight made by A. Vollmer in Jena, Germany. Despite their many innovations, Sharps went into liquidation in September 1881—about the same time that

the buffalo population disappeared from the Great Plains, casualties of this deadly weapon.[137]

Colt Model 1860 Army Revolver

Pistols were clearly secondary weapons on the expedition, although nearly every frontiersman had one. The Colt Model 1873 US Army Colt Revolver was just entering the production line and it is doubtful that more than a handful of men on the wagon train owned this new weapon, although it appears that Henry Calfee did. The Model 1860 Army Colt was a percussion revolver on its introduction, but beginning in 1871, some 1,200 weapons were converted to use the army .44 centerfire cartridges. Undoubtedly, some of these Model 1860s were present with the wagon train, as were Colt Richards Conversions, also in caliber .44. This cartridge used 23 grains of black powder to propel a 210 grain bullet. The percussion original model could well have been present as well, as the federal government had procured 127,000 of them during the war.[138] The weapon was a popular one in the Old West; at the Gunfight at the OK Corral, Frank McLaury and Billy Clanton carried Colt Model 1860s. Confederate

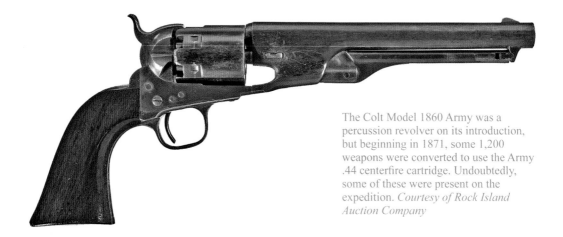

The Colt Model 1860 Army was a percussion revolver on its introduction, but beginning in 1871, some 1,200 weapons were converted to use the Army .44 centerfire cartridge. Undoubtedly, some of these were present on the expedition. *Courtesy of Rock Island Auction Company*

raider John Hunt Morgan also carried two of these pistols, as did Frank James at one point; so, supposedly, did "Liver-Eatin" Johnston.

Remington Army Revolvers

The Remington Army Revolver Model 1858, Model 1861, and New Model 1863, percussion weapons could also have been present among expedition members—and perhaps the warriors as well. It featured quick-change cylinders for reloading in less than thirty seconds. Some

110,000 New Army Revolvers were produced beginning in 1862. With an octagonal barrel, and in .44 caliber, it was a sturdy weapon.[139]

1851 Colt Revolving Belt Pistol of Naval Caliber

The Colt Revolving Belt Pistol of Naval Caliber is more popularly called today the Colt 1851 Navy or Navy Revolver. Designed by Samuel Colt between 1847 and 1850, it was a percussion weapon of .36-caliber. Total

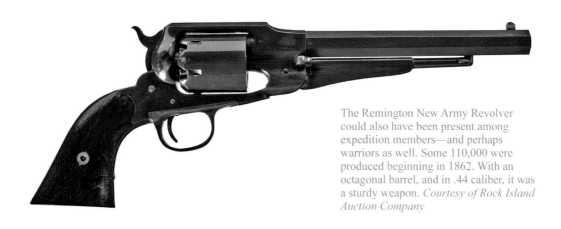

The Remington New Army Revolver could also have been present among expedition members—and perhaps warriors as well. Some 110,000 were produced beginning in 1862. With an octagonal barrel, and in .44 caliber, it was a sturdy weapon. *Courtesy of Rock Island Auction Company*

production was about 250,000 units. The model remained in production until 1873 (it was discontinued in part with the introduction of the Colt Model 1873) when revolvers using metallic cartridges came into widespread use. The .36 caliber round lead ball weighed 80 grains and had a muzzle velocity of 910 feet per second. The men who used the pistol read like a *Who's Who* of steely-eyed characters of the Civil War and the Wild West: William "Bloody Bill" Anderson, John "Oswatomie" Brown, Nathan B. "Old Bed" Forrest, John Wesley "Wes" Hardin, Wild Bill Hickok, John Henry "Doc" Holiday, Frank James, Jesse James, William Clarke "Will" Quantrill, Jack Slade, and Cole Younger.[140]

Shotguns

It would be logical to assume that some of the men took shotguns on the expedition. First, these weapons could be used to kill gamebirds for food once winter turned to spring. Secondly, shotguns could be used as close-in weapons if the warriors penetrated the laager positions at night.

Colt 1851 Navy, or Navy Revolver. Designed by Samuel Colt between 1847 and 1850, it was a percussion weapon of .36 caliber. This weapon was manufactured in 1865 and is serial number 184713. *Courtesy of a private collector*

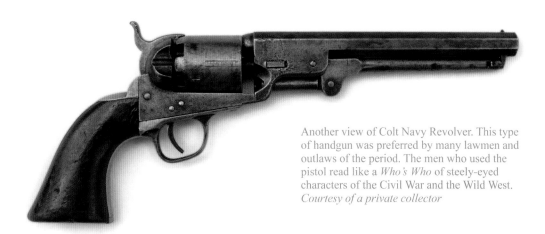

Another view of Colt Navy Revolver. This type of handgun was preferred by many lawmen and outlaws of the period. The men who used the pistol read like a *Who's Who* of steely-eyed characters of the Civil War and the Wild West. *Courtesy of a private collector*

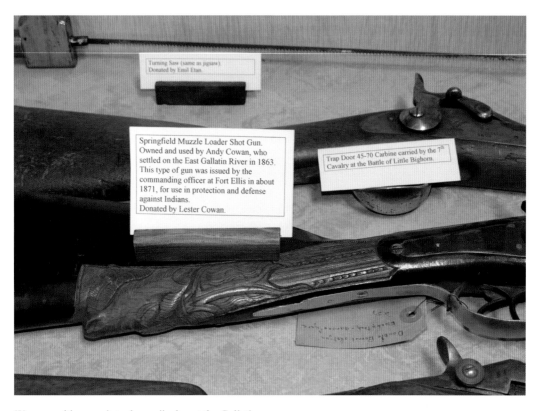

Weapon with carved stock, on display at the Gallatin County Courthouse in Bozeman, is a Springfield muzzle-loading shotgun belonging to Andy Cowan. He may have taken it on the expedition for close-in fighting and gamebird hunting. *Author photograph at Gallatin County Courthouse, October 2013*

Artillery

The leaders of the 1874 Yellowstone Wagon Road and Prospecting Expedition decided to take two artillery pieces with them, and this decision would prove significant. Expedition member Joe Cook later described the artillery pieces of the expedition:[141]

Fort Ellis gave us a six pounder cannon and ammunition to go with it. Colonel Bozeman [had earlier] brought an iron piece of four-inch caliber. We had to make the ammunition for this piece. We got some blue flannel and made sacks to fit the muzzle, and about ten inches long to hold the powder, and for shells we went to the tin shop and had cans made to fit the bore

View of Fort Ellis, Montana Territory, taken in July 1871. Members of the expedition "procured" the mountain howitzer outside the fort shortly before the expedition started. *William Henry Jackson, courtesy of National Park Service, Public Domain*

of the gun. For projectiles, we went to the blacksmith shop and got all the old scraps of iron horse shoes and cut them up to fill the cans. I want to record that when we fired this gun, the cans bursted when they left the muzzle of the gun, the pieces of iron not being the same shape or size, each and every one of them had a tune of its own, as it passed through the air.

James Gourley added these details about the artillery on the expedition: [142]

> … the two guns we had—one a twelve-pound howitzer and the other a twelve-pound Napoleon. Unfortunately, however, we had but little ammunition which could be used in the Napoleon.

These descriptions have led to some confusion over the years. Charles Avery, who was on the expedition, later recalled that the Big Horn Gun was made of brass and the mountain howitzer was black and probably made of iron.[143] First, the "six powder" recalled by Cook is probably a misnomer for a six pound cannon. Secondly, we know that the two guns were not the same caliber, as James Gourley described. Don Weibert, the first modern writer to publish a detailed description of the expedition, stated that Fort Ellis furnished a mountain howitzer, while the town of Bozeman provided a small Mexican War cannon that became known as the "Big Horn Gun" and may have been procured much earlier by John Bozeman as asserted by Joe Cook.

The US Army used Napoleonic style bronze 6-pounder field guns (Models of 1835, 1838, 1839, and 1841) in the Mexican War and early in the Civil War, although they became outdated due to the small size of the shot. There were even a few older Model 1819 cannons made of iron. The smoothbore bronze 6-pounders had a bore of 3.67 inches, a cannon length of sixty inches and a weight of 884 pounds. They fired 6.1 pound projectiles, using a gunpowder charge of 1.25 pounds—giving a muzzle velocity of 1,429 feet per second

M1819 6-pounder Iron Field Gun displayed at the post office of the Wisconsin Veterans Home at King, Wisconsin. *Courtesy of John Anderson, as posted on War Memorials of Wisconsin*

and a range (when elevated to 5°) of 1,523 yards. The Model 1819 6-pounder, also a smoothbore, had a cannon length of 72 inches.

The mountain howitzer was probably the M1835 or M1841 Mountain Howitzer, which was in service use from 1837 to 1870; therefore it was in use during the Mexican War. Ordnance engineers designed the smoothbore weapon to be light weight (220-pound gun tube; 500 pounds overall) and highly portable. Because of this—and its ease of disassembly into three components—it did not require roads for transportation. This made it well suited for Indian fighting and mountain warfare. However, its shorter effective range (1,005 yards) made it unsuitable for dueling with enemy field artillery—a non-factor on the western frontier. The caliber of the mountain howitzer was twelve pounds, a period measurement that designated in Imperial pounds of round solid iron shot of diameter to fit the bore, which measured 4.62 inches. The gun tube was made of bronze and measured thirty-three inches in length.[144]

The weapon, known in army circles as the "Bull Pup," using a half-pound black powder charge, could fire solid cannon balls, spherical case (an iron anti-personnel projectile containing an interior cavity packed with lead or iron round balls, around a small bursting charge of sufficient force to break open the

M1819 6-pounder Iron Field Gun mounted to a replica wooden gun carriage. *Courtesy of John Anderson, as posted on War Memorials of Wisconsin*

M1819 6-pounder Iron Field Gun view of the muzzle. *Courtesy of John Anderson, as posted on War Memorials of Wisconsin*

thin-walled iron projectile,) or canister shot (an anti-personnel projectile which included many small iron round shot or lead musket balls in a metal can that broke up when fired, scattering the lethal shot throughout the enemy personnel, like a huge shotgun).[145]

The major difference between spherical case and canister shot, each weighing about 8.9 pounds, was that a spherical case exploded downrange hundreds of feet, while canister effects started almost immediately after leaving the muzzle. The spherical iron ball was hollow; inside were several .69-caliber lead balls, a powder charge, and a thin zinc fuse. This fuse stuck out of the ball and was ignited by the explosion of the main powder charge behind the iron ball in the barrel of the cannon. An experienced gunner knew how long the fuse needed to be to cause the ball to explode at certain distances after it left the muzzle. Added to his task, the gunner had to know to what elevation to raise the gun tube, so the ball would fly and hit the target directly—or at least come very close.[146]

In addition to the pack carriage—with the gun tube carried on one mule, the carriage and wheels on a second animal and an immediate load of ammunition on a third pack animal—a prairie carriage was available, with the gun with carriage assembled and drawn by two horses or mules. This versatility permitted its use in areas where roads were little more than paths, a condition the expedition found during most of its journey. These small howitzers provided artillery support for forces where it would otherwise be unavailable. However, their shorter range made them unsuitable for dueling (known as counter-battery fire) with other field artillery.[147]

Author Don Weibert described that the Big Horn Gun was a small piece of Napoleonic design, speculating that it may have been used in the Mexican War and then found its way over the Santa Fe Trail; this hypothesis adds an additional speculation that the cannon could have been in the Mexican Army, although Weibert stated that the piece was not a military weapon, nor did it have any military production markings. The cannon appeared in history at Fort Kearny, Nebraska (named for Stephen Watts Kearny, and not to be confused with the fort in Wyoming)—owned by John Talbotte, the founder of Kearny City. In 1870, the town ceased to exist after the railroad passed on the opposite side of the Platte River. The cannon somehow arrived at Cheyenne, Wyoming Territory. Shortly thereafter, a Big Horn Expedition formed at Cheyenne.

The endeavor was originally slated to explore the Black Hills region for gold.

After the commander at Fort D.A. Russell (outside Cheyenne) prohibited the expedition from going to the Black Hills, it set its sights on the Big Horn Mountains. After discovering none of the precious metal, most of the prospectors returned to Cheyenne, while a few men continued to Bozeman, Montana Territory—taking the cannon with them. A group of citizens of Gallatin County subsequently purchased the piece for frontier defense against marauding warrior bands.[148] This scenario would have occurred after the death of John Bozeman.

Author Phyllis Smith has added additional information concerning the gun. She wrote that in 1870 the gun came under the care of miller Perry McAdow, and added that allegedly Gen. Zachary Taylor had used the small cannon on the Chihuahua and Santa Fe Trails in the Mexican War.[149] Her source for this information was a letter written by the granddaughter of Walter Cooper. Phyllis Smith also opined that the cannon could have been used by the Confederacy during the Civil War.

In 1874, William D. Cameron, a Civil War veteran, assumed command of the gun.

Reconstructed Big Horn Gun in the Gallatin History Museum of Bozeman. The wooden carriage and wheels burned in a fire at Fort Pease. Over one hundred years later, Don Weibert made a new undercarriage and wheels of laminated cottonwood and refurbished the gun. *Author photograph at Gallatin History Museum of Bozeman, October 2013*

Front view of reconstructed Big Horn Gun in the Gallatin History Museum of Bozeman. *Author photograph at Gallatin History Museum of Bozeman, October 2013*

View of the rear of the gun tube of the reconstructed Big Horn Gun in the Gallatin History Museum of Bozeman. Note the touch hole into which a fuse was placed to fire the gun. *Author photograph at Gallatin History Museum of Bozeman, October 2013*

Close-up view of the muzzle of the reconstructed Big Horn Gun in the Gallatin History Museum of Bozeman. The diameter of this cannon measured 3.375 inches. *Author photograph taken at Gallatin History Museum of Bozeman, October 2013*

He determined that what was needed were shrapnel filled projectiles, although in the Montana Territory there were probably few of these munitions to be found. Using his imagination, Cameron discovered several cases of canned oysters in the Tuller, Rich, and Willson General Store, owned by Lester S. Willson. However, Lester S. Willson was no ordinary shopkeeper, not by a long shot.

Born in Canton, New York, on June 16, 1839, to Ambrose and Julia Hill Willson, Lester Willson attended the Canton Academy and became a store clerk before he enlisted in the Union Army in 1861, rising through the ranks in the 60th New York Volunteer Infantry Regiment to become a colonel by 1865. During the war, he fought at Antietam, was severely wounded in the left thigh at Chancellorsville, and fought at Lookout Mountain, Atlanta, and Savannah. Col. Willson received the surrender of Savannah from Mayor Dr. Richard Arnold and was the first officer to enter that city at the head of his own regiment. Two years after the war, Willson

Brevet Brig. Gen. Lester S. Willson in 1865; he was later the owner of the Tuller, Rich, and Willson General Store and assisted William D. Cameron develop shrapnel rounds for the Big Horn Gun. *Courtesy of Montana State University, Special Collections Library, Collection 1407 – Lester S. Willson Family Papers, 1861–1922*

The Tuller, Rich, and Willson General Store in 1866. Just before the expedition departed in 1874, the owner, Brevet Brig. Gen. Lester S. Willson, found several cases of canned oysters, the diameter of the cans were a perfect fit to serve as canisters for artillery shrapnel rounds for the Big Horn Gun. The building was demolished on August 17, 1882. *Courtesy of Montana State University, Special Collections Library, Collection 1407 – Lester S. Willson Family Papers, 1861–1922*

received a brevet promotion to brigadier general, "for gallant and meritorious services under Gen. William T. Sherman, resulting in the fall of Atlanta, Georgia."[150] Shortly after the war, Willson heard a speech by Speaker of the United States House of Representatives Schuyler Colfax about the prospects of the West and told his two best friends, "Boys, let's go to Montana!" They did, reaching Montana on September 1, 1866, where he became a prominent businessman and politician.[151] When Cameron told him what

he needed, Willson knew just what the doctor ordered and offered the canned oysters.

Cameron and Willson donated the appetizers to the enthusiastic general public of Bozeman and filled the empty cans with nails, pieces of chain, and scrap iron. As Charles Avery would later say, that included "ox shoes and any old thing that we could put into it." The two men cut the tops of the cans—which were about eight inches tall—to form metal tabs around the edge and after the cans were filled with shrapnel, the original lids were put back into place and crimped tightly. The pair also found a ream of blue flannel which they cut and sewed into powder charge bags. Ten inches long and filled with black powder, these charge bags formed a snug fit, when rammed down the muzzle of the cannon, and ensured that the shrapnel canisters would fly a long way. As Jack Bean recalled of these rounds and their prospective targets:[152]

> Whenever this gun was fired every piece takes a direction of its own, saying, "where is yee—where is yee—where is yee!"

Previously, Walter Cooper, master gunsmith, owner of the Walter Cooper's Armory and Gun Manufactory at Bozeman, and the largest distributor for the Sharps Arms Company in the Montana Territory, examined the cannon and got it into operational condition.[153] According to Cooper, the caliber of the cannon was 4.62 inches. He termed it a "9-pounder."[154]

Walter Cooper did not go on the expedition, but he played a pivotal role in its success. In addition to giving one of the cannons a clean bill of health, Cooper undoubtedly provided several of the buffalo hunters (and other men for that matter) with their Sharps rifles in the years leading up to February 1874. Walter Cooper was born on July 4, 1843, at Sterling, Cayuga County, New York, the son of Andrew Cooper and Sarah McGilvra. His father died of pneumonia after a boat accident, when Walter was eight. Sent to live with an aunt in Lansing, Michigan, his adventurous spirit led

Example of the special "oyster can" round for the Big Horn Gun on display at the Gallatin History Museum of Bozeman. The height of the oyster can shrapnel shell measured 6.50 inches. *Author photograph taken at Gallatin History Museum of Bozeman, October 2013*

Another example of the special oyster can round for the Big Horn Gun on display at the Gallatin History Museum of Bozeman. This round has split and shrapnel pieces inside can be seen. *Author photograph taken at Gallatin History Museum of Bozeman, October 2013*

View of the top of a special oyster can round for the Big Horn Gun on display at the Gallatin History Museum of Bozeman. The diameter of the round was measured at 3.125 inches. Note how tabs were created on the side of the can and after the shrapnel was loaded, the lid was replaced and the tabs folded down to secure it. *Author photograph taken at Gallatin History Museum of Bozeman, October 2013*

Walter Cooper in 1859; he was later a Sharps gun dealer in Bozeman and arms expert that refurbished the Big Horn Gun before the expedition. *Photograph by George D. Wakely, Pac 99-69.2, courtesy of Montana Historical Society Research Center Photograph Archives*

him to go west and in 1858 he reached Leavenworth, Kansas, where supposedly he met Jim Bridger. The following year saw Walter Cooper travel to Pikes Peak; in 1860 he joined a prospecting expedition to the San Juan Mountains in southwest Colorado, where legend has it that he visited "Kit" Carson. Two years later, Cooper went to Colorado Springs, where he worked as a scout for the 1st Regiment of Colorado Volunteers. In November 1863, he headed north to the Montana Territory, arriving in Virginia City in February 1864.[155]

After several years of mining and moving freight by steamboat, Walter Cooper settled in Bozeman in 1868 and established his armory and gun manufactory. His occupation in 1870 in Bozeman, Gallatin County, was obviously listed as gunsmith.[156] Walter Cooper's first order to Sharps for rifles was made in September 1871. He soon wrote to Sharps Arms the following letter:[157]

Those four guns you sent me take the eye of everyone. They outshoot anything ever brought to this country. I won a bet of ten dollars the other day on penetration against an army musket—called the Springfield Needle Gun here. Shot the same powder and shot two inches deeper into wood.

Cooper's gunsmiths soon began rebuilding and rebarreling Sharps rifles. Numerous existing weapons were then chambered for the .44-90 Sharps Bottleneck (2⅝") and later the .45-110 Sharps (2⅞"). Many of these modified-by-Cooper Sharps rifles had extra heavy barrels and special buckhorn rear sights; in short, Cooper catered to the particular preferences of individual hunters.[158]

Tactics

Outstanding weapons are useless if combined with inefficient tactics. Fortunately for the Yellowstone Wagon Road and Prospecting Expedition, the tactics employed were close to perfect with respect to the nature of the enemy, the terrain, the weather, and the capabilities and weapons of the frontiersmen. Joe Cook later recounted that when the wagon train was traveling there was a front and rear

Wagon train with Murphy wagons circa 1880s. *Photo offered for sale on Online Collectibles Auctions*

guard of twenty men in each squad, and a left and right flank guard of the same number that moved with the train, from a quarter to a half mile distance from the train all owing to the lay of the country through which they were traveling. Additionally, the wagon train had an additional belt of security in the form of two men each day that would be selected as hunters, to provide game for the next evening. This pair would ride a full one mile ahead of the advance guard, partly to spot elk or deer before they were spooked by a group of twenty mounted men, but also this point element could give really advance warning of any groups of warriors.[159] Addison M. Quivey later commented on the precautions taken by the frontiersmen:[160]

During the whole trip, every precaution was observed to guard our wagons. We drove in double line wherever practicable, with the pack animals well in hand; and when moving we always had a guard in front and rear, and on each flank. We entrenched all our camps from the time we passed the mouth of Big Horn, going down, until we crossed it (about sixty-five miles from its mouth,) coming back.

When the wagon train entered a defile, additional security measures came into play. Before the column entered these narrow passes, groups of riflemen climbed the heights on either side and remained in the high ground in firing positions until the wagons had passed through the defile below.[161]

Each afternoon that the wagon train was on the move, Frank Grounds would personally select a campsite on high ground, with no higher terrain in the vicinity from which warrior snipers could fire down into the camp. Each campsite was large enough for the men to place all the wagons in an oval and chain them together. At dusk, the frontiersmen would drive all the livestock into the center of this oval; every man knew that if these animals were killed or driven off in the night, disaster would follow. In many places, this center position

Conestoga wagon on display at the High Plains Western Heritage Center. *Author photograph, October 2013*

Wagon Train on the Move

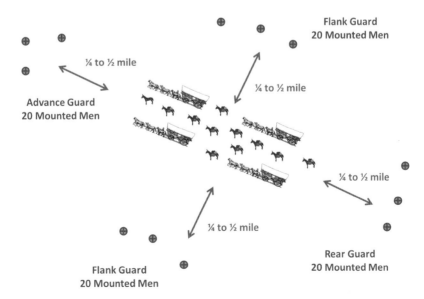

for the livestock was in a slight depression, where the animals could be corralled.[162]

Joe Cook stated that when the wagon train was halted for the night, the men would dig a trench about two feet wide and two feet deep as breastworks for the protection of the pickets on both sides of the corral. They would then dig individual position holes 200 to 300 hundred yards from the camp. Each man cut a "head log" from eight to ten inches in diameter and about three feet long. They would lay these on the embankments and dig small post holes under the logs, so that the Indians could not shoot them in the head, while the frontiersmen were shooting from these small covered positions. Whenever any of these pickets fired a shot, all the other pickets would come into camp as soon as possible.[163]

In 1942, M.G. O'Malley, in a newspaper article, "Thrilling Frontier Experiences in Montana," reported that Charles E. Avery later told his brother Albert "Bert" Avery that apparently one or two of the expedition wagons had special platforms on the top of them and that the two cannon could be lifted (or perhaps rolled up a makeshift ramp) onto the platforms and fired from this elevated stand—although no other source on the expedition has confirmed this.[164] Avery added in his reminiscences that no campfires were permitted after dark.[165] This made it difficult for any warriors at a distance at night to estimate the strength of the wagon train. 1st Lieutenant James Bradley, himself an infantryman and expert at frontier fighting wrote about the defensive tactics of the expedition:[166]

After passing the mouth of the Big Horn, they had taken the precaution to fortify all their camps; and while some took care of the stock, prepared the supper, others were busy with axe, pick and shovel and in a short time their position was securely environed in a line of rifle pits that would afford them ample protection in case of attack.

The tactics of the men on the wagon train were clearly visible to their opponents. Lakota warrior

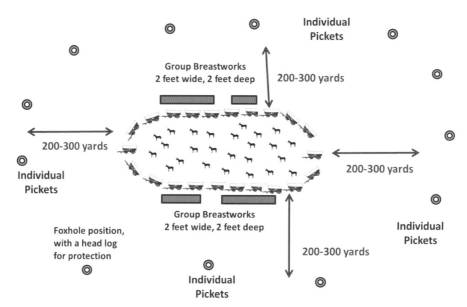

Wagon Train in Laager

Individual Pickets

Group Breastworks
2 feet wide, 2 feet deep

200-300 yards

200-300 yards

200-300 yards

Individual Pickets

Foxhole position, with a head log for protection

Group Breastworks
2 feet wide, 2 feet deep

Individual Pickets

200-300 yards

Individual Pickets

Individual Pickets

Stands-With-Horns-In-Sight described them many years later to Judge Frank B. Zahn:[167]

> Their wagons loaded with food and equipment were formed in a large circle with all the stock inside. The white men dug long cellars or trenches holding about 6 to 8 men and they were deep. We called them by the Sioux name, Maka-ti-oti (dug-out dwellers.) From these dug-outs they shot at the warriors as they rode close to these mounds. The white men were excellent shots.

The men were ready; the weapons were formidable; and there was plenty of ammunition. Now, the expedition just had to get moving.

Notes

1. Carter, *An Oldtimer's Story*, 31.

2. Letter from William C. Barkley to Walter M. Camp dated January 20, 1914, Denver Public Library, Western History Department.

3. "The Story of a March," 12-13.

4. Elmer Keith, "The 'Big Fifty' Sharps," *The American Rifleman*, Volume 88, Number 6, June 1940, published by the National Rifle Association of America as found in http://www.americanrifleman.org/article.php?id=14150&cat=3&sub=0&q=1

5. Bradley, "Bradley Manuscript," 108.

6. US Civil War Pension Index Card, BARKLEY, William, as found on Ancestry.com; Weibert, *The 1874 Invasion*, 59; and Camp Manuscripts, Box 4: Folder 5, Envelope 6—Barkley statement of 1874, gold expedition from Bozeman; odometer on Rosebud River, September 1913; Bozeman expedition, 1874.

7. Rachel Hergett, "Mixed-race pioneer has place in Bozeman history," *Bozeman Daily Chronicle* (Bozeman, Montana,) 21 February 2010; "John Anderson, Who Broke Sitting Bull's Heart," *The Angelica Advocate*, Angelica, New York, 1918, as found at http://fultonhistory.com/Newspapers%2021/Angelica%20NY%20Advocate/Angelica%20NY%20Advocate%201915-1919/Angelica%20NY%20Advocate%201915-1919%20-%200072.pdf; Montana State University Library, Special Collections Library, Bozeman, Montana, Collection 1250 -Walter Cooper and Eugene F. Bunker Papers, 1886–1956, Series 2: Box 2A, Folder 2—Second Big Horn Expedition; and 1880 United States Census for Gallatin County, Montana Territory.

8. 1870 US Census for Gallatin County, Montana Territory.

9. Ancestry.com, US Army Record of Enlistments, 1798-1914, Volume 1816-1862, A-G, ASHMEAD, Henry; and National Park Service, The Civil War, Soldiers and Sailors Database at http://www.nps.gov/civilwar/soldiers-and-sailors-database.htm

10. *Progressive Men of the State of Montana*, Chicago, Illinois: A. W. Bowen and Company, 1901, 1631.

11. 1870 US Census for Gallatin County, Montana Territory; Find-A-Grave, William Awbrey.

12. Email from Rachel Phillips, research coordinator, Pioneer Museum, Bozeman, Montana, August 15, 2013; James U. Sanders, editor, Society of Montana Pioneers, Constitution, Members, and Officers, with Portraits and Maps, Volume 1—Register, Helena, Montana: Society of Montana Pioneers, 1899, 96; Leeson, 1101-1102; and Montana Historical Society Research Center, Montana Pioneers Records, 1884–1956: William H. Babcock, Box 1/Folder 2.

13. 1860 US Census for Dakota County, Minnesota; 1880 US Census for Gallatin County; and Ancestry.com, William D. Bassett.

14. Don L. Weibert, *Buckskin, Buffalo Robes & Black Powder: Fifty Years in the Old West*, San Jose, California: John L. Bean Publishing, 1997, vi-viii, 1-10.

15. Collection 1250, Folder 2.

16. Email from Rachel Phillips, August 15, 2013; Sanders, Society of Montana Pioneers, Volume 1—Register, 97; Leeson, 1104; Joachim Miller, *Illustrated History of The State of Montana*, Chicago: The Lewis Publishing Company, 1894, 372; and "Reports of Receipts and Expenditures of Gallatin County, Montana,

from March 1, 1873 to March 1, 1874," *Avant Courier* (Bozeman,) March 20, 1874, 2.

17. Find-A-Grave, Green B. Blakeley.

18. 1870 US Census for Missoula County, Montana Territory.

19. Also at the Crow Agency was Mitch Bouyer (of later Little Bighorn fame) who served as interpreter from April to June 1873 and possibly later; he worked as a laborer there from November 1873 to February 1874; Bouyer was employed as messenger at the Crow Agency from March 1874 to August 1874.

20. Gray Research Papers, Box 16, Folder 136, Scouts; Mocavo Genealogy Website: 1873 Official Register of the United States at http://www.mocavo.com/Official-Register-of-the-United-States-1873/228899/347; 1860 US Census for Saratoga County, New York; 1855 New York State Census for Saratoga County; and Clyde McLemore, "Fort Pease: The First Attempted Settlement in Yellowstone Valley," *The Montana Magazine of History*, Volume 2, Number 1 (January 1952,) Helena, Montana: Montana Historical Society, 1952.

21. Carter, 32; and John S. Gray, *Custer's Last Campaign: Mitch Boyer and the Little Bighorn Reconstructed*, Lincoln, Nebraska: University of Nebraska Press, 1991, 15, 138.

22. Camp Manuscripts, Box 4: Folder 5, Envelope 6—Barkley statement of 1874; 1860 US Census for Scott County, Kentucky; 1880 US Census for Gallatin County, Montana Territory; Collection 1250 Folder 41, 19.

23. Jeanette Prodgers, *The Champion Buffalo Hunter: The Frontier Memoirs of Yellowstone Vic Smith*, Guilford, Connecticut: The Global Pequot Press, 2009, 109; and James Willert, *After Little Bighorn: 1876 Campaign Rosters*. La Mirada, California: James Willert, 1985, 2.

24. 1900 US Census for Park County, Montana; Montana Pioneers Records, 1884–1956: Joseph Brown, Box 1/Folder 4; "Uncle Joe Brown, Pioneer Miner and Everybody's Friend, Passes Away," *The Daily Enterprise*, Livingston, Montana, July 5, 1913; and Joey Bunch, "Downfall of Colorado's Jack Slade: Bottle did what the outlaw's shotgun could not," *Denver Post*, August 20, 2012.

25. Weibert, *Buckskin*, 4-11.

26. 1900 US Census for Fergus County, Montana, and Weibert, Buckskin, 4-11.

27. Leeson, 1109.

28. 1870 US Census for Gallatin County, Montana Territory.

29. Hutchins, "Poison in the Pemmican," 18; Collection 1250, Folder 41, 18; and Ancestry.com, Henry Bird Calfee.

30. Carter, 35; 1870 US Census for Gallatin County, Montana Territory; Weibert, *Buckskin*, 9; Collection 1250, Folder 2; Montana Pioneers Records, 1884-1956: William D. Cameron, Box 1/Folder 5; US Civil War Pension Index Card, CAMERON, William D. Fold3; and "Another Pioneer Called by Death," *The Livingston Enterprise*, Livingston, Montana, December 6, 1921.

31. 1870 US Census for Jefferson County, Montana Territory.

32. 1880 US Census for Gallatin County, Montana Territory.

33. Ibid.

34. Collection 1250, Folder 41, 2.

35. Ibid, 4.

36. 1870 US Census for Gallatin County, Montana Territory.

37. Brown and Willard, 558.

38. 1870 US Census for Gallatin County, Montana Territory.

39. 1870 US Census for Gallatin County, Montana Territory; Sanders, Society of Montana Pioneers, Volume 1—Register, 99; and Leeson, 1115-1116.

40. The weapon is on display at the Gallatin County Court House next to the Gallatin History Museum.

41. 1870 US Census for Gallatin County; 1880 US Census for Gallatin County; and Ancestry.com, Franklin D. "Doc" Cowan; Collection 1250, Folder 2; and Leeson, 1116.

42. Collection 1250, Folder 41, 19; 1852 California State Census for Placer County; 1880 US Census for Dawson County, Montana Territory; and McLemore, "Fort Pease," 29.

43. 1870 US Census for Macomb County, Michigan.

44. Collection 1250, Folder 2; Gray, *Custer's Last Campaign*, 105; and Elizabeth

A. Watry and Robert V. Gross, Livingston, *Images of America Series*, Charleston, South Carolina: Arcadia Publishing, 2009, 10.

45. 1870 US Census for Gallatin County, Montana Territory; Collection 1250, Folder 2; and *Progressive Men of the State of Montana*, 126.

46. Collection 1250, Folder 41, 2; and Ancestry.com, Benjamin Rush Dexter.

47. Collection 1250, Folder 2.

48. 1880 US Census for Madison County, Montana Territory; Ancestry.com, US Civil War Pension Index: General Index to Pension Files, 1861–1934 for John Dillabaugh; Ancestry.com, 1890 Veterans Schedules for John H. Dillabaugh.

49. 1870 US Census for Missoula County, Montana Territory.

50. 1870 US Census for Gallatin County, Montana Territory; George B. Herendeen Papers, SC 16, 2; and Avery Reminiscence, SC 372, 1.

51. "Nine Big Horn Survivors Clasp Hands in Bozeman," *The Weekly Courier* (Bozeman, Montana,) August 12, 1914; 1920 US Census for Deer Lodge County, Montana; and Montana Pioneers Records, 1884-1956: Hugh Early, Box 2/Folder 7.

52. Collection 1250, Folder 2.

53. 1870 US Census for Gallatin County, Montana Territory.

54. 1870 US Census for Lewis and Clark County, Montana Territory; Ancestry.com, Robert Henry Evans; and Montana Pioneers Records, 1884-1956: Robert Henry Evans, Box 2/Folder 8.

55. 1870 US Census for Gallatin County, Montana Territory.

56. Leeson, 79; and Collection 1250, Folder 41, 19.

57. Collection 1250, Folder 41, 21.

58. Montana Hyalite Chapter Daughters of the American Revolution, "Old Tombstone Records in Gallatin County, Montana Cemeteries," 1957; 1870 US Census for Gallatin County, Montana Territory; Collection 1250, Folder 2; and Progressive Men of the State of Montana, 1060.

59. 1880 US Census for Gallatin County, Montana Territory.

60. 1870 US Census for Deer Lodge County, Montana Territory.

61. Collection 1250, Folder 41, 7; and 1870 US Census for Jefferson County, Montana Territory.

62. 1880 US Census for Gallatin and Deer Lodge Counties, Montana Territory and Weibert, *The 1874 Invasion*, 16; Camp Manuscripts, Box 4: Folder 5, Envelope 6—Barkley statement of 1874.

63. Eugene Sayre Topping, *The Chronicles of the Yellowstone*, Minneapolis, Minnesota: Ross & Haines, INC., 1968, 258; Collection 1250, Folder 2.

64. Topping, 258; www.brucegourley.com.

65. Carter, 3; Weibert, *Buckskin*, 12-13; and "The Story of a March," 12.

66. 1850 US Census for Fulton County, Arkansas.

67. Richard Parker and Emily Boyd, "The Great Hanging at Gainesville," *New York Times*, October 16, 2012; and telephone discussions with Patricia Adkins-Rochette, historian and author of *Bourland in North Texas and Indian Territory during the Civil War: Fort Cobb, Fort Arbuckle & The Wichita Mountains*.

68. Ibid.

69. Robert M. Utley, *Lone Star Justice: The First Century of The Texas Rangers*, New York: Oxford University Press, 2002, 1863; and telephone discussions with Patricia Adkins-Rochette.

70. Ibid.

71. 1870 US Census for Gallatin County, Montana Territory; and "The Story of a March," 12.

72. Topping, 122.

73. Carter, 5, 39; Weibert, *The 1874 Invasion*, 13; Hutchins, "Poison in the Pemmican," 11; Alpheus H. Favour, *Old Bill Williams Mountain Man*, Norman, Oklahoma: University of Oklahoma Press, 1962, 140; William T. Hamilton, *My Sixty Years on the Plains: Trapping, Trading and Indian Fighting*,

New York: Forest and Stream Publishing Company, 1905; Montana Pioneers Records, 1884-1956: William T. Hamilton, Box 2/Folder 18; "Pioneer Succumbs," *The Billings Daily Gazette*, Billings, Montana, May 26, 1908, 1; Folder containing loose papers concerning William T. Hamilton, Museum of the Beartooths, Stillwater County, Columbus, Montana.

74. Find-A-Grave, Green Hampton; 1880 US Census for Meagher County, Montana Territory; and US Headstone Application for Military Veteran, HAMPTON, GREEN A., May 23, 1936.

75. Carter, 5, 30, 32, 39; Ida McPherren, *Imprints on Pioneer Trails*, Boston: Christopher Publishing House, 1950, 144-145; Joe De Barthe, *Life and Adventures of Frank Grouard, Chief of Scouts*, U.S.A., St. Joseph, Missouri: Combe Printing Company, 1894, 506-507; and Ancestry.com, Oliver Perry Hanna.

76. Ibid.

77. Mocavo Genealogy Website: 1873 Official Register of the United States at http://www.mocavo.com/Official-Register-of-the-United-States-1873/228899/347.

78. 1860 US Census for Noble County, Indiana; 1860 US Census for Geauga County, Ohio; George B. Herendeen Papers, SC 16, 1-2; Gray Research Papers, Box 16, Folder 136, Scouts.

79. 1850 US Census for St. Lawrence County, New York; 1870 US Census for Deer Lodge County, Montana Territory; and Find-A-Grave, William C. Hickey.

80. 1870 US Census for Gallatin County, Montana Territory.

81. Collection 1250, Folder 2; 1850 US Census for Erie County, Pennsylvania; 1870 US Census for Gallatin County, Montana Territory; and 1880 US Census for Gallatin County, Montana Territory.

82. 1870 US Census for Gallatin County, Montana Territory; Bob Moore, "Buffalo Bill Cody's Cinnabar Cowboys," *The Montana Pioneer*, Livingston, Montana: Montana Pioneer Publishing, March 2008; Collection 1250, Folder 2; Ida McPherren, *Imprints*, 17, 28, 96, 117, 123, 128, 144,

178; "Death of Hugo J. Hoppe," *The Livingston Enterprise*, Livingston, Montana, September 14, 1895, 4; and Lee H. Whittlesey, *Gateway to Yellowstone: The Raucous Town of Cinnabar on the Montana Frontier*, Guilford, Connecticut: Twodot Publishing, 2015, 15-22.

83. Weibert, *Buckskin*, 22; and 1870 US Census for Gallatin County, Montana Territory.

84. "Yellowstone Expedition," *Avant Courier* (Bozeman,) February 20, 1874, 2; 1870 US Census for Gallatin County, Montana Territory; and 1880 US Census for Gallatin County, Montana Territory.

85. Leeson, 1137-1138; Gail Schontzler, "Bozeman's wild West days captured in diaries of pioneer Peter Koch," *Bozeman Daily Chronicle*, Bozeman, Montana, July 27, 2010; and Ancestry.com, Peter Koch.

86. Montana Hyalite Chapter Daughters of the American Revolution, "Old Tombstone Records in Gallatin County, Montana Cemeteries," 1957; Gail Schontzler, "A mix of old and new at Malmborg," *Bozeman Daily Chronicle*, Bozeman, Montana, May 23, 1998; and 1900 US Census for Gallatin County, Montana.

87. 1850 US Census for Switzerland County, Indiana; and 1860 US Census for Switzerland County, Indiana.

88. Collection 1250, Folder 2; 1865 New York State Census for Richmond County; and 1870 US Census for Gallatin County, Montana Territory.

89. Brown, *The Plainsmen of the Yellowstone*, 212; Weibert, *Buckskin*, 43; Find-A-Grave, Paul McCormick; Barbara Fifer, *Montana Battlefields, 1806–1877: Native Americans and the US Army at War*, Helena, Montana: Farcountry Press, 2005, 36; and Montana Pioneers Records, 1884–1956: Paul McCormick, Book 3/Folder 4.

90. 1910 US Census for Gallatin and Deer Lodge Counties, Montana Territory; Camp Manuscripts, Box 4: Folder 5, Envelope 6— Barkley statement of 1874; Collection 1250, Folder 2; and Montana Pioneers Records, 1884-1956: Archie McDonald, Box 3/Folder 4.

91. 1870 US Census for Gallatin County, Montana Territory; and 1880 US Census for Gallatin County, Montana Territory.

92. 1870 US Census for Gallatin County, Montana Territory.

93. 1850 US Census for Andrew County, Missouri; 1860 US Census for Andrew County, Missouri; 1870 US Census for Gallatin County, Montana Territory; Genealogy.com William Carroll Officer/Fanny Elizabeth; and telephone discussions with Steve Florman, great-great-grandson of William Officer, June 2015.

94. 1870 US Census for Jefferson County, Montana Territory.

95. Collection 1250, Folder 2; and 1900 US Census for Gallatin and Deer Lodge Counties, Montana Territory.

96. "Death of A. M. Quivey," *Avant Courier* (Bozeman,) 13 July 1895, 3; "Addison M. Quivey," *The Billings Gazette* (Billings, Montana,) 13 July 1895; and Weibert, *The 1874 Invasion*, 7.

97. Weibert, *The 1874 Invasion*, 149.

98. Weibert, *The 1874 Invasion*, 26; and Ancestry.com, Herbert F. Richardson.

99. Topping, 107.

100. Collection 1250, Folder 41, 7.

101. Collection 1250, Folder 2.

102. Email from Rachel Phillips, August 15, 2013; 1870 US Census for Gallatin County, Montana Territory; Sanders, editor, Society of Montana Pioneers, Volume 1—Register, 114; and *Progressive Men of the State of Montana*, 826.

103. 1870 US Census for Gallatin County, Montana Territory.

104. Topping, 258; and "Con Smith Dies at Boulder Home; Pioneer of State," *The Helena Independent*, Helena, Montana, June 24, 1925, 1.

105. 1870 US Census for Gallatin County, Montana Territory.

106. 1880 US Census for Deer Lodge County, Montana.

107. 1870 US Census for Meagher County, Montana Territory.

108. Collection 1250, Folder 2 and Folder 41, 21; 1870 US Census for Gallatin County,

Montana Territory; and Find-A-Grave, John H. Stevens.

109. Collection 1250, Folder 2; and Weibert, *The 1874 Invasion*, 103.

110. "Founder of Famous Stage Station of 'Seventies Recalls Picturesque Characters of Early Days," *Billings Gazette* (Billings, Montana,) June 30, 1927, 10.

111. 1870 US Census for Jefferson County, Montana Territory.

112. Phyllis Smith, *Bozeman and the Gallatin Valley: A History*, Guilford, Connecticut: Twodot Publications, 2002, 133; Don L. Weibert, *The 1874 Invasion*, 16.

113. 1870 US Census for Gallatin County, Montana Territory.

114. Carter, 5, 39; and Tom Stout, editor, *Montana: Its Story and Biography*, Volume 3, Chicago: The American Historical Society, 1921, 1374.

115. Camp Manuscripts, Box 4: Folder 5, Envelope 6—Barkley statement of 1874, gold expedition from Bozeman; odometer on Rosebud River, September 1913; Bozeman expedition, 1874; and 1870 US Census for Humboldt County, Nevada; Ancestry.com, Eli B. Way; and Find-A-Grave, Eli Britton Way.

116. Collection 1250, Folder 2.

117. Carter, 35.

118. Collection 1250, Folder 40; 1875 New York State Census for Niagara County; and Montana, County Marriages, 1865-1950, WILLSON, Henry A., as found in Ancestry.com.

119. 1870 US Census for Gallatin County, Montana Territory.

120. Topping, 257; Sanders, editor, *Society of Montana Pioneers*, Volume 1—Register, 216; Leeson, 1174; and Montana Pioneers Records, 1884-1956: William M. Wright, Box 5/Folder 4.

121. 1870 US Census for Jefferson County, Montana Territory.

122. Hutchins, "Poison in the Pemmican," 21; 1870 US Census for Jefferson County, Montana Territory; and Collection 1250, Folder 41, 15.

123. Quivey, "The Yellowstone Expedition of 1874," 269-270.

124. Brown and Willard, 559.

125. Carter, 31.

126. "The Story of a March," 12.

127. Annotated Manuscript of Jack Bean on the 1874 Yellowstone Wagon Road and Prospecting Expedition, undated, unknown editor, Gallatin County, Montana Pioneer Museum Archive, 15; and Weibert, *The 1874 Invasion*, 25.

128. Camp Manuscripts, Box 3: Folder 8, Rosebud, Battle of, 1874.

129. Quivey, 269-270.

130. George Markham, *Guns of the Wild West: Firearms of the American Frontier 1849–1917*, London: Arms & Armour Press, 1991 103-105; R. Stephen Dorsey, *Guns of the Western Indian War*, Eugene, Oregon: Collectors' Library, 1995, 137, 177; Douglas C. McChristian, *The US Army in the West 1870–1880*, Norman, Oklahoma, University of Oklahoma Press, 1995, 113; folder containing loose papers concerning William T. Hamilton, Museum of the Beartooths, Stillwater County, Columbus, Montana.

131. McChristian, 113; Dorsey, 63, 83, 139; and Frank C. Barnes, *Cartridges of the World*, 9th Edition, Iola, Wisconsin: Krause Publications, 2000, 83.

132. Markham, 105-107; Dorsey, 151-152; and Glenn W. Sunderland, *Lightning at Hoover's Gap*, New York: Thomas Yoseloff, 1969, 42-43.

133. Markham, 119-121; Dorsey, 181; and McChristian, 111-116.

134. National Park Service, Springfield Armory.

135. Joseph G. Rosa, *Guns of the American West*, New York: Crown Publishers, 1985, 156-157, Sellers, 33-341; and Mike Venturino, *Shooting Buffalo Rifles of the Old West*, Livingston, Montana: MLV Enterprises, 2002, 125, 128, 137, 160 and 164.

136. Rosa, 158.

137. Markham, 111.

138. Dorsey, 185-189.

139. Ibid, 186-187; and Dennis Adler, "Top 12 Western Classics," *Guns of the Old West*, Fall 2014, New York: Harris Publications, 74.

140. Multiple discussions with Wes Pietsch, noted American West gun collector.

141. Brown and Willard, 559.

142. "The Story of a March," 12.

143. Avery Reminiscence, SC 372, 2.

144. James C. Hazlett, Edwin Olmstead and M. Hume Parks, *Field Artillery Weapons of the American Civil War*, rev. ed., Urbana: University of Illinois Press, 1983, 134-137, 218.

145. Weibert, *The 1874 Invasion*, 43.

146. Ibid.

147. Hazlett, Olmstead and Parks, 218.

148. Weibert, *Buckskin*, 8-9.

149. Smith, *Bozeman and the Gallatin Valley*, 113.

150. William H. Powell, Lt . Col., US Army, editor, *Officers of the Army and Navy (Volunteer) Who Served In The Civil War*, Philadelphia, Pennsylvania: L.R. Hamersly and Co., 1893, 50.

151. Kim Allen Scott, "The Willson Brothers Come to Montana," *Montana: The Magazine of Western History*, Volume 49, Number 1, 58-70.

152. Avery Reminiscence, SC 372, 2; Weibert, *Buckskin*, 9-10; and Annotated Manuscript of Jack Bean, 9.

153. Weibert, *Buckskin*, 10.

154. Walter Cooper, *A Most Desperate Situation*, edited by Rick Newby, Helena, Montana: Falcon Publishing, 2000, 355; and Collection 1250, Folder 43.

155. Larry Len Peterson, editor, "The Footrace: From the Frontier Adventures of Walter Cooper," *Montana: The Magazine of Western History*, Volume 50, Number 2, 50-62.

156. Ralph A. Heinz, "Montana Sharps," *Man at Arms: The Magazine of Arms Collecting-Investing*, Volume 3, Number 6, November/December 1981, St. Providence, Rhode Island: Mowbray Company, 25; 1870 US Census for Gallatin County, Montana Territory.

157. Heinz, 28.

158. Ibid, 26-28.

159. M.G. O'Malley, "Thrilling Frontier Experiences in Montana"; and Brown and Willard, 563-564.

160. Quivey, "The Yellowstone Expedition of 1874," 282.

161. Hutchins, "Poison in the Pemmican," 13.

162. Ibid; and Weibert, *The 1874 Invasion*, 25.

163. Brown and Willard, 561-562.

164. O'Malley, "Thrilling Frontier Experiences in Montana."

165 Avery Reminiscence, SC 372, 3.

166. Bradley, "Bradley Manuscript," 111.

167. Statement from Stands-With-Horns-In-Sight made to Judge Frank B. Zahn.

CHAPTER FOUR

The Trek

The following timetable shows the significant events of the 1874 Yellowstone Wagon-Road and Prospecting Expedition for the weeks leading up to the Battle of Lodge Grass Creek. Although several frontiersmen recorded engagements with the warriors, general comments on the weather and a rough route of travel, with occasional laager locations, it does not appear that anyone maintained a really detailed journal. As a result, while we know what happened, it is very possible that some of these events occurred a day or two earlier or later than recorded here. Following each date is the location—often with latitude and longitude coordinates—where the expedition laagered that evening, or was believed to have laagered. All times will be in military time: 0720 is 7:20 a.m., 1720 is 5:20 p.m. etc.

Monday, February 2, 1874 **(Outside Bozeman)**
According to Tom Allen, the expedition began to receive men outside of Bozeman; eighty men reported on this day.[1]

Tuesday, February 3, 1874 **(Outside Bozeman)**
Ford's four horse team with four men, Graham's four horse team and three men, the Gallatin City pack outfit of ten men, and the Piper Central Park four yoke team with eight men departed Bozeman for the expedition assembly area.[2]

Friday, February 6, 1874 **(Outside Bozeman)**
According to Oliver Perry Hanna, J.L. Vernon came to the camp every day, making speeches about the rich gold deposits he "knew" were out there. The *Avant Courier* published the following article this day:[3]

THE EXPEDITION MOVING TO THE FRONT!

This week the streets of Bozeman have been enlivened by the passage among them of pack trains, mule teams, ox team and miners with their picks, shovels and grub on the backs of restless steeds on their way to the Yellowstone, preparatory to starting with the great Wagon Road and Prospecting Expedition. The men are well equipped and look the hardy pioneers they are. This is the greatest expedition ever outfitted in Montana, and will be productive of great benefit. These pioneers go to open the front door to the rich fields of our Territory, and upon their success hangs much of our future prosperity, and the men who go feel the responsibility of their proportions and mean business. They will do their duty. Their friends expect them to fulfill the high expectations entertained from the undertaking and a great deal depends on their conduct and enterprise. We have great faith in the caliber of the men composing this expedition, and we trust they will exert themselves to accomplish great results. They depart with the best wishes of those they leave behind for their health and the highest degree of accomplishment of all they desire and wish.

The entire expedition will assemble at Quinn's Ranch on the Yellowstone, some fifteen miles from Bozeman, and start about the tenth of this month.

A good many of them are out there now, and several large trains left yesterday.

The expedition is moving to the front in fine order and condition, and in splendid spirits.

***Saturday, February 7, 1874* (Outside Bozeman)**

Teams of men traveled through Bozeman and camped in the snow some six miles from the town. The men built roaring campfires to keep warm and passed bottles of "Snake-Bite Medicine" around to cut the chill of the night.[4]

***Sunday, February 8, 1874* (Quinn's Ranch) [N 45° 39.704', W 110° 40.310']**

The lead elements of the expedition loaded supplies onto sleds and crossed the Bozeman Pass to the east. The expedition would be a logistical challenge; in addition to all the ammunition, the wagon train needed prodigious amounts of food, as initially in the dead of winter, living off the land would be problematic. Men at heavy work in extremely cold conditions in the era typically consumed 8,000 to 10,000 calories per day.[5] By noon the men had crossed the high snow and began arriving at Quinn's Ranch, where they turned out the livestock and ate supper. The wind blew all night and it was "quite cold."[6]

***Monday, February 9, 1874* (Quinn's Ranch) [N 45° 39.704', W 110° 40.310']**

The wind continued to blow hard all day as men visited other campfires and found old acquaintants. Undoubtedly, some of the veterans started "Stuffing the Tenderfeet"

(telling blood-curdling tails of Indian atrocities to junior, inexperienced men.) The frontiersmen began to discuss whom they might select as leaders of the expedition; there seemed to be consensus that Bill Wright should receive a significant position. [7]

***Tuesday, February 10, 1874* (Quinn's Ranch) [N 45° 39.704', W 110° 40.310']**

The last wagon teams, carrying the reserve ammunition for the expedition departed Bozeman for Quinn's Ranch, as did a delegation of the executive committee, who would speak to the men just before the start of the endeavor. Several of the camp groups moved to clumps of brush to seek some protection against the wind, finding their new positions much warmer.[8]

***Wednesday, February 11, 1874* (Quinn's Ranch) [N 45° 39.704', W 110° 40.310']**

Sunrise was 0723. Roughly 149 members of the expedition gathered at the cabin of Ed Quinn and then moved the camp one mile away. The ranch was located sixteen miles from Bozeman, halfway to the mouth of the Shields River, east of Bozeman Pass, a few miles down Billman Creek. Some of the men saw some Crow Indians who were peaceable, as they were mortal enemies of the Lakota. In fact, the previous summer, the Apsaàlooke, under Sits in the Middle of the Land, along

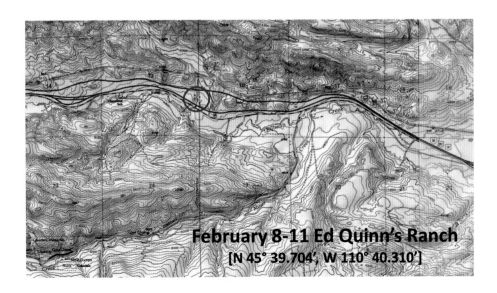

February 8-11 Ed Quinn's Ranch
[N 45° 39.704', W 110° 40.310']

View of the area believed to be the location of the Quinn Ranch in 1874. In the background, looking westward is the Bozeman Pass area. The expedition gathered there from February 8–11, 1874, to elect leaders and make final preparations. *Author photograph, October 2013.*

Close-up of believed Quinn Ranch area, looking west. Location is [N 45° 39.704', W 110° 40.310'] between the separated lanes of US Highway 90 between Livingston and Bozeman. *Author photograph, October 2013*

with forty lodges of Nez Perce, battled Crazy Horse and his Lakota band along the Pryor and Fly Creeks in an action that became known as the Battle of Pryor Creek. Sunset occurred at 1735.[9]

Thursday, February 12, 1874 (**Benson's Landing**) **[N 45° 41.397', W 110° 31.751']** Sunrise was at 0721. In the morning, the members of the expedition elected the leadership for the journey. These positions included:[10]

Captain	Benjamin Franklin Grounds.
Lieutenant	William Wright.
Adjutant	Ely B. Way.
Signal Officer	Hugh O'Donovan.
Secretary	B.P. Wickersham.

The men also selected a council that presumably would represent the men's interests in major decision-making, if conditions allowed such deliberation. The following members of the expedition were members of this body: Fred B. Wilson, T.C. Burns, William C. Langston,

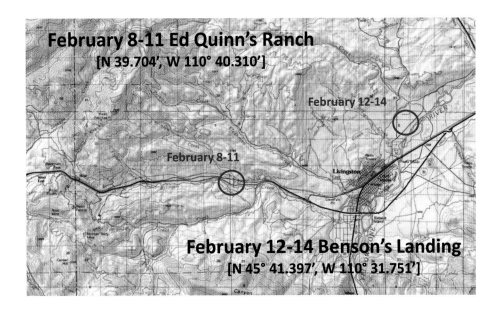

February 8-11 Ed Quinn's Ranch
[N 39.704', W 110° 40.310']

February 12-14

February 8-11

February 12-14 Benson's Landing
[N 45° 41.397', W 110° 31.751']

Addison M. Quivey, G.A. Yates, George H. Miller, A.B. Ford, James Hancock, and Joseph Brown.[11] As Addison M. Quivey recalled the event two years later:[12]

> From this time material was contributed, and men came forward rapidly, until the 12th of February when about one hundred and thirty men were assembled at the rendezvous near Quinn's ranch (half way between Bozeman and the Crow agency,) at which place officers were elected, and final arrangements made for the march.

Joe Cook added:[13]

> We organized on the Yellowstone River, on the 12th of February, electing Frank Grounds, captain; William Wright, lieutenant, and Eli Way, adjutant. Way's duties were to detail the guard night and morning. The guards stood six hours on and then six off.

The expedition then departed Ed Quinn's ranch to the "booming of artillery." It moved down a small drainage creek toward the

Maj. Pease Cabin; at the head of the big spring just south of modern-day Livingston, this cabin was built of the wide thick boards cut with a whip saw. The expedition passed by north of the cabin on February 12, 1874. *Photo #2006.044.1939, Whithorn Collection, courtesy of Yellowstone Gateway Museum, Livingston, MT.*

Yellowstone River, turned to the east and moved along the benchland on the north side of the Yellowstone. In the late afternoon, it arrived at Benson's Landing and made camp just east of modern-day Livingston and some thirty ground miles from Bozeman. Given that Tom Allen years earlier had helped organize the cow camp, near the later ferry crossing, at the conclusion of Nelson Story's massive cattle drive from Texas, the men knew exactly where to establish their own campsite. Sunset was at 1737.[14]

Friday, February 13, 1874 (Benson's Landing) [N 45° 41.397', W 110° 31.751']

Sunrise was 0720. It was very cold, with a fierce wind blowing. Two wagons were damaged and had to be repaired. Frank Grounds crossed the Yellowstone River on the ferry and met with George Herendeen in an attempt to persuade him to join the expedition. The rest of the frontiersmen rested at Benson's Landing and perhaps "wet their whistles" with the whiskey from the runners that periodically arrived with their wares after Dan Nailey and Amos Benson had built a saloon there the previous summer; Frank "Buckskin" Williams, later a renowned stage driver on the Billings to Benton line, was the first to build a cabin for a saloon and trading post in the area in 1870. Benson's Landing was truly a wild and wooly place, even being mentioned in one unverified Wild West story as the location that on September 25, 1873, Martha Jane "Calamity Jane" Canary gave birth to a daughter after marrying Wild Bill Hickok, ostensibly the baby's father, earlier in the day! Sunset occurred

Fort Parker, the location of the first Crow Agency, shown in 1872, opposite Benson's Landing, where the expedition made camp on February 12-14, 1874. *Public Domain photograph*

at 1738. Addison M. Quivey wrote of the events that day:[15]

> On the 13th we commenced our march down the north side of the Yellowstone, our objective point being the mouth of Tongue River, near which place rich mines of gold were supposed to exist, and it was also supposed that steamboats could ascend the Yellowstone to that point. We followed the route traveled by the trains of Colonel Baker accompanying the Northern Pacific Railroad survey of 1872.

Saturday, February 14, 1874 (Benson's Landing) [N 45° 41.397', W 110° 31.751']

Sunrise was at 0718. The weather was cold; snow covered the ground. George Herendeen, who had been working at the Crow Agency at Fort E.S. Parker on the south side of the Yellowstone River from Benson's Landing—on the advice and permission of Assistant Indian Agent Capt. Robert Cross—took Grounds' offer, left his job, and joined the expedition; Herendeen probably brought William Hamilton and Taylor Blevin with him.[16] George had written his family the night before about the adventure. Sunset occurred at 1740.[17]

During some of these early days, Frank Grounds organized drills to simulate a warrior attack on the laager. The men organized the wagons to form a circular or oval corral. The herders led the stock animals to a grazing area outside the corral, while fifty men quietly walked to a nearby hill. These men would then start firing their weapons, yelling and running toward the animals. The stock herders responded by rushing the animals inside the corral. After several practice drills, the animals would head on their own to the corral whenever they began to hear gunfire.[18]

Sunday, February 15, 1874 (North of the Yellowstone River)

Sunrise occurred at 0717. The weather was bitter cold, although a "Chinook wind" had taken away most of the snow.[19] Once past the mouth of the Shields River, the expedition

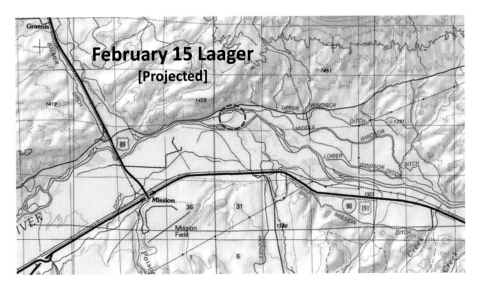

Projected or estimated laager locations are shown with a dashed circle.

turned north along the old 1872 Baker Expedition trail and paralleled the river about one mile to its north. There were several reasons for shifting away from the large waterway. First, there were numerous swampy bottomlands near the river, frozen but treacherous to traverse. Second, the size of the wagons made crisscrossing the Yellowstone a hazardous proposition. Last, all land south of the river belonged by treaty to the Apsaàlooke. The expedition probably made about ten miles before laagering for the night. Sunset was at 1741. A "king bolt" (which held the front axle to the body of the wagon) broke and George Chadbourne road back to the Crow Agency to get a replacement. The blacksmith shop was not open, so the frontiersman stole one. That night the wind howled "terribly."[20] Oliver Hanna later said that the farthest the wagon train ever traveled in a single day was about twenty miles.[21]

Monday, February 16, 1874 (**Hunter's Hot Springs**) [N 45° 45.502', W 110° 15.248']

Sunrise was at 0715. The column awoke early, packed their equipment, yoked the oxen to the wagons, and continued east. After another ten miles, the expedition reached Hunter's Hot Springs adjacent to Hunter's Creek, a mile north of the Yellowstone River and opposite today's town of Springdale. Hunter's Hot Springs was (and is) one of the largest flows of hot water in Montana, with more than 1,300 gallons per minute of 139-degree water flowing from three primary and a dozen lesser springs over rolling foothills. Dr. Andrew Jackson Hunter, the owner, was a physician born in Virginia and later living in Kentucky, who had served as a surgeon for the Confederate Army in the Civil War (6th Louisiana Volunteers, 38th North Carolina Volunteers, and Stuart's Horse Artillery.) In 1864, after being released from Union captivity and enamored by stories of gold fields in the Montana Territory, Dr. Hunter and his family headed west, arriving near the Yellowstone River, about forty-six miles from the new settlement of Bozeman.[22]

Finding an encampment of Crow Indians near the hot springs, the physician staked a claim on the land and then headed to Bozeman. After trying his hand for four years in the gold mining business at Virginia City and Helena, Dr. Hunter returned to the springs, built a log

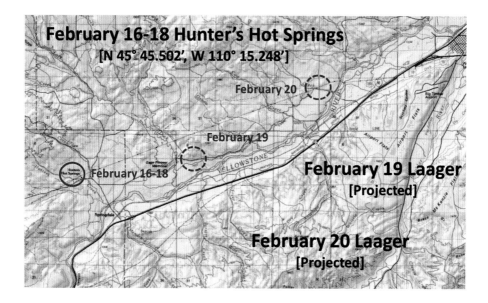

cabin and dammed the hot creek runoff, creating a large pool for bathing. During the early years, Crow Indians flocked to the springs seeking medicinal cures; at times a visitor could count 1,000 teepees in the immediate area. The presence of the Crow kept hostile Lakota bands away from the area. Sunset occurred at 1743.[23] It had taken all day to round up some stray livestock. That evening, Frank Grounds published the expedition's First General Order and took the first roll call. B.P. Wickersham sent a note back to Bozeman and the executive committee that the expedition now had 112 men and nineteen wagons. He added that the expedition planned to stop for one day at Little Timber so that any outfits or individuals still behind could catch up with the main body. Wickersham gave this message to Charles E. King, who rode back and arrived at Bozeman three days later.[24]

***Tuesday, February 17, 1874* (Hunter's Hot Springs) [N 45° 45.502', W 110° 15.248']**
Sunrise was at 0713. The expedition remained at Hunter's Hot Springs, waiting for stragglers, washing up, and preparing for the rugged trail ahead.[25] Sunset occurred at 1744. As Addison M. Quivey later described: [26]

Dr. Andrew Jackson Hunter, owner of Hunter's Hot Springs. The expedition laagered at his location [N 45° 45.502', W 110° 15.248'] from February 16-18, 1874. Hunter had been a surgeon in several prominent units in the Civil War. *Source: F. Jay Haynes, courtesy of Museum of the Rockies Photo Archives, Catalog Number: 84.128.27*

About forty-five miles from Bozeman, on our route, is an extensive group of hot springs, differing from most of the hot springs of the country, in containing little or no lime, silica, or magnesia, but some sulphur and alkalies. They are now occupied by Dr. A.J. Hunter, who has given them the name of the 'Yellowstone White Sulphur Springs.' Dr. Hunter is making improvements, and in time the Yellowstone White Sulphur Springs will become a health-giving resort, famous throughout the land.

***Wednesday, February 18, 1874* (Hunter's Hot Springs) [N 45° 45.502', W 110° 15.248']**
Sunrise occurred at 0712. The expedition continued to rest at Hunter's Hot Springs. Sunset was at 1745.[27]

***Thursday, February 19, 1874* (North of the Yellowstone River)**
Sunrise was at 0710. The weather turned extremely cold, probably reaching thirty to forty degrees below zero. The expedition departed Hunter's Hot Springs, heading east along the north side of the Yellowstone River toward Shed Creek, some nine miles away; they probably laagered a few miles

short of this destination. Sunset occurred at 1747.[28]

***Friday, February 20, 1874* (Shed Creek)**
Sunrise occurred at 0709. Given the bitter weather, the expedition probably did not reach Shed Creek until the afternoon. Sunset was at 1748.

***Saturday, February 21, 1874* (North of the Yellowstone River)**
Sunrise was at 0707. The expedition probably departed Shed Creek in the direction of Little Timber Creek. Sunset was at 1750. The scribe Addison M. Quivey later discussed the land he had seen: [29]

The first one hundred miles from Bozeman we traveled through a fine grazing country, with a large amount of good farming lands, and but little snow in winter. There is a narrow valley along the Yellowstone; also along Shields River, Big Timber, Sweet Grass, etc., with cottonwood along the streams, and pine, fir, etc. In the mountains, the rocks are limestone, sandstone, trap, clay, slate, etc.; in some places showing signs of volcanic action. Between Shields River and Big Timber are extensive veins of feldspar, in a friable trap formation.

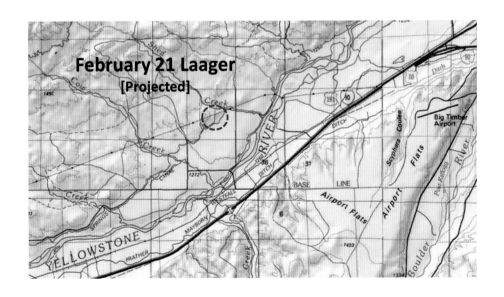

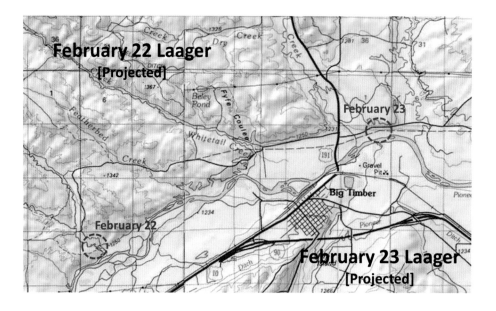

Sunday, February 22, 1874 (**Little Timber Creek**)

Sunrise occurred at 0705. The expedition likely arrived near the mouth of Little Timber Creek. The water in this location was so alkaline as to be practically undrinkable.[30] Sunset was at 1751.

Monday, February 23, 1874 (**Big Timber Creek**)

Sunrise occurred at 0703. The expedition moved to a campsite one-half mile east of Big Timber Creek, some sixty-four ground miles from Bozeman.[31] The water at this location was much better, although the wind was a perfect "hurricane." There was plenty of grass and wood. Jack Bean and Buck Buchanan joined the expedition from their hunting camp in the Crazy Mountains. The gunners of the Big Horn Gun and the mountain howitzer test fired their guns, the loud noise booming down the valley. Sunset occurred at 1753. Jack Bean wrote of the meeting.[32]

> The leaders [of the expedition] knew of me and my partner in the Crazy Mountains so brought provisions for us to join them. They made camp on Big Timber Creek and we accidentally came into their camp. They were glad to find us and invited us to join them.

Addison Quivey sent an update back to the *Avant Courier*. He mentioned that the strength of the expedition was now 142 men, with nineteen wagons. He also mentioned that some of the livestock had moved away from the laager area and the herders had to look for them. The flying dust, as the wind had been blowing strongly since the expedition started, was almost as unpleasant as the snow had been. At the time he was writing the note, Quivey stated that the wind was twenty-seven knots per hour.[33]

Tuesday, February 24, 1874 (**North of the Yellowstone River**)

Sunrise was at 0702; it began to snow again. The expedition moved east into the high country over the prairie to avoid the high bluffs north of the Yellowstone River and headed toward Sweet Grass Creek (some seventy-four ground miles from Bozeman,) arriving at 1500.[34] Sunset occurred at 1754. Addison M. Quivey described the immediate plan of action.[35]

The Crazy Mountains as seen from Big Timber. Jack Bean and Stewart Buchanan were hunting in this region and joined the expedition near Big Timber Creek on February 23, 1874. *Author photograph, October 2013.*

… leaving the Yellowstone at the mouth of Big Timber creek, crossing Sweet Grass creek (twelve miles) about five miles from its mouth; thence following up a small right-hand branch of Sweet Grass to the summit of the divide or table-land between the Yellowstone and Musselshell rivers, which we followed for eight days (two of which we lay by,) descending to the Yellowstone again a few miles above the mouth of Prior's creek, and near the place where Colonel Baker and his command had their fight with the Indians in 1872.

Wednesday, February 25, 1874 (Sweet Grass Creek)

Sunrise was at 0700. The expedition probably remained at Sweet Grass Creek, while Frank Grounds rode ahead to find a good route east of the creek.[36] Sunset occurred at 1755. George Herendeen later recalled the situation in the bitter cold: [37]

> We had to run our stock around nights to keep them from freezing to death. It was the coldest spring I ever saw.

Thursday, February 26, 1874 (Divide between East Fork of Sweet Grass Creek and East Fork of White Beaver Creek)

Sunrise was at 0658. The expedition headed to the divide between the East Fork of Sweet Grass Creek and the East Fork of White Beaver Creek. One wagon tipped over and several others were damaged during the march. The wind was from the northeast and again it was quite cold.[38] Sunset occurred at 1757. Tom Allen later reported that Charles Gale and another man slipped away from the expedition at this point in the journey.[39] Once again, Addison M. Quivey later discussed the land through which he had traveled:[40]

> After leaving Sweet Grass; sandstone, clay, slate, and other sedimentary rocks predominate, often worn by the elements into strange, fantastic forms. In one place especially, the sandstone is worn in cones from ten to twenty feet in height, having very much the appearance of a vast collection of Indian lodges on a smooth grassy plain. To the left of our route are a number of shallow, slightly alkaline lakes, having no outlets, which are a great summer resort for the Crow Indians in pursuit of buffalo and other game which abounds in that locality.

Friday, February 27, 1874 (Canyon Creek)

Sunrise was at 0657. The expedition camped at Canyon Creek. Elisha Terrill sent a report back to Bozeman on the progress of the endeavor, but incorrectly identified their laager site as Duck Creek. He wrote, "We have experienced the most disagreeable weather I have ever saw."[41]

It was more than disagreeable. Terrill reported that some men were suffering severe frostbite and frozen toes. However, that was the least of their problems. A report reached Frank Grounds that a significant amount of ammunition was missing from the wagons. He ordered a search to be made, but the men did not find any of the missing ammunition cases; they may never have been loaded at Bozeman, but receiving that information this far into the expedition was crushing news, as nothing could be done about it.[42] Sunset occurred at 1758.

Saturday, February 28, 1874 (Canyon Creek)

Sunrise occurred at 0655. The expedition remained on Canyon Creek, while an advance party scouted ahead. Charley, a young black man, was found to have frozen toes.[43] Sunset occurred at 1800. J.L. Vernon joined the expedition at this point.[44] However, his presence would not be for long. Joe Cook later recalled the shifty Vernon: [45]

> [Vernon] and three other men left Bozeman three or four days before we all got together on the Yellowstone. The day before we got to his camp he said he would wait for us on the Yellowstone River. The day before we arrived at his camp, we met two of his men going back to Bozeman after a supply of flour, as they said they were about out of flour. The next day at noon we got to his camp, and in the afternoon he made us a nice long speech, telling how to go on and that as soon as his men got back from Bozeman he would overtake us.

Elisha Terrill wrote a summary of the expedition to this point and an unnamed man rode back to Bozeman with it. Elisha estimated that the expedition had 250 horses and mules, fifty head of cattle, twenty-one wagons and 30,000 to 40,000 rounds of ammunition. Some 153 men were now present. One steer had run off during the night and could not be found, despite a thorough search. Terrill added that some of the men routinely stayed awake until midnight, telling yarns. Now another man, Blue Dick was suffering from frostbitten toes.[46]

Sunday, March 1, 1874 (North of the Yellowstone River)

Sunrise occurred at 0653. The weather was windy and very cold. The expedition traveled about eight miles to the east, before halting in the afternoon and establishing a laager for the night not far from a large beaver dam.[47] Sunset was at 1801. Temperatures during many of the nights dropped to well below zero.

Monday, March 2, 1874 (North of the Yellowstone River)

Sunrise was at 0651. The expedition traveled about eight miles to the east, before halting in the afternoon and establishing a laager for the night. Several men shot deer or antelopes and someone shot an old bull bison for food.[48] Sunset was at 1802. It was fortunate that most of the men came from professions that required them to routinely sleep in frigid weather. There were only a few tents on the expedition and therefore most men slept on "Tucson Beds" (in the open, without tentage) after throwing a couple of buffalo robes on the ground, putting on all the clothes they had, pulling down the ear flaps of their caps and curling up under the robes.[49]

Tuesday, March 3, 1874 (North of the Yellowstone River)

Sunrise was at 0649. The expedition traveled about eight miles across hilly terrain to the east, before halting in the afternoon and establishing a laager for the night, possibly near White Horse Creek. The weather had moderated; areas of snow were still two to six inches deep, but in other areas the snow had melted completely. The men killed one antelope and another bison.[50] Sunset occurred at 1804. Every day was tough going for the expedition, because in some areas the snow had drifted. James Gourley remembered the journey this way: [51]

> The most trouble we had on the way down was caused by heavy snow drifts. Through these we had to shovel our way, and occasionally we struck hard steep hills where it would take about fifty men with ropes attached to the wagons to help pull the wagons and teams up the hills.

Wednesday, March 4, 1874 (North of the Yellowstone River)

Sunrise occurred at 0648. The expedition traveled about eight miles to the east, before halting in the afternoon and establishing a laager for the night. Frank Grounds issued the expedition's Third General Order. It stated that unless a man was appointed as a hunter, he would not shoot at game from the wagon train or leave the formation in search of food. Failure to abide by this order would result in the offender standing extra guard duty at night. Prior to this ruling, many men went hunting, but returned with little game—a waste of ammunition, and putting these individuals at risk of ambush should unfriendly warriors be lurking. After issuing the order, Grounds divided the expedition into twelve-man groups. Each group would appoint its own hunter by vote.[52] Sunset was at 1805.

Thursday, March 5, 1874 (North of the Yellowstone River)

Sunrise was at 0646. The expedition traveled about eight miles to the east, before halting in the afternoon and establishing a laager for the night. Sunset occurred at 1807.

Friday, March 6, 1874 (North of the Yellowstone River)

Sunrise was at 0644. The expedition traveled about eight miles to the east, before halting in the afternoon and establishing a laager for the night. Sunset occurred at 1808. Back in Bozeman, the *Avant Courier* printed a long article on the expedition that included: [53]

> As for finding gold on this expedition, everyone feels confident of success…one thing is certain, the country is gold-bearing and in case we fail in our expectations at our point of view, there is a majority as willing to and will prospect the country to the head of Wind river or find diggings, and shall not visit Bozeman before Christmas. Gold is what we want and gold is what we must have.

Saturday, March 7, 1874 (Five Mile Creek) [N 45° 52.995', W 108° 36.351']

Sunrise was at 0642. The expedition traveled about eight miles to the east, before halting in the afternoon and establishing a laager for the night near Five Mile Creek (northwest of present-day Billings.) Sunset was at 1809. [54]

Sunday, March 8, 1874 (Alkali Creek)

Sunrise occurred at 0640. The expedition traveled about 8.5 miles east-southeast, passing

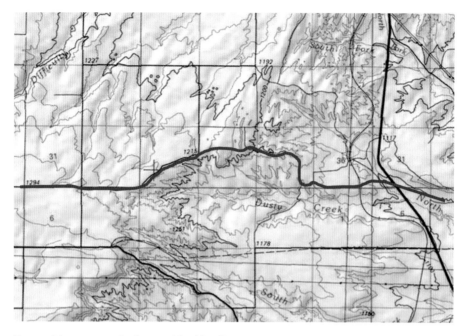

Route of the wagon train shown with a blue line.

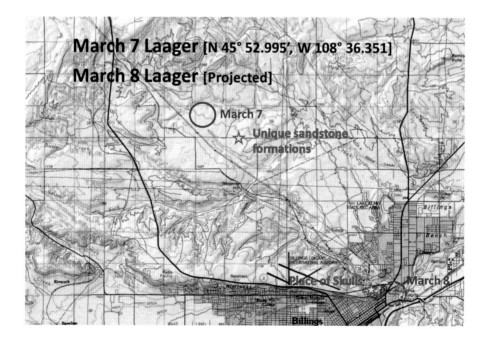

Yellowstone valley from Skull Bluff, 1882. The
expedition passed by here on March 8, 1974.
*Photograph by F.J. Haynes, H-746, Haynes
Foundation Collection, courtesy of Montana
Historical Society Research Center Photograph
Archives, Helena, MT*

near several unique sandstone formations, and
made camp near the mouth of Alkali Creek
and the Yellowstone River. About this point
in the expedition, J.L. Vernon made his escape
along with James Rockfellow, not far from
the "Place of Skulls," also known as "Skull
Bluff," which derived its name from the
massive Crow burials there (after smallpox
epidemics killed four of every five members

of their population in the 1840s.)[55] Sunset was
at 1811. Oliver Hanna picked up the action
and the ephemeral Vernon.[56]

Mr. Vernon disappeared at this point and
we never heard of him afterward. We had
become suspicious of him and he knew
it. We were nearing the Porcupine stream
where he had told us he found the gold

and he knew, if he failed to make good on his promises, a rope would soon encircle his neck. So he made his get-away.

Monday, March 9, 1874 (Baker's Road)
Sunrise occurred at 0638. The weather began with clouds, but the sun soon dispersed them. Even so, the temperature remained cool. The expedition traveled ten to twelve miles to the northeast along Baker's Road toward Stanley's Road in the general direction of Pompey's Pillar, before halting in the afternoon and establishing a laager for the night. Designated hunters killed a number of bison for supper.[57] Sunset was at 1812.

Tuesday, March 10, 1874 (Intersection of Baker's Road and Stanley's Road)
Sunrise occurred at 0636. The expedition traveled ten to twelve miles to the northeast, before halting in the afternoon about 1330 at a small creek near the intersection of Baker's Road and Stanley's Road and establishing a laager for the night.[58] Sunset occurred at 1813.

Wednesday, March 11, 1874 (Stanley's Road)
Sunrise occurred at 0635. The expedition traveled ten to twelve miles to the northeast in the general direction of Pompey's Pillar along Stanley's Road, before halting in the afternoon and establishing a laager for the night. The men melted snow for water and killed several antelope and one sheep. Two more wagons joined the expedition at this late date.[59] Sunset was at 1815.

Thursday, March 12, 1874 (Pompey's Pillar)
Sunrise occurred at 0633. The expedition probably arrived to a laager site north of Pompey's Pillar late in the afternoon, probably at Fly Creek. The expedition was now some 214 ground miles from Bozeman.[60] The men set up their usual security and then ate supper. The grass was very poor and the men spotted almost no game animals. The weather was partially cloudy and cold.[61] Sunset was at 1816.

Friday, March 13, 1874 (Pompey's Pillar)
Sunrise occurred at 0631. Several men road from the campsite, crossed the Yellowstone River, and visited Pompey's Pillar on the southern side of that river. Hugo Hoppe reportedly carved his name into the rock formation as did Thomas E. Rea and Edward Farnum.[62] The party then re-crossed the Yellowstone and returned to camp. The rest of the men rested at camp during the day, while the livestock herd attempted to graze on the frozen ground. Sunset was at 1817. Back in Bozeman, the executive committee reported

Pompey's Pillar in good weather. Data base onsite does not record any names of members of the expedition whose names still remain on the constantly eroding rock formation. *Author photograph, June 2015*

View of the Yellowstone River to the west from Pompey's Pillar about 1906. The expedition laagered near here from March 12-13, 1874. *Layton A. Huffman, Catalog Number: x80.15.25, courtesy of Museum of the Rockies Photo Archives,*

in the *Avant Courier* that it had received no news since Elisha Terrill's February 27/28 letter that had been published the week before.[63]

Saturday, March 14, 1874 (North of the Yellowstone River)

Sunrise occurred at 0629. The expedition traveled about ten miles to the northeast in the general direction toward the mouth of Buffalo Creek at the Yellowstone River, before halting in the afternoon and setting up the positions for the night. A.B. Ford found some coal and put chunks of it on the campfires that burned nicely.[64] Other men undoubtedly used prairie coal (dry buffalo chips burned as fuel.) Sunset was at 1819.

Sunday, March 15, 1874 (North of the Yellowstone River)

Sunrise occurred at 0627. The wagon train traveled about ten miles to the northeast, before halting in the afternoon and establishing a laager for the night. The men killed two or three buffalo for food.[65] Sunset was at 1820.

Monday, March 16, 1874 (North of the Yellowstone River)

Sunrise occurred at 0625. The men traveled about ten miles to the northeast in the general direction toward the mouth of Buffalo Creek at the Yellowstone River, before halting in the afternoon and establishing a laager for the night. Sunset was at 1821.

Tuesday, March 17, 1874 (**North of the Yellowstone River**)
Sunrise occurred at 0623. The expedition traveled about ten miles to the northeast, before halting in the afternoon and establishing positions for the night. Sunset was at 1823.

Wednesday, March 18, 1874 (**Mouth of Buffalo Creek**)
Sunrise occurred at 0621. The expedition traveled about ten miles to the northeast and arrived at the mouth of Buffalo Creek at the Yellowstone River, before halting in the afternoon and establishing a laager for the night. Eli Way put out an order not to leave the main body to hunt and to put all camp fires out before darkness. He knew that the expedition was approaching areas of likely Lakota activity. Sunset was at 1824.[66]

Thursday, March 19, 1874 (**Mouth of Buffalo Creek**)
Sunrise occurred at 0619. The expedition remained in camp near the mouth of Buffalo Creek at the Yellowstone River. Some of the men explored the sandstone cliffs in the area; Thomas Rea cut his name into the side of one of the cliffs. Sunset was at 1825.

Friday, March 20, 1874 (**North of the Yellowstone River**)
Sunrise occurred at 0617. The expedition traveled about ten miles to the northeast, before halting in the afternoon and establishing a laager for the night. The terrain had been very difficult; there were numerous gulches and ravines.[67] Sunset was at 1827. The rookie frontiersmen would have a difficult time sleeping that night. Jack Bean later recalled that many wolves had come north of the Yellowstone and were howling so much that "the tin dishes in the camp would vibrate."[68] Back in Bozeman, the *Avant Courier* published an update on the progress of the expedition, but erroneously stated that the men were determined to build a stockade, a task that was never attempted at any point during the endeavor. In the same edition, an enterprising businessman placed the following advertisement in the paper: [69]

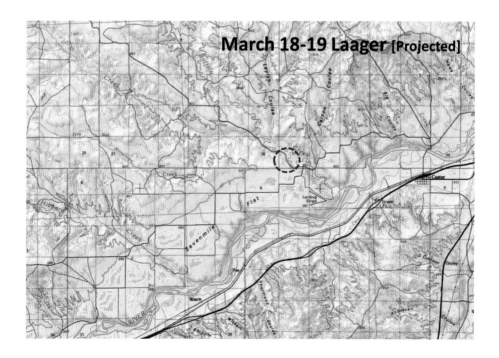
March 18-19 Laager [Projected]

The Yellowstone Expedition

Ordered from William's & Murray's Mammoth Saloon a large stock of choice whiskies, brandies, wines, etc. Fifty boxes of the choicest cigars were also forwarded. Reader, go thou and see if the Y.E. did not exhibit good taste in patronizing Williams & Murray.

***Saturday, March 21, 1874* (North of the Yellowstone River)**

Sunrise was at 0615. The expedition traveled about ten miles to the northeast along the old Stanley Road, before halting in the afternoon and establishing a laager for the night. The men who had earlier gone back to Bozeman to deliver news returned and rejoined the expedition. The returnees brought mail and news from Gallatin County.[70] Sunset occurred at 1828.

***Sunday, March 22, 1874* (Froze to Death Creek)**

Sunrise was at 0613. The expedition traveled about ten miles to the northeast, before halting in the afternoon and establishing a laager for the night near the mouth of Froze to Death Creek. Sunset occurred at 1829.[71] The wagon train was now 249 ground miles from Bozeman.[72]

***Monday, March 23, 1874* (North of the Yellowstone River)**

Sunrise was at 0612. It snowed early in the morning. The expedition traveled about ten miles to the northeast, before halting in the afternoon and establishing a laager for the night. Sunset was at 1831. During the night, a warrior—tribe unknown—shot at one of the pickets and the frontiersman returned fire but no one was hit in the small melee.[73]

***Tuesday, March 24, 1874* (Big Porcupine Creek)**

Sunrise occurred at 0610. The expedition traveled about ten miles east, arriving close to the mouth of Big Porcupine Creek, where they made camp. The expedition was now 267 ground miles from Bozeman.[74] The men saw numerous bison and antelope. Stands of cottonwood trees abounded.[75] Scouts likely rode, while it was still daylight, the short

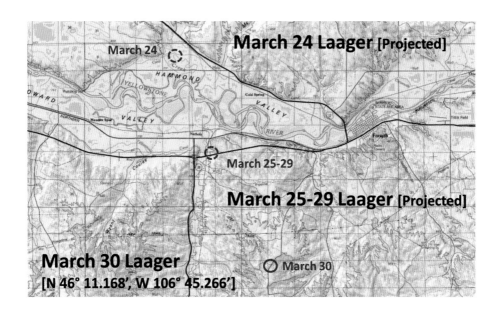

distance down to the Yellowstone River to conduct a reconnaissance for the next day's crossing. Sunset occurred at 1831.

Wednesday, March 25, 1874 (Crossing the Yellowstone River/Armells Creek)

Sunrise occurred at 0608. The weather was excellent, with a clear blue sky. The expedition crossed the Yellowstone River on the ice, which George Herendeen estimated was four or five feet thick, to the south shore near the mouth of Armells Creek, making camp a mile south of the Yellowstone. Jack Bean later stated that there were now 149 men on the expedition; he added that the crossing area had also been used by large numbers of bison, so there was little grass for the horses to eat on either side of the river. The men allowed the horses to strip bark off the long-hanging cottonwood tree limbs. The group rested, while a party of twenty-five men with thirty-eight horses and five days' provisions, under Zack Yates, went back across the Yellowstone about 1800 to the north and made a prospecting trip up the Great Porcupine and Little Porcupine creeks. Oliver Hanna went with this group as well.[76] In a letter to the *Helena Herald*—written by Hugh Hoppe after the expedition on May 9, 1874—this laager area on the south side of the Yellowstone was described as "a beautiful bottom covered with fine grass and timber."[77] Sunset occurred at 1833. Addison M. Quivey recorded the events of the day:[78]

> We soon after left Baker's road, and struck across the country, intersecting the road made by Gen. Stanley accompanying the Northern Pacific Railroad survey of 1873, which road we followed until we arrived at a point about three miles above the mouth of Big Porcupine Creek, where we crossed the Yellowstone on the 21st of March [he was probably off by four days.] Here we laid by four days.

Joe Cook's recollection focused on the wily Vernon:[79]

> We traveled down the north side of the Yellowstone until we got to Goose Creek, this being the creek that Vernon said that he found the gold on. We prospected this creek from its mouth to its source and did not find even a hat full of gravel, as it runs through a gumbo soil all the way. After finding Vernon's statement all a hoax, we crossed to the south side of the river with the view of prospecting the streams on the south side."

1st Lt. James Bradley later wrote:[80]

> The expedition kept to the north of the Yellowstone, following Baker's trail of 1872, and Stanley's of 1873, until they reached a point on the Yellowstone about two miles above the Great Porcupine, having traveled leisurely and encountered much severe weather. Here on the 21st of March they crossed the river on the ice and going into camp, laid over four days to enable prospecting parties to visit and examine the two Porcupine and O'Fallon's creeks.

Thursday, March 26, 1874 (Armells Creek)

Sunrise occurred at 0606. The expedition remained in camp. It snowed all day and was cold. Zack Yates and his prospectors remained north of the Yellowstone, exploring the Great Porcupine and Little Porcupine, but the prospectors sent no messages to the main wagon train regarding their progress.[81] Sunset occurred at 1835. Addison M. Quivey, ever the naturalist, recorded what he saw:[82]

> After leaving what is known as "Baker's battle-ground" (which is a few miles above where Prior's Creek comes into the Yellowstone from the south side,) the country becomes more barren, with but little grass or water, and all the country between the Yellowstone and Musselshell east of the above point seems to be a very low formation, full of marine fossils, mostly, I think, of the different orders or

varieties of *articulate*—many having the form of the common coiled snail-shell, being from two to three feet in diameter; some of them having the appearance of ammonites; others more the appearance of articulate animals coiled up in that form.

In one place I found fossil fishes, but they were so broken and crushed that no good specimens could be obtained, and many shells, the enamel of which was as bright and brilliant in color as the shells gathered on the ocean beach of to-day. What are known as the Bull Mountains are composed of sedimentary rocks, and are an elevated table-land, extending far toward the junction of the Missouri and the Yellowstone. All the country along the north side of the latter stream is inconceivably barren, being almost destitute of grass, water, or timber, except a narrow strip along the river, which alone is capable of cultivation.

Friday, March 27, 1874 (**Armells Creek**)
Sunrise was at 0604. It rained and snowed during the entire day. The expedition remained in camp. Zack Yates and his prospectors continued prospecting north of the Yellowstone, exploring the Great Porcupine and Little Porcupine, but again sent no news to the main camp.[83] Sunset occurred at 1836. Addison M. Quivey apparently traveled with Zack Yates and the prospectors based on his following later account:[84]

We explored the Big and Little Porcupine creeks, which make an imposing show on the maps, following them nearly to their sources, and found them to be only wet-weather rivers, their beds being dry during the greater part of the year. In fact, I do not believe that the Yellowstone has one single tributary on the north side, from "Baker's battle-ground" to its mouth, which runs water during the dry season of the year. The country is valuable for neither agriculture, grazing, nor minerals, but may be interesting to the geologist or

naturalist. The country is evidently a marine formation, and from its present appearance I should think it admirably formed for the last home and burial place of the horrible monsters [dinosaurs] of the earliest animal creation.

Back in Bozeman, the *Avant Courier*, republishing an article from the *Helena Herald*, took Gen. George A. Custer to task for his actions concerning the expedition.[85]

General Custer from Fort Abraham Lincoln, Dakota Territory, February 25th, sends a report to the War Department, adversely criticizing the Prospecting Expedition, which recently moved from Bozeman toward the Tongue River country. It is the opinion of General Custer that this expedition will embarrass proposed military operations, and precipitate difficulties with the Indians. In which opinion, we do not join, believing that the General himself will see and confess his mistake in a short time.

The *Avant Courier* went on to state that it would like to see more actual military operations than all "these *proposed* operations."

Saturday, March 28, 1874 (**Armells Creek**)
Sunrise occurred at 0602. It rained and snowed a great deal during the day; in the afternoon the sun came out and started melting the snow. No warriors were encountered. The expedition remained in camp. Zack Yates and his prospectors remained north of the Yellowstone, exploring the Great Porcupine and Little Porcupine.[86] Sunset was at 1837. Jack Bean later described a special security measure that had been implemented:[87]

We had three men with us whose job in the morning was to saddle up and take a little turn around before we turned the stock out to feed—which was not a very comfortable job to do. Often they came back to camp and reported lots of signs which consisted of pony tracks—and occasionally a head over a hill.

Sunday, March 29, 1874 (Armells Creek)

Sunrise was at 0600. It rained and snowed during the day before turning warmer and no warriors were encountered. Zack Yates and the prospectors crossed the Yellowstone south and returned to the main camp at 1600, reporting that their search for gold had been fruitless.[88] Sunset occurred at 1839.

Monday, March 30, 1874 (East of Armells Creek) [N 46° 11.168', W 106° 45.266']

Sunrise was at 0558. It had rained and snowed during the previous night. The men cleared the snow off the wagons and their belongings. The expedition struck camp, followed an Indian trail and started toward Rosebud Creek. Finding the direct route blocked by a narrow canyon flanked by steep bluffs, the wagon train turned south into the Badlands to search for a safe detour. Suddenly, Bill Hindman and Charles Dryden—who had been far forward of the column hunting—raced back to the group, closely followed by seventeen Lakota warriors. The advance guard of the wagon train, which on this day included Oliver Hanna,

turned the tables on the advancing Lakota with accurate gunfire and later found the warriors' supplies a half mile away in a gulch. The expedition traveled a difficult eight miles through the several feet of wet snow on the ground and made camp at noon. The column halted on a high ridge and dug firing positions, while water carriers rode to a gulch three-fourths of a mile away to fill canteens.[89]

In the afternoon, a small party moved forward to conduct a short reconnaissance for the next day's movement. Frank Grounds put out the pickets about 1600. One mile from camp, as the group was ascending a steep hill topped by pines, George Herendeen spotted a warrior—later referred to in the frontier slang of "Lo"—running through woods, a possible precursor to a warrior assault. As the warriors attacked, the reconnaissance party from the wagon train conducted a fighting withdrawal—while one group of men laid down intense rifle fire, a second group withdrew fifty yards and then began firing while the first group withdrew fifty yards, leap-frogging the second group. As the withdrawing men approached the main camp, Grounds and Way deployed reinforcements and drove the warriors away. What the frontiersmen did

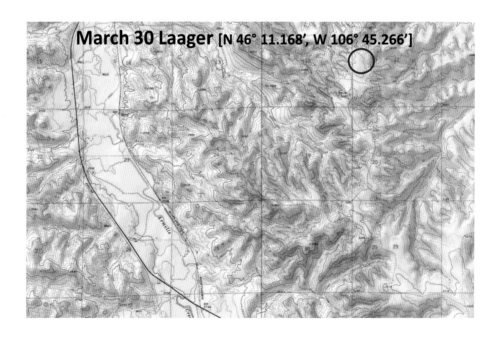

March 30 Laager [N 46° 11.168', W 106° 45.266']

not know was that the attackers were from a large combined camp of Sitting Bull's Hunkpapas and Minneconjou led by Flying By and Makes Room.[90]

Meanwhile, Henry Bostwick had been stationed on his horse on another ridge to the right of the camp. Eight mounted warriors approached—although Bostwick could see only two. Bostwick emptied his Winchester rifle at the attackers with no visible results, although a later report suggested that he may have hit one of them. In any case, the warriors proved better shots, hitting Bostwick four times during the chase back towards camp. Jack Bean saw the encounter and rode toward the action, but his horse slipped on the ice in a gulch, fell, and broke its neck. Bean, now on foot, grabbed his Sharps buffalo rifle, and fired, smashing the arm of a warrior that was preparing to shoot an arrow into the luckless Bostwick. Zack Yates quickly arrived and added his own covering fire to that of Bean, while a group of other men carried the wounded Bostwick back to camp.[91] Addison M. Quivey described the hot action:[92]

We saw them [the warriors] no more until the 30th, when, after we had camped, our captain and a few others were taking a look at the country ahead, and when about one mile from camp they were fired at by a small party of Indians concealed in a ravine. They returned the fire, but not knowing the number of their assailants, returned to camp. Shortly after, one of our pickets (Bostwick, from Deer Lodge County,) seeing an Indian a short distance from his post, who seemed desirous of talking with him, started out to interview the "red brother," when he was attacked by four others, who were concealed in the brush. He turned his horse to run, but received four wounds, and was even struck on the head with their whip-stocks, but he held to his horse, and finally escaped, aided by some of our party, who heard the firing and went to his assistance. He recovered from his wounds, but carries

two of the bullets in his person yet. From blood found, and one revolver and bow and arrows picked up, it was supposed that one or more Indians were killed or wounded. During the early part of the night, one of our pickets fired at and wounded an Indian, as much blood was found where he had lain, but he was probably carried away before morning.

Joe Cook recalled the events on March 30 in this way:[93]

The morning we left the Yellowstone to go across lots to the Rosebud, we encountered thirteen Indians. As we were going up a draw, a young fellow, I think his name was Davis, who rode a buckskin horse, was a half mile ahead of the train, was the first to see them. He had gone over the ridge out of sight of the train. The Indians had seen him first and had stripped their horses of everything, such as provisions, blankets and other things. I think they intended to take him alive, for they never shot at him during the race. Davis' horse was a plug race horse and he rode away from them. As soon as the Indians got to the top of the ridge, and saw the train they stampeded up the mountain, and we got their pile of stuff. This little band of Indians harassed us every day by shooting at us from behind ridges and trees and then getting out of the way.

Joe Cook continued, discussing the peril in which Bostwick soon found himself:[94]

We were camped in a gulch and just in the gray of the morning they fired several shots at us before we were out of bed. About sun up we put out pickets and turned the horses out of the wagon corral to feed. About one-half mile from camp we had four horsemen on a ridge, about another half mile still further out a lone Indian who was riding a good looking sorrel horse, came out in the open, and flashed a small mirror, thereby expressing a desire to talk to one of the pickets. There was a ridge extending out to where he was. One of the pickets said he would ride out there and kill this Indian and get his horse. The three other guards remonstrated and tried to keep him from going. He would go, and as the lay of the land was uneven he did not see the Indian disappear. He rode on out to where the Indian had been, when he started back six Indians that were secreted, surrounded him. As they ran, he [Bostwick] emptied his Winchester at them, but did not hit any of them. The Indians rode so close to him that they struck him several times with their quirts in the face. He was shot through the upper part of the shoulder and once through the right foot, the bullet going in at the instep and coming out through the sole.

Hitting Bostwick with their quirts was the warriors' way of counting coup and was considered an act of great bravery when done against a living foe. 1st Lt. James Bradley later wrote about the incident:[95]

The expedition was not molested during the ensuing three days, but on the 30th of March a small party were ambuscaded and fired upon but escaped without harm. Later in the day, W.A. Bostwick, while a picket, saw an Indian not far from his post, who appeared to wish to talk with him, and riding forward to meet him, fell into an ambuscade and was fired upon at short range, receiving four wounds. Bostwick fled at the best speed of his horse, but the Indians overtook him, and might easily have killed him, but thought to amuse themselves first by beating him with coup sticks and pony whips as he ran. They were then drawn within range of the picket guards concealed behind a ridge about half a mile from camp. Jack Bean fired and knocked an Indian out of

his saddle when they ceased the pursuit and withdrew.

Bostwick clung to his saddle until within the protection of the guard when he fainted and fell to the ground. His wounds were considered mortal, yet in a few days he was so far recovered as to be able to take part in a general engagement with the Sioux. Undo exposure brought on a relapse and upon the return of the expedition, he was for some time an inmate of the military hospital at Fort Ellis, but ultimately recovered, still bearing two bullets in his body. During the night an Indian was wounded by the guards and in the morning the Indians annoyed the camp for some time by firing at long range from the neighboring hills. The fire was returned when daylight came, whereupon the Indians withdrew, without having wrought any harm.

Finally, James Gourley added the following, which described how the Lakota and Cheyenne warriors counted coup on an enemy with their whips:[96]

It was here that one of the party, who was more anxious to secure horses than prudent in his method, rode up to get a horse that had been put out for a decoy and when the Indians got him where they wanted him, they opened fire on him and wounded him in several places. Then riding up on him commenced circling around him and beat him with their whips, but the plot was discovered in time by some of the pickets, who got close enough to get in some good shooting at the Indians and drove them off and prevented the Indians getting either the horse or the man, who afterwards got well.

Sunset occurred at 1841. The men, who melted snow for drinking water, tried to treat Bostwick's wounds as best they could. During the night, Herbert Richardson—the butcher from Bozeman—spotted a warrior and shot him. Addison M. Quivey continued with his version of events:[97]

> The first hostile Indians we encountered … were a small party, who, discovering one of our advance guard, 'stripped' for fight, and gave him a lively chase; but others going to his rescue, they ran away, leaving blankets, robes, provisions of dried meat, etc.

Tuesday, March 31, 1874 (Sheep Creek Camp) [N 46° 5.314', W 106° 39.512']

Sunrise was at 0556. Expedition members found traces of blood in the snow from Richardson's shot, but could not locate a body. Hugh Hoppe also wrote that the men found pistols and bows and arrows.[98] Quivey picked up the action:[99]

> Before daylight in the morning, they opened a lively fire on our camp at long range from the surrounding hills, many bullets striking about our corral, but doing no damage. They retired as soon as it became light enough to return their fire with effect.

It rained and snowed during the day. The expedition made ten miles. As he would for the remainder of the expedition, the seriously wounded Henry Bostwick—unable to mount a horse—rode in the back of a wagon. Once again, the night laager was away from water and Eli Way had to send water carriers to retrieve sufficient quantities for drinking and cooking. The pickets, water party, and guards encountered no warriors.[100] Sunset occurred at 1841. Addison M. Quivey later explained the general route the expedition had recently followed:[101]

> When we resumed our march, leaving the Yellowstone, taking a south or southeasterly course (but necessarily a very crooked one) until we crossed the Rosebud Creek, probably twenty-five miles above its junction with the Yellowstone; thence we followed up the Rosebud Creek or river about forty miles; then crossed the country in a southwesterly direction to the streams tributary to the Big Horn river, crossing the Little Horn, Grass Lodge, Rotten Grass, and other streams, finally reaching the old emigrant road, about twenty miles

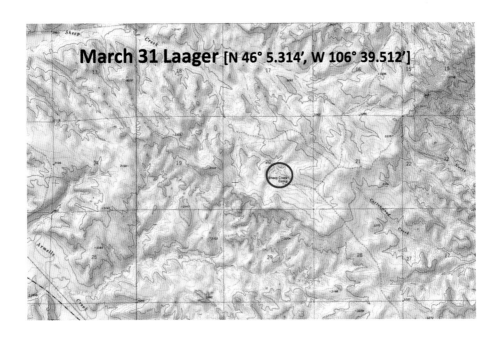

March 31 Laager [N 46° 5.314', W 106° 39.512']

southeast of old Fort Smith, at which place we crossed the Big Horn River, and followed the old Bozeman road to this place, being absent about ninety days.

Wednesday, April 1, 1874 (Smith Creek) [N 45° 59.701', W 106° 34.278']

Sunrise occurred at 0554. At about this time, according to George Herendeen and later recorded by Walter Mason Camp, the men started to leave behind bread as they left each campsite. The bread had been poisoned with strychnine.[102] The trick did not sit well with all the men. Charles Avery was one of those who did not like the tactic and later wrote:[103]

We got so mad at those Indians that we poisoned the pemmican and left it for them to eat. That was, no doubt, a mean trick and should not have been done.

It rained and snowed during the day. No warriors were encountered. The expedition moved south and camped at Smith Creek. Sunset was at 1843.

Thursday, April 2, 1874 (Spring Creek) [N 45° 56.776', W 106° 29.953']

Sunrise occurred at 0552. Buck Buchanan, Yank Evarts, and Harry Wilson made a scout around the area before the livestock were released from the corral to graze. It rained and snowed during the day. No warriors were encountered during the movement of the expedition, which began at 0800, and continued south. The wagon train camped at Spring Creek, on ground higher than any bluffs in the area. Several warriors were observed in the distance.[104] Sunset occurred at 1844.

Quivey went on to record that the terrain changed again in this area, a description that provided substance to the opinions that the eastern portion of the Montana Territory was rich in many types of mineral deposits, if not gold:[105]

After crossing the Yellowstone, we were six days traveling to the Rosebud River. We had much better grass, but the only water we found was from melted snow in the ravines; and I think it would be impossible

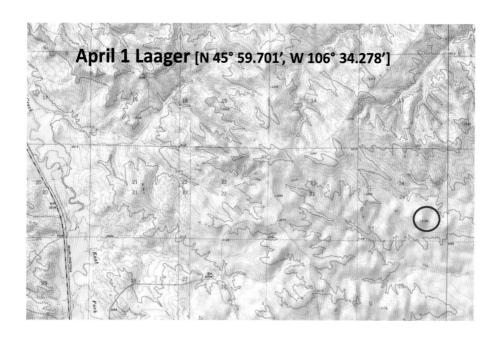

April 1 Laager [N 45° 59.701', W 106° 34.278']

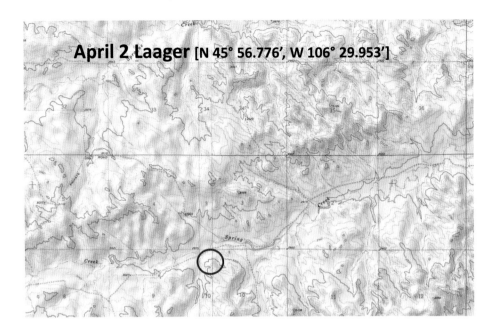

April 2 Laager [N 45° 56.776', W 106° 29.953']

to travel the same route in summer, for want of water. On this part of our journey, we were making our own road; and, until we reached the old Bozeman road, we followed an entirely new route. Between the Yellowstone and Rosebud, the country abounds in coal and iron ore, and in places limestone, but no granite or other primitive rocks, and is cut up by deep, impassable ravines, and our road was necessarily very crooked. In places, the ground was covered with cinders; and in others it appeared that veins of coal had been burned out, leaving beds of ashes, cinders, etc.

Friday, April 3, 1874 (Entered the Rosebud Valley/Rosebud Creek) [N 45° 50.188', W 106° 24.563']

Sunrise occurred at 0551. From a high ridge some 800 yards from the campsite, a warrior fired at the men, but return fire drove him away; later recollections indicated that up to thirteen warriors were shadowing the wagon train. Buck Buchanan, Yank Evarts, and Harry Wilson again made a scout around the area before the livestock was released from the corral to graze. Apparently the trio was

becoming a good team together. The frontiersmen made coffee and ate breakfast. The expedition departed camp about 0800, heading for the divide between Sheep Creek and Cottonwood Creek, and entered the valley of the Rosebud at a point thirty-two miles south of the Yellowstone River in the afternoon. The wagon train crossed several small dry creek beds with cottonwood and ash timber in them. The men pulled up on the first bench land east of the Rosebud Creek and began making camp; they had made nine miles that day. The bench land was fifteen feet above the valley floor, some 400 yards east of the creek. During the movement, the men saw evidence of an Indian campsite of up to 200 lodges, although Hugh Hoppe thought it could have been upward of 300 to 500 lodges.[106] The men dug rifle pits around the outside of the corral for defense against a possible night attack.[107] Sunset was at 1845. Back at Bozeman, the *Avant Courier* on this day wrote that no further contact had been made with the expedition and no messages had been received from it.[108] 1st Lt. James Bradley later wrote about the defensive positions taken by the expedition before each night:[109]

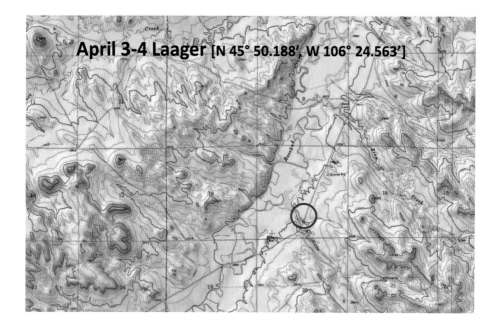

April 3-4 Laager [N 45° 50.188', W 106° 24.563']

They were upon the brow of what is known in the West as the 'First bench' where the ground breaks off abruptly to the depths of several feet to the low ground (bottom) to which the timber in western valleys is confined, and through which the river flows. The first bench was here from 15 to 20 feet above the valley proper, the rifle pits on the river side crowning its verge. In front (and toward the river) at the distance of about 150 yards was a bench growth of ash and cottonwood timber, on the left two ravines sloped down from the hill, uniting about 75 yards from the camp and terminating the bench upon that side. On the right and in the rear the ground was open and level to the distance of several hundred yards, affording no cover for an enemy, so that it was from the timber and ravine that an attack was to be apprehended. Four small rifle pits, designed as cover for the outposts, were advanced some 75 yards on the different sides of the camp, the one on the upper side being located upon the brow of the bench opposite the intersection of the two ravines already described.

Addison M. Quivey later described the day:[110]

"We arrived at and crossed the Rosebud on the 3d of April, camping on the bench above the creek bottom, the bluff being perhaps twenty feet high, having, as usual, thrown up rifle pits or entrenchments around our camp (which we had done since leaving the mouth of the Big Horn,) at night corralled our stock, with the exception of a few horses, which were tied to the outside of the corral, and posted pickets and guards as usual. No Indians in sight, but we were encamped upon a trail, over which a large party, with many lodges, had passed a few days before."

Saturday, April 4, 1874 (**Rosebud Creek/ Battle of Rosebud Creek**) **[N 45° 50.188', W 106° 24.563']**

Based on all the recollections of the wagon train participants and previous historical analyses, the Battle of Rosebud Creek of the 1874 Yellowstone Wagon Road and Prospecting Expedition unfolded in the following manner. The wagon train made camp on the first bench

View from laager area to the southwest. *Author photograph, June 2015*

View from laager area to the west-southwest. *Author photograph, June 2015*

of land next to the Rosebud Creek, some fifteen or twenty feet in elevation before the valley floor in mid-afternoon on April 3. The frontiersmen dug four rifle pits on the edges of the bench, each some seventy-five yards from the camp, although the farthest pits were later found to be 465 feet from the center of the laager. Two men were at each position. Each rifle pit had a head log that the men cut, which was three feet long and eight to ten inches in diameter; this protected the men from being shot in the head when they fired

View from laager area to the west. *Author photograph, June 2015*

from small observation loopholes beneath them. On both sides of the corral, the men dug two trenches, each two feet wide and two feet deep for breastworks. These would be perfect for men to shoot their rifles from the kneeling position, much more accurate than firing from a standing position in the open.

Some 150 yards from the camp, towards the river, was a growth of ash and cottonwood timber; to the south were two ravines sloping down from the hill, uniting about seventy-five yards from the camp and terminating the bench upon that side. The width of the ravine was fifty to sixty feet. Between this draw and the corral for the livestock, sage brush grew to a height of eighteen inches. The river was 350 yards to the west of the timber described. To the north and east, the ground was open and level to the distance of several hundred yards,

affording no cover for an enemy. Frank Grounds probably thought that any attack on the camp would come from the timber and ravine. The waning gibbous moon, with 93% of the moon's visible disk illuminated, rose at 2044 on April 3; it would not set until 0646 on April 4.

Tom Allen was on picket duty; at his position was also a frontiersman named Jones. At about 0010 (April 4), two pickets reported that they had shot at several mounted warriors, possibly killing one horse. Less than two hours later, at about 0200, 300 to 400 warriors attacked up the ravine, forcing the two pickets there to abandon their position and flee back to the main camp. If any frontiersman was still asleep, he awoke at this point from all the noise and remained vigilant the rest of the night. The warriors began firing into the camp at about 0215 from a range of seventy-five to

View from laager area to the west-northwest. *Author photograph, June 2015*

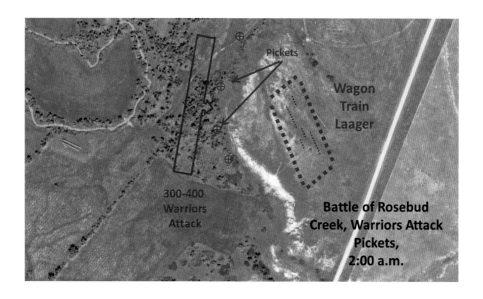

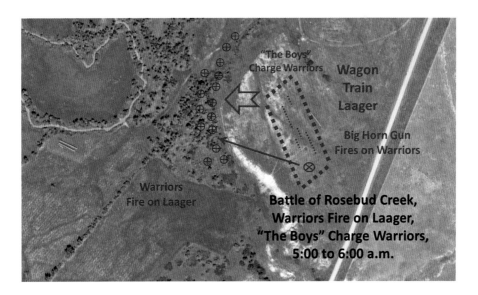

"The Boys" Charge Warriors

Wagon Train Laager

Big Horn Gun Fires on Warriors

Warriors Fire on Laager

Battle of Rosebud Creek, Warriors Fire on Laager, "The Boys" Charge Warriors, 5:00 to 6:00 a.m.

one hundred yards. Tom Allen later told researcher Walter Camp that warrior chief Gall (Allen did not know this warrior's identity at the time) called out during the firing for the Lakota to save their ammunition until daylight when they would "get them all." Allen also recalled that fourteen horses of the expedition were outside the laager and that the warriors killed all of them, while George Herendeen later reminisced that twelve fine mules were killed also.[111] Whoever gave this order to conserve ammunition, the warriors probably temporarily stopped firing within a few minutes. Stillness would reign for perhaps two hours, during which time a few men probably tried to catch a catnap—if that was possible.

The beginning of morning nautical twilight (BMNT) commenced at 0436 and with slightly increased visibility, the frontiersmen discovered that the warriors occupying the picket holes were doing most of the shooting, which had just recommenced. By 0450, the warriors in the coulee began to lower their aiming points and with this adjustment, they shot a frontiersman, Tom Woodward, through his wrist as he was lifting a stick or shovel on top of the earthworks while attempting to dig a hasty firing port. He learned the hard way that while a rotten log was easier to cut, it would

not provide nearly as much protection as good wood. About this same time, the frontiersmen noticed that one warrior was rolling an ash log in front of him as he crawled along the ground, making rifle fire against him ineffective. They probably notified Frank Grounds (who retained tight control on the firing of the artillery pieces,) about 0500 concerning the advancing warrior. At some point in the early light, warriors killed a yellow dog belonging to Archie McDonald and ate it. They also killed another dog that belonged to Charlie Johnson.

Grounds probably took a few minutes to decide that he would launch a combined artillery and dismounted infantry attack—one artillery piece would neutralize the lone warrior sniper behind the log, and about thirty frontiersmen would charge the warriors in the ravine. It took a few minutes for the gunner, Billy Cameron, to lower the angle of fire for his artillery piece (he took the unscientific approach of jumping on the top of the gun tube to depress it.) About this time, other frontiersmen observed a single mounted warrior riding slowly toward a group of fellow warriors at the foot of a hill about one-half mile from the camp. That probably occurred at 0515.

At about 0530, the dismounted charge, which included Bill Calfee and Oliver Hanna,

View from laager area to the northwest. *Author photograph, June 2015*

View from laager area to the north-northwest. *Author photograph, June 2015*

and possibly led by Hugh Hoppe, raced toward the coulee; the warriors were probably driven out of this location by 0549, which was sunrise. Hanna later recalled that the men on the charge all carried repeating rifles and pistols, and that the men kept six foot intervals from each other to prevent bunching up. This was the time and location where an old warrior, whose leg had been blown off by the shrapnel round of the Big Horn Gun, was killed by a .50-caliber Springfield round, while Bill Calfee shot another warrior in the face with a pistol. Lakota warrior Shoot the Bear attempted to sneak into the laager and steal a horse that happened to belong to Jimmy Crane. Several men began firing at Shoot the Bear; the men later estimated they expended fifty rounds in the fusillade, but did not hit him. Oliver Hanna had an opportunity to shoot one of the warriors who became trapped in the melee, but could not

pull the trigger, so Zack Yates shot the man. Other frontiersmen attempted to "buffalo" the opposing warriors by striking them in the head with their pistols as clubs (known in modern terms as pistol whipping.)

No later than 0600, a second charge by the frontiersmen to the north and east drove the warriors from their cover on those sides of the camp. This movement was covered by fire from Edward C. Wilson manning the Big Horn Gun. That second charge and defense probably lasted until 0630. By this time, the frontiersmen had killed seven warriors in the ravine in close combat fighting and perhaps dispatched several other warriors by artillery and long range rifle fire. Scattered combat probably lasted until 0800, after which about 600 warriors gathered on the opposite side of the Rosebud and subsequently moved away from the laager. The expedition suffered one

View from laager area to the north. *Author photograph, June 2015*

View from laager area to the east. *Author photograph, June 2015*

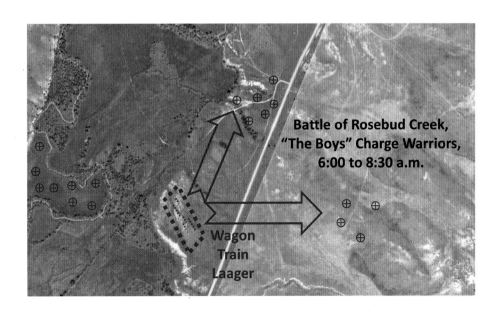

man wounded and between twelve and twenty-one horses and two oxen killed. The frontiersmen expended between 800 and 900 rifle rounds of ammunition and about thirty rounds of artillery shell and canister. The expedition remained in this laager location the rest of the day and night.

Historian Robert M. Utley concluded in his book on the Lakota chief, that Sitting Bull probably led these attacks. This was later confirmed by Red Hawk in an interview with Walter Mason Camp; Camp also noted that Sitting Bull's forces may have suffered 200 casualties, although thirty casualties are probably more accurate. Hugh Hoppe later estimated that there had been 800 warriors in the fighting that day. He further calculated that "not over 200 had shooting irons and very few had needle guns." He also opined that the frontiersmen had killed twenty-five to thirty.[112] Checking the area after the warriors had departed, Charles Johnson found a badly wounded warrior, according to Tom Allen. Remembering what had happened to his dog, Johnson beat the warrior to death with the stock of his rifle.[113] Sunset came at 0646. Joe Cook later provided the lead-in to what the expedition would later call the "Battle of the Rosebud," which this text has slightly modified to avoid confusion with the 1876 battle:[114]

The next day's travel after this brought us to the Rosebud. The first thing that engaged our attention was the wide road that the Indians' travois made going up the creek just a day or two before we got there. Right here I want to describe their mode of transportation. Their tepee poles are from sixteen to eighteen feet long. They bore one-half inch holes in the little end of each pole through which they pass a stout piece of buckskin or elk skin. They drag these tepee poles by tying the little ends to their pack saddles, and the big ends drag on the ground, six or eight feet on each side of the pony. Behind the pony they tie a couple of cross pieces, on which they have a wicker work made of willows

for a platform, on which they carry their goods and small children. From the size of the tracks, they had made we concluded that the whole Sioux tribe had gone up the valley, so we expected an attack that night and at midnight we were surrounded by them.

James Gourley added a lengthy description of the day's events:[115]

One more hard day's travel and we crossed the Rosebud River. On the river bottom we crossed a fresh Indian trail of 400 or 500 lodges of Indians who had passed up the river that day. Then the music commenced, and a great many were pulling their hair and wondering what they were doing in that country. We made our camp on a bench about 500 yards from the Rosebud, on the east side, dug breastworks and arranged for the truest possible use of the two guns we had—one a twelve-pound howitzer and the other a twelve-pound Napoleon. Unfortunately, however, we had but little ammunition which could be used in the Napoleon. We had two picket posts in holes dug for that purpose, two men in each hole, to cover the coulee below us. The coulee was about thirty feet from the breastworks. Another picket post was put out for protection from the river bottom, at the point of the bench we were camped on, and near the mouth of the coulee our earthworks ran along.

About two o'clock in the morning the pickets from both holes were driven in and the coulee occupied by 300 or 400 Indians, with other Indians at points in two or three directions, who probably intended to cut us off in case we made an attempt to run. Shortly after getting into the coulee, they commenced firing on us, riddling our wagon sheets, tents and lodges. A party of them occupied the picket hole near the mouth of the coulee, and from that point they had a very good chance to shoot into the mouth of our

Laager area; ground to the immediate front would have been a good position for one of the artillery pieces, offering excellent fields of fire. *Author photograph, June 2015*

corral, which couldn't be better protected on account of the formation of the country. They killed twenty-one of our horses during the night. We might have held them down by continuous shooting, but only fired every time we saw the flash of a gun, as we didn't want to waste any ammunition, and thought we could better afford to lose some stock.

About gray daylight in the morning we discovered that the Indians occupying the picket holes were doing the most shooting. One fellow we saw lying behind an ash stick which he was rolling up ahead of him as a protection from our shots. About this time it grew lighter and the Indians in the coulee commenced to shoot a little lower than they had been, and shot one of our men through the wrist while he was lifting a stick on top of the earthworks so as to make a hole underneath it to shoot through. It was not very long before we had ten Indians shot above the eyes, and the others in the coulee commenced to shoot at random, holding their pistols over the edge of the coulee. While they were doing this a number of their hands were shot off in that game. This we afterwards learned from a half-breed who was with them at the time.

We soon found that the Indians had to be charged out of this coulee, and a party of about thirty men got ready. Before this, however, we turned our attention to the Indian who was behind the ash stick. We thought a shell from the howitzer would settle him, but the gunner from his position couldn't take a sight at him. So, in order to help him out, we commenced shooting all around in order to keep them down, while the gunner jumped on top of the gun so as to get the location accurately, and while we held the Indians down he sighted the gun, cut his fuse and loaded the howitzer, and the next minute turned the gun loose. There was an explosion as the shell struck the stick, and we afterwards found pieces of blanket and Indian, and saw patches of blood.

Instantly on the discharge of the piece there was a scattering of Indians, and the charging party of thirty men jumped on top of the Indians in the coulee. They were the worst lot of paralyzed Indians I ever saw. They staggered around like a lot of fool hens, and didn't have strength enough to run. We got thirteen of their scalps that time and following up the charge captured twenty-three of their horses, making us good for all they had killed. We laid over at that point the next day, but took the precaution to put a picket post across the coulee, so as to prevent any further occupancy of it by the Indians while we were there. We also loaded a lot of rifle shells, such as we thought would fit their guns, by extracting part of the powder and adding a little giant powder in its place, and scattered these around so that the Indians might find them. We also captured a large lot of their pemmican in the coulee and dosed it pretty strong with strychnine. We afterwards had some proofs of its effects. Two men who had followed us up to get news of us discovered four Indians laid away in a tree with no signs of any wounds on them.

The booby-trapped rifle cartridges were obviously intended to be used in the rifles of the warriors and when fired would explode in the chamber due to the increased powder charge. The use of strychnine in the pemmican (lean, dried meat) speaks for itself and probably

killed these four warriors found in a tree. Addison M. Quivey continued his description:[116]

A short time after the guards were changed at midnight, two shots were fired, and two of our pickets reported that they had shot at some mounted Indians, and had killed one horse. Everything became quiet, and the camp was soon wrapped in slumber; but the quiet was of short duration, for about two o'clock several shots were heard in quick succession. Our pickets were driven in, and a rapid fire was opened from a coulee or ravine on the left of our position (facing the creek bottom,) at a distance of from seventy-five to one hundred yards; also from a steep bank on our right front at about the same distance, as well as from other points further off.

It was so dark that the Indians could not be seen, and their locality was only revealed by the flash of their guns. But few shots were fired in return. A few rounds of shell and canister were fired at points where they were supposed to be under cover of brush, ravines, etc. The fire of the enemy began to tell on the horses tied outside the corral, and six were soon killed; and occasionally an unusual commotion on the inside of the corral gave notice that some damage was being done there; but most of their shots went too high. We could hear the Indians talking and laughing, evidently thinking they were going to have it all their own way. Daylight began to appear, enabling the Indians to take better aim, but also giving us a chance to do the same, so that whenever one showed himself within range, he was made a target for our needle-guns.

Just as it was becoming daylight, one Indian made his appearance on our right, perhaps two hundred and fifty yards distant, riding slowly toward a large body of Indians, who were massed at the foot of a hill about half a mile away. The boys opened fire on him, but he did not change his pace or appear to pay the least attention to us until his horse began to falter, and fell dead, when the rider raised partly to his feet and hobbled away, evidently badly wounded, and in a few rods disappeared. Afterward his track was followed by blood to where he had been picked up and carried away. After the fight was over, I looked at the horse and found that it was pierced with nine bullets. Soon a charging party was made up by our adjutant to drive the Indians out of the ravine on our left, which was successfully done, the charging party being covered by a heavy fire of artillery and small arms, which kept the enemy down. The Indians were panic stricken, and only tried to escape. Seven were killed in the charge, and eight or nine horses captured, our men escaping unhurt. At the same time, a party of our men charged out on the right, driving the Indians from their cover on that side, and the fight was over, although a scattering fire was kept up for some time longer at long range, and we followed them up for half a mile, but without result, as the Indians were evidently badly whipped.

The Indians collected their forces (at least six hundred in number) about one mile above, on the opposite side of the creek, and soon moved away, some remaining in the vicinity, as the next morning, when we moved, we saw them in our camp before we were a mile from it. Seven scalps were taken, and, from blood and other evidence, many were killed and wounded, who were carried away. Nine horses were captured; also several guns, pistols, bows and arrows, etc.

Our loss was one man wounded, twelve horses and two oxen killed and a number wounded, and one horse, too poor to either tie up or put in the corral, captured. Our wagon-covers, tents, etc., were riddled with bullets, and if the Indians had aimed lower, much more damage would have been done.

Careful inquiry showed that we had expended between eight and nine hundred cartridges for small arms, and about thirty rounds of shell and canister. The Indians fired over three shots to our one. During the fight the Indians had killed a dog belonging to our party, and had roasted and eaten it in the ravine, within one hundred yards of our corral.

Years later, Joe Cook recalled the attack on April 4 by the Lakota warriors:[117]

I am going to describe this fight more definitely as it was our longest and the most disastrous to the Indians. We camped in the bottom about 400 yards from the creek. Our corral was about sixty yards from a hay draw that ran from the foothills to the stream. It was about fifty or sixty feet wide. Sage brush about 18 inches high grew between the corral and the draw. We had dug a trench about two feet wide and two feet deep on both sides of the corral for breastworks for the protection of our pickets. We dug holes out from two to three hundred yards from the camp. Each man cut a head log from eight to ten inches in diameter and about three feet long. We laid this on the embankment and dug a little post hole under the log, so that the Indians could not shoot us in the head while we were shooting. Our rule was that whenever any of the pickets fired a shot all the other pickets were to come into camp as soon as they could.

Near midnight on the 4th of April the pickets next to the creek saw something they took for Indians, and they fired on them. All the pickets came rushing in and the entire camp was routed out of bed. All of us stood around shivering and finally went back to bed and the pickets were sent out to their posts. My bed-fellow was on picket on the bank of the draw. He did not quite get to his picket hole when there were a dozen shots fired at him, but he was not hit by any of them. By this time there was a constant stream of fire from the draw which lasted until after sun up.

Several horses were killed, but only one man was wounded. His head log was rotten and in adjusting it a bullet went through it and made a flesh wound in his arm between the wrist and the elbow. After sunrise, we charged on the draw and killed ten Indians. One old buck, who must have been eighty years old and weighed at least three hundred pounds, had his right foot shot off just above the ankle, and his foot was hanging on by the skin on the inside of his leg. He was trying to get away, by jabbing the bones of his leg in the ground every step he took. Someone put an end to his misery by shooting him in the back with a .50 caliber needle gun.

Another young Indian, about thirty years old, was found in a little patch of brush, apparently dead. A fellow by the name of Bill Coffee [Bill Calfee], after looking at the Indian a while said, "I think I will shoot him once more for luck." He understood what Bill said, and he raised up to a sitting position and commenced to beg for his life, when Bill stuck his Colt 45 in his face and fired, blowing some of the Indian's teeth out, the bullet coming out of the back of his head. We stayed in this camp one more day. We had two big fat Newfoundland dogs that must have run to the bank of the draw to bark at the Indians for after the fight was over, the dogs' bones were lying about the fire where they were cooked. For the benefit of some of the readers of this I must tell them that a fat dog is one of the greatest luxuries that a Sioux Indian enjoys. We stayed in camp expecting the Indians to come and get their dead, but they failed to make any appearance.

Stands-With-Horns-In-Sight made the following comments to Judge Frank B. Zahn in 1956, based on what several warriors had told him when he was a little boy:[118]

Some of the warriors rode very close and it was then that dogs would come out between the wagon wheels and take after them. The warriors shot several of them [the dogs] with arrows. When the firing got too heavy the warriors retreated behind hills and small knolls and from behind these hills the warriors would hold up their coup-sticks as targets and the bullets would hit the scalps. *Wan-tan-yeya-pelo* (straight-shooters.) One warrior tied a red eagle feather to a long stick and held that up as a target and the bullets would hit the feather.

1st Lt. James Bradley compiled his account much sooner after the battle, based on recollections of the frontiersmen and from some of the warriors he interviewed at Fort Peck:[119]

An Indian sharp shooter by rolling a log before him succeeded in gaining the protection of the nearer ravine where he occupied the further side of the rifle pit abandoned by the outpost at the beginning of the fight. From this point he kept up an annoying fire, killing four horses in succession and sending his after shots in such close proximity to the men in the works that it became highly desirable to dislodge him. The fire of several good marksmen was concentrated upon him whenever he was seen to rise, but a moment afterwards would come the flash of his own gun and the zip of his bullets proving that he was still unharmed. It became a mystery how he escaped the aim of so many good marksmen; but presently it occurred to S. C. Burns to examine his position with a field glass and after a moments close survey he exclaimed: "Boys, he is fooling us with a buffalo robe." He would elevate his robe into view, draw the fire of his foes and when in comparative safety would deliver his own shot with careful aim.[120]

As daylight drew near, the prospectors made all arrangements to dislodge the Indians by a charge, 15 men being enrolled for the attempt, with Adjutant Way at their head. Both guns were charged with canister, the howitzer being aimed at the timber and the six-pounder at the ridge and simultaneously fired. As their heavy boom rolled over the valley, the charging party leaped over the works, covered by a general fire along the line, crossed the first ravine, scaled the ridge and were upon the Indians in the further ravine before they comprehended the movement. Such boldness took the Indians entirely by surprise and panic stricken they thought only of flight. A wild stampede followed from the ravine and at the same moment, encouraged by the success of the attempt, a considerable number leaped over the works and swept the Indians from the timber. Seven of the Indians were overtaken and killed, sixteen horses and many articles of personal equipment were captured and the vicinity of the camp was entirely cleared of the foe.

Oliver Hanna recalled a small piece of the action involving his tent partner, Elisha Terrill:[121]

To show how cool our men were during the fighting I will relate an incident which occurred. I was out of ammunition and crawled into a tepee for some that was in my saddle bag. There lay old Elisha Terrill running his hands into the warm ashes where we had had a fire before the Indians attacked us. I yelled, "My God, man, get out of here! You'll get killed!" He very calmly answered, "I'd as soon get shot as to lay out there and freeze to death." The bullets were whizzing through the tepee.

It was not all bravado, as Hanna continued with a discussion of the effects of artillery fire had in support of the defensive laager:[122]

There was a big cottonwood log along the brow of the gulch. The Indians rolled it over toward our camp more than twenty feet, then hid behind it and, when daylight came, they would center their fire between the wagons and were killing a lot of our horses. It took the cannoneer some little time to get his gun centered on the log, as he had to expose himself to sight the cannon, but when he did and fired the shell struck that log in the center and tore the Indians and log to pieces, throwing some of them several feet in the air. After the battle we found fragments of Indians and log.

Many years later, Jack Bean described the end of the day's fighting:[123]

The Indians had one warrior up on a point who governed their fighting and when he had seen that they were whipped he fired three shots to close the fight. We do not know how many Indians we really killed but we saw them packing off the dead on horses towards the hills at daylight. We found signs of more Indians being killed in the direction the old black gun threw its canister. Among the horses we found the intestines of one of them, but no Indian and at the little gulch which they fortified, we found a bullet hole through the log and brains all over the log but no Indians.

After the fight, many of the men reflected on their close call with real danger and combat. James Gourley reported on the schism creeping into the expedition:[124]

Here the party had a bitter trial; those who didn't know much about Indians were anxious to take the back track and get out of the country as quick as they could, but a small number of the party who knew better, and were aware that any attempt to turn back was infinitely more dangerous than to go ahead, finally persuaded the others to keep on. We then continued our way up the Rosebud nearly to the head waters, made a camp and laid over a day with the view of looking up a road through the Wolf Mountains. A party of thirty men went out to hunt up a road that day, and the Indians expecting that we were going that way had ambushed the road for the train; and we afterwards learned they had those thirty men completely in their power, but wanted to capture the whole outfit together.

Sunday, April 5, 1874 (Rosebud Creek) [N 45° 46.877', W 106° 32.425']

Sunrise occurred at 0547. The weather was rainy and foggy. Apparently the men burned three wagons that were no longer needed or that perhaps were severely damaged. The expedition moved on, leaving the bodies of the warriors where they fell; after the frontiersmen were some two miles from their old camp, warriors and non-combatant villagers swarmed over the previous entrenchments and laager. Sometime during the day, it appears that the wagon train passed by the scaffolds of a Lakota burial ground. There were several bodies on the platforms; the men threw ropes around the corner posts and pulled them out, collapsing the structures and then scattered the bodies and burial effects. This was a brutal cultural fight. In the afternoon, the expedition camped at what is today known as Lee Cemetery, a distance traveled of about twelve miles. The

frontiersmen observed warriors tracking them. The men constructed their fortifications as usual. Sunset occurred at 1848. Addison M. Quivey discussed the land and vegetation in the Rosebud valley in greater detail:[125]

Along the Rosebud, we found a narrow valley of fertile land, timbered with cottonwood, box-elder, etc. As we travel up the stream, the grass becomes better, but the geological character of the country continues nearly the same until we arrive at the Little Horn, where we find a beautiful valley, with a fine growth of white ash and other timber along the streams; and from thence to the Big Horn we have a succession of fine valleys along the creeks, and the hills and bench-lands are covered with a fine growth of grass, and the abundance of plum-bushes, grape and hop vines, prove the country to be adapted to the cultivation of the hardier fruits as well as grain and vegetables. And taking it all together, I think it the most desirable country for settlement in Montana.

The country is well watered, and we found gold wherever we prospected; but our prospecting was only on the surface,

April 5 Laager [N 45° 46.877', W 106° 32.425']

Location of expedition laager on April 5, 1874, near Rosebud Creek. The cemetery was not there in 1874 [N 45° 46.877', W 106° 32.425']. *Author photograph, October 2013*

and the gold we found was light or fine. But the character of the rocks had changed, and quartz boulders and gravel were abundant, having been brought from the mountains by the water; and I have no doubt that rich mines exist in the Big Horn Mountains, south of the Big Horn River.

Monday, April 6, 1874 (Rosebud Creek) [N 45° 45.578', W 106° 36.275']

Sunrise was at 0545. The weather was rainy and foggy. The livestock had not been grazing well lately, so Frank Grounds decided to remain in the laager until after noon. The wagon train finally got moving and traveled along the east side of the valley. Expedition members observed warriors tracking them. The valley constricted and after four miles,

Frank Grounds decided to make camp close to Rosebud Creek. The men formed a laager, but not all the livestock could be driven inside of it due to limited space. The frontiersmen tied their horses outside the corral to the wagons. Other men dug trenches. Sunset occurred at 1849. No attacks occurred during that night.[126]

Tuesday, April 7, 1874 (Rosebud Creek/ Lame Deer Creek) [N 45° 40.341', W 106° 41.685']

Sunrise occurred at 0543. The weather was bright and clear. Snow remained on the north slopes of the hills. The wagon train departed at about 0900 and marched all day. During the day, Frank Grounds observed warriors along some high bluffs, within rifle range,

Location of expedition laager on April 6, 1874, near
Rosebud Creek [N 45° 45.578', W 106° 36.275'].
Author photograph, October 2013

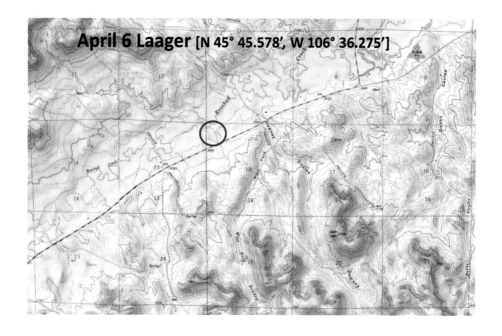

April 6 Laager [N 45° 45.578', W 106° 36.275']

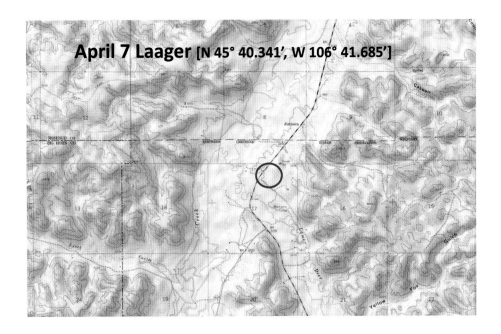

April 7 Laager [N 45° 40.341', W 106° 41.685']

near the valley. He called Billy Cameron forward and directed him to unlimber the mountain howitzer. Cameron and Charlie Wilson placed the howitzer in a good battery position and fired several rounds at the warriors on the bluff. As they were shelling the target, Frank Grounds organized about fifty men to form a charge and the group ran towards the bluff. Before they could arrive at the high ground, however, the warriors vanished over

the high ground and into the woods. The expedition resumed the march and continued into the afternoon, making some eight miles, before the wagon train camped near the mouth of Lame Deer Creek. The men observed that the grass was starting to turn green with a little warmer temperatures and that there were considerable numbers of pine trees on the bluffs. These bluffs were not as high as those previously encountered and the country was

Location of expedition laager on April 7, 1874, near the mouth of Lame Deer Creek on Rosebud Creek [N 45° 40.341', W 106° 41.685']. *Author photograph, October 2013*

Location close to the April 7, 1874, laager location, where two years later Sitting Bull conducted his famous Sun Dance before the battles against the United States Army. *Author photograph, October 2013*

more open. Two years later, Sitting Bull would perform his ritual Sun Dance shortly before the Battle of the Little Bighorn, just a few hundred yards from this location. Sunset occurred at 1850. The men had to be vigilant at night. Years later, in a previously unrecorded incident, William Officer recalled the following story to William Hamilton, as recalled by his son, Guy: [127]

Dad recounted to Hamilton one happening on the trip. Dad was sleeping in a tent with some other men. Dad's bedfellow was next to the [tent] wall. Dad said, "Bill, I don't know what woke me up, but I came out of a sound sleep standing up and I guess every hair on my head was standing up too." An Indian crawled past the sentries,

cut a hole in the tent, stabbed the man sleeping beside Dad and got away.

Wednesday, April 8, 1874 (Rosebud Creek) [N 45° 33.979', W 106° 54.337']

Sunrise came at 0541. The weather changed again and was now rainy and foggy. The wagon train began moving at 0830, crossed Lame Deer Creek and followed Rosebud Creek to the southwest. The going at first was fairly smooth until the expedition reached Muddy Creek, whose steep banks caused some delay for the wagons. By the afternoon, the valley had opened up once again and the men could get their first glimpse of the dark Wolf Mountains to the south. The wagon train passed several small creeks; the country was rolling and grassy. After traveling thirteen

Lakota rock carvings at location of Sun Dance;
expedition camped near here on April 7, 1874. *Author
photograph, June 2012*

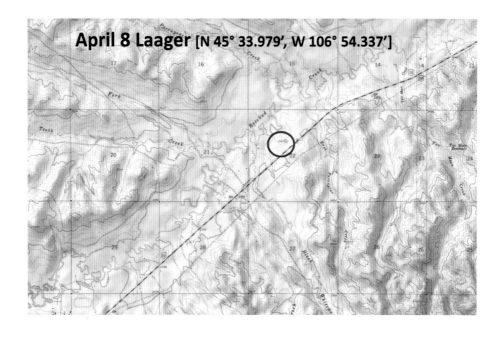

Location of expedition laager on April 8, 1874, near
Rosebud Creek [N 45° 33.979', W 106° 54.337'].
Author photograph, October 2013

miles, the expedition made camp three and one-half miles from present day Busby. Grounds located the camp in a draw protected by two ridges; it was only 200 yards from water. The men quickly dug their firing pits and trenches before the sun set at 1852.[128]

Thursday, April 9, 1874 (Davis Creek)

Shortly after sunrise at 0539, a warrior fired from a hilltop about one-half mile to the southeast of the laager, but no one was hit; the warrior quickly disappeared. The frontiersmen finished breakfast and the wagon train started moving. The weather was clear and sunny. In the early afternoon, the expedition had traveled six miles and had crossed Rosebud Creek, just south of the mouth of Davis Creek. Here they made camp, probably about noon. Frank Grounds held a short council with the leaders of the expedition to discuss whether to continue to the west up Davis Creek or to turn south and remain in the Rosebud valley. Grounds dispatched a mounted reconnaissance party of twenty-eight men to explore the country to the south. While the scouting party was gone, the rest of the men constructed rifle pits and trenches. During that afternoon, a single warrior

on a far hill fired into the area; several men returned fire with no result on either side.[129]

Sunset occurred at 1853. Later in the evening, some of the scouts returned with news that a few miles to the south, the terrain in the Rosebud valley would be impassable for the wagons and the two cannon. Frank Grounds and William Wright, the two senior officers of the expedition, held a meeting and told the men that they both believed it would not be wise to continue into the Wolf Mountains without the cannons, which they would have to do, given the terrain in that direction southward. The men took a vote and agreed with Grounds and Wright. One small group wanted to secede from the expedition and go on its own, but was talked out of this risky idea. Shortly afterward, the rest of the scouts returned; they had intercepted a small herd of buffalo, killed several and had packed out their horses with the meat—leading their mounts by foot back to camp, where everyone had enough to eat.[130]

Friday, April 10, 1874 (Head of Davis Creek) [N 45° 27.487', W 107° 8.895']

Sunrise occurred at 0537; the weather started out foggy with rain. After eating breakfast, the

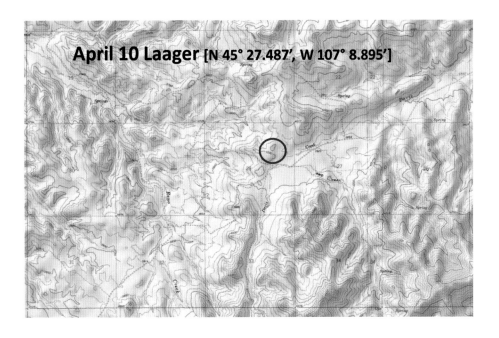

April 10 Laager [N 45° 27.487', W 107° 8.895']

frontiersmen broke camp and the wagon train headed up Davis Creek. Frank Grounds rode ahead of the main body and selected the night's campsite near the head of Davis Creek along the divide between the Rosebud and the Little Bighorn. The camp had a hollow in the middle for the laager, while the surrounding ground was suitable to dig fighting positions. In the afternoon, the weather improved. As the visibility grew greater, the flank guards spotted more and more warriors. Sunset occurred at 1854. After dark, around the campfire, Joe Cook played his violin, while Blue Dick sang. However, Billy Cameron and Charlie Wilson had more serious tasks to attend. The two artillery pieces had been firing more ammunition over the last few days than had been anticipated. The two men took stock of the remaining cannon rounds and the news was not good—they found that there were less than three cases left of the special "oyster can" canister rounds for the Big Horn Gun and only a dozen shells of the spherical case rounds for the mountain howitzer.[131]

***Saturday, April 11, 1874* (South Fork of Reno Creek) [N 45° 23.183', W 107° 13.149']** Sunrise was at 0536. After initial cloudiness, the weather turned for the better as the day progressed with bright sunshine and increased temperatures. The men opened the corral and allowed the livestock to graze a half-mile northeast of the camp in a small valley. It generally took about thirty men to guard the livestock, while the animals were feeding. On a small hill near the livestock, Oliver Hanna pulled guard duty. After riding up on his horse, he dismounted and soon observed thirty warriors approaching him some 200 yards away. Oliver remounted and attempted to flee when the warriors opened fire, hitting his horse at least once, but he made it to an outcropping of rocks and dismounted. The warriors cautiously approached and Hanna opened fire with his .50-caliber Springfield rifle. Before the warriors could close, several men at camp—seeing Hanna's predicament—mounted their horses and quickly rode to his rescue, chasing the warriors away.[132]

Frank Grounds let the livestock continue to graze after the melee until late morning, when the expedition formed up and began moving southwest to the headwaters of Ash Creek. Over the years, this tiny waterway has been known by several monikers. The Lakota called it Great Medicine Dance Creek, after originally referring to it as Spring Creek. The

April 11 Laager [N 45° 23.183', W 107° 13.149']

Crows named the stream Ash Creek, while some white settlers at the time knew it as Sundance Creek. Trail Creek, Yates Creek, and Little Wolf Creek have been transitory names of this rivulet. After George Custer's defeat at the Little Bighorn in 1876—just a few miles away—new names came into the picture of this terrain feature, initially Benteen Creek. Finally, the stream received the designation of Reno Creek—named for the second in command of the 7th Cavalry, Major Marcus Reno. Reno Creek is the name that appears on modern maps, and it is this name the study uses concerning laager locations to facilitate those wishing to visit them.

The route kept the column one mile from the bluffs to eliminate potential warrior snipers on the high ground. The wagon train reached and crossed the South Fork of Reno Creek, which had a substantial level of water in it from the melting snow runoff. Grounds selected a suitable laager site; it was not the best defensive terrain, but the best of several options. Five hundred yards to the south was a small east-west ridge and all around was thick, tall, knee high grass. To the northwest was a second hill, higher than the campsite and some 800 yards away, which probably worried the wagon train boss. The camp, however, was close to water, which facilitated its defense.

To ensure that every frontiersman had a good field of fire as they were preparing their rifle pits, Grounds ordered that all the grass in and around the campsite be burned, much to the consternation of some of the teamsters, who thought that their animals should be grazing on the grass instead. Some of the picket positions were 550 feet from the center of the laager. Sunset occurred at 1856; as the last light of day faded, the men observed roughly 300 head of buffalo charge out of the mouth of the main canyon. Grabbing their rifles, the frontiersmen killed three of the large animals. However, what the men did not know at the time was that a Lakota warrior named Red Hawk and a small band of fellow hunters had come across the bison farther up in the narrow

portion of the canyon and had started to drive them into open terrain to better kill the beasts. Red Hawk and the warriors had no idea that the expedition was close at hand until they were next to their quarry, looked up, and saw the campsite. At this point, the warriors hurried hastily away into the timber along the creek, but not before one warrior spotted Oliver Hanna and fired at his horse, striking it several times, but at the same time revealing the presence of the warriors to the frontiersmen.[133]

In the twilight, several frontiersmen rode out from the laager and killed several buffalo, providing meat that night for the entire expedition. However, the other foodstuffs were running low and Frank Grounds began rationing canned provisions. Soon, even the "Cincinnati Chicken" (salt pork,) "Embalmed Beef" (canned beef) and "Corned Willie" (corned beef) would be gone. After the meal, the men went to sleep; the weather was warm enough that they did not need to use the few tents they had packed in the wagons. All the while, Red Hawk and several other warriors were 200 yards away in the timber—watching them.[134] 1st Lt. James Bradley later wrote this summary of the day:[135]

On the 11th of April, they arrived on the first branch of the little Big Horn (now Custer) River, a dry creek with water standing in pools…the Wolf Mountains lay in their front, something like three quarters of a mile distant, cut by three dark canyons, sheltering a heavy growth of timber.

Addison M. Quivey later wrote about an incident that happened sometime that night:[136]

On the night of the 11th of April, one of our pickets fired at what he supposed to be an Indian, but nothing more being seen, the night passed quietly.

Hanna's horse died during the night of its wounds.[137] Unknown to Frank Grounds and the other men on the expedition, Hump and about 600 warriors rode through the rough terrain toward the camp, dismounted out of earshot, and quietly took up hidden positions in the timber around the laager. A few days before, the wagon train had been lucky during the night attack by the Lakota. Tomorrow would be different.

***Sunday, April 12, 1874* (South Fork of Reno Creek/Battle of Great Medicine Dance Creek) [N 45° 23.183', W 107° 13.149'] (later Little Bighorn) [N 45° 18.217', W 107° 22.140']**
Based on all the recollections and previous analyses, it's believed the second major battle between the warriors and the wagon train occurred at this location. Thirty-five years later, Tom Allen referred to it as the South Fork of Reno Creek. Given that at the time of the battle that name for the stream was not in use, this study has chosen to term the engagement the Battle of Great Medicine Dance Creek in honor of the participants that fielded the greatest number of men in the fight.

The Battle of Great Medicine Dance Creek of the 1874 Yellowstone Wagon Road and Prospecting Expedition unfolded in the following manner. During the night, one of the men on guard as a picket thought he saw a warrior in the darkness (he probably actually did) and fired, but could not be sure if he hit his target. The waning crescent moon, with 20% of the moon's visible disk illuminated, rose at 0402; it would not set until 1355. The men woke up and climbed out of their firing positions no later than 0515 to be prepared for any potential attack at dawn by the warriors. Sunrise occurred at 0534. Probably about 0600, herders took the livestock to water at several pools below the laager. After watering, perhaps at 0620, the herd crossed the stream and began grazing on a large flat area to the east—the night before having been spent on ground where the grass had been burned the afternoon before. About twenty men, standing in small groups, guarded the herd as the sun continued to rise in the Montana sky. The men cooked breakfast; no pickets saw any of the several hundred warriors, who had crept closer and closer to the laager.

The actual fighting began about 0800—when three groups of mounted warriors rushed the horse herd. The overall fight lasted four hours, although combat was not continuous throughout the morning. The two cannons

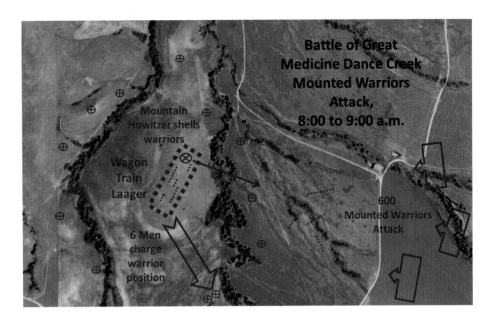

probably commenced firing at 0815, about the same time that Adjutant Eli Way called for volunteers to charge the warrior positions. The first round from the mountain howitzer exploded extremely short, which caused some of the loose horses of the frontiersmen to stampede in the wrong direction away from the laager. The men out on the picket lines abandoned their positions in the face of the mounted enemy charge and ran toward the laager. At 0820 six frontiersmen dashed from the laager south some 250 yards to a small hill that the warriors were attempting to occupy to give them a position of advantage against the camp. The frontiersmen probably gained the summit at 0835, putting the warriors there to flight within about ten minutes.

About 0900, a group of warriors took possession of a ridge that was higher than the camp and north of it (bullets and empty cartridge casings indicated warrior positions 650 yards southeast of the laager, 700 yards northwest of the laager and 900 yards north of the laager as well) and began to fire into the camp. After initially returning fire for a few minutes, at perhaps about 0915, Frank Grounds, Eli Way, and other leaders would have held a quick discussion and decided to

launch two attack parties against this key terrain and expel the warriors with a charge. The two parties may have been formed, briefed, and ready to move by 0940. The plan was for one party to move directly against the ridge and the other group to diverge to the east and intercept the warriors in their retreat. Given the distance, the two groups of attacking frontiersmen were probably on the ridge by 1000. In the group of frontiersmen that attacked directly toward the warriors were Eli Way, Oliver Hanna, Doc Wickersham, Archie Campbell, Tom Allen, and John Anderson. Only two frontiersmen from the other group reached good firing positions to intercept the fleeing warriors. This portion of the fighting was probably over by 1015.

At about this time, a warrior chief, possibly of the Brulé sub-tribe (Sičháŋu Oyáte), dressed in a war bonnet and buckskin jacket and riding a black horse rode up the ridge. The six frontiersmen, under Eli Way, fired at the chief, wounding his horse and knocking the warrior to the ground. As the men approached the fallen Lakota, other warriors began firing toward the area to protect their chief. John Anderson closed on the chief, firing his pistol that finally killed the warrior's horse and

165

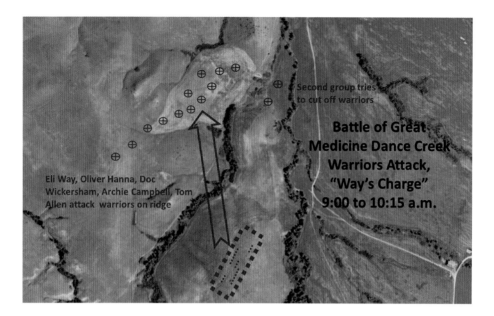

Eli Way, Oliver Hanna, Doc Wickersham, Archie Campbell, Tom Allen attack warriors on ridge

Second group tries to cut off warriors

Battle of Great Medicine Dance Creek Warriors Attack, "Way's Charge" 9:00 to 10:15 a.m.

causing the chief to jump to his feet. The Lakota chief then drew his knife in an attempt to kill the strange-looking "white man." Meanwhile, the warriors stopped firing for fear of hitting their leader and the two men engaged in a titanic death struggle in which only one man would remain alive.

Anderson was finally able to grab the chief's wrist and wrenched the warrior's knife free, and in an instant used the weapon to kill him. That energized the nearby warriors, who opened a withering fire and in a feat of strength, Anderson lifted the chief's dead body and used it as a shield against the warrior gunfire, as he quickly scrambled to a nearby coulee to find cover. After this seminal incident, the remaining warriors fled from the hill. Anderson subsequently scalped the dead chief—after Doc Wickersham and Archie Campbell had tried to do so—and took his ornate jacket, leaving the body in the coulee. Several warriors later turned around and rode hell for leather at the gallop, recovered the body of the fallen chief and retreated with it for a later proper burial.

The fighting continued at other locations around the laager. Probably about 1030, a group of mounted warriors rode close to the herd animals and attempted to capture them.

At this key moment, Jack Bean stripped the buckskin cover from his Sharps rifle and ran toward the warriors, until he got ahead of the herd, at which time he began whipping the animals back toward the wagons with his gun cover. Seeing the warriors continue their advance toward him, Jack paused long enough to shoot the closest warrior from his horse. Seeing Bean in the lead, several comrades ran from the laager to his position and joined in the fire. Within minutes, the mounted warriors swerved away from the camp. Bean probably shot and killed two of them during this part of the fight. However, losses were not solely among the Lakota and Cheyenne. Reports on when Zack Yates was killed vary. Many described that he died instantly, shot through the heart. However, Tom Allen recalled that the wound was higher up, that it took Yates twenty minutes to expire, and that the warrior who had shot Yates was subsequently wounded.

No later than 1100, the Battle of Great Medicine Dance Creek was over. One of the frontiersmen found a new Sharps carbine left by the warriors, an indicator that fresh warriors were coming from the reservations better armed—a phenomenon that would occur many times in future battles between the Lakota and

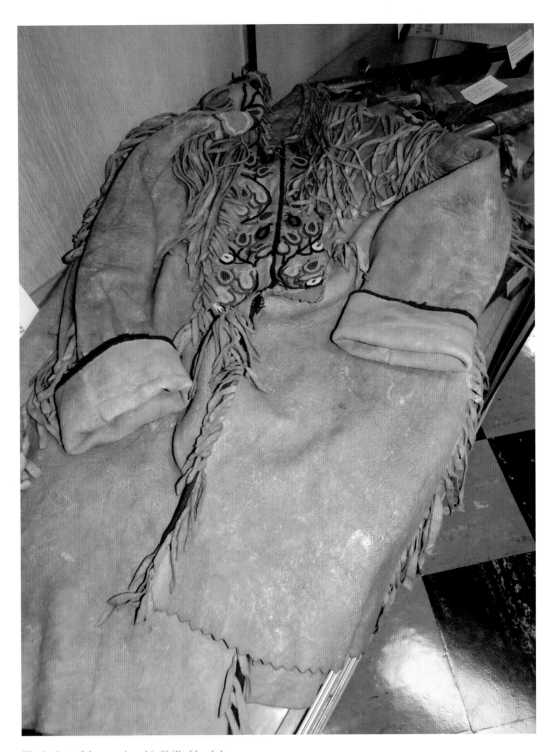

The jacket of the warrior chief killed by John
Anderson is on display at the Gallatin County
Courthouse. *Author photograph, October 2013*

Photograph of the jacket worn by the warrior killed by John Anderson at the Battle of Great Medicine Dance Creek on April 12, 1874. *Author photograph, October 2013*

Another photograph of the jacket worn by the warrior. John Anderson went to his grave believing that the warrior chief he vanquished was the son of Sitting Bull. *Author photograph, October 2013*

the US Army. A few minutes later, a somber group of frontiersmen gathered, and a spokesman—perhaps Frank Grounds— apparently said a few words of remembrance for Zack Yates; someone suggested naming the small creek leading off to the north as Yates Creek, a name that would last only a few years. The men then hitched the mule and oxen teams to the wagons and formed up the wagon train; they placed the remains of Yates in one of the wagons for later burial. Just before noon— perhaps at 1130—the expedition hit the trail and moved out to the southwest. It appears that the expedition left one tent at the campsite;

perhaps it had been damaged by the gunfire. Although the weather was good, the frontiersmen could see storm clouds off in the distance. The men crossed several drainages throughout the afternoon and by late evening they had traveled thirteen miles, crossing the Little Bighorn Valley at the mouth of Gray Blanket Creek. The expedition made camp on the edge of a large plateau some 800 yards west of the Little Bighorn (south-southwest of the current town of Lodge Grass.) The men then dug trenches around the positions and constructed rifle pits.

Sunset occurred at 1857. After dark, the men assembled near the largest rifle pit,

A third photograph of the jacket worn by the warrior. Jack Bean wrote that he believed the fallen chief was the son of Black Moon. *Author photograph, October 2013*

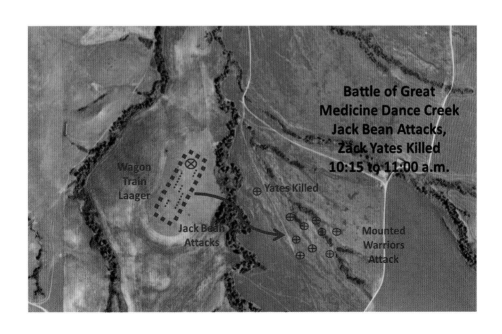

Battle of Great Medicine Dance Creek Jack Bean Attacks, Zack Yates Killed 10:15 to 11:00 a.m.

Wagon Train Laager

⊗

⊕ Yates Killed

Jack Bean Attacks

⊕ ⊕ ⊕ ⊕
⊕ ⊕
⊕ ⊕ ⊕

Mounted Warriors Attack

Laager area was in the center and left about 200 yards in front of the barbed wire fence. *Author photograph, June 2015*

carrying the body of Zack Yates. The men wrapped the body in a buffalo robe, place it in the pit and covered it with earth. They took the dirt from the pit and disguised it as a defensive berm near a second rifle pit, and buried an iron picket a foot below the ground at the head of the grave. At some point, the men held a short service at the grave; they then laid out their blankets and buffalo robes and slept in the open; a few men slept in tents. During the night, a heavy storm moved into the area, soaking everything.[138] 1st Lt. James Bradley later wrote the most complete summary of the day's action:[139]

Preparatory to moving, the stock attended by the herders had been driven down to water, many of the animals after drinking, having crossed to the opposite side of the creek while the remainder were huddled in the bed of the stream. At this moment dense swarms of mounted Indians suddenly emerged from each of the canyons and dashed at full speed across the intervening ground toward the herd. The alarm was sounded, and while efforts were made to gather and drive in the herd, the prospectors seized their arms and ran down the slope toward the Indians, firing as they went. At the same time the cannons were rapidly served, delivering their fire on the high ground on which the camp was pitched, over the heads of the force in front. The steep bank of the creek rendered it difficult to get the herd in motion toward the camp while the side of the bank running down

Laager area was in the low ground to the right. Warriors occupied the three hillocks in the center of the photo until routed during "Way's Charge." *Author photograph, June 2015*

toward them from the camp and the noise of their guns caused many of the animals to break away in the opposite direction and run directly toward the Indians, who still came on with confidence.

They were now getting so near that some of the herders became alarmed and began to abandon the herd and but for the courage of one man, many of the animals would undoubtedly have been lost. This was Jack Bean who from his uniform prudence, in providing against danger, had been deemed timid by his comrades, but who now, as such men are apt to in the presence of eminent peril, rose to a sublimity of courage. Stripping the cover from his gun, he ran toward the Indians at the top of his speed until he had got in

advance of the herd, and began whipping the animals back with the gun cover, running from one to the other, and exerting himself with such energy, that, at last, he changed their course toward the camp.

Keeping his eyes on the Indians he saw that they were crowding upon him and paused long enough to shoot the foremost headlong from his horse, which dashed on and joined the herd. Bean had taken this advanced and perilous position without knowing whether his comrades would sustain him or not, but fortunately for him and to their honor, they did and following as closely as their speed would admit now began to arrive just in time to check the advance of the Sioux, ere they reached the herd. A few more directed

Small depression is last evidence of a firing pit dug by a frontiersman on the high ground overlooking the laager. *Author photograph, June 2015*

shots at short range caused the Indians to swerve from their course. Then the herd was safely corralled and the prospectors fell back within the protection of their works. During the fight outside with the herd, Zack Yates was shot through the heart and instantly killed; his comrades carrying his body back to the works upon their retreat.

The Indians now spread themselves around the camp and taking to the ridges and ravines opened fire which the whites returned whenever a fair mark was presented. South of the camp and near the creek about 250 yards distant stood a small hill, which as it commanded the camp, the Indians were anxious to occupy, but could only do so by running the gauntlet of a severe fire from the whites. By riding rapidly in a circle on the plains beyond, until near the hill and then dropping forward at full speed, several Indians had successively gained its cover until gathering confidence with numbers, one of them raised and fired, killing a horse. "We must charge that hill at once," cried Adjutant Way, and called for volunteers to make the attempt. Some half dozen offered themselves and as they dashed over the intervening space their advance was covered by a rapid fire from the camp, which kept the Indians down and prevented them from discovering the movement.

Rolling terrain to the north, west, and south provided the warriors with numerous concealed routes that enabled them to approach the laager unseen. *Author photograph, June 2015*

As they reached the summit the firing ceased and a moment after to the consternation of the Indians, they were upon them. They opened fire at short range while the Indians fled for their lives and notwithstanding they had to traverse a space of several hundred yards, exposed to the bullets of their foes, all but one gained the cover of a distant ridge, apparently unharmed. The fire had ceased from the camp, all remaining silent but excited spectators of the race, amid the bullets of the charging party, the last Indian whipping furiously was about to pass the ridge and in an instant more would have been safe, when he was seen to bound upward from his saddle and fell to the ground amid tumultuous cheers from the camp.

The fight had now lasted for about an hour, the Indians having done most of the firing after the herd was saved. North of the camp at a distance of some 500 yards was situated a ridge rather higher than camp, behind which a considerable force of Indians had gathered. It was the only position from which their fire was at all annoying and at last it was resolved to expel them from it by a charge. Two parties were formed—one to move directly against the ridge and the other to diverge to the right and intercept the Indians in their retreat. The conformation of the ground rendering it probable that they would flee in that direction when dislodged. This plan was carried out and as the Indians did not see the parties start, it would but for an untoward accident have taken them completely by surprise. An old mare with her colt had been permitted to range loose around the camp and when the charge was made, the mare took fright and led the way over the ridge. At her sudden appearance among the Indians, being on the further slope, they knew that it boded some mischief to them and without waiting to learn its character, mounted and fled in hot haste.

Before the charging party reached the ridge, the ground was entirely cleared of their foes, many of them did not draw rein within the space of two miles. As had been expected, a large number of the Indians fled along the ridge in the direction taken by the second party and had the latter been able to get into position sooner many of the Indians must have fallen under their fire. As it was, only two men arrived on the ground and they only in time to get a shot at the rear of the retreating Sioux. Their retreat was covered by a savage known as the Brule chief, who reined in his horse and tried to check the panic of his warriors. But it was in vain and as if ashamed of their cowardice, he turned to look at his pursuers, inclined not to leave the field.

But his temerity cost him dear for a shot grazed his neck and brought him to the ground. John Anderson, a colored man, whose great strength had enabled him to keep the lead during the charge, ran forward to scalp him, but at that moment the chief recovered and arose upon his feet. His warriors had by this time, gained cover not far distant, when they checked their flight and opened fire. The bullets fell thick around Anderson, but he kept on, threw his left arm against the chief, and with his right gave him a fatal stab with his knife. The chief fell and Anderson gained the cover of the

ridge unharmed. Several attempts were made to secure the scalp, but the Indians fired briskly upon the parties attempting and balked them for a time. It was obtained however in a fragmentary condition, as well as the chief's headdress or war bonnet as it is usually called on the frontier.

The charging parties then returned to camp and the Indians gave them no further molestation. The body of the chief had scarcely been quitted by the whites when two young warriors mounted upon fine spirited steeds rode to the spot and after maneuvering for a few minutes as if to see whether they were to be fired upon, together raised it from the ground, without quitting their saddles, and bore it away. The loss sustained by the Indians in this action is unknown, but at one time six of their number were borne from the field either killed or badly wounded. The only casualty among the whites was the killing of Yates, but several horses were killed and wounded.

Joe Cook later provided a description of the fighting that cost Zack Yates his life:[140]

About four days afterwards, they tried to get our horses, we had just turned them out to graze in the morning, and just as they began to feed the Indians came out of the mountains north of us, and tried to stampede the herd. They are great bluffers. As soon as they came in sight, they began yelling and shooting, thereby thinking to intimidate our herders. In the melee one of our boys shot one of the Indians off his horse, and the horse came into camp with our horses. About ten of us started out to scalp the Indian, and when we were about half way, an Indian about five hundred yards up the creek fired at the bunch of us, killing Zack Yates. Zack was walking behind me and a little to the left. Someone said, 'Zack is shot.' I looked around and he was lying on his back with his legs drawn up against his stomach and his hands clasping his stomach. I stooped down and asked him where he was hit, but he made no reply, and in three or four seconds he began to straighten out his limbs and with a quiver of his body, life was extinct.

Four of us picked him up and started to the camp. I presume the Indians wanted us to leave him where he fell so they could get his scalp, for they poured their bullets around us like hail until we got out of gun shot. We hauled his body that day, and after dark we buried him. We filled his grave that was dug right alongside of a rifle pit, so that the mound over his grave was a part of the breastworks on that side of the corral. We had to do this to keep the Indians from digging him up and scalping him. Mr. Yates was the only man that was killed, and only two were wounded.

Addison M. Quivey picked up on the action that followed:[141]

In the morning the stock was turned out to graze as usual, attended by a guard; and while most of us were eating our breakfast, an alarm was sounded, and a large force of Indians were seen coming out of ravines at the head of a little valley to the south of our camp (which was on a hill,) and coming like a whirlwind down upon our herd, evidently expecting to stampede our stock. Our herders were immediately reinforced, and fire opened on the Indians as they came within range. Some corralled the stock, while others fought the Indians back. In doing so, one man, Z.T. Yates, from Boulder Valley, was killed, but was carried into camp by his companions.

The Indians quickly took to the ridges and ravines on all sides of camp, and opened fire, which was returned whenever it was possible to do so effectively. A large number of the enemy took possession of a hill about two hundred and fifty yards

south of our corral, and firing rapidly, were doing some damage, when a party of our men charged them and drove them with loss, as several were seen to fall from their horses as they were running away. In this charge a new Sharps cavalry carbine, fifty caliber, was picked up, which an Indian had dropped.

Shortly after, a charge was made to the north of our camp, and several Indians killed; one, evidently a chief, fell into our hands. The enemy soon after left. During the charge on our herd at the commencement of the fight, one Indian was shot from his horse, which ran into our herd and was captured. Our loss was one man killed, and several horses killed and wounded. Of the Indian loss we know but little; only one scalp was taken, but at one time we saw them carrying away six, who were either killed or badly wounded.

Addison M. Quivey continued his description:[142]

We soon broke camp and moved on, and in the afternoon reached the Little Horn [Little Bighorn], crossed it, and camped on a bench overlooking the valley. Here, during the night, we buried our comrade, Yates, in our trenches, and so effectually concealed his grave that there was no danger of the Indians finding it. Here a storm set in, and we were obliged to lay over, after which we had almost constant storms for nearly two weeks, and the country was almost impassable for wagons. Indians were all the time in sight during the day.

James Gourley added his own interpretation to what happened in this Battle of Great Medicine Dance Creek that day:[143]

We next crossed over to another fork of the Rosebud where there was open country and made camp on a low bill that was almost surrounded by a valley. In this camp about nine o'clock in the morning, while our horses were turned out to graze, the Indians in three columns made a dash on the herd. Fortunately, perhaps, our horses were worn out, and so many had the epizootic [possibly equine flu] that they failed to stampede them. They came after them in Indian fashion, swinging their blankets, whooping and yelling, making all the noise they could. But our men were too prompt in getting around the herd and turning the stock into the corral. We didn't lose a horse. We captured one of their horses, his rider having been shot off, and the horse running and joining our herd.

Here we had one very exciting little scene. An Indian had been knocked off his horse by a bullet, being creased, not badly hurt, but came too about the time some of the boys were trying to get his scalp off. As there was no other way out of it, Anderson stuck his knife into the Indian and, then took his scalp. One young fellow who had been listening to the stories of the old mountaineers and frontiersmen around the camp-fires on the way down the Yellowstone about the scalping they had done, used to comment on the brutality of such a thing, and would get disgusted as he heard the stories told. It so happened, that he was one of the parties who attempted to scalp the Indian on this occasion, but failing to do that, cut off the Indian's ears as a memento. He was a nice, well-educated boy, and had been a druggist in Bozeman.

While this was going on, there were not less than 300 Indians within 400 yards shooting at them. It was a very dangerous piece of work. In an attempt to secure the scalp of an Indian that had been knocked off his horse, one of our best men, Zack Yates, got shot through the heart, dying almost instantly. In packing him to the corral, we concealed his death as well as we could, but hardly hoped to do so completely, because the Indians are very apt to discover such things. Here we buried

Yates in the breastworks so that the Indians couldn't find him.

James Gourley continued to recall the day in this manner; he mistakenly mentioned the Rosebud instead of the Little Bighorn:[144]

After the fight was over we proceeded to hitch up, and pulled out as though nothing had happened. We crossed the Rosebud that day and made camp on a level bench about 600 yards from the creek, where we thought we were pretty safe. We laid over there a day to recuperate our stock. The travelling was fearful, the wagons rolling up great coils of gumbo, so that we had to stop every little while and cut it off with axes and shovels.

Finally, in a letter to researcher Walter Camp in 1912, Tom Allen, a participant in the expedition, wrote:[145]

The second fight of which you speak took place on South Fork of Reno Creek, where Yates was killed. After the second battle we moved down Gray Blanket and crossed Little Horn at the mouth of Gray Blanket. We buried Yates on the Little Horn and layed there one day.

Monday, April 13, 1874 (Little Bighorn) [N 45° 18.217', W 107° 22.140']

Sunrise was at 0532. The storm continued to rage and the rain turned to snow that melted as it hit the ground. During the day, several herders attempted to take the livestock to water, but at each attempt, groups of warriors appeared along the timber lines. As there were no trees near the laager, woodcutters had to travel several hundred yards to cut firewood for cooking, but once again the warriors appeared and the woodcutters subsequently had to be escorted by large numbers of men to and from their work. Inside the laager, the precipitation, nature of the heavy clay soil and heavy traffic by the large animals and many men made the earth a deep "sea of

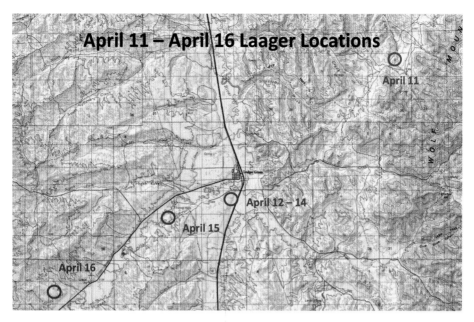

April 11 – April 16 Laager Locations

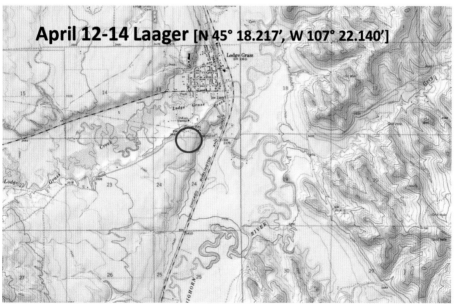

April 12-14 Laager [N 45° 18.217', W 107° 22.140']

gumbo" that clung to every wagon wheel, hoof and foot and made movement ponderous and difficult. Frank Grounds determined that sending anyone out—to hunt large game for food—further than where the woodcutters had been, would be too dangerous and the men started dipping in to their meager reserve rations.[146] After a miserable day, sunset occurred at 1858.

Tuesday, April 14, 1874 (Little Bighorn) [N 45° 18.217', W 107° 22.140']

Sunrise occurred at 0530. The storm had continued through the night, returning to wet, heavy snow as temperatures dropped. The morning was stormy and cold, with temperatures hovering around freezing. It snowed all day. On the plateau where the expedition had laagered, the wind was whipping about in all

Location of expedition laager from April 12–14, 1874, near the Little Bighorn River and present-day Lodge Grass [N 45° 18.217', W 107° 22.140']. *Author photograph, October 2013*

directions. It remained impossible to take the herds to water and undoubtedly some of the animals were becoming sick and weak. Frank Grounds concluded that the expedition should now turn back to Bozeman, given the increasingly bad weather and the ever-increasing presence of warriors. The expedition leader expressed his concern to a gathering of the men. William T. Hamilton, who already possessed a stellar résumé as a scout and Indian fighter, wanted to continue south and not turn back, as did Eli Way—who by now had an excellent reputation among the men. Many of the younger men, led by Hugh Hoppe, also wanted to continue south and head for Goose Creek in the Big Horn Mountains, which he reckoned was forty-five miles south

in the Dakota—later Wyoming Territory. Hoppe mesmerized "the boys" with tales of the elusive—and fabulously lucrative—Lost Cabin Mine.[147]

The Lost Cabin Mine became one of the most famous lost gold mine legends of the entire West. The story went that in 1863 three prospectors, Allen Hurlbert, a man named Cox, and a third miner named Jones, ventured into the wilds in what would become northeastern Wyoming, in quest of gold– the exact location was in the Wind Rivers, the Big Horns, or Crazy Woman Creek. Finding traces of the mineral, they built a cabin and a sluice to work their discovery. Lakota or Cheyenne warriors ambushed the miners and all but Hurlbert were killed. In October of that

Another view of the center of the laager from April 12–14, 1874 [N 45° 18.217', W 107° 22.140']. The men buried the body Zach Yates somewhere near here. *Author photograph, October 2013*

year, this lone survivor finally made it out of the wilderness and ran into army troops; he showed the troopers some 370 ounces of gold nuggets, worth $7,000 at the time.

At this point, the legend had two alternative endings. In the first, Allen Hurlbert sickened and died without providing a map or good directions to the mine, leaving future prospectors to speculate on where it might be. The second version maintained that he assembled a group of partners to accompany him back to the mine, but on their journey, a group of warriors massacred them, leaving no survivors.

Other embellishments to the story appeared over the years. Jim Bridger supposedly rediscovered the mine, while in another tale, Belgian Roman Catholic priest Father Pierre-Jean De Smet was involved. This version stated that Father De Smet was in the Big Horn Mountains in search of a Lakota tribe to which he planned to preach. Stopping to water his horse, the padre noticed a small cabin nestled along the side of a hill. Entering, he saw a decaying corpse and a pile of gold on the wooden floor. Saying a prayer for the deceased, the father then left, keeping his find secret until 1873, when he was preparing to leave the Wyoming Territory and return to St. Louis. In failing health (he would die in St. Louis later that year) De Smet confided in an old Indian friend known as Running Deer and told him the story of the cabin. Old Running Deer, with a new spring in his step, bid Father De Smet farewell and hurried to the Wyoming

Territory town of Buffalo, where he found a prospector and old friend named Joe "Old Joe" Svenson, who had spent considerable time searching for the cabin himself. In a secluded location, Running Deer told Old Joe the story of the Catholic priest. After he finished, Running Deer was surprised when he suddenly saw Joe's revolver pointed at him; he never knew what hit him when Old Joe pulled the trigger to ensure the secret remained with him. Leaving the dead Running Deer, Old Joe made his way to the Wyoming Saloon on Buffalo's Main Street, but accidentally was struck by a passing stagecoach and died in the street. It was all very confusing— Kit Carson, for example, before his death in 1868, was convinced that the mine and cabin were in the Black Hills, not the Bighorn Mountains. Most of the stories, however, hinted that the mine was some three days travel from the ruins of Fort Reno; it was on a running stream; a cabin had been built, which was still standing some years later, and that a sluice had been built along the stream.

Hoppe did not state that he knew exactly where the Lost Cabin Mine was located, but his description of the untold riches it might contain was almost as exciting a story. Grounds suggested that a vote be taken concerning where the expedition should go next. By a vote of 129 to 16—with the officers not voting—the men decided to head south toward Goose Creek and perhaps find the Lost Cabin Mine. Frank Grounds, knowing that if the expedition split up, the warriors would destroy both elements piecemeal, said that he would take the wagon train toward Goose Creek as the majority wanted, but suggested that the best route to travel was to initially head west, hitting the old Bozeman Trail, at which point they could turn south on a much-better trail. The men agreed. The weather began to clear at 1730.[148] Sunset occurred at 1859. 1st Lt. James Bradley later wrote of the conditions that day and the discussion about what to do next.[149]

The epizootic, then so prevalent throughout the United States had broken out among their horses and the draft animals were hardly able to stagger through a five or six mile march, while few of the saddle horses were required to do more than carry themselves. Nearly all the more experienced frontiersmen were convinced of the propriety, almost necessity of immediate return, and a canvass of the opinions of other members of the expedition showed this to be the opinion of the majority. At this juncture, a German of the party came forward with a story that he had passed through the country a few years previous in company with three California miners, who had obtained rich returns of gold in Goose Creek. He had seen them sink the hole, wash from pans of the dirt and afterwards accompanying them to an assay office with the yield, which proved to be $1.10 to the pan. He thought he could go to the spot and the enthusiasm created by the story was such that when upon the evening of the arrival in this camp a vote was taken on the question of their [immediately to Bozeman] return, and only 16 voted affirmative.

In Bozeman, a mail carrier that had been sent to the expedition returned after he could not find it.[150] Some 225 miles north of the Yellowstone River at Fort Benton, J.L. Vernon and James Rockfellow arrived from the expedition. Sensing that something was amiss in their story, Deputy US Marshal Charles D. Hard sent a messenger to Fort Shaw, directing that a telegram be sent to Bozeman requesting clarification of the role that these two men had on the expedition.[151]

Wednesday, April 15, 1874 (Lodge Grass Creek) [N 45° 17.158', W 107° 25.662']

Sunrise occurred at 5:28 a.m. The storm had stopped, but the ground remained extremely muddy. Many of the horses refused to budge, having come down with the epizootic. The wagon train did not start moving west until noon, heading southwest in the general direction of the Bozeman Trail, which the day before

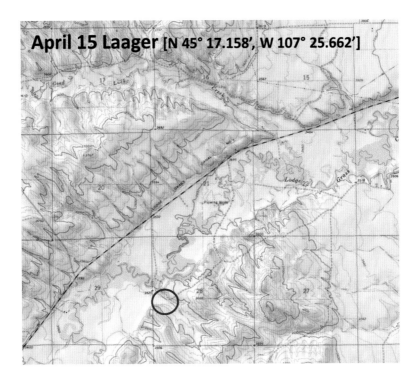

April 15 Laager [N 45° 17.158′, W 107° 25.662′]

the men had agreed would be their next goal. As the livestock passed any grass, the animals strained to move toward it, as they had not eaten in days. The expedition became strung out, as healthy animals tried to move through the "gumbo," while the sick and weak livestock lagged to the rear. By evening, the expedition had made only four miles before Frank Grounds led the wagon train to high ground just south of Lodge Grass Creek, less than one-half mile from that stream. A deep coulee ran through the middle of what would become the laager area, so the train's draft animals could be taken directly to water and return to a grassy slope to try and graze. Because of the condition of the oxen, the men burned two wagons.[152] Sunset occurred at 1901.

After dark, several men began constructing a fake grave, first digging a large hole. At the bottom, they placed one of the spherical cannon balls. Billy Cameron very carefully loosened the fuse and unscrewed it from the projectile. One could not be too careful building a booby trap or it might explode prematurely and kill everyone around. Billy then placed a friction primer—normally used to detonate the propellant charge in the mountain howitzer—through the fuse hole and into the center of the projectile. Cameron then carefully attached a long wire to the fuse and gingerly held the wire, as a few other men—equally as careful—put pieces of the iron wheel hubs from the burned wagons, as well as nails, bolts, broken cooking utensils, a broken spur and a few horse shoes for good luck on top of the cannon ball. It is possible that Cameron added a few sticks of dynamite to the mix. The men then covered the booby trap with a layer of dirt, while Billy Cameron fastened the end of the wire to the bottom of

Location of the laager for April
15, 1874. *Author photograph,*
October 2013

Another view of the likely location of the laager for
April 15, 1874 [N 45° 17.158', W 107° 25.662'].
Author photograph, October 2013

a newly made cross. He finished by gingerly pushing the cross into the fresh mound and packing dirt around the bottom of it to hold it upright and in place.[153]

Given the frequency that he had seen warriors over the last several days, Frank Grounds posted a reinforced guard force. Although he did not realize it, Grounds and the wagon train may have been under the observation of Sitting Bull, based on events that would soon unfold. Addison M. Quivey picked up on the action that followed:[154]

Our next day's travel was not more than three miles, when we lay over another day on a high point near Grass Lodge Creek. At this place, in the afternoon, the Indians attempted to drive in our pickets, who were quickly reinforced, when the Indians left. Here we were obliged to leave two heavy wagons, our teams being so reduced we found it impossible to take them farther.

James Gourley recalled the day in this manner; he used the name Long Creek instead of Grass Lodge Creek (Lodge Grass Creek) in his description:[155]

We next travelled about three miles over to a little point close to Long Creek. While we were resting the stock here, we dug a grave and proceeded apparently to bury a body. We thought that the Indians knew that they had probably killed one of our men. But instead of burying a body we buried a loaded shell, over which we placed log chains and a few sticks of giant powder and such other missiles as we thought would take effect in case the Indians attempted to open the grave. The gunner fixed the primers and laid a board over the shell and other things, and arranged it so that if any one attempted to lift the board up at either end, it would be certain to explode the charge. We afterwards found out that four or five Indians were killed there in trying to open the grave.

1st Lt. James Bradley later wrote of the day; he pegged a close encounter with two pickets on the evening of April 14. Other sources described that it actually happened the next morning:[156]

The next day a camp was made upon Grass Lodge Creek, a march of only three miles. The camp was pitched upon a high point overlooking the valley, but fortified as usual, notwithstanding the material strength of the place, a sham grave was here made, in which a loaded shell was placed so arranged that it would explode, in case the grave was disturbed. At this camp two heavy wagons were burned, to increase the teams upon those retained. Two members of the picket guard had this evening a narrow escape; they were lying carelessly on the slope of the hill, paying little attention to the country in their front, when five mounted Indians stealthily descended the opposite slope and were almost upon them, ere they discovered their approach. They had barely time to throw themselves into their saddles, ere the Indians dashed over the summit, and commenced firing at close range. The guards fled for the camp at full speed, and the Indians gave them a hard chase for several hundred yards, firing upon them at every step, but the speed of the horses kept them in front, till they neared the camp when the Indians drew off.

The next morning would bring the events that caused the story of the 1874 Yellowstone Wagon Road and Prospecting Expedition to pass from story to saga.

Notes

1. Camp Manuscripts, Box 4: Folder 5, Envelope 6—Barkley statement of 1874.

2. "Report of the Executive Committee of the Yellowstone Wagon Road & Prospecting Expedition," *Avant Courier* (Bozeman,) February 6, 1874, 3.

3. Carter, 31; and "The Expedition Moving to the Front," *Avant Courier* (Bozeman,) February 6, 1874, 2.

4. Collection 1250, Folder 41, 1.

5. Marga Lincoln, "History in the Baking: Savor Montana's early recipes with 'A Taste of the Past' presentation," *Independent Record* (Helena, Montana,) March 24, 2013.

6. Collection 1250, Folder 41, 1.

7. Ibid.

8. "Report of the Executive Committee of the Yellowstone Wagon Road & Prospecting Expedition," *Avant Courier* (Bozeman,) February 20, 1874, 2; and Collection 1250, Folder 41, 1.

9. Collection 1250, Folder 41, 2; Topping, 104; and Weibert, *The 1874 Invasion*, 11-12.

10. Quivey, 269.

11. Ibid.

12. Ibid.

13. Brown and Willard, *Trails*, 9.

14. Collection 1250, Folder 41, 2; Hutchins, "Poison in the Pemmican," 10; Weibert, *The 1874 Invasion*, 12; and Jim Annin, *Horace Countryman—Unsung Hero*, self-published. 8.

15. Quivey, 270.

16. The agency was established in 1869 a few miles below the great bend of the Yellowstone River, on the opposite side of the Yellowstone from Benson's Landing and near the mouth of Mission Creek. In 1875, the Bureau of Indian Affairs moved the facility to the Stillwater Valley near the junction of the East and West Rosebud Rivers in order to get away from the plethora of whiskey peddlers at Bensons Landing. Eight years later, the agency moved to its current location near Hardin.

17. Weibert, *The 1874 Invasion*, 13.

18. Carter, 31.

19. A Chinook wind is a dry, warm, down-slope wind that occurs in the downwind side of a mountain range especially in the Great Plains and Northwest.

20. Collection 1250, Folder 41, 2-3; Carter, 3; and Weibert, *The 1874 Invasion*, 13-14.

21. Carter, 32.

22. Annin, 8.

23. Jeff Birkby, *Touring Montana and Wyoming Hot Springs*, Guilford, Connecticut: Morris Book Publishing, 1999, 103-106.

24. Collection 1250, Folder 41, 3; and "Yellowstone Expedition," *Avant Courier*

(Bozeman,) February 20, 1874, 2.

25. "From the Yellowstone Expedition," *Avant Courier* (Bozeman,) February 27, 1874, 2.

26. Quivey, 269.

27. Weibert, *The 1874 Invasion*, 14.

28. Ibid.

29. Quivey, 271.

30. Weibert, *The 1874 Invasion*, 14.

31. Annin, 8.

32. Weibert, *The 1874 Invasion*, 15; and Annotated Manuscript of Jack Bean, 4.

33. "From the Yellowstone Expedition," *Avant Courier* (Bozeman,) February 27, 1874, 2.

34. Collection 1250, Folder 41, 4; and Annin, 8.

35. Quivey, 270.

36. Collection 1250, Folder 41, 4.

37. Weibert, *The 1874 Invasion*, 17.

38. Collection 1250, Folder 41, 4.

39. Camp Manuscripts, Box 4: Folder 5, Envelope 6—Barkley statement of 1874.

40. Quivey, 272.

41. "From the Expedition," *Avant Courier* (Bozeman,) March 6, 1874, 2.

42. Collection 1250, Folder 41, 4.

43. Ibid.

44. Weibert, *The 1874 Invasion*, 16.

45. Brown and Willard, 559.

46. "From the Expedition," *Avant Courier* (Bozeman,) March 6, 1874, 2.

47. Collection 1250, Folder 41, 4.

48. Ibid.

49. Weibert, *The 1874 Invasion*, 17.

50. Collection 1250, Folder 41, 5.

51. "The Story of a March," 12.

52. Collection 1250, Folder 41, 5.

53. "From the Expedition," *Avant Courier* (Bozeman,) March 6, 1874, 2.

54. This date was extrapolated backwards from March 25, 1874, which is the date that this study accepts for the expedition crossing the Yellowstone River.

55. Camp Manuscripts, Box 4: Folder 5, Envelope 6—Barkley statement of 1874.

56. Carter, 32.

57. Collection 1250, Folder 41, 7.

58. Ibid.
59. Ibid.
60. Annin, 8.
61. Collection 1250, Folder 41, 7.
62. Weibert, *The 1874 Invasion*, 21.
63. "Yellowstone Expedition," *Avant Courier* (Bozeman,) March 13, 1874, 2.
64. Collection 1250, Folder 41, 7.
65. Ibid.
66. Ibid, 8.
67. Ibid.
68. Annotated Manuscript of Jack Bean, 5.
69. "Yellowstone Expedition," *Avant Courier* (Bozeman,) March 20, 1874, 2.
70. Collection 1250, Folder 41, 8.
71. Annotated Manuscript of Jack Bean, 4.
72. Annin, 8.
73. Collection 1250, Folder 41, 9.
74. Annin, 8.
75. Collection 1250, Folder 41, 9.
76. Hutchins, "Poison in the Pemmican," 14-15; "Yellowstone Expedition," *Avant Courier* (Bozeman,) May 15, 1874, 2; Herendeen Papers, SC 16, 2; Collection 1250, Folder 41, 10; and Carter, 32.
77. Hugh Hoppe, Letter to *Helena Herald* concerning expedition, Bozeman, May 9, 1874, as found in the Gray Research Papers, Box 16, Folder 136-137, Scouts. The letter appears to have been published on May 14, 1874.
78. Quivey, 270-271.
79. Brown and Willard, 559-560.
80. Bradley, "Bradley Manuscript," 109.
81. Hutchins, "Poison in the Pemmican," 14; Collection 1250, Folder 41, 11.
82. Quivey, 272.
83. Collection 1250, Folder 41, 11.
84. Hutchins, "Poison in the Pemmican," 14; and Quivey, 273.
85. "The Eastern Montana Expedition," *Avant Courier* (Bozeman,) March 27, 1874, 2.
86. Hutchins, "Poison in the Pemmican," 14; Collection 1250, Folder 41, 11.
87. Annotated Manuscript of Jack Bean, 14.
88. Topping, 105; Collection 1250, Folder 41, 11.
89. Topping, 105-106; Annotated Manuscript of Jack Bean, 6; and Carter, 32.
90. Carter, 32; Hoppe, Letter to *Helena Herald*; and Utley, *The Lance and the Shield*, 118.
91. Topping, 106-107; and Carter, 32.
92. Quivey, 276-277; and Annotated Manuscript of Jack Bean, 6.
93. Brown and Willard, 560.
94. Ibid, 560-561.
95. Bradley, "Bradley Manuscript," 110.
96. "The Story of a March," 12.
97. Quivey, 275.
98. Hoppe, Letter to *Helena Herald*.
99. Quivey, 277.
100. Topping, 106; and Hoppe, Letter to *Helena Herald*.
101. Quivey, 271.
102. Camp Manuscripts, Box 2: Folder 2, Bozeman Expedition of 1874.
103. Avery Reminiscence, SC 372, 2.
104. Collection 1250, Folder 41, 12.
105. Quivey, 273-274.
106. Hoppe, Letter to *Helena Herald*.
107. Hutchins, "Poison in the Pemmican," 16; Collection 1250, Folder 41, 12-13; and Weibert, *The 1874 Invasion*, 28.
108. "Yellowstone Expedition," *Avant Courier* (Bozeman,) April 3, 1874, 2.
109. Bradley, "Bradley Manuscript," 111.
110. Quivey, 276.
111. Camp Manuscripts, Box 4: Folder 5, Envelope 6—Barkley statement of 1874, gold expedition from Bozeman; odometer on Rosebud River, September 1913; Bozeman expedition, 1874; and Herendeen Papers, SC 16, 3.
112. Hoppe, Letter to *Helena Herald*.
113. Camp Manuscripts, Box 4: Folder 5, Envelope 6—Barkley statement of 1874, gold expedition from Bozeman; odometer on Rosebud River, September 1913; Bozeman expedition, 1874.
114. Utley, *Sitting Bull*, 118; Brown and Willard, 561; and Camp Manuscripts, Box 3: Folder 8, Rosebud, Battle of, 1874.
115. "The Story of a March," 12.
116. Quivey, 276-278.
117. Brown and Willard, 561-563.
118. Statement from Stands-With-Horns-

In-Sight made to Judge Frank B. Zahn.

119. Bradley, "Bradley Manuscript," 113-114.

120. Bradley was likely referring to T.C. Burns, not S.C. Burns.

121. Carter, 33.

122. Ibid.

123. Annotated Manuscript of Jack Bean, 12.

124. "The Story of a March," 12.

125. Quivey, 274.

126. Weibert, *The 1874 Invasion*, 58.

127. Collection 1250, Folder 41, 14; Weibert, *The 1874 Invasion*, 58-59; and "Happenings and Remembrances of the Officer Family, as Written and Told by Guy C. Officer," September 1964 (Transcribed by Karen Officer Dean, 1971.)

128. Collection 1250, Folder 41, 14; Weibert, *The 1874 Invasion*, 61-62.

129. Ibid.

130. Ibid, 63.

131. Ibid, 63-64.

132. Ibid, 65-66.

133. Carter, 36; and Weibert, *The 1874 Invasion*, 67-71.

134. Weibert, *The 1874 Invasion*, 70-71.

135. Bradley, "Bradley Manuscript," 116.

136. Quivey, 278.

137. Carter, 36.

138. Letter from Tom Allen to Walter M. Camp, dated April 23, 1912, Denver Public Library, Western History Department; and Weibert, *The 1874 Invasion*, 58, 82-83.

139. Bradley, "Bradley Manuscript," 116-120.

140. Brown and Willard, 563.

141. Quivey, 278-279.

142. Ibid. 279-280.

143. "The Story of a March," 12-13.

144. Ibid, 13.

145. Letter from Tom Allen to Walter M. Camp, dated April 23, 1912, Denver Public Library, Western History Department.

146. Weibert, *The 1874 Invasion*, 83, 85.

147. Hoppe, Letter to *Helena Herald*; and Weibert, *The 1874 Invasion*, 85-86.

148. Collection 1250, Folder 41, 16; and Weibert, *The 1874 Invasion*, 86-87.

149. Bradley, "Bradley Manuscript," 120-121.

150. "Yellowstone Expedition," *Avant Courier* (Bozeman,) April 17, 1874, 2.

151. "Yellowstone Expedition," *Avant Courier* (Bozeman,) April 24, 1874, 2.

152. Weibert, *The 1874 Invasion*, 87-88.

153. Ibid, 89.

154. Quivey, 280.

155. "The Story of a March," 13.

156. Bradley, "Bradley Manuscript," 121.

CHAPTER FIVE

The Battle of Lodge Grass Creek – April 16, 1874

Thursday, April 16, 1874

Based on the recollections of those present and previous analyses by other historians, this study has concluded that the Battle of Lodge Grass Creek of the 1874 Yellowstone Wagon Road and Prospecting Expedition transpired in the following manner. Sunrise was at 0526. Shortly afterward, warriors attempted to cut off two pickets, who had their horses with them out on security duty. The warriors were well-mounted, but the pair of frontiersmen were able to mount up and ride into camp at a dead run. Hearing the cries for help from the pair of men, several frontiersmen in camp mounted up and raced in the direction of the warriors in a counter-charge. The men from the camp drove the warriors out of visual range and re-established the outpost. It is possible that at this time, Uncle Billy Hamilton tried to communicate in sign language to a lone warrior that had appeared on a ridge southwest of camp. While that vignette was transpiring, a couple of men worked their way within 200 yards of the warrior and fired at him. That episode was likely over by 0600, perhaps 0615 at the latest.

One source later pegged another event—a mounted warrior charge from in front of the wagon train—as occurring about 1000. Assessing the time required to move or fight in the other significant events that occurred that morning, we might be able to extrapolate that the wagon train started moving at about 0755. Given the possibility that this one participant could have been mistaken in the

Battle of Lodge Grass Creek; ground condition in the valley after saturation with rain and snow. As wagons rolled through this soil, it became a "sea of gumbo." *Author photograph, October 2013*

exact time, this study has chosen to base the noteworthy actions of the morning on an H-hour sequence. Hence, **H-hour** is whatever time that morning that the wagon train actually began moving, whether that was 0755 or some other time, earlier or later. *H+30* indicates that an event occurred thirty minutes or so after H-hour. *H+240* would describe an event that happened 240 minutes (or four hours) after H-hour. In a combat situation such as this one, time probably seemed to stand still for some men and race by quickly for others. Given the muddy conditions throughout the valley that morning, movement would have been extremely slow.

H-hour. The expedition (which at this point consisted of no more than twenty wagons) began traveling southwest in the Lodge Grass Creek Valley in two parallel columns. The creek was not much more than a small stream. The valley was muddy because of the recent rain and snow. To the right rose the first bench of land, a rolling set of hills that were perhaps fifty feet higher than the valley floor, but fairly easy to climb by riding up one of the many draws. About a quarter of a mile up the elevation was another 150 feet higher. On this day, eight men were riding in the advance guard, probably

four hundred yards in front of the dual columns, because of the sloppiness of the ground. Another eight men rode behind the last wagons, by routine a quarter mile to the rear, although a rear guard sometimes inadvertently closed on the main body if the men were not paying attention to the slower-moving animals to their front; today, this caused the rear guard to be 300 yards from the wagon train.

Along each flank rode sixteen men. Those to the right would have attempted to ride on top of the first series of low hills to the north to get a better view, unless ground conditions were too slippery to climb up the slope. The sixteen men on the left likely rode close enough to the creek that they could see any massing of warriors in the brush along the lowland, but not so close to the creek that they would be ambushed at short range. To cover the movement of the column up to the creek, Frank Grounds directed Billy Cameron to take the mountain howitzer to the top of a small hill overlooking the creek and the valley and provide overwatch, although there was not much more than a handful of rounds left for it.[1]

H+30. The Lodge Grass Creek does not flow continuously along the southeast side of the valley and about one-half mile from where

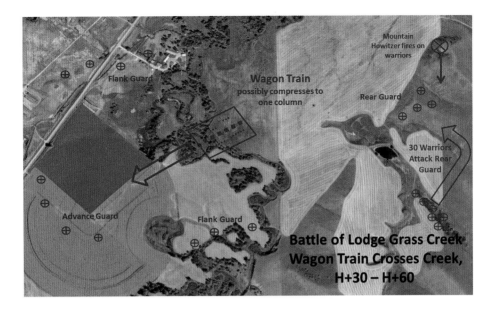

Battle of Lodge Grass Creek
Wagon Train Crosses Creek,
H+30 – H+60

the wagon train entered the valley the creek meandered through the middle of the basin. The first blow by the warriors came from a coulee at the left rear and 300 yards behind. Thirty warriors came out of the coulee and attacked four frontiersmen of the rear guard who were on a small hill. These men returned fire against the attackers. Seeing the assault, the crew of the mountain howitzer on the hill began firing, which caused these warriors to quickly withdraw.

H+60. The wagon train finally crossed the creek after much difficulty. It is likely that the two columns merged to cross the creek at a single crossing site that would have been identified by the advance guard, unless there were two good crossing sites fairly close together. It appears that several of the wagons became stuck and could only proceed after a great effort by the teamsters was made to free them. One ox became hopelessly mired in the mud and had to be shot; however, the drivers were able to get his yoke mate safely out of the muck. After crossing the creek, Frank Grounds took up a position with the left advance guard, while Billy Cameron got the mountain howitzer into limber and raced from

his overwatch position to catch up with the wagon train before he could be attacked on the move by warriors in the area.

H+105. The wagon train then pulled out to the foot of the bench to the right. It struggled along for about a mile, now back in double column, ready to form a corral to get the pack horses and loose stock inside for protection in case of a major attack. By this time in the expedition, the men knew that the warriors often had the goal of killing the animals or attempting to capture them. Given the terrible state of the mud, it probably took at least twenty minutes to travel that one mile.

H+125. The second blow against the wagon train occurred from the left front—about 600 yards from the train—when upwards of 400 to 850 mounted warriors burst out of concealment in the creek bottom and from draws heading into the hills to the front about one mile distant and charged the wagon train. One source stated that this may have occurred at about 1000. According to witnesses, the warriors appeared to be riding at the gallop and that many were wearing bright, white shirts. As the warriors charged, they broke

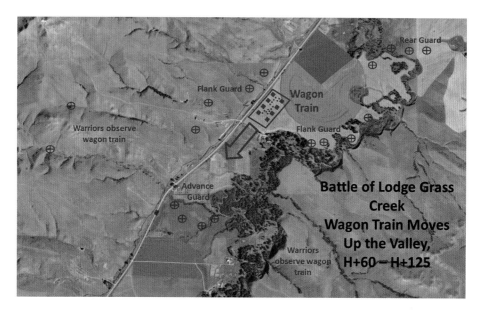

into war yells and raised their rifles above their heads, shaking the weapons. Another source said that these warriors were Northern Cheyenne. Closest to this attack were four men in the advance of the left flank—Neil Gillis, Tom Rea, Irving Hopkins, and French Pete. The quartet was traveling pretty close to the brush near the creek. Frank Grounds and Pat Sweeney soon joined them and the

six men dismounted and sent their horses across the valley with another man to join the wagon train as it pulled into a ravine.

The six frontiersmen would fight on foot. Sweeney attempted to fire his rifle, but a cartridge stuck in his weapon. The other men, armed probably with .50-caliber Springfield rifles, told him to go back to the wagon train and he ran to that location across the valley

Battle of Lodge Grass Creek; view from the valley
center looking north. That morning, the wagon train
approached from the right and hugged the high
ground rising to the front of the photograph. *Author
photograph, June 2013*

Similar view taken in colder weather. *Author
photograph, October 2013*

View from the valley to where the wagon train made an emergency laager (area of larger trees.) *Author photograph, October 2013*

Another view from the valley center looking north. That morning, the wagon train approached from the right and hugged the high ground rising to the front of the photograph. *Author photograph, June 2013*

Another view from the valley to the first level of bluffs where most of the fighting took place. *Author photograph, October 2013*

This spent Henry bullet was found close to the position of the Big Horn Gun on the first bench land. *Author photograph, June 2015)*

This shrapnel from the mountain howitzer was found by Ron Wald in an alfalfa field on his land, where the battle took place. *Courtesy Ron Wald as found when he led Don Weibert around the battlefield circa 1992*

View from the valley center looking north-northwest.
Author photograph, June 2013

floor. As the warriors approached, the remaining marksmen knelt down and began picking their targets. After firing a shot, each man would get up on his feet and advance a few steps toward the enemy. He would then kneel again for another shot. This rolling fire continued until the men were just forty yards from the warriors. At about the same time, the rest of the advance guard rode ahead behind a small ridge in front of a coulee, dismounted and opened fire, which likely frustrated the warrior plan of charging into the wagon train from the front. Most of the warriors finally broke ranks and headed to ravines to their rear, losing some men and horses killed and wounded.

View toward clump of trees where mounted
Cheyenne warriors began their charge. *Author
photograph, October 2013*

Area in Lodge Grass Creek Valley where members of
the Advance Guard met mounted Cheyenne warriors.
Author photograph, October 2013

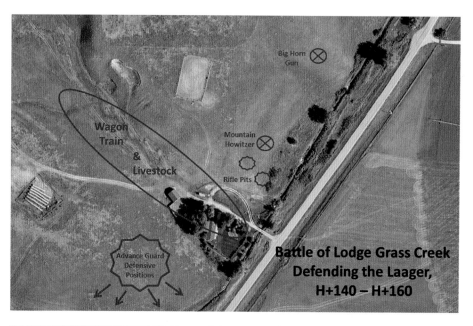

H+140. The advanced guard mounted up and rode back to a ravine—where the wagon train would seek shelter—dismounted and took up firing positions oriented to the southwest. The small hill had no crest, and to get a good sight on a target, each man had to stand up, exposing himself to enemy fire. After the warriors to their front had retreated under their withering fire, Neil Gillis, Tom Rea, Irving Hopkins, French Pete, and Frank Grounds ran to the first bench land and joined the rest of the advance guard there.

Advance Guard Defense on Bluff looking north.
Author photograph, June 2013

Advance Guard Defense on Bluff looking south.
Author photograph, June 2013

Advance guard defense on bluff looking east. Laager area is behind white barn at left. *Author photograph, June 2013*

Ravine from which warriors began firefight against members of the Advance Guard that had assumed defense on bench land. *Author photograph, October 2013*

View toward the Advance Guard positions (today behind white farm building.) *Author photograph, October 2013*

H+150. The third warrior attack of the morning consisted of another party of about 200 to 400 fighters that came up the Lodge Grass Creek bottom land behind the wagon train. This group of warriors, including Red Hawk and possibly High Bear, rode across the prairie and took up firing positions behind the rear guard in a coulee about 150 yards to the right rear of the train, along the first bench. From that vantage point, they could hit the bulk of the expedition's horses, as some of the warriors had Spencer and Winchester and other breech-loaders, although a majority of those with firearms had muzzle-loading rifles and some revolvers. Many of the warriors had bows and arrows in addition to their firearms, which would come into play at closer ranges, although at 150 yards the Spencers and Winchesters could seriously wound or kill a horse, sometimes with only one hit. Later, the frontiersmen would find that the warriors also had "needle-guns of fifty caliber," evidenced from the many battered bullets and cartridges.

The double columns of wagons, with the pack-horses between, quickly closed interval to make ready for an immediate defense in the open—Frank Grounds' least preferred option, but one he might have to take if the pressure from all sides increased. Warrior fire killed at least one horse and wounded several other animals.

H+160. The wagon train pulled into the ravine on the first bench and the teamsters attempted to lead the animals to defilade positions, in which it was difficult for warrior fire to hit them. By this time, the rear guard had withdrawn from its position to another small hill and began firing at the warriors, who were now in the former position of the rear guard. The rear guard's fire was accurate and heavy and this checked the advance of the warriors from this position, although at 750 yards away from the wagon train in the ravine, they could still range to that position with albeit ineffective fire. Bullets began to strike several of the wagons. Bostwick was still prostrate in the back of one of the wagons—not fully recovered from his wounds eighteen days earlier—and the bullets passed just over his body, making him try and get as flat to the wagon floor as he could. Pack horses tied to the wagons also began to have their packs hit by the fire of the warriors, causing the animals to get skittish.

The wagon train pulled into this ravine from the valley floor and established a defense. *Author photograph, June 2013*

A similar view from the laager area in the ravine toward the ridge from where warriors later began firing. *Author photograph, October 2013*

Another view of the warrior ridge. *Author photograph, October 2013*

Photo is taken from the firing pits of the frontiersmen looking across the valley; the creek is in the trees at the base of the bluffs. *Author photograph, June 2013*

Another view across the valley; Big Horn Mountains are far in the background. *Author photograph, June 2013*

Another view across the valley in colder weather toward the Big Horn Mountains. *Author photograph, October 2013*

H+165. Sensing that there was little time to waste, Frank Grounds and Eli Way called for volunteers to form a thirty-man party to charge from the main body northeast toward the rear to attack the warriors in the coulee next to the old rear guard position; it appears that Hugh Hoppe led the charge. Eli Way, Charles Avery, Johnny Jones, and Joe Cook definitely were part of the effort. One historian has posited that only six men were in this assault party, but witnesses and the nature of the odds dictate that the outfit was closer to thirty in strength. To provide covering fire, a second group of thirty men that had been in the rear guard climbed up the lowest hills and started firing. The objective of the charge was to advance into the coulee and fight the warriors at close quarters. Halfway to their objective, the charging frontiersmen gained the protection of a ravine midway between their supporting fire and the warriors' positions. They paused at this location for probably five minutes to recover their breath, check their ammunition count, and re-orient on the enemy.

The warriors, who seemed to be one hundred in strength at the far coulee, began screaming war chants, thinking the frontiersmen had lost courage and gone to ground for good. However,

Hoppe and his comrades popped back into the attack and soon the men reached the coulee, where the melee began, and the warriors slowly withdrew. The number of casualties at the coulee remains uncertain; one source says that ten warriors died, while one frontiersman recalled a dying warrior attempting to continue to use his bow and arrow while on the ground against Hugh Hoppe, who was carrying a pistol. Finally, a frontiersman known only as "Blackhawk," shot the warrior. Hoppe probably scalped the fallen warrior. Then Johnny Jones, after spitting out a large spray of tobacco juice, and his big butcher knife went to work.[2] Another man, the nephew of Zack Yates,[3] found another dying warrior, pulled out another large knife and disemboweled the man, saying "Now I am even for the killing of my uncle."[4]

H+170 to H+180. Once the frontiersmen maneuvered the horse-drawn mountain howitzer and Big Horn Gun up to two higher elevations southeast of the wagon train in its ravine, the men unlimbered both pieces of artillery. Billy Cameron, from his position, observed that there were dozens of warriors—maybe more— south across the valley in the cottonwood groves adjacent to the Lodge Grass Creek.

Battle of Lodge Grass Creek
"Hoppe's Charge,"
H+165 – H+180

100 warriors

5 minute rest at coulee to re-orient on objective

Covering Fire
(30 men)

Photo is taken from the firing pits of the frontiersmen looking north; warriors attacking from the rear of the wagon train took up firing positions just to the left of the white farmhouse in the left center of the photograph. *Author photograph, June 2013*

Cameron probably estimated that to the center of the largest and nearest grove of trees was about 1,000 yards. His first round, a spherical case shot with an internal explosive charge, hit the valley floor 800 yards distant from the howitzer and shortly afterward exploded, sending deadly iron fragments in all directions, but probably not hitting any warriors. After several subsequent rounds struck the timber, observers could see perhaps as many as several hundred warriors abandon the area. At the conclusion of this artillery fire, Billy Cameron made the disturbing observation that he had completely run out of ammunition for the mountain howitzer. Only the Big Horn Gun could save them now.

Marker emplaced by Don Weibert and Ron Wald at the estimated location of the Big Horn during the battle. *Author photograph, June 2013*

Marker emplaced by Don Weibert and Ron Wald at the estimated location of the Big Horn during the battle. *Author photograph, June 2013*

H+185. Back on the ridge of hills higher and to the northeast of the wagon train, while the warriors in this coulee were attempting to escape, what appeared to be a significant chief mounted on a fast horse rode prominently back and forth on a hill about 150 yards away. It was apparent to the frontiersman that this warrior was putting his own personal safety in severe peril, endeavoring, and also succeeding, in drawing the fire of many of the dismounted expedition's best shots. At that distance, one of the men firing a Springfield "Big Fifty" or Sharps buffalo gun dropped the chief's horse, but failed to hit the rider. At the time, the men did not know who he was but information later obtained by 1st Lt. Bradley in interviews indicates that it was the great Sitting Bull.

This study believes that it was not Sitting Bull, but Crazy Horse, who rode in the path of almost certain danger. His village was clearly in the vicinity of the trail of the wagon train. With at least 1,000 Lakota warriors participating in the fight at one point or another, it is inconceivable that Crazy Horse would have missed the combat. However, most convincing is that this extremely courageous action was almost a mirror image of what he did in December 1866 at the Fetterman Massacre and what he would do just two years

later when Crazy Horse rode through the 7th Cavalry lines on Battle Ridge during the climactic moment of the battle against Custer's wing at the Battle of the Little Bighorn. The action on the ridge overlooking Lodge Grass Creek on the morning of April 16 was "pure Crazy Horse." Perhaps no other warrior in the entire Lakota nation possessed this level of *sangfroid*, although certainly the Lakota would not have used these types of words to describe Crazy Horse's brave actions.

H+195. The fourth warrior attack occurred roughly at the same time, or a few minutes later, as that the chief was creating a diversion higher on the hills. The wagon train, by this time, had reached a coulee between two low hills on the first bench land and had been successfully driven into it. While herders were organizing the wagons for a final defense if the warriors overran the defensive positions around it, a large number of warriors came at the position from the front from the southwest. They made it to a coulee about 300 yards in front of the position covering the corralled animals. The ground was open and the deadly fire pouring from the frontiersmen's position made any advance almost impossible by the warriors. By this time, the men in the hillocks surrounding the depression protecting the wagon

**Battle of Lodge Grass Creek
Close Fighting in the Coulee
H+185 – H+195**

Lone Chief, drawing enemy fire

Hoppe's Charge defeats warriors in coulee, Joe Cook and Ely Way shoot warrior

Warriors mount horses and retreat

View from behind Big Horn Gun position across the valley toward Lodge Grass Creek. At the end of the battle a warrior standing on the ridge across the valley was engaged by Jack Bean. *Author photograph, October 2013*

train were digging in and scraping out rifle pits that would give them some protection from the enemy and that would allow them to fire from the prone position for increased accuracy.

H+215. The warriors began to flank the wagon train from the high ground to the north. Frank Grounds first organized two dismounted groups of marksman to move between the wagon train and these warriors to bring them under fire. Some of the warriors fired .50-70 rifles and began hitting some of the livestock. When the first group of frontiersmen failed to drive the warriors off the ridge, a second group moved closer.

H+230. Sensing that the rifle fire was not driving the warriors away, Frank Grounds organized a mounted party to ride from the corral area to the higher hills northeast in an effort to disperse the remaining warriors and prevent them from massing.

H+240. After the mounted men cleared the immediate area, the teamsters hitched the wagons to their yokes of oxen and began

Frontiersmen assumed positions at this location after warriors moved to the hill to the front and began firing at the wagon train that was in a ravine to the rear of where this photograph was taken. View is looking northwest. *Author photograph, June 2013*

Battle of Lodge Grass Creek
Warriors Outflank Positions
Mounted Attack Against Ridge
H+215 – H+240

Third Warrior
Flanking Position

Second Warrior
Flanking Position

First Warrior
Flanking Position

Warriors shoot at
oxen and horses

Second
Counter-
fire
Position

Mounted Attack to clear ridge

Big Horn
Gun shells
creek area

Mountain Howitzer
out of ammunition

First Counter-
fire
Position

Wagon
Train

Frontiersmen assumed positions at this location after
warriors moved to the hill to the right in the distance.
View is looking west. *Author photograph, June 2013*

View from behind Big Horn Gun location toward ridge where warriors gathered to snipe at the wagon train in its ravine. *Author photograph, October 2013*

View to the far heights northeast of the battlefield. The mounted charge would head in this direction. *Author photograph, October 2013*

View from the rear guard position of the frontiersmen looking east where the wagon train would have been in the ravine on the far side of the small pond. *Author photograph, June 2013*

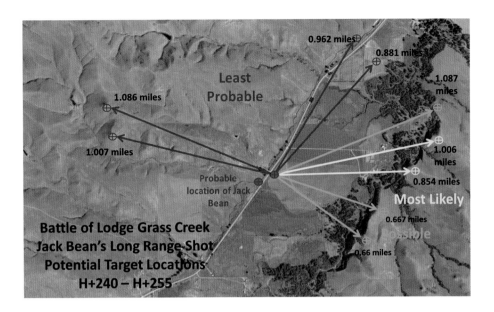

Battle of Lodge Grass Creek
Jack Bean's Long Range Shot
Potential Target Locations
H+240 – H+255

maneuvering the wagon train out of the ravine and onto the valley floor. Other men herded the pack animals in the same direction, while dismounted frontiersmen found their horses, mounted up, and rode onto the valley floor themselves. Considering that the wagon train had been facing toward the hills and not the valley floor, this maneuver was a lot more complicated than first imagined and it may have taken thirty minutes to get the wagon train to the valley floor, organize it in two columns, and put all the individual pack animals between the columns.

H+265. After Hugh Hoppe and his men drove the warriors out of the coulee to the rear of the wagon train at about H+165, several of the Lakota—including Red Hawk and probably High Bear—rode east to the area where the wagon train had camped the night before. The group found the mound of dirt and the cross. Red Hawk urged caution, but High Bear started to dig. He pulled the cross out of the ground, but nothing happened. A little farther down in the ground, High Bear found the wire and gave it a strong tug. The bomb exploded.

Red Hawk was thrown backward, dazed. Five or six Indians were killed (but not High Bear) and more were wounded; it is possible that some of the victims were Lakota women, looking for supplies left by the whites. Witnesses later recalled that No Flesh was another warrior believed to be present when the bomb exploded. However, a detailed measurement indicates that the distance between the warriors and frontiersmen near the wagon train and the old campsite was 3.184 miles, so any witnesses near the wagon train could not have identified even the number of people at the old campsite, let alone their identities.

Additionally, a small spit of high ground along the line of sight may have blocked viewing the ground level at the old campsite. What probably happened was that the frontiersmen heard the explosion, looked back toward their old laager and saw a plume of black smoke from the explosion, but no other details. Two years later, the cavalrymen at Weir Point at the Little Bighorn were 3.258 miles from Last Stand Hill and they too had difficulty determining what was happening.

H+270. When the wagon train was about ready to move on the valley floor, two warriors approached about a mile away. The accounts are similar concerning the distance to the wagon train, but vary with respect to the warriors' actual location. One warrior, accompanied by his fellow Lakota warrior Shell Necklace, *Pankeska Napin*, took up a firing position and fired one round in the general vicinity of the pack herd. The round struck no target, but the impact was noticed by several of the frontiersmen as striking between the front hooves of a horse. The warrior then stood up.

Some accounts indicate that the two warriors were on one of the small hills on the first bench on the northern side of the valley. Another possibility is that the warrior who fired the shot was on a small elevation on the floor of the valley near the creek. The third possibility is that he was across Lodge Grass Creek on the high ridge that is almost one

hundred feet higher than the valley floor. A fourth possibility is that one of the warriors returned to one of the higher hills that had previously been cleared by the mounted frontiersmen forty minutes earlier. The ultimate authority, frontiersman Jack Bean, stated that the men were "across the bottom and up on the hill." The commonality of all possibilities is that the warriors were on a ridge.

Whatever the location of this unnamed warrior, Jack Bean had him in his sights. Bean took out his Sharps Model 1874, the caliber of which was .44-90 according to some sources. Previously, most accounts postulated that mounted on top of the rifle was a thirty-inch telescopic sight. However, in his written account many decades later, Jack said that he gave his peep sight of his "old Sharps" a

Estimated location from where Jack Bean took his long-range shot against a warrior on a range, probably in the background of this photograph.
Author photograph, October 2013

"pull" and used a wagon wheel to rest his rifle for support.

The peep sight was probably tang, not barrel, mounted. Most Sharps 1874 Sporting Rifles came out of the factory with some type of Lawrence high notch or buckhorn open rear sight on top of the barrel, through which the marksman looked through a notch and lined up the front sight to get the correct sight picture. A tang sight was a tall (usually folding) aperture/peep sight, mounted to the upper rear tang (where the butt stock meets the receiver) of the Sharps, which was adjustable over a wide range of elevation, making the rifle extremely suitable for long range shooting. When not in use, the sight simply folded down towards the rear of the stock, thus it had to be pulled up to the vertical position, matching Bean's description. The peep sight often used a rectangle or disk about the size of a dime that had a pinhole-sized aperture in the middle.

The mechanics of the sight were/are that the human eye will automatically center the front sight, when looked through the rear aperture, which will increase accuracy. The small aperture, or pinhole in the disk, provides a much darker image of the target and a greater depth of field to produce a much sharper image of the target. Vernier sights—and Bean did not say that he had this type—then in use allowed adjustment down to a single minute of arc over the full range of the sight. This was important because black powder used in the cartridges then was not capable of propelling a bullet at high velocity. The .45-70 cartridge, for example, as tested by the army for accuracy at ranges of up to 1,500 yards, required $3\frac{1}{3}$ degrees of elevation to travel to that range. Regular peep sights could be adjusted but not to the refinement of a Vernier sight. Dr. Richard J. Labowski, an expert at Sharps rifle production, has opined that Jack Bean's rifle probably had either a buckhorn sight or a traditional peep sight, but not a Vernier model.[5]

With several frontiersmen watching through binoculars, Jack Bean used his experience to calculate whatever wind there was to help drift the shot and carefully squeezed

the trigger, sending the ounce of lead bullet toward the target through the large puff of smoke belching out the muzzle of the Sharps. Shell Necklace later stated that he thought the distance was so great that there was little danger that he or his companion would be hit. Shell Necklace thought wrong.

The men said that suddenly the warrior dropped out of sight. Shell Necklace said that he saw the rifleman shoot and was ready to ride away, when his friend jerked violently backwards and fell on the ground, mortally wounded. The speed of sound is 1,116 feet per second, which is constant. The muzzle velocity of Jack Bean's rifle was probably 1,270 to 1,400 feet per second at the muzzle, but this would have dropped to 990 feet per second at 375 yards, so the warrior may have heard the shot that killed him, but would not have had time to duck or jump aside. The men on the expedition heard the shot and gave a large cheer when they saw the target drop. The wagon train then departed to the southwest, with the warrior dead next to his horse on a "barren hilltop." Hugh Hoppe later wrote that they had captured several needle guns after this battle.[6]

After the fight, the wagon train covered three miles before making camp northwest of the valley floor. The laager location was on the end of a ridge and the pickets could see around them in every direction [N 45° 14.305', W 107° 32.060']. The men dug their positions and Bill Cameron set up both cannons on the southern tip of the ridge, ensuring that they were not camouflaged, but that they could be seen—hopefully as a deterrent—as the mountain howitzer had no more ammunition. Sunset occurred at 1902.

Several participants in the battle wrote about their experiences or agreed to be interviewed years after the event. James Gourley continues his description of the Lodge Grass Creek fight:[7]

That morning we were very well aware that we had to fight during the day from signs we had seen and information brought

April 16 Laager [N 45° 14.305', W 107° 32.060']

in by the pickets and scouts. In the camp on the point overlooking Long Creek an amusing incident occurred. The Indians attempted to cut off two of our pickets, who were Gallatin Valley farmers and had lazy horses under ordinary circumstances. The Indians were well mounted, but had no chance to catch up with those two men, who came into camp on the dead run, although several of our men were going in the direction of the Indians just as fast as they could go. The men from the camp drove the Indians back, however, and re-established the outpost.

We moved from this hill and got down into the creek bottom, and about a half mile from where we struck the bottom had to cross the creek. This was really the most dangerous point of the whole expedition. From the coulee on the left, and in the rear of where our train was,

about 300 yards from the train, four of our party held a point behind a small hill at the mouth of the coulee. From this point the Indians evidently intended to make their attack. While that point was being held, about thirty Indians were seen coming into the coulee, and undoubtedly had they not been held in check they would have opened fire on the train.

We would have been hardly able to dislodge them unless through active use of the howitzer. However, the train, after much difficulty, got across the creek. We had to kill one ox because he was hopelessly mired, and we dragged his mate out by a great deal of exertion, and finally succeeded in getting the wagons and teams across. The train then pulled out to the foot of the bench to the right. We were moving along peacefully for about a mile, in double column, ready to

Location of expedition laager on April 16, 1874, after the "Battle of Lodge Grass Creek." *Author photograph, October 2013*

pull into corral form, so as to get the pack horses and loose stock inside in case of an attack.

At this point we had four men in the advance of the left flank, probably about 600 yards in a straight line from the train. They were traveling pretty close to the brush, when 850 Cheyennes charged them. Here probably the bravest and coolest work that men ever did in any extremity those four men did. One of the men attempted to discharge his Winchester as the savages came crushing towards the train, but he got a cartridge stuck in his gun and had no means of getting it out.

One of his companions told him to go to camp, as he could be of no use. The men undoubtedly expected to die there;

they never flinched, but as the Indians approached knelt down and shot into the charging mass of savages. After firing they would get up and scatter wider apart and take a few steps in advance, and then kneel again for another shot. They so continued until probably there were not forty yards between them and the Indians. This was probably different fighting than the Indians expected to see. The four flankers were Neil Gillis, Tom Ray, Irving Hopkins and a Frenchman named Pete.

At about the same time the advance guard ran ahead behind a little ridge—a wash-out from a coulee—got down and commenced shooting. This broke up the entire Indian plan of riding into the main on that line.

Another view of the location of expedition laager on April 16, 1874 after the "Battle of Lodge Grass Creek." *Author photograph, October 2013*

At the same time, another party of about 400 Indians came up the river bottom behind us and took a position in a coulee about 150 yards in the rear of the train. From this point they could hit the bulk of our horses, and there was very little time to lose if we saved the train, so we formed a charging party of about thirty men. To protect them in their charge on the coulee, another party of thirty men on higher ground kept the grass cut down with their bullets. The object of the charge was to get right into the coulee and fight them at close quarters, as we had found out that Indians wouldn't fight under such circumstances. And here, as on the Rosebud, when we got into that coulee, the Indians didn't have strength enough

to run; they were simply paralyzed. At the first shots men missed Indians who couldn't have been more than twenty feet away, being out of wind from running.

One Indian who was knocked down made desperate attempt in his dying struggles to shoot arrows at the parties nearest him, but he was so far gone he could hardly throw an arrow twenty feet. The Indians got away very slowly. They were so scared they couldn't run. I don't know how many we killed or wounded.

While the Indians were escaping, Sitting Bull rode back and forth on a hill about 150 yards away mounted on a fast horse, endeavoring, and also succeeding, in drawing the fire of our men from the Indians who were within thirty feet of us, trying to knock him off his horse. We succeeded in killing the horse, but failed to hit the Sioux chief. We didn't know at the time, who he was, but learned it afterwards. Another movement was going on at the same time in a big coulee just ahead of where the train was corralled. A very large body of Indians attempted to come down there, but was held in check by the positions our parties occupied, making it a sure thing that a good many Indians had to die before they could reach the train.

It was a remarkable thing that during this fight none of our men were seriously hurt; the most serious hurt anyone received was by being hit with a spent bullet. But probably there was not a man in the fight that didn't have dirt thrown on him from bullets striking the ground, and as an instance of this, one man attempted to dig a rifle pit and had taken out three or four shovels of black loam, when two or three bullets struck in the hole. He jumped out of that pretty quick, declaring very emphatically that if the Indians wanted that hole they could have it; he didn't need it any more. One man got his eyes filled with dirt from bullets striking close to him as he was lying down. We had several of our horses shot slightly and

several head of cattle hurt, but they were all in shape for use.

The following is an account from Addison M. Quivey, "The Yellowstone Expedition of 1874," *Contributions to the Historical Society of Montana*, in 1876. Quivey probably had the date incorrect, but the rest of his account was highly informative:[8]

On the morning of the 18th, we moved out of camp and crossed Grass Lodge Creek (the Indians being in sight on the hills,) and moved up the valley of that stream, keeping near the bluffs on the north side. We had proceeded thus about two miles, when a large body of Indians poured out of the timber on the creek about one mile distant, and a little in our advance, coming at full speed, but with the order and regularity of a regiment of cavalry. As they came within range, our advance and left-flank guard dismounted and opened on them, when they quickly broke and took to the hills and ravines, losing some men and horses killed and wounded. At the same time another large body of Indians crossed the creek in our rear, and came across the prairie to attack us on that side.

View from the rear guard position of the frontiersmen looking across the Lodge Grass Creek Valley. *Author photograph, June 2013*

As we drove our wagons in double column, with the pack-horses between, our train was soon closed up and ready for them. Our rear-guard checked them in their career, although there could not have been less than four hundred in that column, and they, too, took to cover and opened fire from every quarter on our train, which was corralled next to the bluff, upon which our artillery was soon posted, and our men stationed to the best advantage for offensive or defensive operations as opportunity might offer. The fire of the Indians was terrific from every point, but their aim was bad, or rather those who were near enough to shoot with certainty took no aim at all, as they were afraid to raise high enough to do so; yet it seemed strange that no one was killed, as the balls fell thick all around.

Soon, however, a party of our men charged the Indians to the north and east of our position, and drove them in every direction, capturing one scalp and one fine horse and trappings, and one breech-loading rifle. Immediately after, a mounted party (all other charges were made on foot) scoured the hills, scattering the Indians in every direction. At the same time our artillery shelled them out of the timber on the river, and the fight was over.

The Indians were completely demoralized, and molested us no more, although a few were seen for several days after. Our loss was but one horse killed and several wounded. The Indian force could not have been less than one thousand, and

View from the rear guard position of the frontiersmen looking north toward where the warriors were massing and firing from. *Author photograph, June 2013*

many of them had needle-guns of fifty caliber, center fire, as we picked up many battered bullets of that size, and found a good many metallic shells that they had used. They also had Spencer and Winchester and other breech-loaders, but probably a majority of them had muzzle-loading rifles and many revolvers. Many of them had bows and arrows in addition to their fire-arms. Most of them were well mounted—much better than we were.

Over the next two years, 1st Lt. James Bradley—who was not on the expedition—interviewed wagon train men and warriors and developed this account of the fight:[9]

The following morning…the expedition resumed the march in the usual order, the wagons being in two parallel lines, with the pack horses between them, protected by an advanced guard of eight men, a rear guard of the same strength, and a flanking party of sixteen on each side. They had descended the valley and crossed the stream to the left bank, and ascending the valley along the foot of the bluffs had gained a distance of about two miles from their camp, when suddenly from nearly every side, they were charged by hundreds of mounted Indians, who burst upon them in swarms, that literally darkened the land. The train was hurried forward about 100 yards and rapidly corralled, while the cannoneers seized their guns and rushed them forward to the top of the ridge in front, which had been gained by the advance guard just as the attack began.

The advance guard were charged by about two hundred Indians, who rode down upon them with the utmost confidence, but the gallant eight never flinched, delivering their fire with such coolness, precision and rapidity that their assailant soon began to waver and finally fled, the flanking party on the left of the train were attacked by overwhelming numbers, who had been concealed in the timber along the stream, but coolly sat down in their places and opened so hot a fire upon the savages that they speedily ceased their advance and fled to cover, the flanking party on the right and the rear guard were attacked by at least 400 warriors, and unable to maintain their ground against such tremendous odds, were retiring, slowly firing as they went, but by this time the train had been corralled, and the entire force turned out to fight, and within a few minutes after the attack began, the chargers were everywhere repulsed and the Indians driven with severe loss to the cover of the ridges, timber and ravines.

"All this time," says Mr. Quivey (and he is sustained by my authorities) "the fire of the Indians was terrific from every point, but their aim was bad, or rather those were near enough to shoot, must certainly have taken no aim at all, as they were afraid to raise high enough to do so, yet is seemed strange that no one was killed as the balls fell thick all around." A considerable force of Indians had affected a lodgment in a ravine a couple of hundred yards below the train, from which they were amusing themselves by firing into the open end of the corral, for the purpose of disabling the stock. One horse was killed and several wounded, when it was resolved to dislodge them by a charge. As usual the charging party was small, consisting only of half a dozen men led by H.J. Happy [Hugh Hoppy] who stripped themselves of most their clothing and prepared for hot work.

When all was ready they advanced at a run covered by a general fire from the line, and gained the protection of a ravine midway between their friends and the Indians' positions. The Sioux received the movements with shouts of defiance, and appeared to be determined to remain and resist the advance, and when the charging party paused a moment in the first ravine to recover breath, the Indians, thinking that they had lost courage, burst forth with cries and cheers; they were about 100 strong and well covered by the ravine, but un-appalled by such tremendous odds, Happy and his brave command soon arose from their concealment and rushed resolutely on. The Sioux received them with a brisk fire, but such un-paralleled audacity seemed to bewilder, seemed to confuse the most of them and they stood watching the movement in silent, dazed amazement, apparently helpless to act. But there was no hesitation or uncertainty on the part of the brave little band that the Sioux watched in such amazement and their comrades at the train in breathless suspense.

On they went at their best speed; as they drew near the ravine the rifles soon began to tell upon the red mass gathered there. Each individual Sioux saw in their determined bearing, death for his particular self, and taking a last look, turned and fled in wild dismay. They ran the gauntlet of a severe fire, several received wounds, but only one was killed. He fell in the ravine and his body was the only one that the whites got possession of in the fight. Was there ever a more gallant act performed than this charge of half a dozen men upon a hundred, well-armed, strongly posted savages; no wonder that Sitting Bull

declared afterward that he had never seen such men.

Immediately after this exploit, a mounted party swept the remaining savages from the vicinity of the corral, while the artillery shelled them out of the timber along the stream and the fight was at an end.

Several decades later, Joe Cook—who had charged the warrior position northeast of the wagon train laager in the ravine—provided his own recollections of this final battle, naming the small creek Rotten Grass instead of Lodge Grass:[10]

The next and last general battle we had was on a stream called Rotten Grass. It was about 10 o'clock in the morning when one of our left flank guards came to the train and reported the timber along the creek full of Indians. As we were in the middle of the valley, the captain ordered us to move over to the foothills, thereby preventing the Indians from having the timber and foothills both to shoot from. The Indians, seeing what we were going to do, started in to checkmate us. About three hundred of them came out of the timber on horseback and on the dead run started for the train, thinking our left flank

Ravine between the two hills is where the frontiersmen formed to conduct a charge toward the right. *Author photograph, June 2013*

would stampede for the train. But the men dismounted and kneeling down, they sent such a storm of lead into them that the Indians turned off and went into the foot hills. About eighty of them left their horses behind, and crawled up behind a ridge, and were killing our horses.

Eli Way called for a detachment to charge the ridge, and here I got my Indian. About twenty-five of our boys ran across a plateau and Eli Way and I were in the bottom. The Indians seeing us coming, got to their horses and made a getaway, excepting one. He came out of a little gulch about forty yards from us, and was running away from us. He had on a brand new shirt made of white domestic sewed with black thread and his pants were black woolen stuff. I had a .50 caliber needle gun and Way said, "Is your gun loaded? Shoot the son of a gun." Thinking that I would not miss, I drew a bead on his body just where his pants and shirt met. I hit him in the right hip joint and the bullet came out in his groin. This charge ended the last fight we had with them.

"Happenings and Remembrances of the Officer Family, as Written and Told by Guy C. Officer," September 1964, has proven to be a valuable source concerning William Officer and the expedition. It describes that while reminiscing about the battle in about 1903, William Officer told William T. Hamilton the following story (It would appear that Officer served as one of the flank guards moving down the valley.)

Another incident that they talked about and which I felt was the highlight of the whole visit, was about the time that fourteen men were sent out on a scouting party. The men were riding single file along a side hill, about four hundred yards from a creek bottom. Dad had stopped to attend to a call of nature; the rest of the men rode on. They estimated two or three hundred Indians came out of the brush charging up the hill. All the men but one

carried repeating rifles. So many Indians and horses were knocked down that the charge was broken. One Indian was starting a swing to hit Dad on the head with a war club when Hamilton spurred his horse and shot the Indian off his horse with a cap and ball pistol. Dad was riding a not too well broke pinto. Hamilton said, "Bill, was you scared?" Dad said, "Hell, I was so busy holding my britches up with one hand and holding that damn pinto with the other I didn't have time to get scared."

As Tom Allen later told researcher Walter M. Camp:[11]

Our little cannon did great business.

According to Don Weibert, during the night, Sitting Bull held a council of war with Hump and the other warrior leaders. He recommended that the Lakota and Cheyenne separate and not attack the wagon train again, as they were losing too many valuable warriors.[12] Sitting Bull understood the price of victory.

Notes
1. Brown, *The Plainsmen of the Yellowstone*, 217.
2. Avery Reminiscence, SC 372, 3.
3. It is possible that Jones was confused with Ki Yates, as the two incidents seem eerily similar.
4. Gray Research Papers, Box 16, Folder 136, Scouts.
5. Telephone discussion with Dr. Richard J. Labowski, September 3, 2013.
6. Hoppe, Letter to *Helena Herald*.
7. "The Story of a March," 13.
8. Quivey, 280-281.
9. Bradley, "Bradley Manuscript," 121-124.
10. Brown and Willard, 564.
11. Camp Manuscripts, Box 4: Folder 5, Envelope 6—Barkley statement of 1874.
12. Weibert, *The 1874 Invasion*, 106.

CHAPTER SIX

The Return Home

After the fighting at Lodge Grass Creek, the Lakota and Northern Cheyenne would follow the wagon train, but never again would they close with it for battle. However, Frank Grounds did not know the intent of the shadowing warriors and thus maintained a high security level as the column moved southwest.

Friday, April 17, 1874 **(Rotten Grass Valley) [N 45° 13.580', W 107° 36.824']**

Sunrise occurred at 0525. It apparently had rained during the night as many of the men were wet. There was a fog or mist that combined with a temperature near 32°F that coated almost everything with a white frost. It was quite cold. In the mountains, some 4,000 feet high, snow was visible to the frontiersmen. Later the sun shone through the fog until 1030,

when the fog began to raise. About this time, the expedition moved out of its laager and re-formed on the valley floor. Ground conditions on the route were mud and snow, which would make progress difficult.

After just a few miles, the wagon train hit an offshoot of the Bozeman Trail. Frank Grounds stopped the column and faced southward on his horse. He looked back at the column, knowing that a few days earlier—before the massive fight along the creek—the men had voted to head south at the trail crossing he was now located. It was a ragged bunch: animals sick and dying, little reserves of food (although the men could see thousands of bison in the hills,) little ammunition for the Big Horn Gun and no ammunition for the mountain howitzer.[1]

Marker for the Bozeman Trail in Lodge Grass Creek. *Author photograph, October 2013*

The wagon train reached this point on April 17, 1874. At this point, Frank Grounds motioned for the expedition to return to Bozeman and not head south to the Bighorn Mountains. *Author photograph, October 2013*

Grounds looked at his old friend Bill Buchanan. Buchanan shook his head "no." The head of the expedition then reined his horse around, faced north and began riding. The wagon train followed without complaint, except for Hugh Hoppy who grumbled, but understood he did not now have the votes to reverse course. The column found the old wheel ruts on the grassed-over Bozeman Trail and headed toward the divide between the Lodge Grass and Rotten Grass Creeks. Grounds sent scouts ahead to cross the divide and find a good site to laager near Rotten Grass Creek. At the divide, late that afternoon, the scouts returned with their findings and the wagon train crossed and made its way to the valley. After crossing the creek, the wagon train traveled uphill to the first range of hills and laagered near the end of a ridge. Lakota warriors had been following them at a distance all day.[2]

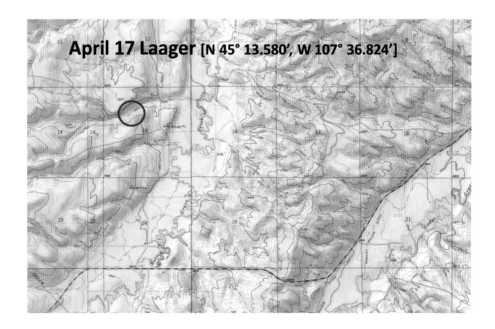

April 17 Laager [N 45° 13.580′, W 107° 36.824′]

Wagon Boss William Wright decided to leave one wagon behind and several men broke it up with sledgehammers and subsequently burned the wreckage. The wagon train now had no more than nineteen wagons. Sometime at this laager, Bill Calfee was fiddling with his Colt Peacemaker and accidentally shot and killed a pony that Conger Smith had captured at the last fight. The men took an inventory of supplies and found that they were almost out of food. To lighten the loads in the wagons for what was shaping up as a potential death march back to Bozeman, Bill Wright decided that all unnecessary items would be jettisoned from the Conestogas. Addison Quivey's collection of fossils and rocks would become one more casualty of the expedition, as only essentials could be carried in the dwindling numbers of wagons. The men posted their reinforced guard in case the warriors were hidden in close proximity.[3] Sunset occurred at 1903. As Addison Quivey painfully recalled several years later concerning his hard-earned acquisitions:[4]

I made quite a collection of fossils, most of which I was obliged to throw away when our teams began to give out during the storms in April, when we were obliged to throw away everything not absolutely necessary to our subsistence.

Saturday, April 18, 1874 (Divide between Dry Soap Creek and Soap Creek) [N 45° 13.541', W 107° 44.041']

Sunrise occurred at 0523. There was some fog on the high mountains; the temperature was cold. The wagon train prepared to move after the men finished their meager breakfast and began to roll at 0800. The column first crossed a coulee to the north of the laager and then moved up a ridge toward the divide between the Rotten Grass Valley and the Soap Creek Valley. The route remained muddy and the column had to halt numerous times for the animals to rest. The steepness of the route became significant and the men were forced to leave the stock that could not make the strenuous climb behind. The expedition finally made the divide and started downhill.[5]

Once in the valley, the wagon train crossed Dry Soap Creek near the mouth of Cherry Creek. After crossing, the column took until dark to travel the single mile to the other side of the valley. Sunset occurred at 1905. The expedition pulled into the next laager site

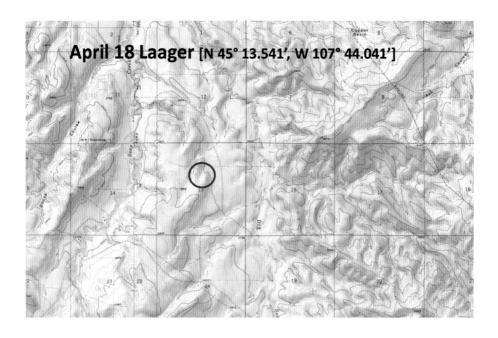

April 18 Laager [N 45° 13.541', W 107° 44.041']

having covered only six miles the entire day. Canned provisions had run out, but at 1730 two bison came into camp, "and in less than ten minutes some of them were being cooked." The men dug several large pits and emplaced the two artillery pieces, but because the laager site was at the edge of a large plateau, where visibility extended for several miles in all directions, the usual picket positions were not constructed.[6]

Sunday, April 19, 1874 (Goose Creek) [N 45° 13.597', W 107° 46.998']

Sunrise was at 0521, but because of the exertion required the previous day, Frank Grounds let the men sleep in. After a meager breakfast, the men hitched up the wagons and the expedition headed through the mud again. At about noon or 1300, the wagons reached Soap Creek, having traveled only a mile and a half. The livestock watered at the creek and then headed on—but only another mile and a half, before Grounds called it a day. The laager was along Goose Coulee, a small drainage flowing into Soap Creek. The men dug shallow positions around the new laager position. Sunset occurred at 1906. Those men not on guard duty dropped off to sleep. exhausted from another day's

backbreaking effort.[7] Back in Bozeman, authorities were becoming worried about the fate of the expedition and dispatched S.S. Bowles and Maj. Alonzo S. Reed to find it.[8]

Monday, April 20, 1874 (War Man's Creek)

Sunrise was at 0519 a.m. It snowed all night and was cold. The snow continued until 1400 in the afternoon. The men continued to lighten the loads on the wagons, throwing away everything that was not needed. The wagon train began moving along the old Bozeman Trail with the goal of getting to the head of War Man's Creek. It arrived at this location in late afternoon and established another laager. The men dug their positions and started drifting off to sleep.[9] Sunset occurred at 1907.

Tuesday, April 21, 1874 (Fort C. F. Smith) [N 45° 18.852', W 107° 54.485']

Sunrise was at 0518. It had rained most of the night. As the men began to move around, they spied the Big Horn River, which immediately improved morale. The trail, which was so muddy that it rolled up on the wheels until it was almost impossible for the wagon to move, finally began to descend and by the afternoon, it had become less broken and the ground

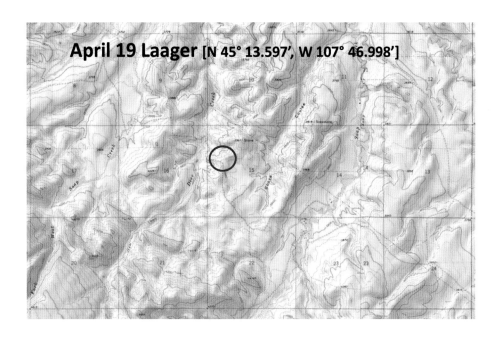

April 19 Laager [N 45° 13.597', W 107° 46.998']

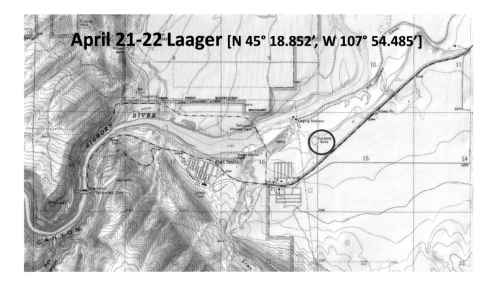

April 21-22 Laager [N 45° 18.852', W 107° 54.485']

began to dry out. For the next ten miles, the expedition made excellent time.[10]

Late in the afternoon, the wagon train approached the Big Horn River and the abandoned Fort C.F. Smith, a casualty of the Treaty of Fort Laramie on July 2, 1868. When the US Army left the following month, Lakota warriors burned the fort down the following day after the troopers' departure. The ruins of the fort lay on benchland 500 yards from the Bighorn River, where that waterway emerged from the canyon. In its prime, the fort included a 125-foot square stockade made of adobe and wood for protection, with bastions for concentrated defense. Now, only the adobe remained.[11]

The wagon train rolled through a gap in the south wall of the uninhabited fort and halted in the center. Frank Grounds posted the picket positions along the ruined walls, which negated the need to dig holes for protection. Many men went to the Big Horn River to wash the trail grime off, and a few may have dipped a fishing line in the water. There would be "Bombay Duck" (fried fish) tonight! The men built campfires.[12] Sunset occurred at 1909. Addison M. Quivey later recalled the condition of Fort Smith:[13]

We found the adobe walls of Ft. Smith still standing, the neatly walled and well-

arranged cemetery nearly as left, except that the Indians had wrenched the gates from the hinges, and the boards at the head of the graves are displaced, and some of these hacked and otherwise defaced; but the names on all of them are yet legible. The beautiful monument in the center of the inclosure, with the names of all the buried—twenty-three in number— engraved upon it, is but little defaced. Nineteen of those buried in this little inclosure were killed by Indians.

Wednesday, April 22, 1874 (Fort C. F. Smith) [N 45° 18.852', W 107° 54.485']

Sunrise was at 0516. The expedition remained at the ruins of Fort C.F. Smith. Many of the men slept in. More men went swimming in the river and the herd of livestock continued to graze and water. Some of the men finally found minute amounts of gold on the riverbed, but in insufficient quantities to pan. The weather was sunny and rest was the priority of the day. However, Frank Grounds and Hugh Hoppe got into a fierce argument; Hoppe still wanted to head south toward Goose Creek and the Lost Cabin Mine. Grounds had had enough and pulled rank on the stubborn Hoppe and the wagon train continued west. Sunset occurred at 1910.

Fort C.F. Smith; abandoned in the Treaty of Fort
Laramie on July 2, 1868, the following month,
Lakota warriors burned down the fort. This is the
view of the remains of the fort in 1910; today it is
just an empty field with prairie grass. *Original
photograph taken by Vie Willets Garber, courtesy of
Bozeman Trail Website*

Location of former Fort C.F.
Smith. The expedition laagered
here [N 45° 18.852', W 107°
54.485'] from April 21-22, 1874.
Author photograph, October 2013

Marker for old Fort Smith. *Author photograph, October 2013*

After the Treaty of 1868, travel along the Bozeman Trail slowed to a trickle. *Author photograph, October 2013*

The Bozeman Trail ran past Fort C.F. Smith until 1868. *Author photograph, October 2013*

Thursday, April 23, 1874 (west of the Bighorn River)

Sunrise was at 0514. The weather was warm and the sky was clear blue, heralding a good day. During the morning, the men buried everything that was not needed for the remainder of the trip in the dilapidated walls of the old fort, so the load on the still weak livestock would be lessened as much as possible. The buried accoutrements included the remaining oyster can canister rounds for the Big Horn Gun. Later in the day, the wagon train left the ruins, traveled several hundred yards to the river and turned downstream. Once Frank

Grounds had found a suitable fording site, the crew of the Big Horn Gun—which now had no ammunition—guarded by twenty men, set up in an overwatch position to protect the wagon train while it was in the water. Watching the wagon train were Lakota warriors on a hill near War Man's Creek.[14]

Once the train had reached the far side, other men provided protection as the Big Horn Gun was limbered up and pulled across the river. The Rich & Willson wagon took two hours to repair after crossing the river. Now the expedition was inside the Crow Reservation. It continued to move northwest until it made

high ground out of the valley. At this location, Grounds designated the laager site. While the frontiersmen were organizing for the upcoming night, a few men spotted a herd of buffalo and several men rode out and shot a few of the animals for meat.[15] Sunset occurred at 1911.

Friday, April 24, 1874 (west of the Bighorn River)

Sunrise was at 0513. The sun shone quite hot. The expedition continued moving, passing Beauvais Creek, where they found a campsite with the remains of two wolf hunters. They identified the men as Joseph Lee and George

Ridge where Lakota warriors observed the wagon train crossing the Bighorn River on April 23, 1874. The warriors did not follow the expedition after this point. *Author photograph, October 2013*

Location near Fort Smith where the wagon train crossed the Bighorn River on April 23, 1874, enroute home. *Author photograph, October 2013*

Ackerly, who six months before had trespassed on the reservation to hunt. Apparently the Crow did not take kindly to the incursion and killed the men as the slept in their tent. Frank Grounds moved the column on, and later the wagon train laagered along the creek. At about 5:00 p.m. there was a small rain shower. Lakota warriors continued to follow the wagon train, but kept their distance.[16] Today, sunset occurred at 1912.

Saturday, April 25, 1874 (Pryor's Gap)

Sunrise was at 0511. The men ate breakfast and then harnessed the oxen and horses to the wagons, commencing movement at 0800. The expedition continued on the Bozeman Trail, encountering many hills and deep ravines, before experiencing rain showers and deep thunder at 1100. At about 1400, the men crossed Pryor Creek and then through Pryor's Gap, before finding a laager site for the night. Soon afterward, there was another lengthy shower. James Crane and another man departed the wagon train and headed out on their own.[17] Sunset occurred at 1914.

Sunday, April 26, 1874 (Fort Smith Road)

Sunrise was at 0509. About 0700, the wagon train headed west along the Fort Smith Road for Clarke's Fork of the Yellowstone, through very broken terrain, when men on the advance guard potted a warrior party approaching. After receiving this information, Frank Grounds organized the wagon train into two columns. The war party veered off and approached the frontiersmen from the left flank. One of the warriors rode up to the wagon train and the men realized the war party was not hostile, but rather composed of the Crow. The wagon train and the Crow rode on together, until a suitable campsite was found.[18]

After the men formed the laager and took care of the animals, they showed the forty Crows several scalps they had collected in the various combats with the Lakota earlier in the expedition. The Crows were delighted to see the trophies of their traditional Lakota enemies and began breaking into a scalp dance. At 1700, Elisha Terrill, the special correspondent from the *Avant Courier*, and Addison Quivey wrote reports of the expedition and gave them to Edwin R. Bradley and Yank Evarts, who left the expedition and rode as fast as they could toward Bozeman. Sunset occurred at 1915. The Crows continued to celebrate late into the night (2200) as the men fell asleep.[19] According to a later interview, Tom Allen stated that the enemy warriors followed the wagon train until the expedition reached Clark's Fork.[20] Addison Quivey wrote of the experience later:[21]

> Stormy weather continued until we arrived at Ft. Smith, after which we had fine weather most of the time until we got through. Before reaching Clark's Fork, a small war party of Crows made their appearance, and concluded not to travel any farther in pursuit of Sioux, but travel with us during the afternoon, and camp with us at night, seeming to be wild with delight at the sight of Sioux scalps and other trophies which our party had brought along, and at night got up a grand scalp dance. They continued far into the night, and the next morning left us to join their main camp, which was moving from the neighborhood of Wind River, where they had been hunting during the winter, and were then on their way to the Crow agency.

Monday, April 27, 1874 (East Rosebud Creek)

Sunrise was at 0508. The men arose and began assembling the formation. Once again, Hugh Hoppe attempted to talk some of the men into heading south with him to the mystical gold fields, but by this time, most of the men could smell the barn at home and wanted to get back to Gallatin County. The Crows gathered in a large circle to smoke a medicine pipe. At 0700 the wagon train started to roll. The country was dry and stony. The wagon train started to fragment, with ox team wagons in one group and mule teams in another.[22] Sunset occurred at 0716. Joe Cook recalled the experience with the Crows:[23]

> We soon came to the old Fort Fetterman and Fort Smith road. After we crossed the

Big Horn River we fell in with the Crows, Black Foot being the chief of this band. We traveled with them until we came to their agency on the Little Rosebud. The Crows boast that they have always been friendly with the Whites.

Tuesday, April 28, 1874 **(Rock Creek)**
Sunrise broke at 0506. The men ate breakfast. At 0630, the wagon train began to move in the direction of Bozeman, before stopping and laagering for the evening. Even now, Frank Grounds imposed strict security discipline just in case hostile warriors returned, although that was now highly unlikely. Sunset occurred at 1918. Addison Quivey recalled this portion of the journey:[24]

Soon after leaving Clark's Fork, the horse and mule teams and packers left the ox teams, arriving in Bozeman a few days in advance. The last teams arrived in Bozeman on the 11th of May. I forgot to mention in proper place that coal makes its appearance in many places between Big Horn and Clark's Fork, and that in one place, southeast of Prior's Creek, I found extensive beds of fossil marine shells, which are all, or nearly all, of one species, but of different sizes, and are much like those which are usually called 'cockle' shells.

Wednesday, April 29, 1874 **(South of the Yellowstone River)**
Sunrise occurred at 0505. The wagon train continued to move toward Bozeman, gaining a full ten miles, before stopping and laagering for the evening.[25] The men ate supper. Sunset occurred at 1919.

Thursday, April 30, 1874 **(South of the Yellowstone River)**
Sunrise was at 0503. The wagon train continued to move sixteen miles toward Bozeman before stopping and laagering for the evening. John Henry Stevens and Edward Farnum left the wagon train to go hunting but did not return. Edwin R. Bradley and Yank Evarts arrived at Bozeman, gave their accounts and provided the reports written by Elisha Terrill and Addison Quivey to the *Avant Courier*.[26] Sunset occurred at 1920.

Friday, May 1, 1874 **(South of the Yellowstone River)**
Sunrise was at 0502. The wagon train continued to move toward Bozeman about ten miles before stopping at 1500 and laagering for the evening.[27] Sunset occurred at 1921. At Bozeman, the *Avant Courier* published a special extra edition at 0300, featuring two stories on the first page, under the banner headlines:[28]

THE EXPEDITION!
The Command Returning!
ONE MONTH'S HARD FIGHTING!
ONE HUNDRED INDIANS KILLED.
One White Man Killed and Two Wounded.
FOUR PITCHED BATTLES AND CONTINUOUS SKIRMISHING.
The Boys Make a Gallant Fight Against Large Odds.

The first article was a reprint of a letter from John V. Bogert to James P. Bruce, permanent chairman of the Yellowstone Wagon Road and Prospecting Expedition:

Sir: Messers. Bradley and Evarts arrived here late last evening with private letters and report as follows: Since the last installment the Expedition has constantly been attacked and harassed by Sioux—in bodies of from 100 to 1000. I regret to state that Mr. Z. Yates of Boulder was killed, and Bostwick of Deer Lodge and Woodward of Gallatin slightly wounded.

The command reached the near vicinity of Tongue River, but on account of the constant Indian attacks but little prospecting was done, and the Expedition was obliged to retreat. When Bradley and Evarts left on the 26th it was near Pryor's Gap, slowly marching this way, probably out of danger and all well. The stock was run down, feeding having been almost impossible; the horse had suffered greatly from epizootic; the roads were very muddy, and the rain had fallen in torrents. Bradley and Evarts report rich prospects on Big Horn, Tongue River, etc. During the trip some twenty horses were lost, but reprisals restored the complement. In no attack, however, were the Indians successful, and many Sioux and horses were killed.

Mr. Quivey writes to Mr. Story endorsing the foregoing, except that, so far as gold is concerned, he mere states that 'rich mines exist in the Big Horn mountains south of the Big Horn—that the first fight occurred near the mouth of the Rose Bud, and that Vernon abandoned the command twenty-five miles above Pompey's Pillar.'

Rouse, Wilson, Roe, [Rowe] Heinze and two others are now on the way to Bozeman and will probably reach us by tomorrow. Evarts asserts that the country is rich and that 300 men can hold the country without trouble.

While the Committee must admit the unfortunate present result of the movement,

it by no means despairs of ultimate success of the attempt in the lower country. A full history of the events of the march will be made you immediately upon the reception of the report to the Council.

For the Committee,
J.V. BOGERT
Secretary and Treasurer

The second article, also on the first page, was the report of Elisha Terrill:[29]

Prior's Gap, April 26, 1874
At this point the Expedition is in camp for the night all in good health save two wounded men (Bostwick and Woodward) who were shot by the Indians but are doing well. This opportunity will not permit my writing at any length or give many particulars of our trip, only that we have been fighting Sioux Indians since the 1st of April and have had four general battles, one four hours, one three, one five and the other about two hours, with several skirmishes. In all the general fights we have got away with their hair. We have invariably whipped them badly.

We fought about twenty-five the first fight; the second about four hundred; the third about six hundred; the fourth about eight hundred or one thousand Indians. We suppose we killed and wounded about one hundred Sioux. We have had the misfortune to lose one of our best men, Mr. Z. Yates, of Radersburg, who was shot through the heart during a charge in the third battle on the Little Big Horn River.

We have been constantly annoyed with Indians for more than one hundred miles. There have been none in sight for several days past.

The first big fight the boys scalped eight of the red devils, but they killed and wounded about twenty-five head of our stock before they could be dislodged. The 16th they charged upon us while moving in two columns of about two hundred each, one in the front and the other in the rear. The boys met them as they came in full charge on horseback, having only about five hundred yards to run before reaching the train, and fired such deadly volleys into them that they turned their course and made for the ravines. At that time the men charged furiously upon them and dislodged them, leaving many dead and wounded. In the fight there must have been, in the charge upon us and nearby, 1000 Indians. We had the luck to get no one hurt—only a few horses shot.

Taking all into consideration, we have had a hard trip. Our stock has had the epizootic badly, and are dying yet.

There is no use talking—give us a few more such men as we have, and we can clean out the whole Sioux nation. Only twenty minutes to write and the courier is slyly going to leave.

Yours,
Terrill

Saturday, May 2, 1874 (South of the Yellowstone River)

Sunrise was at 0500. The wagon train continued to move fifteen miles toward Bozeman before stopping and laagering for the evening, the day having been uneventful.[30] Sunset occurred at 1923.

Sunday, May 3, 1874 (South of the Yellowstone River)

Sunrise was at 0459. The wagon train continued to move toward Bozeman about fifteen miles before stopping and laagering for the evening. John Henry Stevens and Edward Farnum returned to the wagon train from hunting; they had become lost and crossed north over the Yellowstone River before realizing their mistake and returning to the expedition. During the day, the wagon train came across a camp of the Blackfoot Band of the Crow Indians.[31] Sunset occurred at 1924.

Monday, May 4, 1874 (South of the Yellowstone River)

Sunrise was at 0457. The wagon train continued to move at least eighteen miles toward Bozeman before stopping and laagering for the evening.[32] Hugh Hoppe and a few other men reached Bozeman.[33] Sunset occurred at 1925.

Tuesday, May 5, 1874 (Along the Yellowstone River)

Sunrise was at 0456. The wagon train continued to move toward Bozeman. Opposite Hunter's Hot Springs the expedition crossed the Yellowstone River, arriving at the springs at 1000. Some of the men took a hot bath; the wagon train resumed moving at 1400 before stopping and laagering for the evening nearly opposite the Crow Agency.[34] Sunset occurred at 1927.

Wednesday, May 6, 1874 (Quinn's Ranch) [N 45° 39.704', W 110° 40.310']

Sunrise was at 0454. The wagon train continued to move toward Bozeman past Sheep Mountain, before stopping near Quinn's Ranch and laagering for the evening.[35] Sunset occurred at 1928. Back in Bozeman, Gov. Benjamin Potts congratulated the members of the expedition who had already returned ahead of the main body.[36]

Thursday, May 7, 1874

Sunrise was at 0453. Elements of the wagon train continued to move toward Bozeman before stopping and laagering for the evening. Other men split off and headed to their own homes. Sunset occurred at 1929.

Friday, May 8, 1874

Sunrise was at 0451. Elements of the wagon train continued to move toward Bozeman before stopping and laagering for the evening. Other men split off and headed to their own homes. Sunset occurred at 1930.

Saturday, May 9, 1874

Sunrise was at 0450. Elements of the wagon train continued to move toward Bozeman before stopping and laagering for the evening. Other men split off and headed to their ranches. Sunset occurred at 1931.

Sunday, May 10, 1874

Sunrise was at 0449. Stragglers from the wagon train continued to move toward Bozeman before stopping and laagering for the evening. Sunset occurred at 1933.

Monday, May 11, 1874

Sunrise was at 0447. George Herendeen arrived at the Crow Agency and resumed his job.[37] Sunset occurred at 1934.

Tuesday, May 12, 1874

Sunrise was at 0446. Joe Cook later stated that he got back to Bozeman on the 12th of May, having been out just three months. Sunset occurred at 1935.[38]

Wednesday, May 13, 1874

Sunrise was at 0445. Stragglers from the wagon train continued to move toward Bozeman before stopping and laagering for the evening. Sunset occurred at 1936.

Thursday, May 14, 1874

Sunrise was at 0444. The last elements of the wagon train arrived at Bozeman. Sunset occurred at 1938. James Gourley made some final remarks about the expedition:[39]

During the expedition the weather was very cold and sleety. A good many of the Indians got the quinsy [a tonsillar abscess at the back of the throat caused by streptococcus] and by their treatment of it made a good many good Indians. The treatment consisted in putting a patient into one of their sweat houses until he was in full perspiration. Then the patient jumped into the cold water of the creek. A great many died, probably not less than 800.

It had been a titanic chess game. Frank Grounds ensured that the wagon train did not travel so long during any day that there was no time left to build fighting positions around the nightly laager. The warriors probed in the darkness to try and discover weak spots in the defenses through which to attack at dawn. Both Sitting Bull and Grounds realized—almost simultaneously at the conclusion of the Battle of Lodge Grass Creek—that their forces could no longer achieve success.

In a tactical sense, it had been a draw. Yes, the frontiersmen had inflicted more casualties on the warriors then they had received in return. However, the Lakota and Northern Cheyenne still held the field, after the expedition—finally agreeing that discretion was the better part of valor—turned west at Lodge Grass Creek and returned to Bozeman. Yes, the following year, more frontiersmen, many of whom had been on the 1874 expedition, would try and establish Fort Pease along the Yellowstone River. But after several months, the warriors put so much pressure on the outpost that it, too, was abandoned.

At a higher level, unfortunately, both sides were doomed to defeat. The insatiable hunt for gold would not slacken; months after the 1874 expedition had terminated at Bozeman, a larger expedition, traveling from Fort Abraham Lincoln in the east, would arrive at the Black Hills, also searching for maza-ska-zo—except that this second expedition would find the mineral. President Ulysses S. Grant was now in a hard place. By law and treaty, he had a duty to keep gold prospectors out of the Lakota's sacred Black Hills.

But Grant was nothing if not pragmatic. Realizing that the relatively tiny regular army could not surround the Black Hills forming an impenetrable cordon—within months there were an estimated 15,000 miners in the region—and understanding that the electorate demanded the opening of the region, Grant put into motion a plan to wage war on the bands of Lakota that refused to live on the reservations. That decision set in motion the juggernaut that would take the US 7th Cavalry Regiment to its fate at the Little Bighorn.

The Lakota and Northern Cheyenne would emerge on the losing end as well. The showdown on the plains between the American Indians and the newer European-rooted Americans was a struggle between two ways of life that were basically incompatible. As long as the conflict between the Plains tribes and the US government remained a low-grade fever, the tribes could at least hope for a few more years, maybe longer, of roaming off the reservations; after all, the entire US Army at the time was less than 30,000 in strength.

The gold rush into eastern Montana and the Black Hills changed that because now the roaming tribes were in the wrong place at the wrong time; Gen. Phil Sheridan responded in 1876 by sending a three-prong attack into eastern Montana to force the roaming tribes back to their reservations in the Dakotas. Sitting Bull, Crazy Horse, Gall, and Hump responded by defeating, in turn that June, Brig. Gen. George Crook at the Rosebud and Lt. Col. George Custer at the Little Bighorn. After Custer's defeat, the army "got serious" about the Plains tribes and it was only a matter of time before the akicita (soldiers)—backed by tens of millions of workers stoking the giant furnaces of the Industrial Revolution replete with railroads, river boats, and telegraphs—crushed them.

The 1874 Yellowstone Wagon Road and Prospecting Expedition was a wake-up call for that maelstrom.

Notes

1. Collection 1250, Folder 41, 17; Weibert, *The 1874 Invasion*, 107.
2. Weibert, *The 1874 Invasion*, 107-108.
3. Ibid, 109.
4. Quivey, 273.
5. Collection 1250, Folder 41, 17; Weibert, *The 1874 Invasion*, 110.
6. Ibid.
7. Weibert, *The 1874 Invasion*, 110-111.
8. Hutchins, "Poison in the Pemmican," 23.
9. Collection 1250, Folder 41, 18; Weibert, *The 1874 Invasion*, 111.
10. Ibid.
11. Ibid.
12. Ibid.
13. Quivey, 274-275.
14. Camp Manuscripts, Box 4: Folder 5, Envelope 6—Barkley statement of 1874; Collection 1250, Folder 41, 19; and Weibert, *The 1874 Invasion*, 117.
15. Ibid.
16. Camp Manuscripts, Box 4: Folder 5, Envelope 6—Barkley statement of 1874; Collection 1250, Folder 41, 19.
17. Collection 1250, Folder 41, 19; Weibert, *The 1874 Invasion*, 119.
18. Letter from William C. Barkley to Walter M. Camp; Collection 1250, Folder, 19-20; and Weibert, *The 1874 Invasion*, 119.
19. Ibid.
20. Camp Manuscripts, Box 4: Folder 5, Envelope 6—Barkley statement of 1874.
21. Quivey, 281.
22. Collection 1250, Folder 41, 20.
23. Brown and Willard, 564.
24. Quivey, 282-283.
25. Collection 1250, Folder 41, 21.
26. "From the Expedition!" *Avant Courier* (Bozeman,) May 1, 1874, 2.
27. Collection 1250, Folder 41, 21.
28. "The Expedition!" *Avant Courier—Extra* (Bozeman,) May 1, 1874.
29. Ibid.
30. Collection 1250, Folder 41, 21.
31. Ibid.
32. Ibid.
33. Hoppe, Letter to *Helena Herald*.
34. Collection 1250, Folder 41, 22.
35 Ibid.
36 Hutchins, "Poison in the Pemmican," 24.
37 Gray, *Custer's Last Campaign*, 105.
38 Brown and Willard, 565.
39 "The Story of a March," 13.

CHAPTER SEVEN

Fading Away

Once the expedition crossed Clark's Fork, it began to fragment, with groups of men deciding to go home at a faster pace than the wagons. Gold continued to play a role in many of their lives. Over the next two years, twelve men would seek their fortune to the east in the Black Hills: William C. Langston, Robert Henry Evans, Joseph E. Cook, William D. Cameron, William Buchanan, Stewart Buchanan, William Cudney, Zadok H. Daniels, Benjamin R. Dexter, Frank Grounds, George H. Miller, and Joseph A. Ramsdell.

Many men had become friends during the expedition and would have future adventures together. Robert Evans established the first ranch along Spearfish Creek (at present-day Spearfish, South Dakota) along with his friend on the expedition Joseph Ramsdell. Some, like Henry Bird Calfee and Paul McCormick, would become quite successful in business. Many men participated in later expeditions; at least twenty would search for gold or serve as scouts again in the wilds, and five—Henry S. Bostwick, James Edwards, George H. Miller, Patrick Sweeney, and Wesley Brockmeyer later would be killed by warriors in Montana or the Dakotas. Some men got the itch to continue westward; John Anderson, William Awbrey, Jack Bean, Oliver Perry Hanna, Hugh Hoppe, John Johnston, Peter Koch, Tyler McClees and William Wright all died as old men in the sun of California.

Not everyone made it to the Promised Land. Henry Ashmead appears to have died destitute in Livingston; William Polfer died penniless in Helena. In February 1891, Neil Gillis, after a night of binge drinking, was discovered the next day frozen to death in his underwear. In another incident, in 1882, Benjamin Walker got into an altercation in Coulson with a man named Quinn that ended with the latter shooting and killing Honest Ben.

Five men later served as law enforcement officers. Andy Cowan became the sheriff of Gallatin County; Charles P. Blakeley also served in this position. Billy Cameron became the sheriff of Meagher County in 1884; Zadok Daniels served as the deputy sheriff for Park County, while Muggins Taylor later became a deputy in the Custer County sheriff's department, before he was gunned down in September 1882 in Lump's Laundry at Coulson. Other men chose less stressful pursuits—but jobs that would have been appreciated by their brethren on the expedition—such as John Dillabaugh, later owner of the Bit Saloon in Glendale, where "the Kentucky whisky served there was better than some in Butte and offered at half the price!"

And, of course, several men went on to play significant roles on other battlefields with the Lakota and Northern Cheyenne, making it into the history books covering this dramatic era of American history. No fewer than nine frontiersmen on that 1874 Yellowstone Wagon Road and Prospecting Expedition were noted participants in the Great Sioux War of 1876: Jack Bean, Henry Bostwick, Big Spit Hanna, George Herendeen, Paul McCormick, Yank Brockmeyer, Zed Daniels, Uncle Billy Hamilton, and Muggins Taylor.

The following sketches present information that this study has found on the men of the expedition after they participated in that life-changing event in 1874. Again, those names in bold are wagon train participants that have multiple sources showing their participation in the expedition. For those men not listed below, they simply disappeared from the stage of life to whatever fate would bring them.

Tom Allen. Tom Allen took part in the Fort Pease Expedition along the Yellowstone River in 1875. He lived in Yellowstone County in 1890 and applied for his Civil War pension the same year. In his later life, he admitted his original name to historian Walter Mason Camp. Tom Allen/William Barkley died on March 10, 1914, at his homestead just west of Kirby, Montana, near Rosebud Creek. He was buried at the Custer National Cemetery in Plot A, Number 1469A on October 17, 1931.[1]

John Anderson. In 1881, Anderson married Julia Harris in Bozeman; she had been born in Tennessee in about 1849. He was a charter member and Officer of the Guard of the William English Post Number 10, Grand Army of the Republic. He also served as the first custodian of the Elks Lodge in Bozeman and the custodian of the Carnegie Library there. He and his wife later lived in a cottage on the outskirts of Bozeman. He was present at the celebration in 1883 to commemorate the arrival of the Northern Pacific Railroad to Bozeman and honor the members of the 1874 expedition.[2] Anderson also attended a reunion of survivors of the expedition on August 12, 1914, in Bozeman, at which point his residence was listed as Bozeman.[3] In September 1917, he traveled with George Herendeen and two history professors on the

Tom Allen (also known as William Barkley) grave at the Custer Battlefield National Cemetery. He was buried in Plot A, Number 1469A on October 17, 1931. *Author photograph, October 2013*

1874 expedition's actual route along Rosebud Creek. In 1918, John moved to the Soldiers' Home in Sawtelle, California. John Anderson died at the Soldiers' Home in March 8, 1925. He is buried at the Los Angeles National Cemetery in Section 34, Row K in Site 32 next to his wife, who had died in 1920. His headstone states that he had been a sergeant in the Union Army.[4]

Henry "Hank" Ashmead. Hank Ashmead was present at the celebration in 1883 to commemorate the arrival of the Northern Pacific Railroad to Bozeman and honor the members of the 1874 expedition. He appears to have died destitute in Livingston, Montana, on February 13, 1893. Henry Ashmead was buried at the Park County Poor Farm Cemetery in Livingston, which was closed in 1924, causing any marker of his grave to disappear.[5]

Charles E. Avery. Charles Avery returned to Bozeman and that winter made a gold strike at the Norwegian Gulch mining area. He later made one of the valuable discoveries at the Pony Mines and secured interests in the Boss Tweed and other claims. He remained at the Pony Mines for several years, before moving to Butte. He also prospected and mined in Beaverhead, Madison, Jefferson, andSilver Bow in Montana and also in Idaho. In 1900, Charles Avery was listed as a silver miner in Bannack Township of Beaverhead County in Montana. By 1905 he was back in Butte and in 1915 he was believed to have resided in Pony in Madison County.[6] Charles E. Avery possibly died on July 26, 1918.[7]

William H. Awbrey. William Awbrey left Montana within two years after the expedition and traveled to California. He registered to vote in San Jose Township of Santa Clara County, on October 28, 1876. In 1880, he lived in Red Bluff Township of Tehama County, California, with his family and was a farmer. He died on May 17, 1896, in Gas Point, Shasta County. William H. Awbrey is buried at the Anderson District Cemetery, Anderson, Shasta

County, California. His wife Francis died on December 26, 1919.[8]

William H. Babcock. William Babcock lived in Bozeman and built a huge mansion on Church Street for his family, named "the Castle." However, by 1880, his wife had died. Babcock then spent two years in Southern California and Oklahoma, before returning to Bozeman, where he oversaw the construction of the Bozeman Opera House in 1888, and supervised the building of the Bozeman City Hall in 1889.[9] He later lived in Butte and was a carpenter there in 1900. William H. Babcock died in February 1919 at the home of his son in Seattle, Washington. His remains were cremated.[10]

William D. Bassett. William D. Bassett married Elizabeth A. "Bettie" Mulherin in Gallatin County on April 5, 1879. Bettie—probably the daughter of J.H. "Frisky-John" Mulherin—had been born on January 15, 1863, in Clarkesville, Pike County, Missouri. The following year, he lived in the Upper Yellowstone Valley in Gallatin County. William's father committed suicide by drinking poison on May 1, 1884, in Cinnabar, Montana. William and Elizabeth had three sons and three daughters. He was a rancher and blacksmith and described as hard drinking. William Bassett died in Fishtail, Stillwater County, Montana, on

William Aubrey grave at the Anderson District Cemetery, Anderson, Shasta County, California. *Courtesy of Ancestry.com, William Awbrey*

William Basset grave at the Rosebud Cemetery at Absarokee, Montana. *Courtesy of Ancestry.com, William B. Basset*

February 6, 1922. He was buried the following day at the Rosebud Cemetery at Absarokee. Bettie, who remarried in 1927, died on December 7, 1942, in Fishtail.[11]

John "Jack" Bean. After serving in the Great Sioux War of 1876 in the Montana Column, in the summer of 1877 Jack Bean hired on with the army looking for Nez Perce warriors along the Madison River and in Yellowstone Park as a scout with George Herendeen, making $5 a day. That fall he went to Yellowstone Park as a hunting guide for former Confederate Army officer Col. William D. Pickett (Pickett

Jack Bean, center, at hunting camp table with English hunters in 1880s. *Courtesy of John Bean, grandson of Jack Bean*

Jack Bean and wife, Dora. Photograph was taken by Bean's brother-in-law Charles D. Loughrey. *Courtesy of Gallatin Pioneer Museum*

Jack Bean, far right, at extended family picnic. Photograph was taken by Bean's brother-in-law Charles D. Loughrey. *Courtesy of John Bean, grandson of Jack Bean*

Jack Bean's homestead outside Bozeman, Montana, in 1880s. *Courtesy of John Bean, grandson of Jack Bean*

Jack Bean's Bozeman, Montana, cabin in later years. *Courtesy of John Bean, grandson of Jack Bean*

Jack Bean in his office in San Jose, California. *Courtesy of John Bean, grandson of Jack Bean*

Jack Bean's grave in the Old Section of the Oakhill Cemetery in San Jose, California. *Courtesy of John Bean, grandson of Jack Bean*

was one of the earliest members of the Boone and Crockett Club.) Bean was present at the celebration in 1883 to commemorate the arrival of the Northern Pacific Railroad to Bozeman and honor the members of the 1874 expedition.[12] He later married Dora Francis Erskine. In 1889, Bean lived on Rocky Creek, east of Bozeman; his homestead was 160 acres. Bean guided hunters in Montana until about 1900, when he went to San Jose, California. There he started the San Jose Rubber Works with his sons. Jack Bean died on July 23, 1923, in San Jose, California. He is buried in the Old Section of the Oakhill Cemetery in that city. His wife died in 1951.[13]

Charles P. Blakeley. In 1875, Blakeley received a law license to practice in Montana Territory courts and became known as Judge Blakeley. He went on to have a distinguished career, serving as the sheriff for Gallatin County in 1882. When news was sparse in Bozeman, the newspapers listed prisoners in the jail, calling them "Brother Blakeley's Boarders." He served as the Speaker of the Montana House of Representatives in 1889–1890. During his political battles, based on his frenetic conduct, Blakeley was nicknamed "Flying Artillery." Charles P. Blakeley later lost $5,000 in the Gold Hill Mine. He and his wife Elizabeth had a daughter. He died on February 24, 1912, in Absarokee, Stillwater County, Montana. Charles P. Blakeley is buried at Sunset Hills Cemetery in Bozeman.[14]

Green Berry Blakeley. Green Blakeley married Mary Matilda Gilreath in 1880 in Missouri; it appears that they had two girls and three or four boys. The family is listed as residing in Montana in 1900. Green Blakeley attended a fortieth reunion of survivors of the expedition on August 12, 1914, in Bozeman, at which point his residence was listed as Big Timber.[15] He died on May 3, 1925, in Big Timber. Green B. Blakeley is buried at Mountain View Cemetery in Big Timber, of Sweet Grass County [N 45° 49.384', W 109° 58.046']. His wife Mary died in 1952 and is buried next to him.[16]

Anton W. Blank. Anton Blank worked as a teamster in 1909 for the Western Clay Manufacturing Company in Helena. He lived on Wilder Street in Helena in 1918.

Taylor Blevin. Taylor Blevin, George Herendeen, and Yank Evarts went with a Capt. Jackson from Fort Ellis to Yellowstone National Park to reconnoiter trails in the summer of 1874. In May 1875, Blevin left Bozeman with Maj. Fellows D. Pease and more than thirty other men on the Fort Pease Expedition to establish a proposed head of navigation (the farthest point west on the river that could be navigated by river boats) on the Yellowstone River at the mouth of the Big Horn River.[17] He was wounded in the chest on August 28, 1875, but miraculously the bullet did not penetrate his ribcage, but pieced the skin in the front, passed around the ribs, and exited the skin in his back. He left Fort Pease[18] with seven men and returned to Bozeman in February 1876.[19] There is some evidence that Taylor Blevin worked in Laramie City, Wyoming Territory, in 1880 on a government pack train, and that by 1905, Taylor Blevin had returned east to Wilton, Saratoga County, New York. In the state census for that year, a Taylor Blevin is listed as an uncle living with the family of Burton and Ada Green.[20]

Henry/W.A. Bostwick. On the return of the expedition, Henry Bostwick, due to his serious wounds, was admitted as a patient at the military hospital at Fort Ellis, reportedly with several bullets still in him.[21] He then became an interpreter and guide at Fort Shaw. Henry ran into some trouble concerning stolen horses

Green Blakeley died in 1925; he is buried at Mountain View Cemetery in Big Timber, Sweet Grass County, Montana [N 45° 49.384', W 109° 58.046']. *Author photograph, October 2013*

and hid out at Charles Avery's cabin at Norwegian Gulch, until Avery could procure some ammunition for Bostwick, who wanted another fight with the Lakota. In 1876, Bostwick signed on as a guide for the Montana Column in the Great Sioux War of 1876. Henry Bostwick was killed on August 9-10, 1877, in a battle with the Nez Perce at Big Hole, Montana Territory. His remains are buried in a mass grave at the battlefield.[22] His wife Victoria Mercier Bostwick died at Fort Benton, Montana, on January 20, 1894. She is buried at the Riverside Cemetery there.[23]

Edwin R. Bradley. Edwin R. Bradley lived in Bozeman in 1880 and was still a harness-maker, although that year he was unemployed for a great deal of time.

At one point during the research for this study, it appeared that one Edmund Bradley had been the individual on the expedition, not Edwin R. Bradley. A black man from New Haven, Connecticut, Edmund Bradley had come to Fort Benton in the Montana Territory in the early 1870s, built a small ranch, and married a woman from the Gros Ventre, a tribe that was an enemy of the Lakota. They had at least two children. This association would explain why the Bradley on the expedition could understand the Lakota language.

During the 1877 Nez Perce War, Chief Joseph's Nez Perce, enroute to Canada to escape US Army troops, reached the Missouri River and the crossing at Cow Island in north-central Montana on September 23, 1877. Serving as a small army supply base, the location was guarded by eleven soldiers of the US 7th Infantry Regiment. Four civilians were also present. During the fight in the darkness, the warriors killed two civilians and one soldier. Two days later the Nez Perce approached a wagon train at Cow Creek and offered to buy some supplies. At that moment, the 700 warriors spotted an approaching column led by Maj. Guido Ilges, the post commander of Fort Benton, enroute to Fort Clagett. Due to severe personnel shortages at Fort Benton, Major Ilges had but one enlisted

man and thirty-eight volunteer citizens that lived near the small base. After two hours of skirmishing, the trooper and volunteers withdrew. Among those killed was one of the civilian volunteers, Edmund Bradley.[24] Army troops took the remains to Fort Benton; one year later, authorities sent his remains to his mother in New Haven.

Given all the information, the study does not believe that Edmund Bradley and Edwin R. Bradley were the same individual on the 1874 expedition and that Edwin, the harness-maker from Missouri was probably the correct participant, not Edmund.

Braided Locks. Braided Locks, also known as Wrapped Braids—according to Dr. Thomas Marquis was the leader of Northern Cheyenne at the 1874 Battle of Lodge Grass Creek—was wounded by a shot across the cheek on March 17, 1876, when army soldiers raided his village at the Battle of Powder River. Some three months later, he fought at the Battle of the Little Bighorn. He was wounded again at that latter fight. According to one source, he was present at Sand Creek in 1890. Braided Locks later changed his name to Arthur Brady and lived on the Tongue River Agency in the early 1900s. Braided Locks was still alive in 1926 at the Cheyenne River Agency; he reportedly died at age 106.[25] His grandson, Pvt.Raymond Brady Sr., was an American Army combat hero in World War II, jumping into Normandy as a pathfinder with Company G in the 504th Parachute Infantry Regiment of the 82nd Airborne Division; Raymond also fought in the Battle of the Bulge.[26]

Wesley "Yank" Brockmeyer. In June 1876, Yank Brockmeyer hunted buffalo on Squaw Creek with fellow buffalo hunter, scout, and Indian fighter Victor Grant "Yellowstone Vic" Smith. Brockmeyer was killed near the Powder River Depot next to the Yellowstone River on August 2, 1876. A marker commemorates the spot [N 46° 45.303', W 105° 25.747'], although the exact location of Brockmeyer's remains were—by one report—buried on an island in

Bismarck levee; steamers *Nellie Peck* and *Far West* are in the foreground, Bismarck, Dakota Territory, June 1877. Wesley Brockmeyer died of his wounds on the *Far West* on August 2, 1876. *Photograph by F.J. Haynes, H-58, Haynes Foundation Collection, courtesy of Montana Historical Society Research Center Photograph Archives, Helena, MT*

Memorial to Wes Brockmeyer. Brockmeyer actually died about a mile from this site. *Author photograph, June 2015*

Stone on Yellowstone flood plain indicating the way to memorial to Wes Brockmeyer and the separate memorial to US 7th Cavalry Regiment trooper William George. *Author photograph, June 2015*

Joseph Brown died at Livingston, Montana, on July 3, 1913. He is buried at Mountain View Cemetery in that city. *Courtesy of Ancestry.com, Joseph Brown*

the middle of the Yellowstone River to prevent their later desecration.[27]

Joseph Brown. Joseph Brown later lived in Gardiner; he continued mining the rest of his life. Uncle Joe Brown died at Livingston on July 3, 1913. He is buried at Mountain View Cemetery in that city. The newspaper report of his death stated in conclusion:[28]

> A gentleman of the old school; the blazer of trails, the hardy pioneer; the man inured to privation, hardship and suffering; the man without fear or favor, who tells you if he likes you or if he does not; the man who looks you squarely in the eye, tells the truth and demands the truth in return; the exemplification of honesty, sincerity and frankness—a race disappearing with the advance of civilization as rapidly as the buffalo, and destined in a few years more to live as a remembrance and not as a reality.

Stewart Buchanan. After the expedition, Stewart Buchanan went to the Black Hills with his brother, William. In 1877, he fought in the Nez Perce campaign as a scout.[29] In 1881, Stewart and his brother staked a claim in the Iron Gulch Mine. He was present at the celebration in 1883 to commemorate the arrival of the Northern Pacific Railroad to Bozeman and honor the members of the 1874 expedition. In 1900, he lived with his brother in Deerfield, Fergus County, Montana, and listed his occupation as gold miner.[30]

William Buchanan. After the expedition, William Buchanan went to the Black Hills with his brother, Stewart, and Frank Grounds.[31] He was at the celebration in 1883 to commemorate the arrival of the Northern Pacific Railroad to Bozeman and honor the members of the 1874 expedition. In 1900, he lived with his brother in Deerfield, Fergus County, Montana, and listed his occupation as gold miner.[32] He may have died on January 20, 1913.[33]

T.C. Burns. T.C. Burns left Bozeman in the fall of 1876 and moved to the Tongue River, remaining there for three years. He then became a farmer and lived in Lower Yellowstone Valley of Gallatin County in 1880 with his wife Ellen; his ranch was on the White Tail Deer Creek. It appears that he lived next to his brother, who was a stock grower. T.C. Burns was at the celebration in 1883 to commemorate the arrival of the Northern Pacific Railroad to Bozeman and honor the members of the 1874 expedition. He later became the manager of the Montana Lumber Company near Big Timber. It is possible that he was still alive in 1928.[34]

James "Joe" Burrill. In 1880, Joe Burrill was living at West Gallatin Valley with his wife Lena (who had been born in New York); the couple would have five children (Henry, Francis, Evalena, May, and George,) working as a farmer. Joe Burrill was at the celebration in 1883 to commemorate the arrival of the Northern Pacific Railroad to Bozeman and honor the members of the 1874 expedition. The census of 1900 shows the family still on the farm with their children.[35] James Burrill died prior to 1910.

Henry Bird Calfee. In 1877, he helped lead a group of tourists, who had been captured and released by the Nez Perce Indians, out of the wilderness. After the expedition—and through 1881—Henry Calfee visited Yellowstone National Park and took stereographic photographs

The grave of Henry Bird Calfee at the Sunset Hills Cemetery in Bozeman, Montana. *Courtesy of Ancestry.com, Henry Bird Calfee*

of its attractions, amassing 300 views of the newly established national park, and selling them to eager customers across the United States. In doing so, Calfee helped to name many of Yellowstone's landmarks including Lone Star Geyser, Demon's Cave, Pulpit Basins and Fairies' Fall. In the early 1880s, he traveled around the country exhibiting nearly 200 giant views of the park, using oxy-calcium light to project hand-colored lantern slides of his stereographs. He titled this panorama of the park as Calfee's Wonderland and visited San Francisco, New York, Philadelphia, and St. Paul.

Grave of William D. Cameron in Livingston, Montana. *Author photograph, June 2015*

Henry was at the celebration in 1883 to commemorate the arrival of the Northern Pacific Railroad to Bozeman and honor the members of the 1874 expedition.[36] He married Kate Latus (born in England in 1859) in Missoula County, Montana on June 13, 1885. The couple appear to have had a daughter, Nettie, in May 1886 and a son, Frank, in May 1888. In 1895, Calfee was still residing in Missoula; he died at Deaconess Hospital in Bozeman on February 20, 1912. Henry Calfee is buried at the Sunset Hills Cemetery in Bozeman. Kate died on March 27, 1931, in Los Angeles County, California.[37]

William D. "Billy" Cameron. William Cameron went to the Black Hills for two years after the expedition; he visited what would become the Yellowstone National Park in 1878 with James Gourley.[38] Cameron was at the celebration in 1883 to commemorate the arrival of the Northern Pacific Railroad to Bozeman and honor the members of the 1874 expedition.[39] In 1884, he became the sheriff of Meagher County and killed a bandit during a stagecoach robbery. He married his wife Ruth in about 1885; she was from Canada. As he later recalled to Milburn L. Wilson, undersecretary of agriculture, (who visited the route of the expedition in September 1917) concerning the Big Horn Gun, "That's our ace."[40] William Cameron lived in Livingston, Montana, in 1910 and later in Emigrant; his wife served as the postmaster of the village of Chico in 1910. Cameron attended a reunion of survivors of the expedition on August 12, 1914, in Bozeman, at which point his residence was listed as Emigrant.[41]

On November 21, 1921, French Field Marshal Ferdinand Foch visited Livingston on a tour of America. Cameron, wearing his Civil War uniform and representing Livingston veterans, personally welcomed the French hero. It was Billy's last hurrah. William D. Cameron died of apoplexy on December 5, 1921, in Livingston, Park County, Montana.[42] He is buried at the Mountain View Cemetery at Livingston in Grave 13 of Lot 11 in Block

1 [N 45° 39.706', W 110° 35.248']. His gravestone shows a date of birth of 1843 and that he was a member of the Masons.

Archie Campbell. By 1880, Archie Campbell appears to have moved to Lead City in Lawrence County, Dakota Territory. He was still a miner.[43]

Elias "Blacky" Carter. Elias Carter, in May 1875, left Bozeman with Maj. Fellows D. Pease and more than thirty others on an endeavor that became known as the Fort Pease Expedition, to establish a proposed transportation center on the Yellowstone River near the mouth of the Big Horn River. Blacky initially sailed on the flatboat *Bozeman* from Benson's Landing on June 17, 1875, but the vessel soon struck an underwater snag and sank. Carter survived and helped build Fort Pease. On July 12, 1875, he rode back to Bozeman with a letter describing conditions in the fort. He returned to Fort Pease and at the end of January 1876 departed with six other men on a hunting expedition that was attacked by Lakota warriors on January 29. Blacky survived again and returned to the fort; a rescue party under Maj. Brisbin from Fort Ellis helped evacuate Fort Pease entirely on March 6, 1876.[44]

Nelson Catlin. In 1879, Nelson Catlin served as a packer on a hunting trip to the Crazy Mountains. An 1880 census lists a Nelson

The grave of Joe E. Cook. He died on March 16, 1922 in Spearfish, Lawrence County, South Dakota and is buried at Rose Hill Cemetery (Plot B-5-17-7) [N 44° 28.816', W 103° 51.072']. *Author photograph, October 2013*

Catlin living in Bozeman and working as a carpenter. By 1882, Nelson Catlin worked as a packer and guide in Yellowstone Park; in 1886, he applied to Yellowstone National Park for permission to erect a stable and corral at Mammoth Hot Springs.[45] He was at the celebration in 1883 to commemorate the arrival of the Northern Pacific Railroad to Bozeman and honor the members of the 1874 expedition.[46] It is possible that Nelson Catlin later lived in Arizona and in 1910 resided in Spokane, Washington; this Nelson Catlin was listed as a widower.[47]

Joseph E. Cook. Joe Cook was the assistant leader of the March 1876 gold expedition from Bozeman, Montana, to the Black Hills, during which he fought a group of warriors near Devil's Tower. He married Alma Sophia Schulz in 1882; the couple had one son and three daughters. Joe Cook lived in Belle Fourche City, Butte County, South Dakota, with his wife Alma in 1920. Cook later gave his recollections to A.M. Willard for *The Black Hills Trails: A History of the Struggles of the Pioneers in the Winning of the Black Hills*. He died on March 16, 1922 in Spearfish, Lawrence County, South Dakota and is buried at Rose Hill Cemetery (Plot B-5-17-7) [N 44° 28.816', W 103° 51.072']. His wife died in 1948.[48]

Walter Cooper. Walter Cooper was, perhaps, too successful in his gun business. With the passing of the buffalo in 1883, Walter Cooper's

Walter Cooper in 1894. *Courtesy of Museum of the Rockies Photo Archives, Catalog Number: x85.3.178*

Walter Cooper in his Bozeman office in the 1890s.
Courtesy of Museum of the Rockies Photo Archives,
Catalog Number: x85.3.179

Armory and Gun Manufactory at Bozeman soon went out of business. In 1887, Cooper took an interest in the work of James "Yankee Jim" George and his discovery of the first coal vein near Red Lodge. This interest blossomed into the founding of the Rocky Fork Coal Company.[49] In 1901, seeing that regional railroads were increasing in importance, Cooper organized investors and formed the Walter Cooper Company to provide links to the Northern Pacific Railroad lines.[50] Walter Cooper, master gunsmith, owner of the armory, the largest distributor for the Sharps Arms Company in the Montana Territory, and the man who refurbished the Big Horn Gun, died in Bozeman, Montana, on April 28, 1924, after a successful business and political career. Cooper is buried at the Sunset Hills Cemetery in Bozeman. His

The grave of Walter Cooper at the Sunset Hills Cemetery in Bozeman, Montana. *Courtesy of Ancestry.com, Walter Cooper*

recollections later served as the basis for a book, *A Most Desperate Situation.*[51]

Andrew Cowan. One month after the expedition returned, Andy Cowan married Rachel C. "Kate" Tribble (born in Missouri); the couple would have four children. In 1880, the family lived in Flat Head, Gallatin County, next to Doctor Cowan and his family. Andy Cowan became the sheriff of Gallatin County. He died on June 20, 1899, and is buried in Sunset Hills Cemetery in Bozeman.[52]

Doctor F. Cowan. In 1877, Doctor F. Cowan returned to Kentucky and married "Nannie" (Nancy) Hale; they later and had two sons, age two and one in 1880; his daughter's name was Lucy. In 1880, he lived in Flathead next to Andy Cowan. Doctor Cowan later lived in Central Park, Gallatin County and was at the celebration in 1883 to commemorate the arrival of the Northern Pacific Railroad to Bozeman and honor the members of the 1874 expedition. Doc Cowan died on September 11, 1895, in Belgrade, Montana. He is buried at the Sunset Hills Cemetery, Old Section, V 6, 5 in Bozeman.[53]

James S. Crain/Crane. In May 1875, Jim Crane, Maj. Fellows D. Pease and more than thirty other men left Bozeman on what became known as the Fort Pease Expedition to establish a proposed base for navigation on the Yellowstone River at the mouth of the Big Horn River. Jim initially sailed on the flatboat *Prairie Belle* from Benson's Landing on June 17, 1875, but the vessel struck an underwater obstacle on June 20 and had to undergo major repairs. During the expedition, it appears that Crane piloted a skiff in the boat party that helped supply the fort. His boat ran aground at a drift pile. By 1880, James Crain lived as a rancher in Dawson County, Montana Territory. He died at Glendive in 1884.[54]

Crazy Horse. On June 17, 1876, Crazy Horse led 1,500 Lakota and Cheyenne warriors in a surprise attack against Brig. Gen. George Crook (West Point Class of 1852) and 1,000 cavalry and infantry, elements of the US 3rd Cavalry Regiment, the US 9th Infantry Regiment, and the US 4th Infantry Regiment, and a large number of Crow and Shoshone warriors in what would become known as the "1876 Battle of the Rosebud." Crook withdrew his forces, delaying his planned advance north to link up with the northern prongs of the army operation against the Lakota, which contributed to Custer's subsequent defeat at the Battle of the Little Bighorn. A week later, Crazy Horse played a major role in the defeat of the US

Marker for the death of Crazy Horse on September 5, 1877, at Fort Robinson, Nebraska. His actual burial site is unknown. *Author photograph, June 2012.*

Crazy Horse Memorial in the Black Hills [43° 50' 12.44" N, 103° 37' 27.79" W.] Construction depends on private donations. *Author photograph June 2009*

7th Cavalry Regiment, but the victory was short-lived. The army turned its full attention to defeating the Northern Plains Indians after Custer's defeat. On September 10, 1876, Capt. Anson Mills and a force from the US 3rd Cavalry Regiment captured a Minneconjou village at the Battle of Slim Buttes. Crazy Horse mounted an unsuccessful attempt to rescue the village.[55]

On January 8, 1877, Crazy Horse's warriors fought their last major engagement in the Montana Territory at the Battle of Wolf Mountain, along the Tongue River, against Col. Nelson A. Miles and elements of the US 5th Infantry Regiment and the US 22nd Infantry Regiment—some 436 men. With his followers struggling through the brutal winter, Crazy Horse decided to surrender and his band made their way to Fort Robinson in Nebraska, arriving on May 5, 1877. For the next four months, Crazy Horse resided in his village near the Red Cloud Agency.

However, rumors of Crazy Horse's desire to depart and return to the old ways of life started to spread at the Red Cloud and Spotted Tail agencies. Finally, on the morning of September 4, 1877, two cavalry columns moved against his village, but found that it had scattered the previous night. Crazy Horse fled to the nearby Spotted Tail Agency. After meeting with army officials at the adjacent military post of Camp Sheridan, Crazy Horse agreed to return to Fort Robinson with 1st Lt. Jesse M. Lee, the Indian agent at Spotted Tail Agency, and later of Reno Inquiry fame.[56]

On the morning of September 5, 1877, Crazy Horse and Lt. Lee, accompanied by a number of Indian scouts, arrived at Fort Robinson. There they met the post adjutant, 2nd Lt. Frederic S. Calhoun—the younger brother of Jimmy Calhoun, who had been killed at the Little Bighorn. It was an ominous beginning. Calhoun directed Lt. Lee to turn

Crazy Horse over to the officer of the day, Capt. James Kennington. Lee protested and appealed to Col. Luther P. Bradley, the post commander, but to no avail. 1st Lt. Lee transferred Crazy Horse to Capt. Kennington, who was in command of the post guard, and the officer accompanied Crazy Horse to the post guardhouse [jail cells.] Near the entrance of this building, Crazy Horse struggled with a guard, and with Little Big Man, and attempted to escape. One of the guards, Pvt. William Gentles (who had been born in County Tyrone, Ireland) stabbed Crazy Horse with a bayonet, inflicting a mortal wound. Troopers carried Crazy Horse to the post adjutant's office and placed him on the floor after the chief refused to lie on a cot. Assistant Post Surgeon Dr. Valentine T. McGillycuddy saw that the wound was fatal, but tried to ease the pain by giving Crazy Horse a shot of morphine. The Lakota chief died that night about 2340. Crazy Horse's parents took possession of his body and later buried the remains in an undisclosed location. Some pundits believe that the remains are at Porcupine Bluff on the Pine Ridge Indian Reservation in South Dakota; others have posited that Crazy Horse is buried at nearby Wounded Knee; while still others offer that the burial location is in Sheridan County, Nebraska.[57]

An account of a possible grave with some details reportedly came from a warrior named Lone Eagle that was discovered in the Mari Sandoz Collection at the University of Nebraska. According to a summary of that statement, six years after Crazy Horse's death, a trapper named White brought a skull to the Wounded Knee trading post. He said that he had found it with some bones and a set of travois poles between Wounded Knee Creek and Porcupine Creek. Upon examination, the skull showed a bone deformity in the upper jaw below the corner of the nose; a second deformation lay between the eye cavity and the cheekbone. Several Lakota women, who had known Crazy Horse, examined it and stated that it was definitely the skull of the chief. One of the women, Louise Pourier, who claimed to be a relative of Crazy Horse, took the skull to her cabin. After several years, she wrapped the skull in a piece of blue woolen blanket, crushed the bones to fragments and buried the remains in her backyard near present Rockyford, South Dakota.[58]

William "Bill" Cudney. William Cudney went to the Black Hills in April 1875. He prospected for gold at Deadwood Gulch and supposedly staked the first claim at this location with two other prospectors in November

Zadok Daniels died in Livingston, Park County, Montana, on March 8, 1910, and is buried in Mountain View Cemetery. It appears that even after his death, some people insisted that "Zodiac" was one of his names, another anecdote of the Wild West that may never be finally settled. *Author photograph, June 2015*

Zadok H. Daniels in front of Hunters Hot Springs. He is the man just left of the center white post supporting the balcony (hand on hip.) Barely visible is his moustache and watch chain. For many years, some western aficionados believed that this photograph was of famous gunfighters—including Wyatt Earp—but that does not appear to be the case. *Courtesy of Livingston Area Chamber & Visitor Center*

of that year.[59] The area later became famous as Deadwood, South Dakota. Bill Cudney was present at the celebration in 1883 to commemorate the arrival of the Northern Pacific Railroad to Bozeman and honor the members of the 1874 expedition.[60]

Zadok H. Daniels. Daniels became active in establishing several mines in Cooke City. In May 1875, Zed Daniels left Bozeman with Maj. Fellows D. Pease and more than thirty others in the Fort Pease Expedition, to establish a fort and trading post on the Yellowstone River. Zed initially sailed on the flatboat *Maggie Hoppy* from Benson's Landing on June 17, 1875, and arrived at the site for the fort on June 24, 1875; he briefly served as sutler at the fort and also later served as the post sutler at Fort Ellis.[61] Daniels helped lead a party of 200 prospectors that departed the Crow Agency on April 10, 1876 to prospect along the old Bozeman Trail, examining every creek from Fort C.F. Smith to Fort Reno. The group then split into two elements and made their way to the Black Hills.[62]

Daniels served as a scout for Gen. Terry's forces from August to October 1876; he was under the command of Lt. Col. Elmer S. Otis. Zed Daniels was at the celebration in 1883 to commemorate the arrival of the Northern Pacific Railroad to Bozeman and honor the members of the 1874 expedition.[63] He lived in Cooke City from that year until 1894, when he married Margaret Mallon; she had several children from a previous marriage. He became the deputy sheriff for Park County and supervised the first execution in the county. At 0500, on July 13, 1894, Daniels helped hang Robert A. "Bob Fields" Anderson for the murder of Emanuel Fleming, an event that received the following news commentary:[64]

Every point for several blocks that would permit even a distant view over the high jail fence was thronged with eager and expectant persons, some of whom had come long distances for this meagre opportunity to satisfy a morbid curiosity. So dense was the crowd in front of the

East Gallatin County Cemetery, where David Davis is buried. *Author photograph, October 2013*

David Davis is buried at the East Gallatin County Cemetery outside Belgrade, Montana [N 45° 50.482' W 111° 08.050']. *Author photograph, October 2013*

entrance to the jail yard that it was extremely difficult for those who had been invited to reach the gate for admission.

Anderson had assaulted Fleming with an ax and shot him in the abdomen, leading to his death. Zadok H. Daniels died in Livingston, Park County, Montana, on March 8, 1910, and is buried in Mountain View Cemetery at Livingston in Lot 11 of Block 1 [N 45° 39.704', W 110° 35.244'] near Billy Cameron. His gravestone shows that he was a member of the Masons and his first name is shown as Zodiac.[65]

David Davis. On December 23, 1875, David Davis married Candace Wakefield (born in Louisiana.) The couple had five children. He was at the celebration in 1883 to commemorate the arrival of the Northern Pacific Railroad to Bozeman and honor the members of the 1874 expedition.[66] In 1880 the Davis family was listed as residing in East Gallatin Valley. David Davis died on September 5, 1891, in East Gallatin, probably from a heart attack, while working on his threshing machine. He is buried at the East Gallatin County Cemetery at Belgrade, Montana [N 45° 50.482', W 111° 08.050'].[67]

Benjamin R. Dexter. A sleigh ran over Ben Dexter on January 22, 1875, at Fort Benton, but he survived the incident.[68] Dexter went with Maj. Fellows D. Pease and helped establish Fort Pease in June 1875. Ben Dexter fought

Lakota warriors near Fort Pease on January 2, 1876; on January 22, he led seventeen frontiersmen out of Fort Pease and returned to Bozeman, Montana, on February 8, interested in moving on to richer mining areas in the Black Hills.[69]

By 1880, Benjamin Dexter lived in East Gallatin Valley. He then operated a sawmill in Maiden, before operating a store at the Andersonville mining camp. In about 1895, a crazed man named Duncan slashed the throat of Ben Dexter so badly that the miner almost died. However, once again Dexter proved too tough to kill and he resumed his mining efforts. In 1900, Dexter lived next to the Buchanan brothers in Deerfield, Fergus County, Montana, and listed his occupation as millwright. He was at this time divorced. Benjamin R. Dexter finally died while walking on the trail near his last gold prospecting site near Maiden, Montana, on November 8, 1907.[70]

John H. Dillabaugh. John H. Dillabaugh was appointed the US Postmaster for Glendale Township in Beaverhead County, Montana Territory, on November 29, 1875. On January 31, 1876, he was appointed and served as Justice of the Peace for Glendale Township. Later that year, he mortgaged his shoe shop. The *Butte Miner* newspaper, dated October 1, 1877, reported that John Dillabaugh owned the Bit Saloon in Glendale, and that, "the Kentucky whisky served there was better than some in Butte and offered at half the price!" John was a widower. In 1890, he lived in Thompson Falls, Missoula, Sanders County, Montana, and worked as a carpenter. John Dillabaugh died in May 1894 in this area; he had no known descendants.[71]

Morning Star (Vóóhéhéve); Lakota name Dull Knife. Born in about 1810, he was a signee of the Treaty of Fort Laramie in 1868. In 1878, after the tribe was taken to the Indian Territory (modern day Oklahoma) faced with starvation, he led his band north toward the Montana Territory and their old homelands. They were finally intercepted in 1879 with serious losses inflicted by the army. In 1883, Dull Knife died; he is buried next to Little Wolf at Lame Deer, Montana, in the Northern Cheyenne Reservation [N 45° 37.566', W 106° 39.712'].

Hugh Early. Hugh Early later served as a packer in the US 7th Cavalry Regiment. He was married in 1886 to a woman named Annie Hogan from Ireland; they had two sons (Emmet and Henry) and a daughter (Winfred.) Early attended a reunion of survivors of the expedition

Morning Star and Little Wolf Graves at Lame Deer, Montana. *Author photograph, June 2015*

on August 12, 1914, in Bozeman, at which point his residence was listed as Anaconda, Montana.[72] Alive in 1917 in Anaconda, he ran into Walter Mason Camp and George Herendeen, while they were revisiting the route of the expedition. During that encounter, Herendeen did not recall that Early had been on the journey in 1874. Early was listed on the census of 1920 at Anaconda in Deer Lodge County, Montana; he died there on July 1, 1924.[73]

James Edwards. In May 1875, Neil James Edwards left Bozeman with Maj. Fellows D. Pease on the Fort Pease Expedition to establish a fort on the Yellowstone River at the mouth of the Big Horn River; he was a member of the party that traveled by land. On July 12, 1875, Edwards accompanied Blacky Carter to some bluffs a mile from the fort to scan for enemy warriors. As the men were crossing a small washout, enemy warriors fired a fusillade of thirty to forty shots. Carter's horse was hit, but Blacky was lucky and escaped any wounds. James Edwards was not so fortunate; warrior fire struck him at least seven times. As a warrior ran up to scalp Edwards, the dying

man shot him with his pistol. A recovery party later brought James Edwards' remains back to Fort Pease and buried them.[74]

John Engesser. John Engesser was living with his brother in the Lower Yellowstone Valley of Gallatin County in 1880; it appears that his wife died in April that year of dropsy.[75]

Robert Henry Evans. Robert Evans went on the March 1876 gold expedition from Bozeman, Montana, to the Black Hills. He established the first ranch along Spearfish Creek (one mile below Spearfish) the same year, along with his friend on the expedition Joseph Ramsdell. Robert was married to Rebecca Jane Pettigrew and had eight children and became one of the most successful farmers in the state. Robert Evans died on March 16, 1929, at Spearfish, South Dakota. He is buried at the Rose Hill Cemetery there in Plot C-24-17-2 [N 44° 28.816', W 103° 51.072'].[76]

Edward K. "Yank" Everett/Everetts/Evarts. Yank Evarts, George Herendeen, and Taylor Blevin went with a Capt. Jackson from

Robert Henry Evans, right, in the 1920s. *Courtesy of Ancestry.com, Robert Henry Evans*

Robert Evans died on March 16, 1929 at Spearfish, South Dakota. He is buried at the Rose Hill Cemetery there in Plot C-24-17-2 [N 44° 28.816', W 103° 51.072']. *Author photograph, October 2013*

The family grave of Enoch Douglass Ferguson at the Sunset Hills Cemetery, in the Masonic Plot: D 60, at Bozeman, Montana [N 45° 40.519', W 111° 01.548']. *Author photograph, October 2013*

Individual marker for Enoch Douglas Ferguson. *Author photograph, October 2013*

Fort Ellis to Yellowstone National Park to reconnoiter trails in the summer of 1874.[77] Yank saved an Indian woman and her child from drowning on June 5, 1875, when they fell overboard on a ferry navigating the Yel-

lowstone River near where Fort Pease would be established. Evarts fought in the Nez Perce campaign as a scout in 1877.[78] The Edward K. Evarts that served in the 98th New York Volunteer Infantry Regiment is buried at the Oakwood Cemetery in Syracuse, New York.

Enoch Douglass Ferguson. While making a prospecting tour in July 1874, Enoch Ferguson suffered a shotgun accident at Meadow Creek that resulted in the loss of his left hand. Ferguson became the Gallatin County Assessor in 1877. He lived with two cousins in Bozeman in 1880, listing his occupation as a farmer. He married his first wife in 1880, but she died on September 4, 1888. Two years later, he married again (Nettie Lewis) and had one son and one daughter. Enoch Ferguson was at the celebration in 1883 to commemorate the arrival of the Northern Pacific Railroad to Bozeman and honor the members of the 1874 expedition.[79]

Ferguson also attended a reunion of survivors of the expedition on August 12, 1914, in Bozeman, at which point his residence was listed as Bozeman.[80] He was a part owner of the Mountain House Mine and was also a trustee for the Eastern Montana Mining and Smelting Company. Enoch Douglas Ferguson died on August 24, 1922. He is buried at Sunset Hills Cemetery in Bozeman in the Masonic Plot: D 60 [N 45° 40.519', W 111° 01.548'].[81]

Charles Fisher. In 1875, Fisher left Bozeman with Maj.Fellows D. Pease to establish a proposed transportation nexus on the Yellowstone River near the mouth of the Big Horn River. Fisher initially sailed on the flatboat *Maggie Hoppy* from Benson's Landing on June 17, 1875, and arrived at the site for the fort on June 24, 1875.[82]

George Fisher. George Fisher was at the celebration in 1883 to commemorate the arrival of the Northern Pacific Railroad to Bozeman and honor the members of the 1874 expedition.[83]

James Fleming. James Fleming is buried at Sunset Hills Cemetery in Bozeman.[84]

The grave of James Fleming at the Sunset Hills Cemetery in Bozeman, Montana. It has a military style headstone. *Courtesy of Ancestry.com, James Fleming*

Full length studio portrait of Flying By, wife, and son. *D.F. Barry Cabinet Card, Call Number B-213, courtesy of Denver Public Library Digital Collections*

Flying By. Flying By, sometimes known as Struck or Struck Plenty, was reported to be a member of Crazy Horse's warrior society Hokší Hakákta (Last Born Society) and fought at the Little Bighorn two years later. On May 7, 1877, an attack at present-day Lame Deer Creek, led by Gen. Nelson A. Miles, killed chief Lame Deer, Flying By's father. Flying By returned to the battlefield to recover his father's body, finding that it had been decapitated and had seventeen bullet wounds in it. Flying By later fled to Canada, but returned in about 1881 to live on the Standing Rock Reservation. In the mid-1880s, he toured with Buffalo Bill's Wild West Show, participating in reenactments of Custer's Last Stand, but doing no re-creations of the 1874 Yellowstone Expedition. Later known as George Flying By, he died in 1930.[85]

Grave of Chief Gall at Saint Elizabeth Episcopal Cemetery in Wakpala, Walworth County, South Dakota. Small packet at right is pipe tobacco left by a visitor to the grave. *Author photograph, May 2015*

A.B. Ford. Ford took part in the Fort Pease Expedition along the Yellowstone River in 1875.[86]

Charles Gale. Charles Gale apparently returned to Gallatin County after he slipped away a few days after the expedition began. He was a miner in Gallatin County in 1880.[87]

Gall. At the Little Bighorn, two of Gall's wives and three of his children were killed. After the Little Bighorn, Gall crossed over the border into Canada; he brought his group back to the United States in 1880 and surrendered. On May 26, 1881, authorities loaded Gall and his followers on riverboats and shipped then to the Standing Rock Indian Reservation. Gall became a boss farmer at the agency in 1885; he also appeared briefly in

James Gemmell is buried at the Sheridan Cemetery, Sheridan, Madison County, in Montana. *Courtesy of Ancestry.com, James Gemmell*

Close-up of Gemmell headstone. *Courtesy of Ancestry.com, James Gemmell*

George Gibson's grave at the Sunset Hills Cemetery in Bozeman, Montana. *Courtesy of Ancestry.com, George Gibson*

Wild West Shows and became the Judge of the Court of Indian Offenses at Standing Rock. He lived on the Standing Rock Agency—not participating in the Ghost Dance movement— until his death at his home in Oak Creek on December 5, 1894. Chief Gall's remains rest in Saint Elizabeth Episcopal Cemetery off Route 1806 West in Wakpala, South Dakota, overlooking the Missouri River [N 45° 38.530', W 100° 30.886'].

James Gemmell. James Gemmell operated a sawmill and continued to trade with the Crow. He died on April 6, 1881, in Sheridan, Madison County, in Montana. His obituary

mentioned that he had fathered twenty-two children and suffered from alcoholism. Gemmell is buried at the Sheridan Cemetery.[88]

George Gibson. George Gibson died on January 24, 1923. He is buried at the Sunset Hills Cemetery in Bozeman, Montana, next to his wife Mercy.[89]

Neil Gillis. In May 1875, Neil Gillis left Bozeman with Maj. Fellows D. Pease and more than thirty other men on the Fort Pease Expedition to establish a fort on the Yellowstone River at the mouth of the Big Horn River.[90] Gillis was wounded in the thigh near Fort Pease on January

2, 1876, when attacked by warriors. He returned to prospecting and in 1879, in partnership with James Gourley made a rich strike at Bear Gulch that they named the Highland Chief. Gillis was at the celebration in 1883 to commemorate the arrival of the Northern Pacific Railroad to Bozeman and honor the members of the 1874 expedition.[91] Gillis and his partners sold their claim in the mine in 1890 for $5,000 each. The following year, Neil Gillis moved to Livingston, where he began drinking to excess. The *Billings Gazette* reported on February 1, 1891, the following account, after one night of Gillis' binge drinking:[92]

Neil Gillis was found lying at the foot of the bluffs north of the railroad shops at Livingston about 2 o'clock Sunday afternoon [February 2,] frozen to death. Gillis came down from Cooke City last fall, and soon after his arrival made a sale of some mining property. Since then he had been drinking heavily and Friday evening Charles Millard took him to his ranch on the top of the hill to try and sober him up. Sunday morning about 10 o'clock Millard went down town to get some milk to make Gillis a punch. He was unable to find a milkman for a while and when he returned to the cabin Gillis had wandered away. After searching for him awhile Millard went to town and organized a party to look for Gillis. After a short time he was found lying in the snow with only his underclothing on, dead.

James A. "Jim" Gourley. James Gourley has been mentioned as being part of the Fort Pease Expedition, specifically as leaving the fort on October 10, 1875, to return to Bozeman with Zed Daniels.[93] Gourley visited what would become the Yellowstone National Park in 1878 with William D. Cameron.[94] In 1879, in partnership with Neil Gillis, James Gourley made a rich strike at Bear Gulch that they named the Highland Chief. He would sell his share of the claim in 1890 for $5,000. In 1881, James Gourley and R. Rowland sought a US government

lease in Yellowstone Park at the Grand Falls of the Yellowstone for construction of a hotel. He was at the celebration in 1883 to commemorate the arrival of the Northern Pacific Railroad to Bozeman and honor the members of the 1874 expedition.[95] He remained in the Bozeman area, and was Recorder of Gallatin County in 1884, as well as secretary of the Bear Gulch Placer Mine near Gardiner. On August 12, 1914, Jim Gourley attended a reunion of survivors of the expedition in Bozeman, at which point his residence was listed as Bozeman; he was still living in Bozeman in 1920.[96] In 1929, Gourley wrote his reminiscences of the 1869–70 Yellowstone Park Expedition, and on his ninety-second birthday in 1932, he recounted the 1874 Expedition, concluding with:[97]

I don't think there was ever an expedition made into the heart of a hostile Indian country that equaled this. The country was alive with Sioux Indians, and yet we made that march, losing only one man out of 146 that started from Bozeman.

James Gourley died in Bozeman on February 10, 1935, and is buried at the Forestvale Cemetery in Helena.[98]

Gray Earth Tracking/Sounds-the-Ground-When-He-Walks/Noisy Walking. Gray Earth Tracking, the Santee Lakota warrior and son of Inkpaduta, fought at the Little Bighorn in June 1876.[99]

Frank Grounds. After the expedition, Frank Grounds hunted elk and presented over 1,000 elk skins for sale or trade at the Gardiner River Bridge in 1875. In 1876, he staked a mining claim at Montana City in Jefferson County, but soon moved to Central City in the Black Hills, which was about three miles from Deadwood. On July 17, 1876, Grounds accepted leadership of a project to build a direct road from Central City to Deadwood. Frank Grounds died of pneumonia in the Spearfish Valley (current South Dakota) on September 23, 1877.[100]

A 1902 note from Uncle Billy Hamilton to his friend Malcolm Mackay. Hamilton nicknamed Mackay the "Young Chiefton." The note at bottom requests that Mackay buy some matches and tobacco for him; it also admonishes the younger man not to spend the money he receives for the order in the "Red Light district." *Courtesy of the Museum of the Beartooths, Columbus, Montana.*

William Hamilton (left) and Malcolm S. Mackay (right) taken between 1902 and 1908. Mackay, a rancher, had a large collection of Charles M. Russell paintings; he wrote *Cow Range and Hunting Trail* in 1925, detailing some of his western adventures. *Courtesy of the Museum of the Beartooths, Columbus, Montana.*

John Gundorf. John Gundorf was at the celebration in 1883 to commemorate the arrival of the Northern Pacific Railroad to Bozeman and to honor the members of the 1874 expedition.[101]

William T. Hamilton. In 1876, Uncle Billy served as a scout for Gen. George Crook during the campaign against the Lakota and remained with this command through the fighting at Slim Buttes. He left this duty at Fort Laramie. In 1877, Hamilton fought in

William Hamilton died on May 24, 1908, in Billings, Montana. He is buried at the Columbus Cemetery in Columbus, Montana [N 45° 38.493', W 109° 16.448']. *Author photograph, October 2013*

Log cabin of William Hamilton; Hamilton is at the right. *Courtesy of the Museum of the Beartooths, Columbus, Montana.*

the Nez Perce campaign as a scout; in September of that year, he carried dispatches from Fort Ellis to Gen. O.O. Howard in the field for $100.[102] He settled in the small town of Stillwater (Columbus) in 1881. He visited William Officer at Hunter's Hot Springs at least one time in about 1903. William T. Hamilton died on May 24, 1908, at St. Vincent's Hospital in Billings and is buried at the Columbus Cemetery in Columbus, Montana [N 45° 38.493', W 109° 16.448'.][103]

Green Alexander Hampton. The 1880 census listed Green Hampton's occupation as a gold miner in Diamond City. Green Hampton died on April 5, 1922, at Wilsall, Park County, Montana and is buried at Tinkers Hill Cemetery in Park County.[104]

Grave of Green Hampton at Tinkers Hill Cemetery in Park County, Montana. *Courtesy of Ancestry.com, Green Hampton*

Oliver Perry Hanna. Hanna returned to Benson's Landing in June 1874 with Hugh Hoppe. In the spring of 1875, Hanna—with five other hunters and trappers—built flat boats near Fort Benton on the Missouri River and took their furs and buffalo hides down the river to sell in Omaha, after being attacked several times by warriors on the banks of the river. He spent late 1875 and early 1876 back home at Metamora, Illinois. He then went to Denver, Colorado, and subsequently to the Wyoming Territory. Hanna participated in the Great Sioux War of 1876; he then built a cabin on Hanna Creek, in northern Wyoming in

1878. That winter he rode north along the Tongue River and hunted buffalo in some of the same areas that he had seen in 1874. In 1879, Oliver Hanna went to Cheyenne to purchase farm equipment for his ranch. He later helped establish the community of Big Horn City, Wyoming, where he built the town's first boarding-house, which he named the Oriental Hotel. In 1880, a bear seriously mauled him, but Old Spit survived. About this time, Oliver claimed that he had a chance encounter with outlaw George "Big Nose George" Parrott, although his claim cannot be confirmed. In any case, cattle rustler and highwayman "Big Nose George" was hanged on March 22, 1881—his skin being tanned and made into a pair of shoes and his skull

Oliver Perry Hanna; photo location and date are unknown. He appears to be serving on a stagecoach "riding shotgun." The weapon appears to be a Winchester Model 1897 12-gauge "take down" pump shotgun, which would date the photograph to after 1898. *Courtesy of Oliver P. Hanna Photofile, American Heritage Center, University of Wyoming.*

Oliver Perry Hanna in Sheridan County, Wyoming, on August 8, 1926. Sharps Model 1874 rifle he is holding appears to have a thirty-inch octagonal bull barrel, which was the heaviest offered by Sharps and would boost the weight of the weapon to thirteen pounds. *Courtesy of Oliver P. Hanna Photofile, American Heritage Center, University of Wyoming.*

Oliver Perry Hanna in Sheridan County, Wyoming on August 8, 1926. *Courtesy of Oliver P. Hanna Photofile, American Heritage Center, University of Wyoming.*

Grave of Oliver Perry Hanna. *Courtesy of Ancestry. com, Oliver Perry Hanna; Find-A-Grave, Oliver Perry Hanna*

used as an ashtray after his death. Oliver married Eudora "Dora" Myers on June 27, 1885, in Miles City, Montana; they later had two girls and a boy. Hanna moved to Sheridan, Wyoming, in 1891, when he learned that the Chicago, Burlington, and Quincy Railroad might run a rail line through that town. He served as the postmaster for Big Horn City from 1896 to 1900, after he had moved back from Sheridan. The Hanna family moved to California in 1915. In 1926, Hanna returned to Big Horn City for a visit and also attended the Fiftieth Anniversary of the Battle of the Little Bighorn. Oliver Hanna died in Long Beach, California, reportedly on November 2, 1934. Big Spit is buried at Whittier, Los Angeles, California.[105] Eudora died in 1953.

John Hanson. John Hanson was at the celebration in 1883 to commemorate the arrival of the Northern Pacific Railroad to Bozeman and honor the members of the 1874 expedition.[106]

A.E.F. Heinze. A.E.F. Heinze lived in Helena in 1879, possibly working for a jeweler.[107]

George Herendeen. George Herendeen resumed his position at the Crow Agency until June 10, 1874. George Herendeen, Taylor Blevin, and Yank Evarts went from Fort Ellis to Yellowstone National Park to reconnoiter trails in the summer of 1874.[108] He subsequently went to Fort Pease, Montana Territory, on the left bank of the Yellowstone River, in 1875, after having helped build two mackinaw boats, each thirty-six feet in length. After the Fort Pease Expedition, George went to Helena, and then to the Baker's battlefield area and built a winter dugout (winter 1875–76.)[109]

Herendeen assisted Custer on the Rosebud march in June 1876. In 1877, Herendeen fought in the Nez Perce campaign as a scout; he also was at the Little Bighorn to meet with Capt. Henry Nowlan and Capt. Michael Sheridan, as they reburied the Custer dead. Sheridan, who was the assigned commander of Company L of the US 7th Cavalry Regiment, had been on detached duty for years as the adjutant for his brother Phil. After the fight at Big Hole on August 10, 1877, Col. John Gibbon telegraphed Bozeman requesting that George Herendeen and Jack Bean go to Henry's Lake and observe movements of Chief Joseph of the Nez Perce for the period August 17 to August 27 at $5 a day.

The following month, George Herendeen carried dispatches to Col. Samuel D. Sturgis, commander of the US 7th Cavalry Regiment, making $25. Col. Sturgis, who had been the authorized commander of the regiment—but who had been absent from that position for many years—had now returned after the death of Custer and the death of his own son 2nd Lt. James G. Sturgis at the Little Bighorn.

In 1880, Herendeen lived in Bozeman and worked as a store clerk; he was unemployed for two months this year. A year later, he served as a guide in the Yellowstone National Park, where he guided Col. William D. Pickett to shoot a large bear. He was at the celebration in 1883 to commemorate the arrival of the Northern Pacific Railroad to Bozeman and honor the members of the 1874 expedition.[110] He traveled about Montana until 1889, when he settled in Harlem and worked at the Fort Belknap Indian Reservation. He attended a reunion of survivors of the expedition on August 12, 1914, in Bozeman, at which point Herendeen's residence was listed as Harlem.[111]

Herendeen was present in 1916 for the Fortieth Anniversary of the Battle of the Little Bighorn. He would later lead researcher Walter Camp along the Rosebud, showing him camp sites for both 1874 and 1876. Herendeen died at the Sacred Heart Hospital at Havre, Montana, of pneumonia at 0515 on June 17, 1918. George Herendeen is buried in the Harlem Cemetery at Harlem in Blaine County, Montana.[112]

William C. "Bill" Hickey. Bill Hickey married his first wife Matilda White—a native of England—on July 16, 1876, with whom he had three daughters. Matilda died on September 28, 1884. He later married Agnes "Mary" Moran on August 22, 1888, and had six children with her. In 1900, Bill Hickey lived in Helena City, Montana, with Mary, six daughters and two sons; his profession was listed as a "miner of ore." He later moved to Butte. He died of stomach cancer in Butte on April 3, 1911. William Hickey is buried at Saint Patrick's Cemetery in Butte, Montana, in Section H, Row 5.[113]

High Bear. High Bear, the Oglala Lakota who had been born in 1839 or 1840 and had married Yellow Blanket the year before the expedition, went on to have three sons. In the 1890s, he was listed as residing at the Pine Ridge Indian Reservation.

Grave of George B. Herendeen. Herendeen died at the Sacred Heart Hospital at Havre, Montana, of pneumonia at 5:15 a.m. on June 17, 1918. He is buried in the Harlem Cemetery at Harlem in Blaine County, Montana. *Courtesy of Allen Sorenson*

William "Bill" Hindman. William Hindman lived in Upper Yellowstone Valley in Gallatin County in 1880. He was listed as single and a farmer. The entry of Indiana as his place of birth seems to be in error.[114] He was at the celebration in 1883 to commemorate the arrival of the Northern Pacific Railroad to Bozeman and honor the members of the 1874 expedition.[115]

Fred Hollins/Hoelin/Harlan/Harland. Fred Hollins took part in the Fort Pease Expedition on the Yellowstone River expedition in 1875. He was killed near Fort Pease on November 1 of that year.[116]

Irving (Irvin) B. Hopkins. Irving Hopkins lived with his parents in Cottonwood Creek Valley, Gallatin County, in 1880, working as a farmer. In 1910, he lived on his own in Madison County, Montana.[117]

Joseph R. Hopkins. Joseph Hopkins was at the celebration in 1883 to commemorate the arrival of the Northern Pacific Railroad to Bozeman and honor the members of the 1874 expedition.[118]

Hugo J. Hoppe. Hoppe remained in Bozeman until June 1, 1874, when he returned to Benson's Landing with Oliver Hanna. In July 1874 raiding Lakota warriors wounded him in a fight. The following year, Hoppe left Benson's Landing to establish a new saloon on the north bank of the Yellowstone River opposite the mouth of the Stillwater—directly across from the new location of the Crow Agency. In 1876, Hugh bought Quinn's Ranch with thoughts of making it a traveler's way station—this was the same ranch from which the 1874 expedition had started its journey. In 1877, Montana Territorial Gov. Potts appointed Hoppe the first sheriff of Custer County; he moved to Miles City and remained in the position for two years. Hoppe later built a hotel and maintained a freighting company at Cinnabar, Montana; he also established several more of the first breweries in Montana. Hugo Hoppe was at the celebration in 1883 to commemorate the arrival of the Northern Pacific Railroad to Bozeman and honor the members of the 1874 expedition.[119]

The same year Hoppe received permission to operate a dairy herd near the mouth of the Gardiner River and supply milk to the government. On February 23, 1883, in Bozeman at "John Smith's Bar" Hoppe got in an argument over a card game with Patrick H. Walters—fresh in from the Black Hills. The event escalated into a fight, during which Walters struck Hoppe several times with a chair and his pistol butt. Hugh responded by shooting

Grave of William C. Hickey at Saint Patrick's Cemetery in Butte, Montana. *Courtesy of Pat Armstrong*

five rounds, one of which mortally wounded Walters, who died a day later. Hoppe was indicted on charges of manslaughter, but several months later authorities dismissed the case. Moving to the Cinnabar area, in 1887, he hauled freight for the Yellowstone Park Association, as well as assisting Buffalo Bill Cody in auditioning performers for his European tour. In 1888, Hoppe established a saw mill on Hugo Creek. He lived in Livingston, Montana, in 1890 and in 1891 became a Park County Commissioner. Hugh's wife Mary Gee died in 1894; the couple had four sons and a daughter. Hugh Hoppe died of tuberculosis in San Diego, California, on September 18, 1895. He is buried in the Mountain View Cemetery at Livingston, Montana, in the Soldiers' Plot.[120]

Hump. Hump led the Minneconjou Lakota at the Little Bighorn. Hump later went to Canada. By 1881, buffalo and other game were disappearing in the region of Hump's group and the exiles returned to Fort Buford, where they surrendered, making his band probably the last of all the Lakota to return to the United States. From Fort Buford, the United States government transported Hump and his followers by steamboat to Fort Yates; they later were taken to the Cheyenne River Agency in May 1882. Settling at Cherry Creek, when other tribes had adopted white dress and housing, Hump's band maintained the old ways living in lodges and wearing traditional clothing. Hump greatly opposed the land agreements offered by the federal government in 1888 and 1889.

In 1890, the Ghost Dance began and found its most fervent supporters in the Cherry Creek camps. After talking with Capt. Ezra Ewers, a trusted friend of the chief, Hump avoided the Ghost Dance, when the US Army sent troops from Fort Bennett to suppress it.[121] For his service during the year the US government gave Hump 500 heifers and apparently designated him as an Indian Scout for the period of December 1890 to June 1891. He continued to care for his tribe until his death. Hump died on December 10, 1908, at Cherry Creek in Ziebach County, South Dakota. He is buried at the Episcopal Cemetery at the west edge of Cherry Creek [N 44° 36.246', W 101° 30.428']. A few hundred yards away are the remains of White Bull, a prominent warrior at the Little Bighorn [N 44° 37.191', W 101° 30.737'].

George Hurbert. George Hurbert was at the celebration in 1883 to commemorate the arrival of the Northern Pacific Railroad to Bozeman and honor the members of the 1874 expedition.[122]

Hump died on December 10, 1908, at Cherry Creek in Ziebach County, South Dakota. He is buried at the Episcopal Cemetery at the west edge of Cherry Creek. *Author photograph, May 2015*

Inkpaduta. Inkpaduta was the leader of the Santee and Yanktonais at the Little Bighorn. In the summer of 1877, Inkpaduta and Long Dog took their combined thirty lodges away from Sitting Bull's large village and made their way across the Missouri River to Wolf's Point. In early September, Inkpaduta made his away across the border into Canada. Inkpaduta lived shortly at the Oak Lake Reserve near Brandon, Manitoba, but soon moved again, this time to a new reserve for the Wahpekutes at Turtle Mountain (six miles north of the US border.) Now an extremely old man, Inkpaduta fathered his last child in 1878. He reportedly was out hunting in 1879, when he caught pneumonia and died shortly thereafter.[123]

Charles "Charley" Johnson. Charley Johnson was at the celebration in 1883 to commemorate the arrival of the Northern Pacific Railroad to Bozeman and honor the members of the 1874 expedition.[124] He later lived at Miles City.[125]

John "Liver-Eatin" Johnston. Over the next few years after the expedition, Johnston guided some trips into the mountains in south central and southeastern Montana. It is believed that he was a message carrier for Nelson A. Miles out of Fort Keogh and then a scout for Lt. Charles Erskine Scott Wood (West Point, Class of 1874) in the 1877 Nez Perce War. In 1882, John "Liver-Eatin" Johnston replaced Muggins Taylor as deputy sheriff for Custer County, after Taylor was murdered. In 1884, Johnston and Calamity Jane traveled from Billings to Chicago as part of Hardwick's Wild West tour. He later built a log cabin at Red Lodge, at the foot of the Beartooth Mountains, and probably lived there in 1894, serving again as a law enforcement officer. He reportedly traveled numerous times to Hunter's Hot Springs that was about one hundred miles from Red Lodge. In 1899, Johnston moved to a veteran's hospital in Sawtelle, California, where he died of peritonitis on January 21, 1900. He was buried the following day in the nearby Sawtelle National Cemetery. His remains were eventually moved in 1974 to the Old Trail Town Cemetery in Cody, Wyoming.

Charles E. King. Charles King resumed his profession as a brewer. He lived in Bozeman in 1880 and was single.[126]

Peter Koch. In the fall of 1874, Peter Koch went to Mississippi and married his cousin Laurentze. A year later, he served as a trader to the Crow Agency and then returned to Bozeman to work as a book-keeper. In 1876, a grand jury began an investigation into Nelson Story, who was believed to have cheated the federal government concerning delivering supplies to Crow Indians for the winter. The charges included stealing the tribe's cattle, double-counting bags of flour and packing barrels labeled as ham with offal instead. Peter Koch, who now worked for Story, was widely thought to have served as a "bagman" during

Peter Koch in Pasadena, California in 1917. *Courtesy of Museum of the Rockies Photo Archives, Catalog Number: x85.3.556*

the process—delivering a bribe to a witness. Despite a great degree of evidence, the grand jury refused to return an indictment. In 1879, Peter Koch had risen to become a cashier for the bank owned by Nelson Story. He helped found the Montana Agricultural College, which later became Montana State University. Sometime between 1900 and 1910, he moved with his wife and two children to Pasadena, California, believing that the climate would benefit one of his daughters, an invalid. Peter Koch died on January 7, 1918, in Pasadena; he is buried at Mountain View Cemetery in Pasadena, Los Angeles County in California.[127]

William C. Langston. William Langston led the 200-man, March 1876, gold expedition from Bozeman, down the old Bozeman Trail to the Black Hills. He was at the celebration in 1883 to commemorate the arrival of the Northern Pacific Railroad to Bozeman and honor the members of the 1874 expedition.[128]

Little Wolf. Born in about 1820 in present day Montana, Little Wolf was a signee of the Treaty of Fort Laramie in 1868. He was not present at the Little Bighorn in 1876. In 1878, after the tribe, faced with starvation was taken to the Indian Territory (modern day Oklahoma), he led his band north toward the Montana Territory and their old homelands. They were finally intercepted in 1879. Little Wolf later became an Indian scout for Nelson A. Miles. In 1904, Little Wolf died; he is buried next to Dull Knife at Lame Deer, Montana in the Northern Cheyenne Reservation [N 45° 37.566', W 106° 39.712'].

Makes Room. Makes Room, a Minneconjou Scalp Shirt Wearer, was at the Little Bighorn, but like Sitting Bull, did not get into the fight. He was married to Pretty Feather Woman, the younger sister of Sitting Bull. Makes Room died in 1905.[129]

Aime J. Malin. Aime Malin was a clerk of the district court and lived in Bozeman in 1880. He was at the celebration in 1883 to commemorate the arrival of the Northern Pacific Railroad to Bozeman and honor the members of the 1874 expedition.[130]

Olaf Malmborg. Olaf Malmborg went on to have three sons; Alfred, Oscar, and Eduard, with Nellie. He lived in Nebraska in 1881. He was at the celebration in 1883 to commemorate the arrival of the Northern Pacific Railroad to Bozeman and honor the members of the 1874 expedition.[131] Olaf Malmborg died on August 23, 1900, in Chestnut Precinct of Gallatin County. He is buried at Sunset Hills Cemetery in Bozeman [N 45° 40.505', W 111° 01.588'].[132]

Charles Mate. Charles Mate was at the celebration in 1883 to commemorate the arrival of the Northern Pacific Railroad to Bozeman and honor the members of the 1874 expedition.[133]

Olaf Malmborg died on August 23, 1900, in Chestnut Precinct of Gallatin County. He is buried at Sunset Hills Cemetery in Bozeman [N 45° 40.505', W 111° 01.588']. *Author photograph, June 2015*

Tyler McClees. In May 1875, McClees left Bozeman with Maj. Fellows D. Pease in what became known as the Fort Pease Expedition, to establish a trading post on the Yellowstone River at the mouth of the Big Horn River. Tyler initially sailed on the flatboat *Maggie Hoppy* from Benson's Landing on June 17, 1875, and arrived at the site for the fort on June 24, 1875.[134] Tyler McClees lived in Bozeman in 1880 and listed his occupation as a miner; he was unemployed for five months that year. He was at the celebration in 1883 to commemorate the arrival of the Northern Pacific Railroad to Bozeman and honor the members of the 1874 expedition. It appears that by 1900, Tyler had moved to Trinity Center Township in Trinity County in Northern California, where he lived with his older

brother James. Both men were listed as prospectors on the Trinity County census.[135]

Paul McCormick. Paul McCormick participated in another expedition along the Yellowstone River in 1875. In 1876, he and other personnel were surrounded at Fort Pease; he snuck out of the fort during a blizzard and for four days made his way through deep snow to Fort Ellis to seek help. In the Great Sioux War of 1876, on May 28, 1876, McCormick navigated a trading boat down the Yellowstone River, bringing orders from Gen. Alfred Terry to Col. Gibbon to move down the Yellowstone to Glendive Creek and from there to cross the Yellowstone and "cooperate" with the Dakota Column in the campaign against the Lakota that culminated at the Little Big-

Paul McCormick died on January 26, 1921, in Billings, Montana; he is buried in the Mountview Cemetery in the mausoleum [N 45° 46.080', W 108° 33.646']. *Author photograph, October 2013*

Photograph of Paul McCormick's final resting place inside the mausoleum. *Author photograph, October 2013*

horn. He then became a freelance sutler for the Montana Column. After the campaign, McCormick settled at Keogh and ran a business until 1879 when he moved to Junction City. He married Mary Catherine Spear on February 23, 1879, in Helena and had five children; two died in childhood. The same year, he helped form the Custer Cattle Company, which initially consisted of managing large herds of 20,000 cattle and 100,000 sheep on open range land in the Crow Indian Reservation in the area between the Big Horn River and Pryor Creek. Paul McCormick arrived in Billings in 1891 and became general partner in the Donovan-McCormick General Merchandise Company. Later, he became a close friend of Teddy Roosevelt; during one cross-country train trip, Teddy visited Paul in his mansion at Billings. Paul McCormick died on January 26, 1921, in Billings; he is buried in the Mountview Cemetery in the city.[136]

Archie McDonald. Archie McDonald was at the celebration in 1883 to commemorate the arrival of the Northern Pacific Railroad to Bozeman and honor the members of the 1874 expedition.[137] He lived in Bozeman, Montana, in 1910 with his wife Josephine Chavey (they were married in 1891,) who had been born in Paris, France. He attended a reunion of survivors of the expedition on August 12, 1914, in Bozeman, at which point his residence was listed as Bozeman.[138] In 1920, his occupation was listed as a teamster. Archie McDonald died on April 22, 1924, and is buried at the Sunset Hills Cemetery (in the New Section, Field 10, Grave 103) in Bozeman.[139] His wife appears to have died in 1946.

William McDuff. William McDuff married his wife Christena, who was from Nova Scotia. In 1879 they had a daughter, Mary A. In 1880, he and his family lived in East Gallatin Valley, where he was a farmer. William McDuff died on July 11, 1911, or July 11, 1914. He is buried at the Lewistown City Cemetery in Lewistown, Montana.[140]

The grave of Archie McDonald at the Sunset Hills Cemetery in Bozeman. *Courtesy of Ancestry.com, Archie McDonald*

William McDuff died on July 11, 1911. He is buried at the Lewistown City Cemetery in Lewistown, Montana. *Courtesy of Janet Davis*

Duncan McRae. In May 1875, Duncan McRae departed Bozeman with Maj. Fellows D. Pease and thirty other frontiersmen—known as the Fort Pease Expedition—to establish a proposed head of navigation on the Yellowstone River at the mouth of the Big Horn River. Duncan initially sailed on the flatboat *Bozeman* on June 17, 1875, from Benson's Landing, but the vessel soon struck an underwater snag and sank. He survived and helped build Fort Pease.[141] There is a Duncan McRae listed in 1910 as a copper miner living in Butte, Montana. This McRae was born in Scotland in 1852, arrived in the United States in 1869, married a woman named Margaret in 1875, had one daughter born in 1886 and another born in 1890. It is not known if this is the same man on the expedition.[142]

George H. Miller. George Miller went on the March 1876 gold expedition from Bozeman, Montana, to the Black Hills. He was killed during the march by Lakota warriors in a fight west of Devil's Tower and was buried there.[143]

William C. "Bill" Officer. Bill Officer married Fanny Elizabeth Cullom (born in 1860 in Livingston, Tennessee) on March 16, 1879, possibly in St. Joseph, Missouri; they probably were step cousins. Fanny's father, a Confederate soldier, had been killed at the Battle of Atlanta in 1864. Bill and Fanny had one daughter and six sons, all born in Montana; two of the baby boys were stillborn. In 1880, the family lived in East Gallatin, where he worked raising stock. A few years later, Bill was a grocery man; he and his family lived in Hunter's Hot Springs, Montana. He later became the assistant postmaster there (Fanny also served as a postmaster.) He also ran the lower hotel at Hunter's Hot Springs, a position that put him in contact with several former expedition members over the years. According to oral family history by Guy C. Officer, William's son, Uncle Billy Hamilton showed up one day:

Shortly before school started, when I was 12 years old [1903] Bill Hamilton showed up at the house. Four years before this meeting [1899] a bronc jumped over Dad and struck him on the head with a hind foot, slivering the skull. The doctor chiseled the slivered bone away and put in a silver plate where the bone had been. The injury impaired Dad's center of balance so that he staggered when he walked around. It also left him with double vision unless he closed one eye.

This afternoon I spoke of, Dad was sitting on the front porch reading a paper and I was whittling out a kite frame. A

William Officer died on May 11, 1911, at Hunter's Hot Springs. He is buried at Clyde Park Cemetery, Clyde Park, Montana. *Courtesy of Steve Florman and Barbara Sell*

man drove up to the porch driving a sorrel mare hitched to a two wheeled cart. He climbed out of the cart backwards and turned around. Dad said, "Bill Hamilton, God damn your soul" and Hamilton said the same to Dad. They shook hands called one another S.O.B.'s and other cuss words. I thought to myself, "kid like right here is where someone gets hurt." When the so called amenities were over Dad said, "Put that horse away." When I came back they were hard at it recalling things they knew of or took part in. About half past five o'clock Dad said, "Time for you to do your chores." I milked two cows, fed and watered the horses, got in the wood, kindling and coal, fed the chickens, and gathered the eggs. Never in this world did a boy do his chores so quickly. I got in as everyone was sitting down to supper. Dad and Hamilton were recalling incidents all thru the meal and until two o'clock in the morning.

William C. Officer died on May 11, 1911, at Hunter's Hot Springs. He is buried at the Clyde Park Cemetery, Clyde Park, Montana. His wife Fannie died in 1951 and is buried in Big Timber.[144]

Charles Pietsch. Charles Pietsch was a miller in Bozeman in 1880 and married his wife Isabella in 1883. In 1900, he was living in Bozeman, Montana, with Isabella, a son, and daughter and worked as a miller. He attended a reunion of survivors of the expedition on August 12, 1914, in Bozeman, at which point his residence was listed as Bozeman.[145] Charles Pietsch died on December 11, 1920, and is buried at the Sunset Hills Cemetery in Bozeman [N 45° 40.522', W 111° 01.587'].[146]

Charles Pietsch is buried at the Sunset Hills Cemetery in Bozeman, Montana [N 45° 40.522', W 111° 01.587']. *Author photograph, October 2013*

William Polfer. William Polfer died destitute in Helena on January 24, 1889. He is buried at the Lewis and Clark County Poor Farm at Helena.[147]

Benjamin F. Potts. Benjamin Potts served as governor until 1883. He later served in the territorial legislature. He died in Helena, Montana, on June 17, 1887, of an aneurysm of the aorta. Gov. Potts is buried at the Forestvale Cemetery in Helena.

Addison M. Quivey. Addison Quivey later served as a Deputy United States Marshal among the Crows. In March 1880, serving as an interpreter, he traveled with six Crow leaders from the Crow Agency to Washington, DC, where they met President Rutherford B. Hayes. Addison M. Quivey died at the Boykin House

in Billings, Montana, on July 9, 1895, and is buried at the Mountview Cemetery in Billings.[148]

Joseph A. Ramsdell. Joseph Ramsdell went on the March 1876 gold expedition from Bozeman, Montana, to the Black Hills. He built a ranch at the new town of Spearfish, South Dakota. By 1880, he had settled a farm east of Spearfish Creek. In 1900, Ramsdell lived in Crook County, Wyoming; he later lived in Lemon City in Dade County, Florida. Joseph Ramsdell died on February 2, 1917, in Des Moines, Iowa. He is buried at the Colman Cemetery in Colman, South Dakota.[149]

Red Cloud. Red Cloud died peacefully in his sleep at age eighty-eight on December 10, 1909. He is buried in a small cemetery near

The grave of Benjamin Potts at the Forestvale Cemetery in Helena, Montana. *Courtesy of Thomas J. Fisher*

The grave of Joseph A. Ramsdell, at the Colman Cemetery in Colman, South Dakota. *Courtesy of Norb Sonen*

the Red Cloud Heritage Center at the Pine Ridge Reservation [N 43° 04.654', W 102° 34.989'].[150] Not far away is the grave of the famous scout Baptiste "Big Bat" Pourier [N 43° 04.664', W 102° 35.034'].

Red Hawk. Red Hawk was probably born about 1854 and was possibly a brother of Iron Thunder. According to one source, his first war party was with Crazy Horse in 1865. Red Hawk fought at the Little Bighorn on June 25–26, 1876. He is believed to have surrendered with Crazy Horse's band in May 1877. Red Hawk was probably in one of the bands that fled the Red Cloud and Spotted Tail Agencies

Famed scout Baptiste "Big Bat" Pourier's remains are nearby Red Cloud at the Pine Ridge Reservation. *Author photograph, May 2015*

Red Cloud (Makhpiya-Luta) died on December 10, 1909, at the Pine Ridge Reservation in South Dakota. He is buried at the Red Cloud Cemetery. *Author photograph, May 2015*

in late 1877, eventually arriving in Canada. He reportedly married about 1877–78. In later interviews, Red Hawk later recalled that he surrendered at Fort Keogh, probably in 1880. He worked as a scout there for about six months and led a delegation north to persuade his brother Iron Thunder to surrender on August 7, 1880. Red Hawk was later part of the bands transferred to the Standing Rock Agency in 1881 and does appear in the band of his brother Hump on the Sitting Bull Surrender Census. Red Hawk was then transferred to the Pine Ridge Agency in 1882. During the Ghost Dance difficulties, Red Hawk enlisted as an Indian scout and later served with the Indian Police. On September 22, 1915, researcher Walter M. Camp interviewed him about the expedition; Camp noted then that the old warrior was nearly blind. Red Hawk attended the 1926 Little Bighorn Fiftieth Anniversary. Red Hawk died on March 29, 1928, at the Pine Ridge Agency.[151]

Herbert F. Richardson. Herbert F. Richardson married Lulu B. Newman on June 3, 1904. He died on April 22, 1913, in Bozeman. He is buried at the Sunset Hills Cemetery in Bozeman.[152]

Daniel E. Rouse. In 1880, Daniel Rouse lived in Bozeman. He was a saloon keeper and was also married.[153] Rouse was at the celebration in 1883 to commemorate the arrival of the Northern Pacific Railroad to Bozeman and honor the members of the 1874 expedition.

Herbert F. Richardson died in 1913 in Bozeman, Montana. He is buried at Sunset Hills Cemetery. *Courtesy of Ancestry.com, Herbert Richardson*

Daniel E. Rouse died on July 30, 1912, in Bozeman, Montana. Rouse is buried at the Bozeman Sunset Hills Cemetery [N 45° 40.537', W 111° 01.587']. *Author photograph, October 2013*

Daniel E. Rouse died on July 30, 1912, in Bozeman. Rouse is buried at the Bozeman Sunset Hills Cemetery [N 45° 40.537', W 111° 01.587'].[154]

Shell Necklace. Shell Necklace may have been born in 1860, making him quite young during the 1874 expedition, but still old enough to fight. He was reportedly of the Oglala Tribe. He married in 1891; later that decade, Shell Necklace was listed as living on the Pine Ridge Agency in the Medicine Root District and later at the Cheyenne River Agency in 1926.

Shoot the Bear. Shoot the Bear appears to have been born about 1845. In the 1880s, he is believed to have been at Standing Rock Agency. He appears to have been in Gall's lodge circle at Standing Rock in 1885. There is a Shoot the Bear listed as being killed at Wounded Knee, but it's not certain if this was the same person.

Sitting Bull. After the Little Bighorn, Sitting Bull took his tribe to Alberta and Saskatchewan, Canada, allying with bands of the Canadian Blackfeet. In 1881, he returned to the United States and surrendered at Fort Buford. Between the years of 1881 to 1883, he was held in confinement at Fort Randall. After touring from 1883 to 1885 with Buffalo Bill Cody's traveling Wild West Show, he returned to his people. On December 12, 1890, the US Army Department of Dakota ordered the commanding officer at Fort Yates to arrest Sitting Bull for being in open rebellion against the United States, defying the government, and encouraging disaffection during the Ghost Dance movement. Although the arrest was to have been made on December 20, on December 14 authorities received reports that Sitting Bull was preparing to depart the reservation. On December 16, 1890, Standing Rock Indian police entered the camp and proceeded to Sitting Bull's dwelling. Initially, the Lakota chief agreed to the process, but once outside his home—and now surrounded by many followers—Sitting Bull began to call on his tribe to rescue him. Two men rushed the group of police and began firing. Indian Police Lt. Bull Head was struck by a round; he responded by whirling about and shooting Sitting Bull in the left side between his tenth and eleventh ribs. Sitting Bull died almost instantly. He is buried across the Missouri River from

On December 15, 1890, Standing Rock Indian Agency police attempted to arrest Sitting Bull, and he was killed in the process. He is buried at Mobridge in Walworth County, South Dakota. *Author photograph, May 2015*

John Henry Stevens died on November 27, 1890, in Bozeman and is buried at the Sunset Hills Cemetery, Old Section O7. *Courtesy of Ancestry.com, John Henry Stevens*

Mobridge, South Dakota [N 45° 31.017', W 100° 29.111'].[155]

Bannock Smith. Bannock Smith was at the celebration in 1883 to commemorate the arrival of the Northern Pacific Railroad to Bozeman and honor the members of the 1874 expedition.[156]

Conger "Con" Smith. Con Smith became a livestock rancher. In 1888, he married Sara Maguire at Ogden, Utah; the couple raised six children. Conger Smith died on June 26, 1926, at Boulder, Montana.[157]

John Henry Stevens. John Stevens was at the celebration in 1883 to commemorate the arrival of the Northern Pacific Railroad to Bozeman and honor the members of the 1874

expedition. He died on November 27, 1890, in Bozeman and is buried at the Sunset Hills Cemetery, Old Section O7.[158]

Patrick Sweeney. Patrick Sweeney was on the Fort Pease Expedition to establish a proposed trading post and fort on the Yellowstone River just east of the mouth of the Big Horn River; he was definitely at this location in August 1875. Sweeney was wounded in the right breast while hunting near Fort Pease on January 2, 1876, when attacked by warriors. Patrick Sweeney died of his wounds at the fort on January 6, 1876.[159]

Nelson B. Sweitzer. Lt. Col. Nelson Sweitzer continued his distinguished career by taking command of the US 8th Cavalry Regiment in

1877. He was promoted to colonel on January 9, 1886, and assumed command of the US 2nd Cavalry Regiment. Sweitzer retired from the army on October 29, 1888. Nelson Sweitzer died on March 7, 1898, in Washington, DC. He is buried at the Arlington National Cemetery in Section 1, Lot 21-A.

H.M. "Muggins" Taylor. Taylor went to help build Fort Pease on June 24, 1875. He was wounded in the thumb near Fort Pease on January 2, 1876, when attacked by Lakota warriors. Muggins later went on the ill-fated 1876 expedition to the Little Bighorn in 1876 as a scout for the Montana Column, commanded by Col. John Gibbon, and took the news of Custer's massacre, June 25, 1876, from the battle area west to Fort Ellis and Bozeman.

In 1876 two pioneers settled into an area along the Yellowstone River (present day Billings) through which the expedition had traveled just two years before. They and other settlers soon built a sawmill, trading post, and small hotel; the area soon became known as Coulson, from the Coulson Packet Company, which operated a riverboat line between St. Louis, Missouri, and Montana. By 1879, a general store, post office, saloon, and ferry boat station had taken root. Many businessmen hoped that Coulson would become the "Denver of the Prairies," while others believed that it had the potential to become the busiest city along the northern tier of the Great Plains between Minneapolis and Seattle. The busy little town attracted railroad surveyors, farmers, freighters, and Midwestern businessmen ready

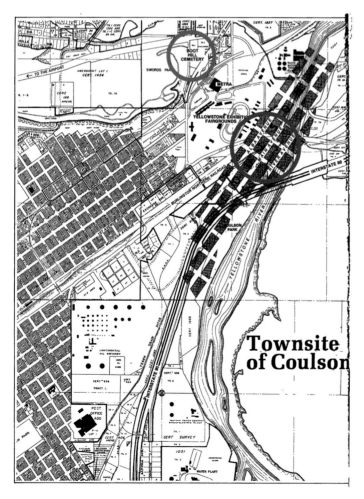

Map of the town of Coulson superimposed over an undated map of Billings. Illustration modified by the author as follows. Blue circle indicates area of McAdow's store, Lump's Laundry, and Skillen & Co.'s Saloon, prominent locations in the shooting of Deputy Sheriff Muggins Taylor in 1882. Red circle indicates Boothill Cemetery, where Taylor was buried. *Courtesy of Myrtle Cooper, From Tent Town to City: A Chronological History of Billings, 1882–1935 as found in Zach Benoit, "YelCo 52: 'Born by the River and killed by the Railroad,'" Billings Gazette, September 13, 2014.*

Skillen & Co.'s Saloon, where bartender P. Folger threw Henry "Hank" Lump out of the establishment. Lump retreated to Lump's Laundry, where he subsequently shot Deputy Sheriff Muggins Taylor. Photo taken in 1882. *Unidentified photographer, #941-075, courtesy of Montana Historical Society Research Center Photograph Archives, Helena, MT*

to invest their life savings. It also served as a magnet for gamblers, prostitutes, gunslingers, and saddle tramps, and sure enough, the town's first murder occurred in 1880, when John Alderson—one of the town's founders—shot and killed Dave Currier—the town's first saloon keeper—over a land dispute.[160]

This mix necessitated a strong law enforcement presence. In walked Muggins Taylor, who became a deputy sheriff in Coulson (probably not in the Custer County Sheriff's Department as Coulson was not in the county jurisdiction.) However, even the vaunted Taylor could not completely tame the wild little river town. He was killed by Henry "Hank" Lump, a wife beater, who according to a report spent his time loafing about saloons and pool halls and depended upon his wife for support. In the fatal

incident, which probably occurred about September 27, 1882, Henry Lump shot at bartender P. Folger who was in the process of throwing him out of (John) Skillen & Co.'s Saloon for unruly behavior, after which Henry retreated to Lump's Laundry. Muggins responded to the escalating disturbance and in a tussle over Lump's rifle, Henry Lump shot Deputy Sheriff Taylor in the side of his chest. The lawman lingered on the edge of death for several days and died between September 27 and September 30. The next day, a large gathering of mourning friends accompanied Taylor to his final resting place. Congregational minister Reverend Benjamin F. Shuart preached Taylor's burial service. Muggins Taylor is buried at Boot Hill Cemetery in Billings, Montana [N 45° 46.163', 108° 33.554'].[161]

Town of Coulson looking east in 1882. McAdow's store and Lump's Laundry are in the foreground. Taylor was fatally shot at the laundry on September 27, 1882. *Unidentified photographer, #941-075, courtesy of Montana Historical Society Research Center Photograph Archives, Helena, MT*

According to a *Billings Gazette* article from 1927, "Somebody called a cowpuncher a liar and right then and there Boot Hill Cemetery was started." In its heyday from 1877 to 1882, some forty people were interred along the scenic Rimrock area of current-day Billings and 1882 was a particularly bad year. One "Dutch Charley" gunned down an eighteen-year-old boy named Joe Dedmond on March 29 in Skillen's Saloon; Dedmond went to Boot Hill and "Dutch Charley" escaped. William "Dutch Bill" Stooltz, a porter in many of Coulson's saloons, died in a drunken fit on May 18; he too went to Boot Hill. Dan Leahy gunned down William Preston, a prominent gambler, behind Leahy's saloon after a quarrel on June 2. Preston went to Boot Hill, while Leahy committed suicide in Miles City by taking an overdose of morphine shortly after he was sentenced to hang. George A. McArthur shot down James D. Russell, a wholesale liquor dealer, on November 3 in Rademacher's Billiard Parlor. Russell went to Boot Hill and McArthur got a hung jury so he didn't hang.

The grave of H.M. "Muggins" Taylor at Boot Hill Cemetery in Billings, Montana [N 45° 46.163', W 108° 33.554']. *Author photograph, October 2013*

Finally, on Christmas Day, Jeremiah Cokeley killed Patrick Dwyer in a gunfight. Dwyer went to Boot Hill and Cokeley disappeared from history.[162]

Henry Lump was quickly apprehended and convicted of Taylor's murder, but the governor pardoned him eight years later. John "Liver-Eatin" Johnston replaced Taylor as deputy sheriff for Custer County.[163]

Elisha S. Terrill. E.S. Terrill left Bozeman with Maj. Fellows D. Pease and more than thirty other frontiersmen in May 1875, in what became known as the Fort Pease Expedition, to establish a proposed trading post on the Yellowstone River near the mouth of the Big Horn River.[164]

Boot Hill Cemetery retains its old character as a windswept ridge. Ben Walker is buried here, but none of the small markers have names. *Author photograph, October 2013*

Benjamin J. "Honest Ben" Walker. Walker later settled on a piece of land along the Tongue River (near modern-day Brandenburg, Montana) Ben Walker got into an altercation on or about June 24, 1882, in Coulson with a man named Frank Quinn. While cleaning his rifle, Quinn became enraged with Walker and loaded a round in the weapon. The gun went off. The discharge caused the metal cleaning rod to pierce Walker's body and he fell dead. Benjamin Walker is buried at Boot Hill Cemetery in Billings [N 45° 46.163', 108° 33.554'].[165]

Timothy C. Ward. T.C. Ward was at the celebration in 1883 to commemorate the arrival of the Northern Pacific Railroad to Bozeman and honor the members of the 1874 expedition. In 1900, he lived in West Bozeman. Timothy Ward died in Bozeman on March 16, 1914, and is buried at the Sunset Hills Cemetery.[166]

Eli B. Way. Eli Way worked as a farmer and lived in Kingman County, Kansas, in 1880 with his wife Elizabeth McBride and his six month old son Frank G. Way. It appears that Eli named his son after Frank Grounds. He had been married in Waterloo, Kansas, on February 15, 1879. Eli B. Way died suddenly of a brain fever on March 3, 1882, in Kingman, Kingman County, Kansas. He is buried at Walnut Hill Cemetery, where his tombstone lists his Civil War rank as sergeant.[167]

White Earth Tracking. White Earth Tracking, the twin brother of Gray Earth Tracking and the son of Inkpaduta, fought at the Little Bighorn in 1876. A Santee–Lakota, he was wounded at the battle and was part of the Lakotas that fled to Canada. He reportedly died of later complications of his wounds—inflicted by Lt. Henry M. Harrington, Company C of the US 7th Cavalry Regiment, at the Little Bighorn—in 1878 in Canada.[168]

B.P. Wickersham. The 1880 United States Census for Pima County, Arizona Territory, shows a B.P. Wickersham, single and a druggist, living in Charleston Village, Pima County, Arizona Territory, in 1880. Charleston was the home to many of the silver miners that worked the mines in neighboring Tombstone. The 1910 United States Census for Cochise County, Arizona Territory, shows a Pierce B. Wickersham in Hereford, fifteen miles southwest of Tombstone. It would seem that this is the same man that was on the expedition. Given that Charleston was only five miles from the Clanton Ranch and nine miles from Tombstone, it is likely that Doc Wickersham knew Ike Clanton, Billy Clanton, Frank McLaury, William "Curley Bill" Brocius, John Peters "Johnny" Ringo, Wyatt Earp, Virgil Earp, and Morgan Earp. And given that both men were in the medical profession, it is also likely that he "Doc" Wickersham was friends with Doc Holiday.

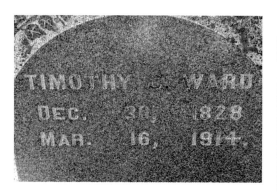

Timothy Ward died in Bozeman, Montana, on March 16, 1914, and is buried at the Sunset Hills Cemetery. *Courtesy of Ancestry.com, Timothy C. Ward*

Eli B. Way died suddenly of a brain fever on March 3, 1882 in Kingman, Kingman County, Kansas. He is buried at Walnut Hill Cemetery, where his tombstone lists his Civil War rank as Sergeant. *Courtesy of Ancestry.com, Eli B. Way*

Henry A. Willson. Henry Willson moved back to Somerset in Niagara County, New York, after the expedition and was listed as living there in 1875. The family still lived there in 1880, as well as in 1900. It appears that his wife died after that and Willson moved with a son to Edinburg in Portage County, Ohio, where he lived in 1910.[169]

Lester S. Willson. After a successful business and political career, including operating several stores, Brevet Brig. Gen. Willson, the man who helped equip the Big Horn Gun with homemade canister ammunition, died on January 26, 1919. His funeral was the largest that the town of Bozeman had ever seen. Lester Willson is buried in the Willson family plot (Plot D,) Sunset Hills Cemetery, Bozeman, Montana [N 45° 40.523', W 111° 01.586'].[170]

Thomas "Tom" Woodward. Thomas Woodward survived his wounded wrist he received at the Battle of Rosebud Creek.

William M. Wright. William M. Wright had his next fight with the Lakota in July of 1874. That month, raiding warriors attacked his ranch and killed his herder, Hardy O'Dare. Wright later lived in Livingston, Montana. He subsequently moved in November 1887 to Ontario, San Bernardino County, California, where he died on April 13, 1909, of heart failure. He is buried in the Wright crypt at the Bellevue Cemetery and Mausoleum in that city.[171]

George Anderson Yates. Andy lived in Canyon Creek, Montana in 1900, and died in Radersburg, Montana, in 1916.

Hezekiah Yates. Ki Yates married Nancy Wetherly on January 24, 1883; they had six children. Ki died on March 10, 1939 in Boise, Idaho.

William Wright moved to Ontario, San Bernardino County, California, where he died April 13, 1909. He is buried in the Wright crypt at the Bellevue Cemetery and Mausoleum in that city. *Courtesy of Ancestry.com, William Wright*

Willson family grave. Lester Willson is buried at the Sunset Hills Cemetery in Bozeman, Montana [N 45° 40.523', W 111° 01.586']. *Author photograph, October 2013*

Individual marker for Lester Willson. *Author photograph, October 2013*

Lost Cabin Mine

In August 1902, reports began filtering out of Wyoming that the ephemeral Lost Cabin Mine had been rediscovered. The *New York Times* reported the following story on August 17:[172]

> Word received to-night from the Town of Buffalo, Wyoming, reports the place as almost deserted, because of the flocking of the miners and prospectors to the Big Horn Mountains, where the fabulously wealthy and long-lost Cabin Gold Mine has been rediscovered.

The report proved false and the elusive gold mine remains undiscovered to this day.

The Big Horn Gun

In June 1875, members of a new Yellowstone Expedition strapped the Big Horn Gun to the deck of the *Bozeman* and sailed east along the river. According to one legend, the boat capsized, sending the gun into the Yellowstone, where it was later recovered. The group established Fort Pease just below the mouth of the Bighorn River and placed the gun inside the fort to contribute to its defense. In 1876, warriors burned the fort to the ground; the blaze left only the gun tube intact.[173] According to another legend, Walter Cooper searched for the gun, found it, and shipped it back to Bozeman. At any rate, Don Weibert located the cannon on a pedestal, built a new wooden carriage for it from laminated cottonwood and refurbished the weapon. It rests today at the Gallatin County Historical Society and History Museum.

However, the mystery continues. According to Walter Cooper—master gunsmith and owner of the Walter Cooper's Armory and Gun Manufactory at Bozeman—when he measured the cannon in the process of preparing the gun for the expedition, the caliber of the cannon was 4.62 inches. When this study examined the cannon, identified as the Big Horn Gun at the museum, in October 2013, it had a caliber of 3.375 inches. The diameter of the oyster can shrapnel shell, identified as ammunition for the Big Horn Gun, at the museum, was measured at 3.125 inches, while the length of the shell was 6.56 inches. Has the diameter of the bore of the cannon "shrunk" an inch and a half over the years, did Cooper err in his original measurement, or is the cannon in the museum not the original Big Horn Gun of the expedition?

Notes

1. Dr. Thomas B. Marquis, "Bozeman Men"; Weibert, *Buckskin*, 44; and Interment Form (QMC Form No. 14) for Interment in the Custer Battlefield National Cemetery for BARKLEY, William, dated January 5, 1932, signed by Victor A. Bolsius, as found on Ancestry.com.

2. "Thanking the Orator," *Avant Courier* (Bozeman,) April 5, 1883.

3. "Nine Big Horn Survivors Clasp Hands in Bozeman."

4. Rachel Hergett, "Mixed-race pioneer has place in Bozeman history,"; Gray Research Papers, Box 16, Folder 136, Scouts; Ancestry. com, California Death Index, 1905-1939, John Anderson; and "John Anderson, Who Broke Sitting Bull's Heart."

5. "Thanking the Orator"; and Find-A-Grave, Henry "Hank" Ashmead.

6. *Progressive Men of the State of Montana*, 1631; 1900 US Census for Beaverhead County, Montana; and Avery Reminiscence, SC 372, 1-4.

7. Montana Death Index, 1868-2011.

8. Find-A-Grave, William Awbrey; 1880 US Census for Tehama County, California.

9. 1880 US Census for Gallatin County, Montana Territory; and 1900 US Census for Silver Bow County, Montana; Gail Schontzler, "Street names keep Bozeman's colorful history alive," *Bozeman Daily Chronicle*, Bozeman, Montana, October 2, 1011; and John N. and Bernice W. DeHaas, "Footlights and Fire Engines," *Montana: The Magazine of Western History*, Volume XVII, Number 4, 34-36.

10. "Pioneer Dies," *The Helena Independent*, Helena, Montana, February 16, 1919.

11. 1880 US Census for Gallatin County, Montana Territory; Whittlesey, *Gateway to Yellowstone*, 149; and Find-A-Grave, William D. Bassett.

12. "Thanking the Orator."

13. Telephone discussion with Mr. John Bean, grandson of Jack Bean, July 30, 2013; and Weibert, *Buckskin*, 40, 41, 74 and 131.

14. Email from Rachel Phillips, August 15, 2013; and 1880 US Census for Gallatin County, Montana Territory.

15. "Nine Big Horn Survivors Clasp Hands in Bozeman."

16. Find-A-Grave, Green B. Blakeley.

17. Gray Research Papers, Box 16, Folder 136, Scouts.

18. Fort Pease was just below the mouth of the Bighorn River not far from the old Fort Lisa that had been abandoned in 1811. The structure was 235 feet square; three sides of the fort consisted of log houses, with the fourth side constructed of poles. In 1876, the army used the site as a logistical base, naming it Terry's Landing.

19. Paul L. Hedren, editor, *The Great Sioux War 1876–77*, Helena, Montana: Montana Historical Society Press, 1991, 116; Weibert, *Buckskin*, 44; and Edgar I. Stewart, "Major Brisbin's Relief of Fort Pease: A Prelude to the Bloody Little Big Horn Massacre," *Montana: The Magazine of Western History*, Volume VI, Number 3, Summer 1956, 24.

20. 1880 US Census for Albany County, Wyoming Territory; and 1905 New York State Census for Saratoga County.

21. Hoppe, Letter to *Helena Herald*.

22. Ronald Hamilton Nichols, *In Custer's Shadow: Major Marcus Reno*, Norman, Oklahoma: University of Oklahoma Press, 2000, 213; Carter, 32; and Avery Reminiscence, SC 372, 2. There is much confusion whether W.A. Bostwick was perhaps the famous Henry Bostwick. The study has decided that Henry Bostwick was the man on the expedition.

23. Find-A-Grave, Victoria Mercier Bostwick.

24. Michno, *Encyclopedia of Indian Wars*, 313; Jerome A. Greene, *Nez Perce Summer 1877: The US Army and Nee-Me-Poo Crisis*, Helena, Montana: Montana Historical Society Press, 2001, 240; and Weibert, *The 1874 Invasion*, 180.

25. Thomas Marquis, editor and interpreter, *A Warrior Who Fought Custer*, Minneapolis, Minnesota: The Midwest Company, 1931, 167, 244.

26. "Raymond Brady, Sr.," *Billings Gazette*, June 2, 2010.

27. Paul L. Hedren, *Traveler's Guide to the Great Sioux War: The Battlefields, Forts and Related Sites of America's Greatest Indian War*, Helena, Montana: Montana Historical Society Press, 1996, 72; Prodgers, *The Champion Buffalo Hunter*, 109; and Willert, *After Little Bighorn*, 2.

28. Montana Pioneers Records, 1884-1956: Joseph Brown, Box 1/Folder 4; and Find-A-Grave, Joseph Brown.

29. Weibert, *Buckskin*, 39, 74.

30. John R. Foster, "Kendall: Twentieth Century Ghost Town," *Montana; The Magazine of Western History*, Volume XXIV, Number 2, 70; "Thanking the Orator,"; and 1900 US Census for Fergus County, Montana.

31. Weibert, *Buckskin*, 39.

32. "Thanking the Orator"; and 1900 US Census for Fergus County, Montana.

33. Montana Death Index, 1868-2011.

34. 1880 US Census for Gallatin County, Montana Territory; Leeson, 1109; and "Thanking the Orator."

35. 1880 US Census for Gallatin County, Montana Territory; 1900 US Census for Gallatin County, Montana; and "Thanking the Orator."

36. "Thanking the Orator."

37. Ancestry.com, Henry Bird Calfee, and Kate Latus.

38. Leeson, 23.

39. "Thanking the Orator."

40. Hutchins, "Poison in the Pemmican," 13.

41. "Nine Big Horn Survivors Clasp Hands in Bozeman."

42. Weibert, *The 1874 Invasion*, 137; Ancestry.com, William D. Cameron; and "Another Pioneer Called by Death," *The Livingston Enterprise*.

43. 1880 US Census for Lawrence County, Dakota Territory.

44. Gray Research Papers, Box 16, Folder 136, Scouts; and McLemore, "Fort Pease," 20, 22, 30, and 31.

45. 1880 US Census for Gallatin County, Montana Territory.

46. "Thanking the Orator."

47. 1910 US Census for Spokane County, Washington.

48. 1920 US Census for Butte County, South Dakota; Find-A-Grave, Joseph Cook; 1900 US Census for Lawrence County, South Dakota; and Weibert, *The 1874 Invasion*, 149.

49. Leona Lampi, "Red Lodge: From a Frenetic Past of Crows, Coal and Boom and Bust Emerges a Unique Festival of Diverse Nationality Groups," *Montana: The Magazine of Western History*, Volume XI, Number 3, Summer 1961, 21.

50. Peterson, "The Footrace," 50-62.

51. Heinz, "Montana Sharps," 28.

52. 1880 US Census for Gallatin County, Montana Territory; and Leeson, 1116.

53. 1880 US Census for Gallatin County; "Thanking the Orator."; and Find-A-Grave, Doc Cowan Montana.

54. Gray Research Papers, Box 16, Folder 136, Scouts; and Leeson, 405.

55. Michno, *Encyclopedia of Indian Wars*, 294-296 and 299.

56. Ibid, 301-302.

57. V.T. McGillycuddy, "Narrative of the life of Crazy Horse," *Nebraska History Magazine*, Volume 19, Lincoln, Nebraska: Nebraska State Historical Society, 1929, 36-38.

58. Lone Eagle Statement, Part II, Box 28, Mari Sandoz Collection, University of Nebraska, as found at http://www.astonisher.com/archives/museum/horn_chips_crazy_horse2.html.

59. Reverend Peter Rosen, Pa-Ha-Sa-Pah, or the Black Hills of South Dakota, St. Louis, Missouri, Nixon-Jones Printing, 1895, 398.

60. "Thanking the Orator."

61. Gray Research Papers, Box 16, Folder 136, Scouts; Watry and Gross, Livingston, 11; and McLemore, "Fort Pease," 18, 20.

62. John S. Gray, *Centennial Campaign: The Sioux War of 1876*, Fort Collins, Colorado: The Old Army Press, 1976, 40-41, 74.

63. "Thanking the Orator."

64. Yellowstone Gateway Museum of Park County Website, The Bill and Doris Whithorn Collection Online Database, http://yellowstone.pastperfect-online.com

65. Find-A-Grave, Zadok H. Daniels; and James Willert, *After Little Bighorn*, 2.

66. "Thanking the Orator."

67. *Progressive Men of the State of Montana*, 126; and 1880 US Census for Gallatin County, Montana Territory.

68. Gray Research Papers, Box 16, Folder 136, Scouts.

69. Stewart, "Major Brisbin's Relief of Fort Pease."

70. 1880 US Census for Gallatin County, Montana Territory; Gray, *Custer's Last Campaign*, 126; 1900 US Census for Fergus County, Montana; Montana Pioneers Records, 1884–1956: Benjamin R. Dexter, Box 2/Folder 3; and "Ben Dexter Dead," *Fergus County Argus*, Lewiston, Fergus County, Montana, November 8, 1907.

71. National Archives and Records Administration (NARA); Washington, DC, Record of Appointment of Postmasters, 1832-Sept. 30, 1971; Roll #: 75, 676; Archive Publication #: M841; and The Hecla Consolidated Mining Company, Welcome to Glendale, Montana at http://www.glendalemontana.com/ and http://glendalemt.com/Biographies/Dillabaugh_John.htm

72. "Nine Big Horn Survivors Clasp Hands in Bozeman."

73. 1920 US Census for Deer Lodge County, Montana.

74. McLemore, "Fort Pease," 20-23.

75. 1880 US Census for Gallatin County, Montana Territory.

76. Weibert, *The 1874 Invasion*, 149; and Ancestry.com, Robert Henry Evans.

77. Gray Research Papers, Box 16, Folder 136, Scouts.

78. Leeson, 636; and Weibert, *Buckskin*, 74.

79. "Thanking the Orator."

80. "Nine Big Horn Survivors Clasp Hands in Bozeman."

81. Montana Hyalite Chapter Daughters of the American Revolution, "Old Tombstone Records in Gallatin County, Montana Cemeteries," 1957; 1880 US Census for Gallatin County, Montana Territory; Leeson, 621; Montana Death Index, 1868-2011; and *Progressive Men of the State of Montana*, 1060-1061.

82. Gray Research Papers, Box 16, Folder 136, Scouts; and McLemore, "Fort Pease," 20.

83. "Thanking the Orator."

84. "Old Tombstone Records in Gallatin County, Montana Cemeteries 1957 Index," Bozeman Public Library.

85. Hardorff, Lakota Recollections, 76; and Gregory F. Michno, *Lakota Noon: The Indian Narrative of Custer's Defeat*, Missoula, Montana: Mountain Press Publishing, 2007, 305.

86. Weibert, *Buckskin*, 44.

87. 1880 US Census for Gallatin County, Montana Territory.

88. Ancestry.com and Find-A-Grave, James Gemmell.

89. Find-A-Grave, George Gibson; and Montana Death Index, 1868-2011.

90. Gray Research Papers, Box 16, Folder 136, Scouts.

91. "Thanking the Orator."

92. "Meets an Untimely Death," *Billings Gazette*, February 12, 1891, 4.

93. McLemore, "Fort Pease," 26.

94. Leeson, 23.

95. "Thanking the Orator."

96. "Nine Big Horn Survivors Clasp Hands in Bozeman"; and 1920 US Census for Gallatin County, Montana.

97. Rachel Phillips, Gallatin County, Montana Pioneer Museum Archive.

98. Weibert, *The 1874 Invasion*, 138.

99. Walt Cross, *Custer's Lost Officer: The Search for Lieutenant Henry Moore Harrington, 7th Cavalry*. Stillwater, Oklahoma: Cross Publications, 2006, 150, 152.

100. Weibert, *Buckskin*, 39; Weibert, *The 1874 Invasion*, 149-150; and "The Story of a March," 12.

101. "Thanking the Orator."

102. Gray Research Papers, Box 16, Folder 136, Scouts; and "Pioneer Succumbs," *The Billings Daily Gazette*, Billings, Montana, May 26, 1908, 1.

103. "Exploits of 'Uncle Billy' Hamilton in Yellowstone Country Like Fiction," *Billings Gazette* (Billings, Montana,) June 30, 1927; Folder containing loose papers concerning William T. Hamilton, Museum of the Beartooths, Stillwater County, Columbus, Montana.

104. Find-A-Grave, Green Hampton; 1880 US Census for Meagher County, Montana Territory; and US Headstone Application for Military Veteran, HAMPTON, GREEN A., May 23, 1936.

105. McPherren, *Imprints*, 182; and De Barthe, *Life and Adventures*, 507-519.

106. "Thanking the Orator."

107. Helena, Montana 1879 City Directory.

108. Gray Research Papers, Box 16, Folder 136, Scouts.

109. Alva Josiah Noyes, *In the Land of Chinook or the Story of Blaine County, Helena, Montana*: State publishing company, 1917, 106-112.

110. "Thanking the Orator"; and 1880 Federal Census for Gallatin County, Montana Territory.

111. "Nine Big Horn Survivors Clasp Hands in Bozeman."

112. Herendeen Papers, SC 16, 4-7; and Willert, *After Little Bighorn*, 2.

113. 1900 US Census for Helena City, Montana; and Find-A-Grave, William C. Hickey.

114. 1880 US Census for Gallatin County, Montana Territory.

115. "Thanking the Orator."

116. Weibert, *Buckskin*, 44.

117. 1880 US Census for Gallatin County, Montana Territory; and 1910 US Census for Madison County, Montana.

118. "Thanking the Orator."

119. Whittlesey, *Gateway to Yellowstone*, 22-28; and "Thanking the Orator."

120. Moore, "Buffalo Bill Cody's Cinnabar Cowboys"; "Death of Hugo J. Hoppe," *The Livingston Enterprise*, 4; and Whittlesey, *Gateway to Yellowstone*, 22-28.

121. The Ghost Dance of 1890 was a religious movement associated with a prophecy of a peaceful end to white expansion and contributed to Lakota resistance on many Indian reservations in the Dakotas. It occurred at roughly the same time as the federal government broke an existing treaty with the Lakota by dividing the Great Sioux Reservation of South Dakota into five smaller reservations. Both occurrences led to Wounded Knee Creek, where on December 28, 1890, the US 7th Cavalry Regiment confronted a small band of Lakota. In the confusion of the moment—which has been termed a massacre by some and a battle by others even to this day—twenty-five U.S. Army soldiers and 153 Lakota—many women and children—lay dead. The Ghost Dance movement fizzled out after the incident.

122. "Thanking the Orator."

123. Johansen and Grinde, *Encyclopedia*, 178; and Beck, *Inkpaduta*, 139, 140.

124. "Thanking the Orator."

125. Camp Manuscripts, Box 4: Folder 5, Envelope 6—Barkley statement of 1874.

126. 1880 US Census for Gallatin County, Montana Territory.

127. Leeson, 1138; Schontzler, "Bozeman's wild West days"; and Schontzler, "Street names keep Bozeman's colorful history alive."

128. "Thanking the Orator"; Gray, *Centennial Campaign*, 74; and Weibert, *The 1874 Invasion*, 149.

129. Hardorff, *Lakota Recollections*, 119-120; and Richard G. Hardorff, *Indian Views of the Custer Fight*, Norman, Oklahoma: University of Oklahoma Press, 2005, 152.

130. 1880 US Census for Gallatin County, Montana Territory; and "Thanking the Orator."

131. "Thanking the Orator"; and 1900 US Census for Gallatin County, Montana.

132. Montana Hyalite Chapter Daughters of the American Revolution, "Old Tombstone Records in Gallatin County, Montana

Cemeteries," 1957; and 1900 US Census for Gallatin County, Montana Territory.

133. "Thanking the Orator."

134. Gray Research Papers, Box 16, Folder 136, Scouts; and McLemore, "Fort Pease," 20.

135. 1880 US Census for Gallatin County, Montana Territory; "Thanking the Orator"; and 1900 US Census for Trinity County, California.

136. Fifer, *Montana Battlefields*, 57, 75; and Gray Research Papers, Box 16, Folder 136, Scouts.

137. "Thanking the Orator."

138. "Nine Big Horn Survivors Clasp Hands in Bozeman."

139. 1910 US Census for Gallatin County, Montana Territory; and Montana Death Index, 1868–2011.

140. 1880 US Census for Gallatin County, Montana Territory; and Find-A-Grave, William McDuff.

141. Gray Research Papers, Box 16, Folder 136, Scouts; and McLemore, "Fort Pease," 20.

142. 1910 US Census for Silver Bow County, Montana.

143. Weibert, *The 1874 Invasion*, 149.

144. 1880 US Census for Gallatin County, Montana Territory; 1900 US Census for Park County, Montana; Genealogy.com William Carroll Officer/Fanny Elizabeth; and telephone discussions with Steve Florman, great-great-grandson of William Officer, June 2015.

145. "Nine Big Horn Survivors Clasp Hands in Bozeman."

146. 1880 US Census for Gallatin County, Montana Territory; 1900 US Census for Gallatin County, Montana Territory; and Montana Hyalite Chapter Daughters of the American Revolution, "Old Tombstone Records in Gallatin County, Montana Cemeteries," 1957.

147. Find-A-Grave, William Polfer.

148. C. Adrian Heidenreich, "The Crow Indian Delegation to Washington, DC, in 1880," *Montana: The Magazine of Western History*, Volume XXXI, Number 2, 56-58; "Death of A.M. Quivey," and "Addison M. Quivey," *The Billings Gazette*.

149. Weibert, *The 1874 Invasion*, 149.

150. Bob Drury and Tom Clavin, *The Heart of Everything That Is: The Untold Story of Red Cloud, An American Legend*, New York: Simon & Schuster, 2013, 363.

151. Michno, *Lakota Noon*, 109, 182, 216 and 252; and Camp Manuscripts, Box 2: Folder 2, Bozeman Expedition of 1874.

152. Find-A-Grave, Herbert F. Richardson; and Montana County Marriages, 1865–1950, Herbert F. Richardson.

153. 1880 US Census for Gallatin County, Montana Territory.

154. "Thanking the Orator"; Find-A-Grave, Daniel Elliott Rouse.

155. Maj. James McLaughlin, Letter to Herbert Welsh, Office of Indian Rights Association, Philadelphia, Pennsylvania, dated January 12, 1891, as found on PBS New Perspectives on The West, website, http://www.pbs.org/weta/thewest/resources/archives/eight/sbarrest.htm.

156. "Thanking the Orator."

157. "Con Smith Dies at Boulder Home; Pioneer of State," 1.

158. "Thanking the Orator."

159. Weibert, *Buckskin*, 47.

160. Zach Benoit, "YelCo 52: 'Born by the River and killed by the Railroad,'" *Billings Gazette*, September 13, 2014.

161. "Muggins Taylor First Officer to Lose Life in Maintaining Order," *The Billings Gazette* (Billings, Montana,) June 30, 1927, 5; Gray, *Centennial Campaign*, 40-41; Weibert, *Buckskin*, 47; Willert, *After Little Bighorn*, 2; and Benoit, "YelCo 52.'"

162. "That Word 'Liar' Started Boot Hill, First Graveyard," *The Billings Gazette*, June 30, 1927, 24.

163. "Muggins Taylor First Officer to Lose Life in Maintaining Order," 5; Gray, *Centennial Campaign*, 40-41; Weibert, *Buckskin*, 47; Willert, *After Little Bighorn*, 2; and Benoit, "YelCo 52.'"

164. Gray Research Papers, Box 16, Folder 136, Scouts.

165. Weibert, *The 1874 Invasion*, 135.

166. "Thanking the Orator"; 1900 US Census for Gallatin County, Montana; Find-A-Grave, Timothy C. Ward.

167. 1880 US Census for Kingman County, Iowa; and Find-A-Grave, Eli Britton Way.

168. Cross, *Custer's Lost Officer*, 150, 152, 231.

169. 1875 New York State Census for Niagara County; 1880 US Census for Niagara County, New York; 1900 US Census for Niagara County, New York; and 1910 US Census for Portage County, Ohio.

170. Schontzler, "Street names keep Bozeman's colorful history alive."

171. Sanders, Society of Montana Pioneers, Volume 1—Register, 216; and Leeson, 1174.

172. "LOST 'CABIN' GOLD MINE AGAIN LOCATED.; Discovery of the Fabulously Rich Mine Causes a Stampede—Wyoming Town Almost Deserted on Account of the Find," *New York Times*, August 18, 1902.

173. Weibert, *Buckskin*, 44-45, 50.

CHAPTER EIGHT

The Impact of the 1874 Yellowstone Wagon Road and Prospecting Expedition on the Little Bighorn Fight in 1876

There were many similarities between the 1874 expedition and the events surrounding the Battle of the Little Bighorn. The first similarity has to do with the terrain. The wagon train camped at many sites along the Rosebud that two years later would serve as overnight resting stops for the US 7th Cavalry Regiment as they marched down that waterway in search of the Lakota and Northern Cheyenne village that was their target. After the 1876 Little Bighorn fight, the bulk of the village moved south along the Little Bighorn to modern-day Lodge Grass and then turned southwest to parallel Lodge Grass Creek, as Sitting Bull moved toward the Bighorn Mountains. This, of course, was the same terrain in which the Battle of Lodge Grass Creek had been fought in 1874. Undoubtedly, many of the warriors that had fought there in 1874 pointed out landmarks to their compatriots as they passed by a second time in two years.

Although not a single frontiersman on the wagon train served two years later as a soldier in the Great Sioux War of 1876, participants on both sides of the 1874 Yellowstone Wagon Road and Prospecting Expedition played significant roles in the Battle of the Little Bighorn. Nowhere is this truer than the contributions made by the Lakota and Northern Cheyenne warriors, even the more junior ones, against George A. Custer and his US 7th Cavalry Regiment.

Warrior Participation in 1876

Gray Earth Tracking and White Earth Tracking

According to author Walt Cross in *Custer's Lost Officer: The Search for Lieutenant Henry Moore Harrington, 7th Cavalry*, Gray Earth Tracking (Noisy Walking)—probable opponent of the 1874 expedition—a son of Inkpaduta and the twin brother of White Earth Tracking, fought with the small Santee band at the Little Bighorn in June 1876. On the Custer wing of the fighting, Lt. Henry M. Harrington, acting commander of Company C—as the nominal commander, Tom Custer, was serving as his brother's aide-de-camp—led a rear guard action, as the men of his company fell back from Calhoun Hill along Battle Ridge. Reportedly wielding two Colt 1873 Single Action Army Revolvers, Harrington assisted several men obtain temporary reprieve in the frantic—and ultimately hopeless—withdrawal. Toward the end of the battle on Custer Hill, Lt. Harrington—an 1872 West Point graduate—led an attempted mounted breakout of five troopers to the east, away from the battle and certain death.

It appears that the other riders did not get far before they were ridden down by their relentless enemies; not so the officer. For several miles, Gray Earth Tracking and White

Earth Tracking chased the army lieutenant, who was riding a strong horse. However, the gap slowly closed and at the end of the chase, Lt. Harrington turned to face his pursuers and severely wounded White Earth Tracking with a gunshot. At almost the same instant, Gray Earth Tracking pulled out a large caliber carbine—possibly a .56 Spencer—and shot Harrington in the left side of his head; the bullet exited the opposite side of the skull, instantly killing the army officer.[1] The brothers counted coup and took the strong steed for their own. They later took Harrington's horse with them to Canada, where the animal lived for several years. After the battle, many warriors credited the soldier (Harrington) who rode swiftly as the bravest in the battle, which would have conferred great honor on Gray Earth Tracking.[2]

Red Hawk

Red Hawk, a documented participant in the 1874 fighting against the expedition, fought at the Little Bighorn on June 25–26, 1876, initially against Reno's forces in the valley, then against 1st Lt. James "Jimmy" Calhoun and his Company L at Calhoun Hill and finally at the last fighting on Custer Hill. His exact actions against Reno in the valley remain in doubt. However, about the time that part of Custer's wing came down Medicine Tail Coulee, we know that Red Hawk crossed the Little Bighorn River to the southeast. Red Hawk recalled that the cavalrymen had moved in three groups. Seeing this, he then crossed Medicine Tail Coulee and headed north toward Butler Ridge. At this position, Red Hawk thought that several warriors around him had been killed, but he did not believe that any soldiers had died yet in this part of the battle. Red Hawk then headed north toward what much later would be called "Nye-Cartwright Ridge." From his position on the elevated terrain there, he could see the cavalrymen being forced back to Calhoun Hill.[3]

Red Hawk then moved to approximately 220 yards east of Calhoun Hill. He appears to have been fairly close to Gall at this time. Red Hawk observed the soldiers on Calhoun Hill and Finley Ridge stand in firing lines and deliver volley after volley into the warrior ranks. He also noted that the firing did not seem to have a perceptible effect on his fellow warriors. Undoubtedly, this was because the 7th Cavalry soldiers were not in the same league as the frontier marksmen that had fought in the 1874 wagon train. The marksmen in that earlier fight had been hitting targets well in excess of the 220 yard range it appears that the troopers on these two positions were firing. And unlike 1874, now—when the soldiers missed shot after shot—the warriors felt impervious and kept closing the distance.[4] Red Hawk kept low on the grassy slopes and made his way north of Calhoun Hill. From that position, he charged toward the cavalry positions, probably those of Company L. As for the results, Red Hawk later stated:[5]

> The soldiers were swept off their feet. The Indians were overwhelming. Here the troopers divided and retreated on each side of the ridge.

Red Hawk then advanced in the low ground to the east of Battle Ridge toward Last Stand Hill. He probably picked up a carbine from one of the dead soldiers and some .45-55 ammunition. Red Hawk saw where the cavalrymen were falling back toward Custer Hill, where they made one more last, desperate fight. After the cavalry position on Custer Hill collapsed, Red Hawk watched the few remaining soldiers retreat south toward Deep Ravine, where he believed they would try to make a third defensive stand. It proved just as futile as their previous attempts that afternoon. Red Hawk believed that none of the cavalrymen made it to the ravine.[6]

Flying By

Flying By, sometimes known as Struck or Struck Plenty, fought at the Little Bighorn as well. After Reno's attack on the village with

Companies A, G, and M, when the troopers left the timber area and retreated toward the Little Bighorn River, Flying By pursued the soldiers, but an enemy bullet dropped Flying By's horse and the warrior tumbled to the ground. Flying By then walked several hundred yards back to the village. When he returned to his tipi area, Flying By saw Hunkpapa and Minneconjou women dismantling their dwellings and preparing to flee away from the soldiers in blue. Seeing the flags of these soldiers coming down toward the river, Flying By ran toward the enemy. He crossed the Little Bighorn River at Medicine Tail Coulee and worked his way north up Deep Coulee. Flying By then approached to about 130 yards from Finley Ridge, which was occupied by part of Company C. Riderless cavalry horses stampeded toward the river and Flying By captured one of the big animals. After he mounted, he rode toward several other cavalry horses and grabbed them by their bridles. Then Flying By temporarily left the battle area to lead the horses down Deep Coulee and back to the village.[7]

After taking the big cavalry horses back to his lodge (cavalry horses were distinctly larger than Indian ponies,) Flying By searched the saddle bags and found ammunition. After a few minutes, he crossed the river, rode back up Deep Coulee and arrived at the battle area some thirty minutes after he had departed. Riding over Calhoun Hill, Flying By also probably picked up a Springfield carbine to go along with the ammunition he had found earlier. He then rode along the east side of Battle Ridge toward the sounds of battle. As Flying By approached Custer Hill, he could see the final few moments of the desperate fight there, later stating that although the soldiers were still firing and seemed to have an adequate amount of ammunition, the warrior numbers were just too great. Flying By observed several soldiers attempting to escape, but believed that only four troopers made it into the gully running downward from Battle Ridge toward the Little Bighorn. Later, at the fighting at Reno Hill, Flying By observed the death of warrior Long Road.[8]

Crazy Horse

This book concludes that Crazy Horse displayed an extremely high level of bravery at the Battle of Lodge Grass Creek. It would not be long before the warrior would have another opportunity to demonstrate his unique brand of courage, and this display of audacity would cement his legacy in the history books. About ten minutes into the fight with Maj. Marcus Reno's forces in the valley (Companies A, G, and M) Crazy Horse emerged from his lodge with his bridle and rifle, looking for his pony. A few minutes later, he was mounted and riding towards the cavalrymen. Leading his warriors from his white-faced pony, Crazy Horse charged toward the positions of the cavalrymen in the timber. Just as Crazy Horse approached the timber, the cavalrymen began to ride out of the woods toward the southeast and east, attempting to reach the Little Bighorn River. Crazy Horse veered off for a moment to catch a riderless black horse and then resumed the lead. He apparently killed several soldiers with his war club and pulled others off their horses as they slowed to cross the steep banks of the river. It appears that Crazy Horse crossed to the eastern side of the Little Bighorn and on his pony scaled a coulee upward to the vicinity of Reno Hill.[9]

On top of the ridge, when Crazy Horse looked to the north, he saw the rear of Custer's column, which was now the major threat to the village. Crazy Horse then rode back down the coulee toward the Little Bighorn, leading several wounded warriors back to the village, before joining the fight again. Perhaps fifteen minutes later, Crazy Horse crossed the Little Bighorn for the third time near Medicine Tail Coulee and rode up the east side of Deep Coulee on his pinto pony. By this time, Crazy Horse could see some of the cavalrymen a half mile to the northeast moving from Nye-Cartwright Ridge toward Calhoun Hill. Crazy Horse, still in the west fork of Deep Coulee, passed some 440 yards to the east of Calhoun Hill and then turned to the north. He was now riding to the rear of the cavalrymen. Crazy

Horse led the warriors with him to almost directly north of Calhoun Hill and moved slightly closer (perhaps 300 yards) to Company L and a position from which he probably could see Company I on the east side of Battle Ridge. Crazy Horse, after giving his pony to Flying Hawk for him to guard, and his men started firing at the soldiers on "Calhoun Hill, also observing that many cavalry horses were on their side of the hill."[10]

After White Bull charged on his horse to the west between Company L on Calhoun Hill and the bulk of Company C, circled Company C, and returned east between Company C and Company I—on Battle Ridge—Crazy Horse decided to go on a second charge with White Bull through the enemy. Now Crazy Horse performed a feat similar to what he had done two years before on a similar ridge along Lodge Grass Creek. Riding between Company C and Company I, Crazy Horse blew on his eagle bone horn as numerous soldiers fired at him, with not a single bullet striking the warrior or his pony. Red Feather said that the warriors believed that the soldiers had fired all their ammunition and immediately followed behind Crazy Horse. The warrior Waterman watched Crazy Horse ride close to the soldiers and thought that Crazy Horse was the bravest warrior he had ever seen.[11]

After the charge through Battle Ridge, the movement of Crazy Horse is more difficult to define. He likely pursued the remnants of Company I, as they attempted to withdraw north up Battle Ridge toward Custer Hill. Near this location, Crazy Horse observed a soldier on foot run off the hill toward the east and gave chase. Perhaps 800 yards later, Crazy Horse killed the man, although the distance could have been much less.[12] Crazy Horse, along with White Bull and many others, had proven his courage at the battle, perhaps gaining some measure of revenge for his inability to defeat the frontiersmen two years before.

Against the wagon train, the frontiersmen put down such accurate fire that not even extreme bravery could break the defenses. At the Little Bighorn, the marksmanship of the cavalrymen was so ineffective that the warriors could fight their style of combat and close with the enemy to a distance that they could record their deeds of bravery, such as counting coup and hand-to-hand fighting. At both fights, Crazy Horse rode a painted pony, was exposed to a hail of gunfire that missed him, and was highly visible in his bravery.

Hump

Minneconjou leader Hump was another warrior chief that fought at the Little Bighorn two years after fighting the 1874 expedition. He had problems from the start of Reno's attack, as the horse he had was not his, nor was it broken in, so Hump could not manage it. By the time he found a pony that he could ride, word flashed through the village that a second group of soldiers was in Medicine Tail Coulee, so Hump rode to that area, disregarding Reno's attack in the valley. Hump crossed the Little Bighorn River and rode up Deep Coulee. He left Deep Coulee, after he had traveled three-fourths of a mile, and moved within 300 yards of Calhoun Hill to the east. Suddenly, bullets from troopers in Company L smashed into his pony. Another bullet hit Hump and the chief—with his pony—slammed to the ground. Knocked almost senseless, Hump examined his wound; the bullet entered just above his knee, traveled up his thigh and exited near his hip. If it had struck the femoral artery, Hump would have had just minutes to live, but Hump was fortunate. As he drifted in and out of consciousness, Hump saw many warriors racing past him on their ponies.[13] After the fighting, non-combatants from the village found Hump and took him to his lodge, where his life was saved.

Warrior Conclusions from 1874

What can we conclude about the experiences that the Lakota and Northern Cheyenne chiefs and warriors took away from their experiences in fighting the 1874 Yellowstone expedition and how would they have applied these experiences two years later at the Little

Bighorn? It is this book's contention that the single most important lesson that Sitting Bull, Crazy Horse, and the other warriors learned fighting against the wagon train in 1874, was that once the frontiersmen were able to dig rifle firing pits, or construct another defensive position with logs or rock piles, they became efficient killing machines and that any attempt to dislodge them would cost many casualties and probably prove unsuccessful.

That observation was accurate as the frontiersmen had hours and hours to prepare these positions, such as those encountered by the warriors at the Battle of Rosebud Creek on April 4 and the Battle of Great Medicine Dance Creek on April 12. However, even on April 16, 1874, at Lodge Grass Creek, the frontiersmen had scraped rifle pits out of the muddy soil just twenty-five minutes after the wagon train had found refuge in a small ravine and even these meager efforts proved sufficient to thwart a warrior force almost ten times larger than the defenders.

Custer's wing at the Little Bighorn never truly had time to dismount and dig positions in their fight. Maj. Reno's initial command—Companies A, G, and M—withdrew from the skirmish line to the timber area and took some initial positions along an old river embankment, but no archaeological evidence exists that they did anything to improve these positions. In any case, Reno ordered his infamous withdrawal order in fairly short order and the remnants of his force hastily departed for the other side of the Little Bighorn, fleeing for their lives.

Reno Hill was a different story. Almost from the beginning of its occupation, troopers tried to scrape depressions out of the rocky soil and piled what they could in the way of boxes and horse tack in front of them. Several Company M soldiers later recalled digging in as best they could, although Capt. Myles Moylan may have taken the cake for the construction of a veritable fortress. Moylan piled mule pack saddles and hardtack boxes so high to his front that he acquired the derogatory nicknames of "*Aparejo* Mickie" (*Aparejo* being a Spanish term for saddle) and "Hardtack Mick."[14]

Despite the derogatory epithets, marksmen behind cover could unleash deadly fire; not only did these breastworks provide protection, but they also served as stable firing platforms, greatly increasing the accuracy and thus lethality of the men firing from them. Sitting Bull knew this. He knew this from many encounters with the whites, the most recent which had occurred during the expedition in April 1874. Sitting Bull also knew that by the morning of June 26, 1876, the cavalrymen at Reno Hill had been on that defensive position for roughly twelve hours and that the cavalry's pack train—with whatever amount of ammunition it carried—had arrived.

It is the assertion of this book that beginning a few hours after the destruction of the Custer wing of the 7th Cavalry—a momentous victory for the Lakota and Northern Cheyenne—Sitting Bull began to counsel with the other chiefs and may have asserted that the victors should not press home the attack on Reno Hill.

Immense glory had already been achieved; many warriors had counted coup on Battle Ridge. Why spoil that victory with what would certainly be large losses against dug-in cavalry soldiers of at least 400 in number? Sitting Bull knew what 150 frontiersmen had done to his warriors, firing from similar defensive positions just two years before. While he may not have known that marksmanship-wise, the young troopers in the cavalry were no match for the seasoned hunters and scouts of 1874, why test that level of proficiency with the blood of his warriors? Sitting Bull knew another force—George Crook's—was still in the south after the Battle of the Rosebud a week before; perhaps even the element just defeated at Greasy Grass was part of that force. There would be other roving enemy columns. Eliminating the cavalrymen on Reno Hill would take time and the village had already been in its current position for two days. It was time to move on.

This book also concludes that Crazy Horse reinforced a personal lesson at the Battle of Lodge Grass Creek that influenced his conduct at the Little Bighorn. Historians have already documented that Crazy Horse was part of the warrior decoy force at the Fetterman Massacre in 1866. He obviously survived that dangerous role and the warriors that day, a decade before the Little Bighorn, achieved a significant victory. On Lodge Grass Creek in April 1874, some three hours into the fight, several dozen warriors in a coulee were attempting to escape a charge of the frontiersmen. A significant chief—this book believes to have been Crazy Horse—rode prominently back and forth on a hill only about 150 yards away from the enemy.

One of the frontiersmen managed to kill the chief's horse, but the unnamed marksman missed the rider—a miss that allowed events two years later to unfold in the manner that they did. Thus, in two previous significant fights—the Fetterman Battle in 1866 and the Battle of Lodge Grass Creek in 1874—Crazy Horse emerged unscathed. With these two experiences in mind, this Oglala chief had no reason to believe that his medicine would not again save him when he charged the cavalry lines on June 25, 1876. And it did.

Frontiersmen Participation in 1876

George B. Herendeen

Determining the influence of the fighting in 1874 had on the 1876 campaign from the warrior perspective is difficult; assessing the participation by the frontiersmen can be better documented. In reading of their aggregate contributions one gets the impression of experienced men, often on their own, scurrying hither and yon to accomplish what might be considered small tasks, but without the efficient completion of these duties, the United States Army would have had a much more difficult time in the Great Sioux War of 1876—and with the Custer debacle, the army did not need any more difficulties.

In the spring of 1876, George B. Herendeen was living in a small cabin along the Yellowstone River just northeast of present-day Billings. As the US 2nd Cavalry Regiment was moving along the Yellowstone, part of Col. John Gibbon's Montana Column, one of

its missions was to remove all civilians from along the river. About March 1, a troop of cavalry arrived at Herendeen's cabin and Maj. James S. Brisbin, the acting commander of the regiment, knocked on the door. When Herendeen walked out, the army officer stated, "George, I came after you." Brisbin, nicknamed "Grasshopper Jim," had been a cavalry officer during the Civil War and had risen to the grade of brevet brigadier general. More importantly now, he was a close associate of George Herendeen. After some negotiations, Herendeen agreed to vacate his cabin and returned to Bozeman.[15]

Shortly afterward, Lt. Joshua W. Jacobs, the quartermaster for Col. Gibbon's column, attempted to hire George Herendeen at Fort Ellis as a teamster for the 1876 expedition, proposing to pay him $16 a month, but the veteran frontiersman scoffed at the offer.[16] However, the Yellowstone was in his blood and George Herendeen departed Benson's Landing with Paul McCormick on a small river boat named the *Fleetfoot* and went back down the river again. At the old Fort Pease, Herendeen ran into Col. John Gibbon and after an argument that Herendeen won concerning who would be the owner of several small boats—that Herendeen maintained he had built earlier—the frontiersman won a position as a boat operator—charged with navigating a large skiff on the river.[17] Meanwhile, on May 2, 1876, about fifty Northern Cheyenne, led by Two Moon, captured a picketed horse and mule of Henry Bostwick during a dust storm near Fort Pease; Bostwick was now a scout for the Gibbons Column.[18]

Later, Maj. Brisbin boarded the watercraft and Herendeen took him past the mouth of the Tongue River to just below the mouth of the Powder River. Brisbin introduced Herendeen to Brig. Gen. Alfred Terry on the river steamer *Far West* at this location on June 8. After several men told the senior officer that Herendeen was exceptionally reliable and competent, the general inquired if Herendeen could ride back up the Yellowstone that night, find Gibbon, and give him the message that he was to stop where he was and wait for Gen. Terry to come up to his location in the *Far West*. George Herendeen took his horse off his boat and rode southwest along the river, finding Col. Gibbon the next morning, June 9, at 0200.[19] Herendeen then returned to the *Far West*, where Terry, Brisbin, Custer, and Gibbon were holding a final council of war on the riverboat on June 21. Here Herendeen picked up the action:[20]

> Custer wanted to know where he could get a good man to guide him to the county where he was going and Brisbin told Custer that he had a man that knew that country. Custer said I would like to see him. So they sent for me and when I appeared, Custer placed his finger on the map and asked me if I could lead them to that particular place, Tullocks Forks. I said "yes." He said, "you are just the man I want." That afternoon we moved right on, we traveled night and day for about three days until we got to the place where Custer had his battle.

An examination of George Herendeen's career indicates that he had been down the Rosebud exactly one time—on the 1874 Yellowstone Wagon Road and Prospecting Expedition. Moreover, during that expedition, he was only on the Rosebud for six days; the day after the 1874 expedition departed the Rosebud, it reached the immediate area of Reno Creek, which would soon prove helpful. Very likely, at some point during the conversation with George Custer, or perhaps previously made by Maj. Brisbin, the fact that George Herendeen had been in the exact area in 1874 was mentioned. George Custer knew of the expedition (he had sent a report on February 25, 1874 about it to the War Department) and the fact that he now had an opportunity to have as one of his guides a recent fighter from that venture should have been viewed as invaluable.

Moreover, George Herendeen, while he could guide along stretches of the Rosebud, also had his own impressions of the 1874

fighting. He had seen the outcome of fighting on the defensive, primarily when the wagon train was laagered and the men had had time to dig firing pits and set up the Big Horn Gun and the mountain howitzer. The situation was much different in 1876. The warriors were not defending their village from an imminent attack in 1874; they were in 1876. Fewer warriors in 1874 had firearms than the warriors had at the Little Bighorn. George Armstrong Custer never went on the defensive, until, perhaps, the last final moments of his fight. With the scout's previous experience coloring his observations, we see George Herendeen picking up the action just before the fighting began on June 25:[21]

> Custer turned to Reno and said take the scouts and lead out. Reno's command was in the timber and the Indians were coming. Reno himself was the one that started the stampede. He started out and the soldiers struggled after him and it was nothing but a mob. In the race Reno lost twenty-eight men before he got to the bluffs where Benteen had taken his position on the hill. This was about two miles from where Custer was killed. We were fighting all the time. In this stamped[e] I had for some reason not seen the men start and I found thirteen soldiers myself managed to join the command, for which some say I have the credit of saving their lives.

Prior to that, George Herendeen had been with the main column with George Custer, when it departed the Yellowstone River at the mouth of Rosebud Creek on June 22. As the regiment was passing Lame Deer on June 24, Herendeen spotted an Indian trail and reported that due to its freshness, the cavalry was overtaking the village ahead. In fact, Herendeen also spotted the gap in the hills that led to the headwaters of Tullock's Fork; he also noted that no Indian trails went in that direction. The guide rode up to George Custer and informed him of this key juncture, but— according to Herendeen—Custer said nothing and continued to ride up the Rosebud valley. Herendeen was perplexed, as when he had first met Custer, he had been asked if he could lead the cavalry to Tullock's Fork. Here was the path to that destination. Like many men that day and the next, who found themselves ignored by their commander, Herendeen resumed his position in the column.

At the second stop on June 25, while Custer went forward to the Crow's Nest, Herendeen found a small secluded ravine and took a nap. Perhaps by this time, he had concluded that Custer no longer needed his services. It was an unfortunate occurrence and his presence at the observation point may have proven valuable. Herendeen awoke when Crow scouts returned; they found fresh pony tracks just 150 yards from where Herendeen lay. Mitch Bouyer told Herendeen that the scouts had spotted the large village some fifteen miles away.[22]

Later in the day, after Reno's detachment charged down the valley toward the village, formed a skirmish line, withdrew to the timber area, and finally began to retreat from the timber toward the Little Bighorn, George Herendeen rode about 150 yards from the wooded area, before his horse stumbled and he was thrown to the ground. Herendeen made his way back into the timber. There he found five troopers from Company G and Sgt. Henry Weihe, Sgt. Patrick Carey, Pvt. George "Cully" Weaver and Pvt. John "Big Fritz" Sivertsen from Company M—all without horses—who had become separated from their units. He reassured the men, undoubtedly telling the soldiers of the battles where the 1874 expedition faced similar odds, and prevailed.[23] Herendeen later recalled the event, praising the conduct of the wounded Sgt. White (Weihe):[24]

Once in awhile while in the timber, I would go to the edge and look, and finally seeing only a few Indians, I told the men we would go out and that we must walk and not run and go across the open flat. There was a wounded corporal or sergeant. On the way out of the timber only one shot was exchanged with these Indians. I told the men not to shoot unless necessary, that I did not wish to stir up a general engagement with them—not to run but to go in skirmish order, take it cool, and we would get out. I told them I had been in just such scrapes before and knew we could get out if we kept cool. I told them I could get out alone, and if they would do what I told them I could get them out also.

The wounded sergeant then spoke up and said: "They will do what you want, for I will compel them to obey. I will shoot the first man who starts to run or to disobey orders." This wounded sergeant helped me out in good shape. When we got to the river, the water was rather deep [chest high] where we forded. This sergeant and I remained on the west bank while the balance forded, and we told them when they would get over to protect us while we forded, and they did so.

As George Herendeen crossed the river, he ran across Lt. Charles Varnum, who was burying 2nd Lt. Benjamin "Benny" Hodgson. Hodgson (an 1870 graduate of West Point) had been serving as adjutant to the portion of the regiment under command of Maj. Marcus Reno. Hodgson had been killed at the ford a little earlier while crossing the Little Bighorn during Reno's retreat.

George Herendeen remained on Reno Hill until Gen. Terry rescued the regiment two days later. His seven-page statement and numerous letters home are on file at the Montana Historical Society in Helena. They show that while George Herendeen was a man of many talents, he was not a man of letters. The statement has been edited to clean up his admitted poor spelling and syntax; the letters show clearly, for example, that George Herendeen could not have possibly written the letter that appeared in the *Helena Herald* on January 4, 1878, accounting what happened at the Little Bighorn and Custer.

In this account, Herendeen stated that after reaching the abandoned lodge during the approach to the village, he heard the Crow scouts call to one another "The Sioux are coming up to meet us." He stated that he understood their language and called to Major Reno, "The Sioux are coming." Another missive that could not have been written by George Herendeen without lengthy full-time assistance is the supposed letter from Herendeen on July 7, 1876, from Bismarck. Again, this is a detailed letter with complete sentences, not the style of letter that George normally wrote that was indicative of perhaps two or three years of schooling at the most. To compare the exact detailing of the battle in the 1876 and 1878 letters with the following known George Herendeen writing sample of January 1877 is to see the difference:[25]

> I do not no when I will come home. It may be for years. I would like to see you very mutch but this contry suits me very mutch.

Finally, from a purely physical standpoint, George Herendeen could not have been in Bismarck to write the July 1876 letter. He was not part of the Dakota column and remained in the Montana Territory.

On July 14, George Herendeen arrived with a group of Crows on the Yellowstone River at Matthew Carroll's supply camp. Carroll was the master in charge of transportation for Col. John Gibbon's Expedition.[26]

On August 27, 1876, Gen. Terry raced down O'Fallon's Creek with the riverboats *Yellowstone* and *Carroll* in an attempt to ferry troopers to key points along the waterway in an effort to prevent the Lakota from moving north. The following day, the general sent George Herendeen—now partnered with Buffalo Bill Cody—to Glendive, some thirty-five miles away, to assess the situation there. George and Buffalo Bill returned from Glendive on August 30, stating that they had seen no warriors, nor had they encountered Gen. Crook.[27]

H.M. Muggins Taylor and Henry Bostwick

While George Herendeen's major role at the Little Bighorn came during the fighting, the significant contributions of H.M. Muggins Taylor occurred just after the battle. His story, however, started several months before. Lt. Joshua W. Jacobs, then a regimental quartermaster in the US 7th Infantry Regiment, hired Muggins Taylor on April 8, 1876, for the operation against the Sioux as a scout for $100 per month. Moving down the Yellowstone River, this Montana Column, under Col. John Gibbon, reached the mouth of the Rosebud. During the march, on May 13, Taylor crossed the Yellowstone and began scouting toward the Rosebud, intending to travel up that stream. However, he mistook a small creek for his target and turned back without reaching the Rosebud; during this escapade, he saw no signs of the Lakota. On June 17, Taylor took a Crow warrior and scouted from the Yellowstone toward the Bighorn River. Later, taking a small skiff across the Yellowstone, Lt. Jacobs, Taylor, and an army sergeant, James Wilson, scouted several miles down the Rosebud, returning the following day with no sightings of Lakota warriors.[28]

Muggins Taylor's co-scout on Gibbon's movement that June was none other than the man that had been seriously wounded on the 1874 expedition, Henry Bostwick. Lt. Joshua W. Jacobs hired Bostwick from his interpreter's position at Fort Shaw in March 1876 for the Gibbon's column of the operation to be a scout and interpreter for $50 per month. On May 7, Bostwick led a scouting mission off the Yellowstone and discovered numerous abandoned Lakota lodges. He was with Taylor on May 13. On June 18, Henry Bostwick nearly drowned. Maj. Marcus A. Reno's scouting column had returned to the mouth of the Rosebud opposite Col. Gibbon's headquarters across the Yellowstone. Frustrated that their hand signals were being misunderstood, Gibbon wrote a message that Bostwick put in a pouch and they attempted to cross the river. Because of the winter snow melt, the river in many places that May was often 300 yards wide. After Bostwick sputtered in the water, two Crow scouts successfully crossed. On June 23, Muggins Taylor and Lt. Gustavus

Doane were scouting ahead of the column and spotted several Lakota on bluffs overlooking the Yellowstone River.[29]

Since that time, events spiraled out of control for Gen.Crook in the south and for George Custer at the Little Bighorn. By June 26, 1876, with Col. Gibbon and his column in tow, Brig. Gen. Alfred Terry moved upstream along the Little Bighorn—the Yellowstone at his back—attempting to find the 7th Cavalry. According to Gen. Terry's understanding, Custer should have dispatched George Herendeen to return to Terry when the cavalry had reached the head of Tullock's Fork. Crow scouts had arrived at Terry's column with unintelligible reports of a potential demise of the flamboyant Custer; nothing was certain.

At 1420, Gen. Terry called scouts Muggins Taylor and Henry Bostwick to report to his position. When they soon did, he offered each veteran of the 1874 expedition a $200 bonus if they would go forward on their own as fast as possible and deliver a message to Gen. Custer. Both scouts accepted the offer. He offered the scouts a further $50 bonus. At this rate, Taylor was going to be able to retire a wealthy man. Taylor rode to the east, scaled a bluff and went down the east side of the river. At 1840, Henry Bostwick raced back to the column opining—according to historian John S. Gray—that the valley was swarming with much more than $200 worth of enemy warriors. At about 2015, Taylor returned breathless to the column, stating that fifteen warriors had come after him, and that he had just managed to escape them. Gen. Terry then called a halt to the march at 2040 and the force went into a nighttime bivouac.[30]

The following morning, Gen. Terry began moving south at about 0730, Muggins Taylor having already departed to try again to gain his bonus. Taylor rode the eight miles to Reno Hill and delivered the message to Maj. Reno that help was on the way. He had passed Last Stand Hill and apparently had picked up a trumpet and pistol that the Indians had overlooked. Gen. Terry and his staff arrived at Battle Ridge about 0900 and subsequently

to Reno Hill at 1100, giving the horrible news to the cavalrymen there concerning the demise of their commander.

Late on the evening of June 27, Brig. Gen. Alfred Terry had digested the extent of the disaster to the 7th Cavalry. He knew that Lt. Gen. Phil Sheridan, back at his headquarters in Chicago, would have to know what happened before the story appeared in the newspapers, which could be in days. Probably while it was still daylight, Terry prepared a dispatch that highlighted the details as he knew them, which he hoped would be sent by telegram from Fort Ellis, Montana Territory, the nearest telegraph office to the Little Bighorn, some 200 miles away. After finalizing the communiqué, Brig. Gen. Terry handed it to Muggins Taylor with instructions to ride quickly.[31]

That first night of June 27, Taylor spotted warriors in the darkness and hid in a rock pile. At dawn the next morning, he made good his escape, but was closely pursued until he reached the vicinity of the *Far West* on the Bighorn River. There, he notified Capt. Grant Marsh that wounded men would soon be brought there for subsequent transportation east to Fort Abraham Lincoln. Taylor remained overnight, procured a fresh horse, and continued his ride on June 29, running into the column of wounded and informing them of the exact location of the riverboat. Henry Bostwick and Pvt. James Goodwin (US 7th Infantry Regiment) stepped forward to deliver the same message and rode out the evening of June 27. They reached the mouth of the Little Bighorn on the morning of June 28, but found no steamboat. Tracing and retracing their steps over the next day, they finally found Capt. Grant Marsh and the *Far West* at 1500 on June 29. Later that evening, they reported back to Gen. Terry, although it remains unknown if they received their bonuses. On July 2, Taylor reached the stage coach station at Stillwater, some one hundred miles from Fort Ellis. He delivered the message to the post commander at Fort Ellis, Capt. Daniel W. Benham, who later filed it with the telegraph office.[32]

On July 15, Muggins Taylor, bringing mail from Fort Ellis, arrived by boat at Matthew

Carroll's supply camp on the Yellowstone. He departed this river location on July 19 with letters from Carroll to Indian Agent Dexter Clapp at Fort E.S. Parker, as well as taking several mules with him.[33]

On August 13, 1876, Muggins Taylor hit the saddle again, this time with a message from Gen. Terry to Gen. Nelson Miles at the mouth of the Tongue River to send another riverboat from Fort Buford to patrol the lower Yellowstone River. Taylor returned to Gen. Terry the next day, having accomplished his mission, but with an erroneous report that 250 Crow volunteers were on their way to join the operation. Nine days later, Muggins found Gen. George Crook and gave him the news that the *Far West* had run aground at Buffalo Rapids (near present-day Terry, Montana) and that there subsequently would be a problem supplying Crook from the river.[34]

Oliver Perry Hanna

Oliver Perry Hanna was one of the scouts for Gen. George Crook on the expedition against the Lakota and Northern Cheyenne and was a participant in the Battle of the Rosebud on June 17, 1876. Crook then withdrew south to Goose Creek (near present-day Sheridan, Wyoming) to lick his wounds. With no requirement for scouting at Goose Creek, Oliver Hanna later stated that he signed on with Lt. Frederick William Sibley and his twenty-five troopers from Company E of the US 2nd Cavalry Regiment, to scout the northern base of the Big Horn Mountains. Hanna and two other scouts, Frank "The Grabber" Grouard and Baptiste "Big Bat" Pourier "sniffed out" a number of Northern Cheyenne war parties converging on Camp Cloud Peak on July 7, 1876. Soon the small group was under attack and the situation turned desperate. Grouard suggested that the platoon tether their horses in sight of the warriors and then quickly hike through the timber and up to the highest elevation of the rocky ridge. The men did and the warriors, happy with the acquisition of so many horses, failed to pursue them. The

cavalrymen and scouts then went on an around the clock fifty-mile forced march before they reached safety.[35]

After learning on July 10 of George Custer's defeat, Gen. Crook sent a detachment of troops and scouts including Oliver Hanna and Buffalo Bill Cody to the Little Bighorn. Cody lost the way, as he had no detailed knowledge of the area, but Oliver Hanna was called forward to set them on the correct trail, knowledge gained—in part—on the 1874 expedition.[36]

Wesley Brockmeyer

August 1876 must have seemed like old home month for many of the men on campaign that previously had been on the 1874 expedition. On August 2, 1876, a small party of Gen. Terry's command, which now included the US 6th Infantry Regiment and the US 17th Infantry Regiment, moved a short distance from their support riverboat *Far West* on the Yellowstone River. The two regiments had reached the region to support Terry in a bid to join forces with Gen. Crook and scour the Yellowstone country for the Lakota and Northern Cheyenne. Maj. Orlando H. Moore (US 6th Infantry Regiment) had the mission to recover forage stolen by warriors at the old depot site near the mouth of the Powder River. In a skirmish near the Wolf Rapids on the Yellowstone River, Oglala warrior Runs Fearless (*Kagi Sni Inyanka*) shot and mortally wounded scout Wesley Brockmeyer, another veteran of the 1874 expedition. Troopers took the mortally wounded scout—who had been hit by a bullet from a Springfield Model 1873 .45 Carbine—to the *Far West* on a blanket. Dr. Henry Porter, who had cared for the wounded on Reno Hill with the 7th Cavalry during the Battle of the Little Bighorn, tended Brockmeyer, but the frontiersman soon died of his wound. The next day, the *Far West* traveled twenty miles upstream and soldiers buried the body of Yank Brockmeyer on an island in the middle of the Yellowstone River, so that warriors would not find and mutilate the body.[37]

Zadok Daniels

Zed Daniels, when last seen departing Bozeman on April 10, 1876, with a column of miners, continued to guide the party of gold prospectors down the Bozeman Trail and east to the Black Hills before he left the group and made his way to the Yellowstone River. On August 7, 1876, 1st Lt. Henry J. Nowlan, the regimental quartermaster of the 7th Cavalry—who was serving during the 1876 campaign as the quartermaster on Gen. Terry's staff and the entire Dakota column—saw Zed Daniels at Terry's headquarters and promptly signed him as a scout through October 7, 1876, at $100 a month, at which point Daniels went to Glendive.[38] During the month, Daniels led Terry's forces in the Powder River area, as Lakota chief Long Dog and his band crossed the Yellowstone and headed north.[39] On August 29, as Gen. Terry's men approached the Missouri-Yellowstone divide, the column sent buffalo hunters "Texas Jack" Omohundro and Zed Daniels to procure some fresh meat. The men ran into warriors from Hunkpapa Lakota Long Dog's village; the encounter caused the Lakota to abandon their lodges and move. Unlike Yank Brockmeyer, Zed Daniels survived this dangerous period.[40]

Paul McCormick

Paul McCormick, never one to miss a business opportunity, got in on the action as well in 1876. After helping George Herendeen ferry trade wares down the Yellowstone to Fort Pease for the troops of the Montana Column in early May 1876, McCormick left on May 9 to ride back to Fort Ellis bearing mail and a dispatch to be telegraphed to Gen. Terry, who was still at Fort Abraham Lincoln in the Dakota Territory. Not wasting a moment in the rear, Mc-Cormick rode back to the Yellowstone and then boarded his mackinaw boat and sailed to Col. Gibbon—now in camp opposite the mouth of the Rosebud—arriving on May 28. In addition to the regular mail, McCormick had brought Terry's telegraph orders of May 15 directing

Col. Gibbon to march to Glendive in an attempt to trap Sitting Bull on the Little Missouri River. Sitting Bull was, in fact, nowhere near the Little Missouri, but Paul McCormick was becoming indispensable as a courier and supply source along the Yellowstone River.[41] At dark on July 18, McCormick arrived at Matthew Carroll's supply camp on the river.[42]

William T. "Uncle Billy" Hamilton

Less is documented about two other "graduates" of the 1874 expedition who fought in The Great Sioux War of 1876. In 1876, William T. Hamilton served as a scout for Gen. Crook during the campaign against the Lakota. He joined Crook's command in early March; he would serve under the command of Maj. Thaddeus Harlan Stanton, chief of scouts. Crook's column had departed Fort Fetterman on February 27, 1876—he hoped to catch the tribes in their relatively immobile winter camps. Hamilton and the command journeyed north to the Tongue River. On March 9-10, Uncle Billy probably went with Frank Grouard to the head of Prairie Dog Creek, but found no warriors. William Hamilton was with Crook at the Battle of the Rosebud" on June 17, 1876. As he said in his book, Crook then "beat a retreat back to Goose Creek." After Gen. Wesley Merritt joined the command, Crook moved back down the Rosebud and then to the Powder River. Hamilton wrote that he remained with this command through the fighting at Slim Buttes, September 9-10, 1876. He added that he then went to White Wood Creek, Custer City, and Camp Robinson, before traveling to Fort Laramie, where he resigned his position as guide.[43]

Jack Bean

In March 1876, Jack Bean became the chief packer—in charge of ensuring all the loads packed on horses and mules were done properly—for the Montana Column, commanded by Col. John Gibbon and thus saw the aftermath of the battle at the Little Bighorn. Before departing Fort Ellis, Bean designed and constructed fifty new pack saddles for the army, which later became known as the "Jack Bean Pack Saddle." Jack referred to his position with Col. Gibbon as "Boss Packer." On May 1, 1876, he accompanied a scouting trip to the ruins of Fort C.F. Smith, where he had been with the expedition just two years before.[44]

Frontiersmen Conclusions from 1874

George Herendeen provided crucial testimony in the Reno Court of Inquiry proceedings in 1879 in Chicago.[45] On January 27, 1879—the thirteenth day of the proceedings—Herendeen was called by the recorder, duly sworn in, and received his first question about 1130. He would continue to testify for over an hour on many aspects of the battle. During this questioning, Herendeen was asked his opinion to the following important quandary:[46]

Question: From your experience in Indian fights, how long could a command of 100 men have held out in that timber with six or seven thousand rounds of ammunition judiciously used?

George Herendeen, who at no point testified that Maj. Reno had asked him his opinion on what should be done during the battle, responded about the timber fight:

Answer: I don't think the Indians could have gotten them out of there at all if they had water and provisions.

The timber position backed against the Little Bighorn River, so adequate water would not have been a problem. We do not know if George Herendeen was factoring in the difference in marksmanship skills between the cavalrymen he saw on June 25 and that displayed by the frontiersmen two years earlier in his other truly significant and prolonged fighting against enemy warriors. The author believes that if any officer that morning had queried Herendeen on what should be done—

and Herendeen later stated that Reno had not spoken to him on the skirmish line or in the timber, nor had he spoken to Reno—the old scout probably would have counseled the men to stay put in the timber, start improving their positions, and make every shot count.

Uncle Billy Hamilton later published his life's story in *My Sixty Years on the Plains: Trapping, Trading and Indian Fighting* and made this short summary of the 1874 expedition:[47]

In 1874 an expedition was organized, consisting of one hundred and forty-eight men. We started in midwinter, going down the Yellowstone River, crossing at lower Porcupine Creek. We then travelled over a broken country to East Rosebud, having two small engagements *en route*. On East Rosebud we had two rifle-pit engagements, repulsing the Indians in every instance with heavy loss. We then went to the Little Big Horn and had two more fights, one on Grass Lodge, where fifteen hundred Indians charged us, but we repulsed them with heavy loss. The people in Bozeman having had no tidings, concluded we were all lost. This was the expedition which brought on the war of 1876 that was so disastrous to General Custer and his command.

Clearly, William Hamilton stressed the construction of the rifle pits and their role in the lethality of the frontiersmen, in perhaps the same way as Sitting Bull might have done with his subordinates the evening after defeating George Custer. Oliver Perry Hanna, meanwhile, had his own observations, which were expressed in even stronger terms than had been by George Herendeen. Hanna later wrote:[48]

The cannons had been our salvation and without them we would not have lasted very long … All that "bunk" written by many "historians" on the Custer Massacre, that if Reno had not retreated on to the hill they would have all been annihilated, is not true, and every experienced Indian

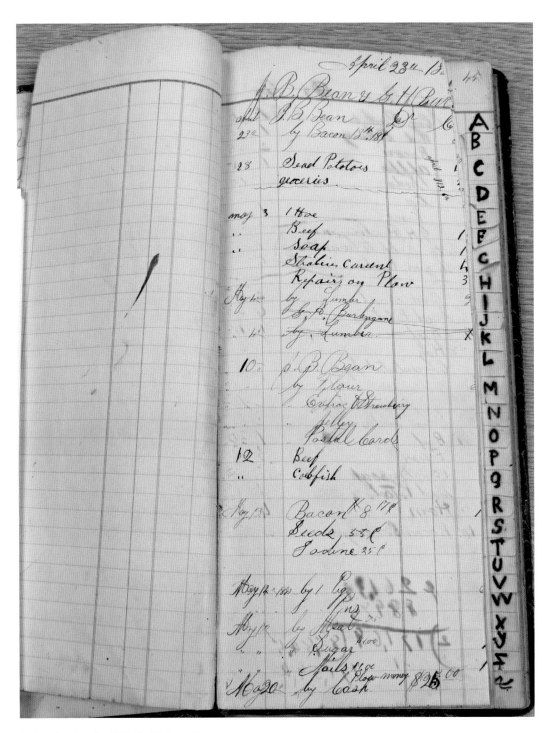

Ledger book at the Gallatin History Museum
showing supply entries for hunter Jack Bean. *Author
photograph at Gallatin History Museum of Bozeman,
October 2013*

fighter says so … Reno was in an old creek bed, which was dry and grown up with cottonwood trees. There was an embankment ten feet high on three sides, a natural breastworks. All that his men needed to have done was to crawl on to the top of the embankment and fire on the Indians. They were camped on level ground. Reno had the greatest advantage imaginable. They could have mowed them down by the hundreds. When Reno turned to run up the valley that gave the Indians the advantage and you know the rest.

Addison M. Quivey, who did not participate in the 1876 campaign, but did write of his experiences in 1874 before Custer's defeat at the Little Bighorn, made the following observation that may or may not have been known by the army officers in the field in 1876:[49]

And we also find that the prowess of the Sioux has been vastly overestimated, and that a small force of frontiersmen can whip the whole tribe at small cost.

1st Lt. James Bradley, who was not present in 1874 on the wagon train, but was an astute observer of history, attempted to cut through the bravado, by contemplating what had transpired in 1874 and contrasting that with the Little Bighorn fight in 1876. The astute junior officer and historian wrote:[50]

It almost justifies the conclusion to which it tempted Mr. Quivey "that the prowess of the Sioux has been vastly over-estimated and that a small force of frontiersmen can whip a whole tribe at small cost." But it has since been found that it makes a great difference whether the Sioux are engaged in offensive or defensive fight. In the latter case, when the safety of their villages, with their wives, children and all that they possess is involved in the issue, they prove themselves able to fight with something of the courage and resolution of civilized men.

Meanwhile, James Gourley, another wagon train veteran, attempted to avoid generalized conclusions and make detailed observations, later opining on the tactical success of the wagon train:[51]

I think our success in fighting them was due to the fact that we always got in the first shot, and they afterward told that we never slept. They said we were neither whites nor Indians, but were like a lot of bull buffaloes; we had no sense. And it was by creating that superstitious feeling of our being bad medicine that we virtually whipped them. During the course of our fights, they lost a great many horses. They attributed this to our bad medicine, and their attempts to shoot the cartridges, which we had scattered around resulted in bursted guns and dead Indians. This made them think that we had stronger guns than they, and was another evidence to them of our bad medicine.

James Gourley further described how the warriors would attempt to stampede the horses of their foes, a tactic done successfully at the Little Bighorn two years later against George Custer's column on Battle Ridge:[52]

They came after them in Indian fashion, swinging their blankets, whooping and yelling, making all the noise they could.

It would seem that the recollections of these men centered on two areas. First, that had Maj. Reno remained in the timber in the valley and had his battalion prepared even rudimentary firing positions, they could have successfully defended against the warriors and inflicted grievous losses. Historians and military officers have debated this point for 140 years, with proponents on each side. Suffice it to say, this study could not find a single frontiersman on the 1874 expedition that later said that Maj. Marcus Reno was correct in his decision to withdraw from the timber, although that does not mean that the frontiersmen were correct in this conclusion. The debate concerning Maj. Reno and the proper tactics to adopt during the valley fight will rage as long as aficionados are interested in the Little Bighorn.

One other assertion is somewhat less precise to compare with the results of 1876. Oliver Hanna and many others in later years opined on the lethality and psychological impact that the mountain howitzer and the Big Horn Gun had during the fighting. Some of this praise for the expedition's artillery bordered on hyperbole—witness the comments made by Judge Horatio Nelson Maguire in 1883 during a speech at Bozeman celebrating the arrival of the Northern Pacific Railroad and commemorating the 1874 expedition:[53]

The now historic "Big Horn Gun"—can I pass it by in silence? It spoke for us through red lips of fire when bullets and arrows filled the air as thick as descending hail: it is entitled to honorable mention now. It has made a proud record in two States and two territories, in citizen campaigns against Indian foes. In Nebraska and Colorado, and then in Wyoming, it followed graders' camps and prospecting parties like a guardian angel. It came to us in the fall of 1872—having been the chief protector of the Prospecting Expedition which in the fall of that year reached Bozeman from Cheyenne by way of the Wind River Valley. It entered the field with the first Big Horn Expedition in 1874, and probably saved it from annihilation— by its thundering tones of defiance, if not by actual execution. It came again to the front in the succeeding Pease Expedition; and finally the fortunes of war consigned it to the depths of the Yellowstone.

But the "Big Horn Gun" has a higher destiny than to rust ingloriously in a quicksand grave. The public-spirited President of the Bozeman Board of Trade had it fished out and brought back home. It is present; and should have been the loudest-mouthed participant on this occasion of congratulation. And why should it not be?

It has been "constant in our ills," and now has a right to be "joyous in our joy." The mission of the "Big Horn Gun" is not yet ended. The dust of our fallen heroes must be gathered together and re-interred in Bozeman, beneath an imposing monument; and surmounting that monumental pile must be the "Big Horn Gun"—its warfare o'er, there let it stand as long as its iron soul endures, a sentinel of peace over the honored ashes below.

Historians have debated for years whether or not George Custer should, or could, have taken several Gatling guns along the march to the Little Bighorn. At the time, George Custer argued that Gatling Guns adversely affected his column's ease and speed of transport. He earlier had problems on his 1874 expedition to the Black Hills, when the guns could not keep up with the rest of his column. The men on the 1874 Yellowstone expedition reported no such problems with the two horse-drawn cannons, although it must be said that the wagon train did not travel as far per day as Custer's column did from June 21 to June 25. While on two occasions along the Rosebud, the cannons were in defensive positions at the wagon train laager, during the Battle of Lodge Grass Creek, the gunners were able to quickly get them into battery and commence firing after they had been in march-mode with the moving wagon train.

The Gatling guns in question in 1876 that were available to Custer were the one-inch-bore versions, designed to reduce defensive emplacements such as log and earth fortifications. The gun itself weighed 650 pounds, versus the 200 pounds for the .45-caliber rifle cartridge model. The weight of the gun carriage for the one-inch version was 1,152 pounds, while the limber and box for the same model weighed 790 pounds—a total march weight of 2,592 pounds. This was probably three or four times the weight of each cannon and carriage taken on the 1874 expedition, so the cannons may have had lesser mobility problems than the Gatling guns.

If taking cannon with the regimental main body racing toward the village proved too difficult, could they have maintained pace with the regimental pack train and helped to subsequently defend Reno Hill? One would think they could have. The terrain was the same during the two expeditions (and the weather was considerably worse in 1874)—much of the 7th Cavalry's route was almost in the same wheel ruts made two years previously. In addition, a mountain howitzer—and the 1874 expedition had one of these weapons—could have been disassembled and carried by pack mules to preclude any mobility problems brought on by pulling a wheeled carriage through rough terrain.

Therefore, perhaps we should add to the glorious Little Bighorn debate by posing the following question, should Custer had taken a few small cannon, or better yet mountain howitzers, with the regiment to the Little Bighorn and use them in the same manner as the wagon train had in 1874? Col. John Gibbon had brought a twelve-pound Napoleon cannon with his column on the campaign, indicating that a possible use for the artillery piece might be found. While a mountain howitzer, transported in the pack train, might not have saved Custer and his five companies on the afternoon of his demise, would they have been able to play a role on Reno Hill in forcing the warriors to withdraw? The range from Reno Hill to the large Lakota/Northern Cheyenne village was much too great to permit mountain howitzers from bombarding the encampment. However, almost every warrior position surrounding Reno Hill—including those on Sharpshooter Ridge—could have been touched by the exploding shells of the Bull Pup and touched heavily. While a definitive answer to this question may elude us, it is interesting to contemplate.

While some questions can never be answered, others are answered incorrectly and in warfare, this latter outcome can have unfortunate repercussions. The frontiersmen, and any army officers that studied the battles fought during the 1874 Yellowstone expedition, may have come to incorrect conclusions concerning the firearms. The weapons used in 1874 and 1876 were all black powder (cartridge, not muzzle-loader.) One of the detriments of this type of propellant was, and is, that it fouls the barrel of the weapon to a great degree, which seriously affects the functioning of the piece (slowing the rate of fire) as well as lessening the accuracy of the bullet. Modern-day black powder shooters overcome this by using a flexible plastic blow tube, placing one end in the empty chamber of the rifle or carbine after each shot and providing four or five sharp exhales through it from the other end. This moist air will go down the barrel from the chamber to the muzzle, causing residual burnt black powder to remain moist. As long as that residue does not dry and cake, the effect on the next round traveling through the barrel is minimal and accuracy does not suffer. If the residue begins to dry, however, the shooter will begin to have problems.

Typical frontiersmen, and this included most buffalo hunters, and army soldiers had no plastic blow tubes nor did they truly understand the magnitude of the problem. On a cool, moist day—typical of almost every day during the 1874 expedition—one might get off many rounds with little problem, as long as the rifleman did not heat up the rifle's barrel too much through prolonged rapid fire. However, on a hot dry day, black powder fouling could cause a decrease in accuracy after only a half dozen to a dozen shots.[54] Many sources would later state that at the Little Bighorn the afternoon of the battle, temperatures rose high into the 90°s and may have even reached 100°. In those temperature extremes, with the magnitude of the numbers of warriors, the black powder fouling may have made almost every cavalry firearm an inaccurate hunk of iron.

Another difference between the experiences of 1874 and 1876 needs to be documented as well. Superior marksmanship won the day in 1874. Almost every man in the wagon train was an experienced shooter. The most plentiful weapons in the wagon train were the Springfield 1868 Rifles, caliber .50. The US Army had their infantry rifles zeroed for 300 yards in those days, with the idea being to aim at the enemy's stomach at shorter range. That prevented the shooter from having a weapon zeroed for 200 yards, which would result in the round striking four feet low when fired at a target 300 yards away. The many hunters on the expedition, using Sharps with adjustable sights for both range and windage, could achieve much more accurate zeros with their weapons. All of this added to a level of lethal fire that kept the warriors at bay in 1874.

Weapons employed had changed by 1876 and the vast majority of soldiers in the 7th Cavalry used the Springfield Model 1873 Carbine, firing the .45-55 cartridge. Because the 55 grains of black powder only gave the 405-grain bullet a muzzle velocity of 1,100 feet per second, the truly effective range of the cavalry carbine at the Little Bighorn was only about 150 yards. This underlying detrimental situation was magnified when we add in black powder fouling on a hot day and the fact that many, many of the soldiers in the regiment had undergone woeful marksmanship training.[55] Therefore, when the scouts in 1876, who had been on the 1874 expedition and knew more about marksmanship than even the best shots in the regiment, were discussing the deadly effects of long-range fire, they were making dangerous conclusions in a later situation in which the parameters of weapons and marksmanship were drastically different.

The most honest interpretation of all concerning the fighting on the 1874 Yellowstone Wagon Road and Prospecting Expedition may have come from Tom Allen, a veteran of that august body of men. Allen was no novice to heavy combat. He had been a private in Company I of the 52nd Ohio Volunteer Infantry Regiment in the Civil War and his unit had been in the thick of the fighting at Chickamauga, Missionary Ridge, Atlanta, Kennesaw Mountain, Jonesboro, and Bentonville. Tom Allen could have told the troopers in the 7th Cavalry what they would encounter when fighting the Lakota and Cheyenne. In 1912, he wrote famed researcher Walter Mason Camp concerning 1874 and ended his letter in this manner:[56]

That is about all the information I can give you because at that time [on the 1874 expedition] I was so badly scared that I didn't know weather [sp] I was in Montana or Idaho.

Notes

1. Army physician Dr. Robert W. Shufeldt discovered Harrington's skull and jawbone in 1877, although he did not correctly identify them, well east of the battle. In 2003, forensic scientists at the Smithsonian Institution were able to make a positive identification of the remains that lay in the museum's anthropological collection.

2. Cross, *Custer's Lost Officer*, 150, 152.

3. Michno, *Lakota Noon*, 109, 116, 128, 136, 139, 147, 172.

4. Ibid, 175, 182.

5. Ibid, 214, 216.

6. Ibid, 250, 252, 263.

7. Hardorff, *Lakota Recollections*, 76; and Michno, *Lakota Noon*, 81, 114, 115, 156, 157, 184, and 186.

8. Michno, *Lakota Noon*, 232, 237, 266; and Richard G. Hardorff, *Hokahey! A Good Day to Die; The Indian Casualties of the Custer Fight*, London: Bison Publishing, 1999, 142.

9. Michno, *Lakota Noon*, 55, 68, 75-77, 81, 82, 84, 96.

10. Ibid, 109, 112 113, 144-146, 164-165, 172, 177, 180.

11. Ibid, 202, 207.

12. Ibid, 264-265.

13. Ibid, 115-117, 161-162.

14. MacLean, *Custer's Best*, 119.

15. Herendeen Papers, SC 16, 4-5.

16. Gray, *Custer's Last Campaign*, 139, 148.

17. Herendeen Papers, SC 16, 4-5.

18. Fifer, *Montana Battlefields*, 72.

19. Herendeen Papers, SC 16, 6; and Gray, *Custer's Last Campaign*, 175.

20. Herendeen Papers, SC 16, 6.

21. Ibid.

22. Gray, *Custer's Last Campaign*, 241.

23. Gray, *Custer's Last Campaign*, 305; Kenneth Hammer, *Custer in '76: Walter Camp's Notes on the Custer Fight*, Provo, UT:

Brigham Young University, 1976, 141; and Richard G. Hardorff, editor, *On the Little Bighorn with Walter Camp; A Collection of Walter Mason Camp's Letters, Notes and opinions on Custer's Last Fight*, El Segundo, CA: Upton & Sons Publishers, 2002, 19.

24. Hammer, *Custer in '76*, 224-225.

25. Herendeen Papers, SC 16, 6. Letter from Bozeman dated January 20, 1877.

26. Matthew Carroll, "Diary of Matthew Carroll, Master in Charge of Transportation for Colonel John Gibbon's Expedition," *Contributions to the Historical Society of Montana*, Volume Two, Helena, Montana: Montana Historical and Miscellaneous Library, 1896, 235.

27. Gray, *Centennial Campaign*, 235-236.

28. Gray, *Custer's Last Campaign*, 139-140, 151 and 380; and James H. Bradley, "Journal of James H. Bradley, The Sioux Campaign of 1876 under the command of General John Gibbon," *Contributions to the Historical Society of Montana*, Volume Two, Helena, Montana: Montana Historical and Miscellaneous Library, 1896, 172, 188.

29. Bradley, "Journal of James H. Bradley," 188, 207, 216.

30. Gray, *Centennial Campaign*, 190-193.

31. Ibid, 194.

32. Gray, *Centennial Campaign*, 193; and Gray, *Custer's Last Campaign*, 139-140, 151, 380.

33. Carroll, "Diary of Matthew Carroll," 235-236.

34. Gray, *Centennial Campaign*, 218-219, 228.

35. Ibid, 198-200.

36. C. Sharps Arms Inc. at http://csharpsarms.com/famoussharps-article/16/Hanna-and-White.html

37. Dr. L. G. Walker, Jr., *Dr. Henry R. Porter: The Surgeon who Survived Little Bighorn*, Jefferson, North Carolina: McFarland & Company, 2008, 65; and Jerome A. Greene, *Battles and Skirmishes of the Great Sioux War, 1876–1877: The Military View*, Norman, Oklahoma: University of Oklahoma Press, 1993, 93-95.

38. Gray Research Papers, Box 16, Folder 136, Scouts.

39. Gray, *Centennial Campaign*, 209.

40. Ibid, 235-236.

41. Ibid, 78, 107 and 108.

42. Carroll, "Diary of Matthew Carroll," 235.

43. Gray, *Centennial Campaign*, 73, 78, 107, 108; and Hamilton, 244.

44. Telephone discussions with Mr. John Bean, July 30, 2013; and Weibert, *Buckskin*, 40, 41, 74, 131.

45. Officially termed: *A court of inquiry convened at Chicago, Illinois, January 13, 1879, by the President of the United States upon the request of Major Marcus A. Reno, 7th U.S. Cavalry, to investigate his conduct at the Battle of the Little Big Horn, June 25-26, 1876.*

46. Ronald Hamilton Nichols, editor, *Reno Court of Inquiry Proceedings of a Court of Inquiry in the Case of Major Marcus A. Reno, Concerning His Conduct at the Battle of the Little Big Horn River on June 25-26, 1876*, Hardin, Montana: Custer Battlefield Historical and Museum Association, 2007, 249-288.

47. Hamilton, 242-243.

48. Carter, 36.

49. Quivey, 282-283.

50. Bradley, "Bradley Manuscript," 124.

51. "The Story of a March," 13.

52. Ibid, 12-13.

53. Text of the speech provided by Rachel Phillips.

54. Discussion with black powder shooting expert Mike Venturino.

55. A previous work by the author, *Custer's Best: The Story of Company M, 7th 7th Cavalry at the Little Bighorn*, postulated that many soldiers in Company M had never fired their carbines until the attack started on June 25, 1875. There is no reason to assume that Company M was different from the other eleven companies in the regiment with respect to rifle marksmanship training or proficiency.

56. Letter from Tom Allen to Walter M. Camp dated April 23, 1912, Denver Public Library, Western History Department.

Postscript

For over 140 years, although reported vigorously in the press, the 1874 expedition has been a neglected portion of the history of the West. In its final report, dated May 22, 1874, and appearing in the *Avant Courier* of that date, John V. Bogert summarized the expedition:[1]

The Command traveled 600 miles; was out 3 months; crossed 57 streams; had four fights; lost (killed) one man; had wounded two men; had wounded 20 horse; lost (killed) two oxen; captured 9 guns, 5 pistols, 12 horses and large amount of camp equipage; took ten scalps; killed (probably) 60 Indians; wounded probably 100 Indians.

The summary added that 125 men on the expedition desired to try it again, but the participants soon faded away to pursue their normal endeavors and no similar expedition was ever mounted. According to Addison M. Quivey, the expedition traveled six hundred miles. It had four significant fights with the Indians during which one man was killed (Zack Yates) and two were wounded. Some seventeen to twenty-five expedition horses were killed and another twenty were wounded. Quivey estimated that the frontiersmen killed about fifty warriors and wounded nearly one hundred; Eugene S. Topping added that the expedition captured twenty-five ponies.[2] Writing within two years after the conclusion of the expedition (but before Custer's defeat at the Little Bighorn,) participant Addison M. Quivey concluded:[3]

The expedition failed in its object, partly because the feed was too short to sustain our stock, so that we moved very slowly going down, and partly because we had not provisions to stay in the country much longer, and men seldom prospect much when harassed by Indians. We are now satisfied that no gold mines exist in the neighborhood of the lower Yellowstone, or in the Little Wolf Mountains; but most of us believe that rich mines exist in the Big Horn Mountains, south of the Big Horn river, and most of our party are desirous of returning to that country the following fall, and exploring it thoroughly.

In regard to the navigability of the Yellowstone River, we know but little more than we did when we went away; but it is very easy to make a good road as far as we went on the north side of the river, and, doubtless, in time it will be the great thoroughfare to the east. Our expedition was a failure, but it has not disheartened the people of Eastern Montana in regard to the Yellowstone route to the east; and while we find a barren country along the Yellowstone, and to the north of it, we find a magnificent country to the south of it; and from what we know of the valleys of Tongue and Powder rivers, we believe them to be among the finest in the West.

With that, the expedition—although remaining fresh in the minds of most citizens in the Montana Territory—became quickly forgotten by the rest of the country—assuming they

J.V. Bogert died on September 28, 1907 in Bozeman, Montana. He is buried at the Sunset Hills Cemetery there [N 45° 40.551' W 111° 01.586']. *Author photograph, October 2013*

knew much about it to begin with. The United States Army had not been involved. Because of that, no military historians and few Western historians tackled those aspects of the 1874 Yellowstone Wagon Road and Prospecting Expedition that needed to be documented and studied. As a result, questions persisted.

Exactly what did George Herendeen, Muggins Taylor, Oliver Hanna, and the other scouts—who had been on the 1874 expedition—*tell* George Custer, George Crook, and John Gibbon during the 1876 expedition against the Lakota? We know what they later *wrote* (although it is doubtful that George Herendeen wrote much on his own,) after George A. Custer met his demise, but what exactly did they *discuss* about the fighting qualities and tendencies of the warriors in the days and weeks leading up to the Little Bighorn, while sitting around the campfire every night?

Perhaps George Custer did not query George Herendeen during the four-day march down the Rosebud; it would not be the first time "The Boy General" failed to take counsel from his associates. Custer's opinion of scouts was that the object of a scout was "not to outrun or overwhelm the Indians, but to avoid both by secrecy and caution in his movements."[4] Additionally, Custer personally did not know Herendeen—who was in the position of a guide—or his capabilities, and we also know what advice he did *not* take from the other scouts. However, George Herendeen certainly counseled the frightened troopers caught in the timber after Maj. Reno retreated from that location (undoubtedly helping to save their lives,) and he probably urged the men to continue to dig fighting positions on Reno Hill.

Was Sitting Bull actually present at any of the fighting? At the time of the event, it does not appear that the frontiersmen had any idea concerning the warrior leaders they were facing. It was only a year or two after the conclusion of the expedition was the name Sitting Bull mentioned; that came about when 1st Lt. James H. Bradley began interviewing Lakota warriors at Fort Benton on the Missouri River. Bradley wrote that the warriors told him that Sitting Bull had been present, although Lt. Bradley could not be sure if those men he interviewed had actually been involved themselves in the battles, or if they had merely told Bradley what they thought the officer *wanted* to hear.

Three acknowledged titans of Little Bighorn research do not share an opinion concerning our search for Sitting Bull. Historian Dr. Thomas Marquis did not believe that Sitting Bull had been involved in the fighting, while historian Robert M. Utley seems to have concluded that Sitting Bull was present. Dr. Walter S. Campbell had no opinion and said that he was not informed about the expedition.

James S. Hutchins, another outstanding researcher, writing in the mid-1950s, did not address the question of Sitting Bull in his excellent article, "Poison in the Pemmican: The Yellowstone Wagon-Road & Prospecting Expedition of 1874." The premier author on the 1874 Yellowstone Wagon Road and Prospecting Expedition, Don Weibert, wrote that Sitting Bull had been present. Some others say he was not, but this study currently concludes that he was—tilted in this direction by old Red Hawk's account of the events to Walter Mason Camp in 1915. And our current era's finest author on the Lakotas, Kingsley Bray, has concluded Sitting Bull (as well as Hump and Crazy Horse) were in the fight against the expedition.

This study will go further and conclude that Sitting Bull, Flying By, and Makes Room were at all three battles with the wagon train. Crazy Horse and Hump, along with their followers, were present at the last two engagements; the location of Gall during the time period of the three battles needs further research before a definitive conclusion can be made; it seems fairly certain that he was at the first fight along the Rosebud at the very least.

If the evidence concerning the presence of Sitting Bull is not unanimous, the facts surrounding the identity of the warrior chief killed by John Anderson are even more ephemeral. Was the chief that John Anderson killed at the Battle of Great Medicine Dance Creek the son of Sitting Bull? That last event certainly sounds like a legend, but can we really be sure how many sons the great Lakota chief sired, and if one could have been killed in 1874?

Clearly, at the time of the expedition, no one had any idea of the identity of this warrior. It was only in later years that the identity started to coalesce that the individual was Sitting Bull's son. We do not know where this theory began or who might have been the source of it. Nelson Story III wrote about John Anderson in 1957. He had known Anderson, and had said that before his death, the old Civil War soldier gave the jacket he took from the dead warrior to Maj. Gen. Walter P. Story (the son of Nelson Story) in Los Angeles. Gen. Story later gave the jacket to his nephew Nelson Story III, who donated it to the Gallatin

County Courthouse, where it remains to this day.[5] Nelson Story III ended his narrative about John Anderson with the following:[6]

> As far as I am concerned this garment belonged to the son of Sitting Bull, and it was acquired exactly as told to me by John Anderson, Pioneer, Soldier, Red and Black, and respected citizen of Bozeman.

Two members of the expedition, John Anderson and Jack Bean, disagreed on the identity of the chief. John Anderson, quite naturally, believed it was the son of Sitting Bull, although a specific name was never attached to the warrior. Jack Bean later wrote that the slain chief was the son of Black Moon.[7] However, nothing in Bean's writings explains how he came to this conclusion. It is more likely than not that the chief was not the son of Sitting Bull, but we cannot be sure either way.

The study also concludes that Crazy Horse may well have been the warrior chief on the ridge during the charge of the frontiersmen against the warriors east of the wagon train during the Battle of Lodge Grass Creek seems vintage Crazy Horse. His village was in the area through which the wagon train traveled; for him to have been elsewhere for several months, during a brutal winter, violates common sense and has never been asserted to this study's knowledge.

On the other hand, other questions do remain. Did "Liver-Eatin" Johnston serve on the expedition? We have only the recollections of the son, Guy, of one of the confirmed expedition members, William C. Officer, as he heard his father recall the expedition with another expedition member, William T. Hamilton. Having said that, the discussion about the mountain howitzer and shrapnel rounds, in that discussion, certainly adds an air of authenticity. Dorman Nelson, who has researched Johnston for almost fifty years and is preparing a massive "tome" on "Liver-Eatin" had this to say to the author concerning the possibility of the legendary mountain man's potential presence on the expedition:

He might have been there, probably was, and we cannot pin him down anywhere else at that time. He was good friends with Uncle Billy Hamilton. One thing we know for sure; he would not have remained with the expedition if he concluded that they were not going to find any gold. He would have left.

Clearly, more research needs to be done on the legendary Johnston before we can say with certainty that he was present. He may have joined after the wagon train left Bozeman and he may have said *adios* before it reached Bozeman on the return trip. Right now, we just don't know and it remains a mystery.

Some visitors to Montana in general and the Little Bighorn Battlefield in particular may be viewing another mystery of the 1874 Yellowstone Wagon Road and Prospecting Expedition and not even be aware of it. In June 1926, Oliver Perry Hanna traveled from his home in Long Beach, California, to southeast Montana to attend the Little Bighorn Battle Semi-Centennial (Fifty-Year Anniversary) Celebration. His journey took him initially to Sheridan, Wyoming, some sixty-four miles south of the battlefield. From here, Hanna drove up the Custer Battlefield Highway next to the Little Bighorn River. Near Lodge Grass, he passed the location where he had helped bury Zack Yates in April 1874. While he did not meet any of his fellow frontiersmen at the semi-centennial, he did meet an old Lakota chief, who through an interpreter, said that the white warriors on the 1874 expedition had been brave and had put up a good fight.[8]

During the 1926 celebration, attendees viewed a military plane fly-over, probably one of the first in the nation. Army Maj. Alson B. Ostrander, acting as a special correspondent for *Winners of the West*, wrote the following description of the crowning moment of the anniversary ceremony on Last Stand Hill:[9]

Slowly they marched to the National Cemetery to the strains of a funeral dirge played by the band of the Seventh [Cav-alry,] concealed in a nearby ravine. From the other side came in a far flung column the hundreds of Indians, led by the nearly 80 Sioux and Cheyenne survivors of the battle headed by White Bull, who as a youth of 20 led a band of Sioux fighters under Rain-in-the-Face. Near the monument the two parties met. White Bull held up his hand making the sign of Peace. General Godfrey replied by dropping his unsheathed sword into its scabbard as he rode forward to meet the Indians. They clasped hands, and to cement the friendship White Bull presented to the General a prized possession—his blanket—while the General gave to White Bull a large American flag.

Also in 1926, a funeral service for an unknown soldier from the 7th Cavalry was conducted at Garryowen, Montana. One source says that the remains had been found the year before near Garryowen, the tiny hamlet now near the Lakota and Cheyenne village over which the 1876 battle was fought. The remains were presumed to be those of one of Maj. Reno's men killed in the opening phase of the battle in the valley fight. Another source indicates that the remains were found while work was being done on an irrigation ditch just east of Garryowen.[10]

These locations are not the same as the information that Oliver Hanna heard when he attended the "Burial of the Hatchet Ceremony" at the granite tomb in front of 50,000 observers. In the tomb were the remains of this unknown soldier. It had been explained to Hanna that workers, excavating for gravel to put on the Custer Battlefield Highway had found the skeletal remains far to the south near the Little Bighorn River, quite distant from the route that Custer's forces took in 1876. On Oliver Hanna's return trip south to Sheridan, he directed his party to stop at the location near Lodge Grass, where in April 1874, the men on the expedition buried Zack Yates. The site was seventeen miles from Garryowen and just 500 feet from the Little Bighorn River.[11]

The party found that gravel had been excavated at the site. They found the iron picket pin that had been buried a foot below the ground that had been used to mark the grave. And they found that the remains of Zack Yates were missing.[12]

As to the content of this entire study, I hope that were they with us today, "Uncle Billy" Hamilton and Sitting Bull, in sign language, would bring their right index fingers to their chins and move them outward at arm's length, the index fingers horizontal—signaling "This is true."

Notes

1. "Yellowstone Expedition," *Avant Courier* (Bozeman,) May 22, 1874, 3.

2. Quivey, 284; and Topping, 121.

3. Quivey, 282-283.

4. Richard Hook, *US Army Frontier Scouts 1840–1921*, Osprey Elite 91, Oxford, Great Britain: Osprey Publishing, 2003, 5.

5. The scalp of the warrior chief was put on display with the jacket at the Bozeman Public Library. It was then transferred to the Bozeman Commercial Club, where a later fire destroyed the scalp.

6. Manuscript on John Anderson of the 1874 Yellowstone Wagon Road and Prospecting Expedition, written by Nelson Story III, February 23, 1957, located at the Gallatin County, Montana Pioneer Museum Archive, 3.

7. Annotated Manuscript of Jack Bean, 14.

8. Carter, 5.

9. Friends of the Little Bighorn, The Next Generation in the Study of Custer's Last Stand, page Custer's Last Fight: Remembered by Participants at the Tenth Anniversary June 25, 1886 and the Fiftieth Anniversary June 25, 1926, as found in http://www.friendslittlebighorn. com/upton50anniversary.htm

10. Tony Perrottet, "Little Bighorn Reborn," *Smithsonian* Magazine, April 2005, Washington, DC.

11. Carter, 38, 40-42.

12. Ibid.

Unknown soldier grave at the Little Bighorn from 1926. According to one expedition member, the remains in this grave belong to Zack Yates who was killed on the wagon train two years before the Little Bighorn. *Author photograph, October 2013*

Epilogue:
The Greatest Shot on the
Western Frontier

Sometimes we are left with only the remembrances of old participants to historical events. At other times, we have the opportunity to use scientific and engineering analysis to determine what historical events are in the range of the possible and which ones must be left to myth. Fortunately, we probably have enough information from 1874 to examine one of the signature events during the 1874 Yellowstone Wagon Road and Prospecting Expedition—Jack Bean's long-range rifle shot at the conclusion of the Battle of Lodge Grass Creek.

Concerning the actual event—a single shot against a single enemy warrior—the principal witness, Jack Bean, later wrote that "no one in our party who judged the distance less than 1,700 yards."[1] This is the equivalent to 0.966 miles. That is a very long distance, especially with black powder cartridges of the day that propelled bullets at relatively low speed. Fortunately, modern replicas of Jack Bean's Sharps rifle exist and allow us to test this account in relative safety—ergo we do not have to obtain a 140-year-old rifle and hope it does not explode when we attempt to shoot it with a maximum black powder load.

A line of sight examination of the Lodge Grass Creek battlefield and found nine potential target locations—based on descriptions of where the warrior was when he attracted Jack Bean's attention—on a crest of a hill or ridge. The ranges of these nine locations—from the presumed position of Jack Bean, close to the coulee branching north of Lodge Grass Creek

valley that had been used as a shelter for the wagon train—were 0.66 miles at the shortest distance to 1.087 miles at the farthest. One potential target was at 0.962 miles distance, but it was not "across the bottom and up on the hill" as Jack Bean recalled later when discussing the event. Three of the potential target locations were on the same side of the valley that Bean was; they are clearly not "across the bottom." A fourth target is on a small rise in the middle of the valley floor; Bean's description seems to rule this potential location out as well.

Bean was most likely correct in his description of the target being across the valley floor and higher in elevation, either a hill or ridge. However, range estimation is difficult under the best of conditions, and it is possible that the frontiersmen could have been off by as much as 10% either way in the conditions present then that included raw spring weather and the stress of an immediate battle fresh in their system. Having said that, frontier hunters of that era, who depended on their shooting prowess to survive, were probably better at this type of calculation than we are today, so a reasonable estimation of range could certainly be 1,500 yards at the near end and 1,900 yards at the far limit.

Next, let us take that bracket and evaluate our potential locations against it. The five potential targets "across the bottom and up on the hill" stand at the following ranges measured by maps: 1.087 miles (1,913 yards), 1.006 miles (1,876 yards,) 0.854 miles (1,503 yards,) 0.667 miles (1,174 yards,) and 0.66 miles (1,161 yards.) The first target seems too far outside our band of possible shots, as do the last two. This leaves two potential targets—at ranges of 1,876 yards and 1,503 yards—as our most likely locations.

Based on Jack's recollections, we know that he was firing a Sharps rifle—probably a Model 1874. This model rifle, at the time the expedition started, was offered in five calibers to Sharps' customers: the .40-90 Bottleneck (2⅝") with a 265 to 370 grain bullet, the .44-77 Bottleneck (2¼") with 380 or 405 grain bullets, the .44-90 Sharps Bottleneck (2⅝") with 450 or 500 grain bullets, the .50-70 Government (1¾") with 425 to 500 grain bullets, and the .50-90 Sharps (2½"), firing 425 or 473 grain bullets. Unfortunately, Jack Bean never elaborated on the caliber of his weapon and his surviving family member does not believe his grandfather ever specified this.

We can reduce the possibilities of determining the correct caliber, however, based on the dates that each caliber was introduced by Sharps. Sharps introduced the .50-70 in 1867, the .44-77 in 1869 and the .50-90 in 1872. The company introduced the .40-90 in 1873, and the .44-90 more specifically in June 1873. Jack Bean's reminiscences indicate that he and his hunting partner, Stewart Buchanan, departed Bozeman in late summer of 1873 and headed to the Crazy Mountains to establish a winter hunting camp. They remained in the mountains, making an occasional short trip to Bozeman to sell meat, until they joined the expedition near Big Timber in February 1874 as previously described.

This study concludes that neither a Sharps rifle .44-90, nor a .40-90, could have been used by Jack Bean on the expedition. First, and most important, is the fact that—according to acknowledged Sharps expert Dr. Richard J. Labowski, the current owner of the surviving production and shipment records for the Sharps Rifle Manufacturing Company/Sharps Rifle Company—no Sharps rifles at all were shipped to Bozeman in 1874.[2] If one were to assume that the Sharps records are possibly incomplete for that year, it would still be unlikely that Bean owned a .44-90. June was the month that the caliber began to be advertised, not necessarily ordered by arms dealers such as Walter Cooper, and could not have been transported from New Haven, Connecticut, to Gallatin County, Montana, prior to Bean's departure in late summer 1873.

Wagon trains from Missouri to Virginia City, Montana Territory, could take up to four and a half months. Riverboats from St. Louis, Missouri, to Fort Benton, Montana Territory might take forty-eight to sixty days, going against the current the entire way.[3] The great clipper ships still in use averaged 117 days transit time from New York City to San Francisco.[4] These shipping times do not include travel from New Haven to New York—in the case of the clipper ships—or rail transit times from New York to St. Louis (five days minimum.) Riverboats plying the Missouri River could not do so in winter, and winter often lasted until late April. Winter conditions also made land transit quite difficult as well. And goods arriving at San Francisco still had to be transported by ground 1,000 miles to Bozeman.

Therefore, this study concludes that Jack Bean most likely carried a Sharps .44-77, a .50-70, or a .50-90 on the 1874 expedition. By 1874, the company had received numerous complaints from buffalo hunters that the .44-77 cartridge was simply too weak to drop a bison with a single shot, although it remained a top seller in the Sharps line.[5] We do not know if Bean felt the same way about this caliber, as at this point in his career, he was primarily an elk hunter. In any case, we can look at the ballistics of all four. According to several sources, the original Sharps .44-77s were actually only loaded with 70 grains of black powder, propelling a 380-grain bullet. In modern performance tests, one veteran shooter, using the bottlenose cartridges with 77 grains of various types of black powder and a 405-grain bullet, achieved three-inch and four-inch groups of five rounds at a target one hundred yards away. Muzzle velocity[6] in the tests ranged from 1,270 to 1,336 feet per second.[7] A round made during the era would have had 1,730 foot-pounds of energy at the muzzle.

The .50-70 Government was the old man of American big game cartridges in the post-Civil War era and was used in Springfield military rifles and Sharps hunting rifles. In fact, probably 95% of the men on the expedition had weapons chambered for this round, although most were Springfields. The same modern shooter that tested the .44-77 also evaluated the .50-70, eliminating the difference between one expert and another. Firing 450-grain bullets from the weapon, using 70 grains of various black powders, the expert was able to shoot five-round groups ranging from 1.875 inches to four inches at one hundred yards. Muzzle velocities measured 1,168 to 1,265 feet per second, making the round a bit slower than the .44-77.[8] Muzzle energy of factory loads of the day was 1,535 foot-pounds with a 425 grain bullet.[9]

The .50-90 Sharps jumped into the firearms scene in 1872, but the caliber was a misnomer. Standard loads were actually 100 grains of black powder, not 90 as might be inferred from the round's nomenclature. This caliber rifle was not the best seller among Sharps Model 1874s; it appears that most customers who bought the rifle in this caliber were true professional hunters. Archaeologists have found .50-90 cases, as well as .50-70 rounds, at the location where the other famous long-range shooting duel happened in the Wild West at the Battle of Adobe Walls, in June 1874. A second expert conducted firing tests with a Sharps Model 1874 with a thirty-inch barrel, produced by Shiloh Sharps in the modern era. Firing a massive 546 grain bullet, using 95 grains of various powders, at a target at 100 yards, the sharpshooter shot groups ranging from 1.5 inches to 2.75 inches, with a muzzle velocity of 1,274 to 1,341 feet per second.[10] A 550 grain bullet, in a factory load of the day, produced a muzzle energy of 1,920 foot-pounds.

In these series of tests, the .50-90 Sharps proved to be the most accurate at 100 yards.

But what about a target fifteen to eighteen times that distance at a different elevation than the shooter? That is what we want to determine in this re-creation on the same ground and in roughly the same atmospheric conditions that Jack Bean faced on April 16, 1874, at Lodge Grass Creek.

The first factor is elevation. If the firing position of Jack Bean was resting his rifle on the top of one of the wheels of a wagon in the valley as a firing support, he would be positioned at an elevation of 3,660 feet above sea level. The elevation of potential targets across the valley on the ridge is generally 3,760 feet—some one hundred feet higher than the shooter. That is beneficial to the shooter with respect to the probability that there will be no visual obstruction between the point the shot is fired and the target is located. However, it may be detrimental in that the speed of the wind could be very different at that higher level than down at the elevation the shooter is standing and this wind speed at the target may not be obvious to the shooter if the target is on a naked ridge where there is no vegetation that might give a clue to wind direction and velocity.

There is a built in error in accuracy when shooting either uphill or downhill at steep angles as well. The effect becomes worse as the velocity of the bullet decreases and as distance to the target increases; it becomes most significant when the shot is up a very steep slope, with a slow moving bullet, at very long ranges. The practical effect is that often the rifle shoots high and the round passes over the target. Fortunately for Jack Bean, he had just spent six months hunting elk in the Crazy Mountains, where probably almost every shot he took was at a target at a different elevation from his own. It must be remembered though that professional hunters most often attempted short-range shots and not long range. They had no desire to hike a long distance to the dead animal or to track a wounded animal if a second shot was necessary.

We know the elevations of the shot, but we do not know the wind conditions; they were never mentioned in later recollections of the participants. It was April and there had been rain and snow in the period leading up to the battle. An examination of historical data over the last fifty years indicates that an accurate average on April 16 of any year at the town of Lodge Grass is a wind from the east or east-northeast at a constant velocity of eight mph, with a maximum sustained wind speed of twenty-one mph and gusts of wind of up to thirty mph.

The larger the projectile, the greater the effect of wind will be on the bullet's trajectory. For example, for a .53-caliber bullet, traveling 1,800 feet per second at a target 100 yards away, a twenty-mile-per-hour wind blowing constantly at right angles to the line of bullet flight, will cause the round to drift twenty-nine inches off target. A wind speed of ten miles per hour will push the bullet almost fifteen inches off course at one hundred yards. At either wind speed, aiming at the center of mass of a man-sized target would result in a miss. Obviously Jack Bean understood "Kentucky windage," which included aiming toward the direction from which a crosswind was blowing and waiting—if possible—for any gust of wind to pass before squeezing the trigger.

The re-creation of Jack Bean's famous long-range shot occurred at the Wald Ranch, several miles southwest of Lodge Grass, Montana, on the afternoon of June 5, 2015. The temperature initially was 72°; it would climb to 80°. Wind at the floor of the valley was from the southeast to the northwest at approximately six miles per hour. Sky conditions were clear. Initially, we planned that four individuals would attempt the shot; no one fired a .44-77, .50-70 or .50-90, but the calibers were very close to that. I was armed with a Shiloh Sharps Model 1874 .45-70 using black powder rounds. The heavy octagonal barrel on the weapon was twenty-eight inches long; the overall length of the weapon is forty-eight inches. This rifle was manufactured in 2002 in Big Timber, Montana.[11] Atop the rifle was a six-power replica of the period Malcom scope. William Malcolm was one of the first names in American riflescopes,

opening for business in 1855 in Syracuse, New York. The company's initial offerings included ½- and ¾-inch-diameter tubed riflescopes, measuring 24 to 30 inches in length. Montana Vintage Arms, in Belgrade, Montana, manufactured this particular scope, a Model 3000, which is twenty-eight inches in length.[12] With the scope, the rifle weighs thirteen pounds and 6.4 ounces.

I selected this caliber and scope several years ago to replicate the Sharps Model 1874 carried by 1st Sgt. John Ryan of Company M in the US 7th Cavalry Regiment at the Little Bighorn; on Reno Hill, with this weapon, he brought effective fire against several warriors firing from Sharpshooter Ridge, about 900 yards away. Jack Bean neither used a .45-70, nor did his rifle have a telescopic sight, but the author's marksmanship skills are so dwarfed by those of Jack Bean that it was thought that this combination might give him a very slight chance to hit the target!

After purchasing the rifle in 2013, I visited the Shiloh Rifle Company, where Kirk Bryan showed exactly how these fine rifles are made in scenic Big Timber. The company employs twenty-three people and turns out from 800 to 1,100 rifles a year. No detail is overlooked and the customer can have one built to his or her own specifications; these masterpieces are in high demand, so waiting times must be factored into the equation—they are worth the wait.

I then visited Montana Vintage Arms in Belgrade, Montana. The company was difficult to locate, but worth the several U-turns. The owner, Bobby Gier, kindly took time to show the author how all the company's sights operated and how they were made. Of great interest was their new Soule XLR. Bobby explained that over the last several years, MVA has been bombarded with requests for a sight that would be capable of keeping the shooter on target at distances approaching one mile. The technicians at Belgrade created a special Soule-type sight that allows for 414 MOA (Minutes of Angle) elevation and 88 MOA of windage adjustment. Bobby went

The Shiloh Sharps Rifle Factory produces high quality Sharps Model 1874 rifles, several of which were used in the re-creation of Jack Bean's historic shot. *Author photograph, October 2013*

This machine at the Shiloh Sharps Rifle Factory helps create barrels for the famous rifles. *Author photograph, October 2013*

distance, the crosshairs of the scope still will have to be placed significantly above the target and that a guess must be made at how much higher this point of aim must be because the target will not even be seen in the bottom of the scope! In a blinding flash of the obvious, I had a feeling that Jack Bean was much more accurate in guessing where to aim than the author will be today!

Hank Adams also used a Shiloh Sharps .45-70 Model 1874. His weapon, on the other hand, did not have a telescopic sight, but rather iron sights. Hank has owned his weapon even longer than I have; ever the practical officer, he selected a .45-70 based on the availability of ammunition components and ease of reloading; in fact, he talked me into buying my own weapon in the same caliber that he had. The weapon has half octagonal, half round barrel. Mounted on it is a Montana Vintage Arms Mid-Range Vernier Tang Sight. The company offers the Sharps Vernier tang sight as a close reproduction of the original Sharps sight, but has incorporated into the design the ability to lock both the elevation and the windage with a simple tightening of the eye disc. It provides 200 MOA elevation and 28 MOA in windage adjustments. This sight will be a much closer approximation to the sight used by Jack Bean than my telescopic sight.

Rich Morris pulled double duty for the event. He first carefully made a silhouette to replicate the target, transported it to Lodge Grass Creek and emplaced it high on the appropriate ridge. For the actual shoot, Rich's weapon was a Shiloh Sharps #1 Sporting Rifle. A nine pound eight ounce .45-70 rifle, it has a thirty-inch octagonal heavy barrel with a pistol grip and shotgun butt. The sights include a Montana Vintage Arms Soule Style Mid-Range rear sight and a spirit level globe front site.

The man the group is counting on to duplicate the shot was Mike Venturino from Livingston, Montana. In addition to writing *Shooting Buffalo Rifles of the Old West*, Mike has authored numerous articles in various gun magazines and won numerous Black Powder

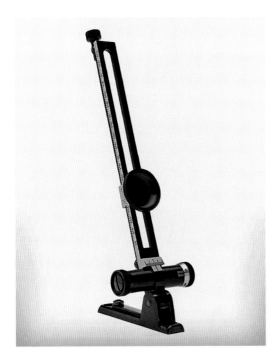

This is the new Montana Vintage Arms Long Range Soule XLR Site. The XLR stands for Extremely Long Range and is designed for shooters engaging targets close to one mile distant. *Courtesy of Montana Vintage Arms*

on to explain that coupled with a spirit level/windage front sight would give the marksman the perfect combination of both accuracy and repeatability at this extended range, by reducing rifle cant and better compensating for windage. The Soule sight looks similar to a Vernier site; the XLR measures a staff height of 6.18 inches; mounted on the tang, it can be folded flat when not in use. Jack Bean clearly did not have this sight—as they did not come into use until the 1880s; 140 years later, we may regret not having this exquisite piece of equipment as well.

However, I had another problem. The silhouette-style telescope mounts (patterned by Montana Vintage Arms after the Malcolm C Mount) on his rifle, when combined with the twenty-eight-inch long scope, will allow for 125 MOA elevation. In layman's terms, this means that even when the author adjusts for maximum elevation for a shot of this

Competitions. Some of these tournaments feature targets at ranges of 1,000 yards. In fact, Mike won the Quigley Match at Forsyth, Montana one year by scoring nine hits in fifteen attempts at that range. Today's target will be a little more distant. In addition, at that Quigley Match, the target was a steel gong in the shape of a bucket, with the top measuring forty-four inches wide and the bottom thirty-six inches wide. The target today will be special and one that none of the shooters has ever previously encountered. In the spirit of historical accuracy, Mike has brought several weapons to the re-creation, including an original Model 1874 Conversion Sharps .45-70, an original Sharps Model 1874 Long Range #2 in .45-90 with a Krieger thirty-inch barrel, and a C. Sharps Model 1874 .45-70 with a Badger barrel of thirty-two inches. Additionally, Montana Vintage Arms has loaned Mike one of the new XLR sights, which is starting to acquire the nickname "Country Mile."

Then the team gets a break. Local southeast Montana long-range black powder shooters Dr. Gary A. Ostahowski, Mike Caprata, and Byron Stimpson arrive. Mike has a Shiloh Sharps #3 .45-90 with a heavy thirty-inch barrel. Gary has a Shiloh Sharps LRE .45-90. Byron has a Shiloh Sharps .45-110. All weapons use sights from Montana Vintage Arms. We

also enlisted the extended Wald family as additional shooters.

We do not know exactly the load of black powder that Jack Bean used for his encounter that April morning, so we are taking Mike's advice on loads that might get us in the vicinity of the target and still remain safe to fire.

The day before the shoot, the team emplaced the silhouette target high on the ridge to the south of Lodge Grass Creek. They then used a Bushnell Elite 1 Mile ARC Laser Rangefinder to establish the distance to the target; the device was developed for long-range shooting. With a seven-power magnification and 26 mm objective lens, this rangefinder can determine ranges from five to 1,760 yards with extreme accuracy. The effective range for deer-size targets in 500 yards; tree ranging performance is effective to 1,000 yards. When the objective has a reflective surface, the distance can be measured to the maximum 1,760 yards. Rangefinder accuracy is plus/minus ½ yard out to 200 yards and plus/minus one yard out to 1,760 yards. The 96x48 Pixel Matrix Display provides bright easy to read displays in all lighting conditions. Taking several readings to ensure the correct target was being measured revealed that the silhouette was a distance of 1,510 yards or 0.8579 miles from the selected shooting location at the historical location for

Close-up view of the target details. It was emplaced on the crest of the ridge and painted white—this was not a test of target acquisition. *Author photograph, June 2015*

the wagon train when Jack Bean fired the shot. Hank Adams, who positioned himself on the ridge, later estimated that the wind was constantly swirling at that elevation, ranging from dead calm to as much as ten miles per hour; the shooters had no way of seeing that due to a lack of vegetation on the ridge.

Although the rangefinder has Angle Range Compensation (ARC) technology, in which shooters can combine information from Bushnell ballistic charts to information displayed on the rangefinder and their specific caliber and load to estimate point of hold, the shooters did not use this feature, as Jack Bean had no outside help for determining where to aim.

Over the course of three hours, thirteen shooters took their turns firing various weapons. None hit the target on the first shot, thus not challenging Jack Bean's feat in any way. In fact, these marksmen (including two women) fired a total of 151 rounds at the silhouette, which was cut slightly larger than real life and painted white to facilitate identification.

Two rounds of the 151 fired struck the target. One bullet, shot by young Connor Wald, struck at the base of the silhouette and ricocheted upward, penetrating the target. Later in the event, Rich Morris hit the silhouette directly with a 530-grain bullet.

Here is what the target looked like to the naked eye at 1,510 yards. It is that small speck to the right of a more-distant hilltop. To help you see it, we have added the red circle at the photo-lab. The firing will be done from the pasture from where the photo was taken. *Author photograph, June 2015*

Bullets that came close; these four projectiles were dug out of the ground immediately in front of the target after the test was completed. *Author photograph, June 2015*

Bullet on the left is from a .44 Henry and was fired in 1874. Four other bullets were fired during the test from various Sharps Model 1874s and are well over twice the weight of the Henry. *Author photograph, June 2015*

Mike Venturino checks his long-range sight from MVA before shooting. *Author photograph, June 2015*

So why did we do this? History should not be a rote memorization of facts, dusted off to read occasionally and then buried in remote stacks in a university or community public library. History is a river that flows; observing the water at one point in the river can help predict how that water will behave farther down the river. Understanding the difficulty in one element of something that happened—in this case Jack Bean's long range shot—can put in perspective the difficulties that participants on both sides faced back in the Montana Territory in 1874. If we find that

the laws of physics, for example, do not make possible a shot of this nature, we can start questioning the accounts of other incidents during the expedition as well.

So what did we learn? First, a typical Sharps Model 1874 that Jack Bean carried on the expedition could have hit a human-size target at this distance. It is not likely that an experienced buffalo hunter would hit on the first shot—it being somewhat easier to adjust fire based on the strike of previous rounds—but it could be done. Second, Jack Bean needed a bit of luck that morning and if the story is

The business end of Byron Stimpson's .45-110! *Author photograph, June 2015*

Connor Wald raised his sight picture just a bit. His shot would ricochet immediately in front of the target and strike the silhouette sideways, but a hit is a hit! *Author photograph, June 2015*

Rich Morris will score a clean hit on the center of the target. *Author photograph, June 2015*

Gary Ostahowski has just fired his .45-90. The white blocks on the shoulder stock are an attempt for such a great range to maintain a decent stock weld—the point of firm contact between the shooter's cheek and the stock of the rifle. *Author photograph, June 2015*

accurate, he got that luck. Third, we used metal detectors to try and find any period cartridges on the ridges that would, at least, indicate where the warrior stood firing at the wagon train, but could not find anything. We, therefore, need to add to our analysis that the warrior could have been somewhat closer, and "war stories" being what they are, the frontiersmen who witnessed the shot either honestly believed the range was one mile (but were in error) or they rounded up a range that was shorter to make it sound better.

Whatever the case, it sure was a long way away!

Three generations of the Wald family. They don't come any better than this. *Author photograph, June 2015*

The target: one hit is shown circled at the center, while the other is circled in the lower right. *Courtesy of Rich Morris*

Looking back from the target area; the shooters are mere specks inside the red circle. The yellow circle shows where the wagon train was when the warriors began harassing fire against it. *Courtesy of Hank Adams*

Notes

1. Annotated Manuscript of Jack Bean on the 1874 Yellowstone Wagon Road and Prospecting Expedition, 16.

2. Telephone discussion with Dr. Richard J. Labowski, September 3, 2013. Dr. Labowski is the current owner of the surviving production and shipment records for the Sharps Rifle Manufacturing Company/Sharps Rifle Company.

3. Francis M. Thompson, *A Tenderfoot in Montana: Reminiscences of the Gold Rush, the Vigilantes, and the Birth of the Montana Territory*, Helena, Montana: Montana Historical Society, 2004, 58; and Krys Holmes, Montana: Stories of the Land, 105-106.

4. A.H. Clark, *California Clippers of 1853, The Clipper Ship Era; An Epitome of Famous American and British Clipper Ships, Their Owners, Builders, Commanders and Crews, 1843–1869*, New York: G.P. Putnam's Sons, 1912, 233–234.

5. John Walter, *The Guns that Won the West: Firearms on the American Frontier, 1848–1898*, London: Greenhill Books, 2006, 131.

6. The speed at which a projectile must travel to penetrate skin is 163 feet per second and to break bone is 213 feet per second. Source: M. Belkin, "Wound Ballistics," *Progress in Surgery*, Issue 16, Basel, Switzerland and New York, 1978, 7-24. However it is the energy of the round that determines lethality and generally the higher the energy the more lethal the round is. Energy is determined by multiplying the mass of the bullet times the square of its velocity. Thus, to a degree, the huge mass of the bullets of this era (often over 500 grains) could somewhat offset their relatively slow speed as compared to more modern firearms, where muzzle velocity is often in the 3,000 feet per second range.

7. Venturino, *Buffalo Rifles*, 128-134.

8. Ibid, 160-163.

9. Barnes, *Cartridges*, 148.

10. Venturino, *Buffalo Rifles*, 164-167.

11. Shiloh Rifle Company, PO Box 279, 201 Centennial Drive, Big Timber, Montana 59011, (406) 932-4266, www.shilohrifle.com

12. Montana Vintage Arms, 61 Andrea Drive, Belgrade, Montana 59714, 406-388-4027, info@montanavintagearms.com

Appendix 1

Lakota and Northern Cheyenne Warriors who likely fought against the 1874 Yellowstone Wagon Road and Prospecting Expedition

Black Twin/Holy Eagle (Wakan): Bad Face band/ Oglala/Lakota

Braided Locks/Wrapped Braids: Northern Cheyenne

Crazy Horse (Tašúŋke Witkó): Hunkpatila band/ Oglala/Lakota

Eagle Elk (Wanbdi Herake)†: Oyuhpe band/Oglala/ Lakota

Flying By/Struck/Struck Plenty (Keya Heyi: Minneconjou/Lakota

Gall (Pizí): Hunkpapa/Lakota

Good Weasel (Hitunkasan Waste)†: Bad Face band/Oglala/Lakota

Gray Earth Tracking/Sounds-the-Ground-When-He-Walks/Noisy Walking (Wahpekute): Santee/ Lakota

High Bear (Sunka Mato): Oglala/Lakota

Hump (Etokeah): Minneconjou/Lakota

Inkpaduta/Red-End-of-Horn (He-inkpa-luta): Santee/Lakota

Iron Thunder (Wakiyan Maza): Minneconjou/ Lakota

Kicking Bear (Mató Wanátake)†: Oyuhpe band/ Oglala/Lakota

Little Killer (Ciqa Wicakte)†: Bad Face band/ Oglala/Lakota

Little Wolf/Little Coyote (Ó'kôhómôxháahketa)#: Northern Cheyenne

Looking Horse†: Minneconjou/Lakota

Low Dog (Sunka Kyciyela)†: Oyuhpe band/Oglala/ Lakota

Makes Room (Kiyukanpi): Minneconjou/Lakota

Morning Star (Vóóhéhéve); Lakota name was Dull Knife (Tamílapéšni)#: Northern Cheyenne

No Flesh: Oglala/Lakota

Red Hawk (Cetan Luta): Minneconjou/Lakota

Shell Boy (Pankeska Hoksila)†: Oyuhpe band/ Oglala/Lakota

Shell Necklace (Pankeska Napin): Oglala/Lakota

Shoot the Bear (Mato Kutepi): Hunkpapa/Lakota

Short Bull (Tataŋka Ptecela)†: Bad Face band/ Oglala/Lakota

Sitting Bull (Tataŋka Iyotaŋka): Hunkpapa/Lakota

Touch the Clouds (Mapíya Ičátagya)#: Minneconjou/ Lakota

White Earth Tracking (Oyemakasan): Santee/ Lakota

White Twin: Bad Face band/Oglala/Lakota

inferred from Lakota oral tradition by Donovin A. Sprague Hump

† inferred from membership in Hokší Hakákta, Last-Born Child Society

Full length studio group portrait of Crow Eagle, Fool Thunder, Slow White Buffalo, and Iron Thunder. Iron Thunder sits in front of the group and holds a peace pipe. Fool Thunder wears feathered headdress and Slow White Buffalo wears fur cap and feathers in hair. *D.F. Barry Cabinet Card, Call Number B-379, courtesy of Denver Public Library Digital Collections*

Red Hawk, (*Cetan Luta*), an Oglala of the Lakota, fought the 1874 Yellowstone Wagon Road and Prospecting Expedition and two years later at the Little Bighorn. *Courtesy of freepages. genealogy.rootsweb.ancestry.com*

Full length studio portrait of Iron Thunder holding peace pipe. *D.F. Barry Cabinet Card, Call Number B-25, courtesy of Denver Public Library Digital Collections,*

Gall in later years. *Courtesy of Smithsonian Institution*

Appendix 2

Frontiersmen from the 1874 Yellowstone Wagon Road and Prospecting Expedition who participated in the Fort Pease Expedition of 1875–76

Tom Allen/William Cable Barkley
Taylor Blevin
Elias "Blacky" Carter
James S. "Old Man" Crain/Crane
Zadok H. "Zed" Daniels
Benjamin R. Dexter
James Edwards (killed July 12, 1875)
A.B. Ford
Neil Gillis
James A. "Jim" Gourley
George S. Herendeen
Fred Hollins/Hoelin/Harlan (killed November 1, 1875)
Tyler McClees
Paul W. McCormick
Duncan McRae
Patrick Sweeney (died of wounds January 6, 1876)
H.M. "Muggins" Taylor
Elisha S. Terrill

Appendix 3

Frontiersmen from the 1874 Yellowstone Wagon Road and Prospecting Expedition who participated in the *Great Sioux War of 1876*

Jack Bean: Chief packer, Col. Gibbon's Montana Column

Henry Bostwick: Scout, Col. Gibbon's Montana Column

Wesley Brockmeyer: Scout, Gen. Terry's Dakota Column (killed August 2, 1876)

Zadok H. "Zed" Daniels: Scout, Col. Gibbon's Montana Column (August 1876)

William T. "Uncle Billy" Hamilton: Scout, Gen. Crook's Wyoming Column (fought at 1876 Battle of the Rosebud and the Battle of Slim Buttes)

Oliver Perry Hanna: Scout, Gen. Crook's Wyoming Column (fought at 1876 Battle of the Rosebud)

George S. Herendeen: Scout, Col. Gibbon's Montana Column, and later for Gen. George Custer's US 7th Cavalry Regiment (fought at Battle of the Little Bighorn)

Paul W. McCormick: Sutler, Col. Gibbon's Montana Column

H.M. "Muggins" Taylor: Scout, Col. Gibbon's Montana Column (rode to Fort Ellis with news of Custer's defeat)

Glossary

Advanced Guard: an element in a moving formation to the front of the main body. The mission of an advance guard is to detect the enemy before the enemy can engage the main body, so the main body has more options to respond to the situation. Generally the advance guard must be within communication range of the main body; in 1874 this meant that usually the advance guard was within visual contact of the main body. A similar force to each flank of the main body is called a **Flank Guard**; one to the rear of the main body is called a **Rear Guard**.

Beginning of morning nautical twilight (BMNT): the time in the morning before sunrise when general outlines of ground objects may be distinguishable. Detailed outdoor operations are not possible and the horizon is indistinct. This time was often when warriors would launch an attack against a stationary enemy.

Bench or benchland: the long, relatively narrow strip of relatively level or gently inclined land that is bounded by a stream or creek and often has distinctly steeper slopes above and below it.

Covered and Concealed: a covered position is one in which the occupant has some level of protection against enemy fire, such as rocks, thick logs, or even a dirt embankment. A concealed position is one that is hidden from enemy view by the use of camouflage, such as cut foliage. A position may provide both cover and concealment or it may just provide one of them.

Covering Fire: shooting at an enemy force to degrade the performance of that force such as causing them to take cover instead of returning fire, or—if they do return fire—it is less accurate. The effects against the enemy are usually only effective for the duration of the covering fire.

Covering fire can often be provided from an **Overwatch** position. Such a position is often higher in elevation, so has direct line of sight into the area that the enemy is expected to be.

Dawn: the first appearance of light in the sky before sunrise, a number of minutes after BMNT.

General Orders: instructions disseminated by the commander of a military, or quasi-military, force that provides standards for important functions to be performed by members of that force. General Orders often address standards to be met while serving as a guard or security force, or concerning departing a formation, use of warming fires, limitations on noise levels. Violations of General Orders can carry significant punishments.

Laager: an encampment protected by a circle of wagons, often with defensive positions outside and outposts farther outside.

Lo: the frontiersman's nickname for an Indian. It came from a poem titled *An Essay on Man*, written by Englishman Alexander Pope in about 1734. The work concerned the social order God had decreed for man:

> Lo, the poor Indian! whose untutored mind
> Sees God in clouds, or hears him in the wind;
> His soul proud Science never taught to stray
> Far as the solar walk or milky way;
> Yet simple nature to his hope has giv'n,
> Behind the cloud-topped hill, an humbler heav'n.

Picket: an individual or individuals placed on a line forward of a position, or outside a position, to warn against an enemy advance, while maintaining a watch. Often pickets are employed in pairs to ensure that one person is always awake.

Bibliography

Archives and Libraries

Bozeman Public Library, Bozeman, Montana
Old Tombstone Records in Gallatin County, Montana Cemeteries 1957 Index.

Denver Public Library, Western History Department
Letter from Tom Allen to Walter M. Camp dated April 23, 1912.
Letter from William C. Barkley to Walter M. Camp dated October 19, 1913.
Letter from Walter M. Camp to William C. Barkley dated January 12, 1914.
Letter from William C. Barkley to Walter M. Camp dated January 20, 1914.

Newberry Research Library, Chicago, Illinois
John S. Gray Research Papers, 1942–1991. Box 16, Folder 136-137, Scouts. Research notes, writings, and correspondence of this Northwestern University physiologist and historian of the American West. Mainly Gray's exhaustive research notes and bibliographies on subjects related to US Indian relations, particularly relating to post Civil War military operations in the West, the fur trade, the Pony Express and other stage lines, and western scouts (including Indian scouts.)

Gallatin County, Montana, Gallatin History Museum Archive
Annotated Manuscript of Jack Bean (14 pages) on the 1874 Yellowstone Wagon Road and Prospecting Expedition, undated, unknown editor.
Manuscript by Jack Bean (11 pages) on the 1874 Yellowstone Wagon Road and Prospecting Expedition, undated.

Manuscript (3 pages) on John Anderson of the 1874 Yellowstone Wagon Road and Prospecting Expedition, written by Nelson Story III, February 23, 1957.
"Thanking the Orator," *Avant Courier* (Bozeman,) April 5, 1883.
Binder entitled "Jack Bean, September 30, 1944—July 1923."

Museum of the Beartooths, Stillwater County, Columbus, Montana
Folder containing loose papers concerning William T. Hamilton.
Folder containing materials related to Jim Annin.

University of Indiana, Lilly Library

Walter Camp Manuscripts
Box 2: Folder 2, Bozeman Expedition of 1874
Box 3: Folder 8, Rosebud, Battle of, 1874
Box 4: Folder 5, Envelope 6—Barkley statement of 1874, gold expedition from Bozeman; odometer on Rosebud River, Sept. 1913; Bozeman expedition, 1874

Montana Historical Society Research Center, Helena, Montana
General Correspondence and Transcripts; Oral History Transcripts, George B. Herendeen Papers, SC 16
General Correspondence and Transcripts; Oral History Transcripts, Charles Avery Reminiscence, SC 372
Montana Pioneers Records, 1884–1956: William H. Babcock, Box 1/Folder 2; Joseph Brown, Box 1/Folder 4; William D. Cameron, Box 1/

Folder 5; Benjamin R. Dexter, Box 2/Folder 3; Hugh Early, Box 2/Folder 7; Robert Henry Evans, Box 2/Folder 8; William T. Hamilton, Box 2/Folder 18; Paul McCormick, Book 3/Folder 4; Archie McDonald, Box 3/Folder 4; William M. Wright, Box 5/Folder 4

Montana State University Library, Special Collections Library, Bozeman, Montana

Collection 561 - Mrs. W.J. Beall Scrapbook, 1867–1929

Collection 1250 - Walter Cooper and Eugene F. Bunker Papers, 1886-1956. Series 2: Box 2A.
Folder 2—Second Big Horn Expedition
Folder 40—Yellowstone Expedition of 1874 (typed transcript of J. V. Bogert)
Folder 41—Yellowstone Expedition of 1874 (typed memorandum of expedition)
Folder 42—Yellowstone Expedition of 1874-1 (handwritten summary by Walter Cooper)
Folder 43—Yellowstone Expedition of 1874-2 (handwritten summary by Walter Cooper)
Folder 44—Yellowstone Expedition of 1874-3 (handwritten summary by Walter Cooper)
Folder 46—Yellowstone Wagon Road

Collection 1407 - Lester S. Willson Family Papers, 1861–1922. Series 5: Photographs, 1865–1910: Box 1
Folder 13—Photo 1 Lester S. Willson 1865
Folder 14—Tuller & Rich Cash Store Bozeman 1866

National Archives and Records Administration (NARA); Washington, DC

Records of the Geological and Geographical Survey of the Territories ("Hayden Survey",) Record Group 57. Letters Received 1867-79. Reproduced as National Archives Microfilm Publication M623; Barlow, John W., to F. V. Hayden. June 3, June 17, November 9, 1871; January 13, January 17, 1872 (M623, roll 2, frames 117-8, 129-30, 170-1, 293-4, 299-300)
National Archives Record Group 77, Map attributed to J. W. Barlow, Rds 108, Roll 1, N.P.R.R. survey in 1872 along the Yellowstone and

Mussell Shell Rivers: Route of party under G.A. Hayden. Escort commanded by Col. E. M. Baker.
Record of Appointment of Postmasters, 1832-Sept. 30, 1971; Roll #: 75, 676; Archive Publication #: M841.

University of Oklahoma Library and Archives

Letter from James S. Hutchins to Dr. Walter S. Campbell dated September 12, 1956, and letter from Dr. Walter S. Campbell to James S. Hutchins, dated September 18, 1956, Western History Collections, University of Oklahoma, Norman, Oklahoma, as found in http://digital.libraries.ou.edu/whc/nam/manuscripts/Campbell_WS_109_3.pdf
Letter from James S. Hutchins to Dr. Walter S. Campbell dated October 4, 1956, Western History Collections, University of Oklahoma, Norman, Oklahoma, as found in
http://digital.libraries.ou.edu/utils/getfile/collection/CampbellWS/id/5792/filename/5774.pdfpage/page/75
Letter from James S. Hutchins to Dr. Walter S. Campbell dated October 27, 1956, Western History Collections, University of Oklahoma, Norman, Oklahoma, as found in http://digital.libraries.ou.edu/utils/getfile/collection/CampbellWS/id/5792/filename/5774.pdfpage/page/77
Statement from Spotted Bear of the Hunkpapa made to Judge Frank B. Zahn, Fort Yates, North Dakota, in October, 1956, as found in http://digital.libraries.ou.edu/utils/getfile/collection/CampbellWS/id/5792/filename/5774.pdfpage/page/81
Statement from Stands-With-Horns-In-Sight made to Judge Frank B. Zahn, Fort Yates, North Dakota, in October, 1956, as found in http://digital.libraries.ou.edu/utils/getfile/collection/CampbellWS/id/5792/filename/5774.pdfpage/page/82

Genealogy Archives of Patricia Adkins-Rochette, Duncan, Oklahoma

Personnel Rosters for Members of Colonel James G. Bourland's Texas Border Cavalry, a unit that was also called; Bourland's Confederate

Border Regiment; Border Regiment; and Bourland's Regiment, Texas Cavalry

Books and Articles

Annin, Jim. *Horace Countryman—Unsung Hero*, Self-published.

Bailey, John W. *Pacifying the Plains: General Alfred Terry and the Decline of the Sioux, 1866–1890*. Westport, Connecticut: Greenwood Press, 1979.

Barnes, Frank C. *Cartridges of the World*, 9th Edition, Iola. Wisconsin: Krause Publications, 2000.

Beck, Paul N. *Inkpaduta: Dakota Leader*. Norman, Oklahoma: University of Oklahoma Press, 2008.

Birkby, Jeff. *Touring Montana and Wyoming Hot Springs*. Guilford, Connecticut: Morris Book Publishing, 1999.

Bradley, James H. "Bradley Manuscript," *Contributions to the Historical Society of Montana, Volume Eight*. Helena, Montana: Montana Historical and Miscellaneous Library, 1917.

Bradley, James H. "Journal of James H. Bradley, The Sioux Campaign of 1876 under the command of General John Gibbon," *Contributions to the Historical Society of Montana, Volume Two*. Helena, Montana: Montana Historical and Miscellaneous Library, 1896.

Bray, Kingsley M. *Crazy Horse: A Lakota Life*. Norman, Oklahoma: University of Oklahoma Press, 2006.

Brown, Jesse, and A. M. Willard. *The Black Hills Trails: A History of the Struggles of the Pioneers in the Winning of the Black Hills*, edited by John T. Milek. Rapid City, South Dakota: Rapid City Journal Company, 1924.

Brown, M. H. *The Plainsmen of the Yellowstone: A History of the Yellowstone Basin*. Lincoln, Nebraska: Bison Books, University of Nebraska Press, 1969.

Carroll, Matthew. "Diary of Matthew Carroll, Master in Charge of Transportation for Colonel John Gibbon's Expedition," *Contributions to the Historical Society of Montana, Volume Two*. Helena, Montana: Montana Historical and Miscellaneous Library, 1896.

Carter, Charles Hanna (editor.) *An Oldtimer's Story of the Old Wild West; The Recollections of Oliver Perry Hanna, Pioneer, Indian Fighter, Frontiersman and First Settler in Sheridan County, Wyoming*, compiled June 1926.

Casemore, Robert. "Muggins Taylor: The Man and the Myth," in *The Way West: True Stories of the American Frontier*, edited by James A. Crutchfield. New York: Forge, 2005.

Clark, A. H. *California Clippers of 1853, The clipper ship era; An epitome of famous American and British clipper ships, their owners, builders, commanders and crews, 1843-1869*. New York: G.P. Putnam's Sons, 1912.

Cooper, Walter. *A Most Desperate Situation*, edited by Rick Newby. Helena, Montana: Falcon Publishing, 2000.

Cross, Walt. *Custer's Lost Officer: The Search for Lieutenant Henry Moore Harrington, 7th Cavalry*. Stillwater, Oklahoma: Cross Publications, 2006.

De Barthe, Joe. *Life and Adventures of Frank Grouard, Chief of Scouts, U.S.A.* St. Joseph, Missouri: Combe Printing Company, 1894.

Dimsdale, Thomas J. *The Vigilantes of Montana*. Norman Oklahoma: University of Oklahoma Press 1953.

Dorsey, R. Stephen. *Guns of the Western Indian War*. Eugene, Oregon: Collectors' Library, 1995.

Drury, Bob, and Tom Clavin. *The Heart of Everything That Is: The Untold Story of Red Cloud, An American Legend*. New York: Simon & Schuster, 2013.

Favour, Alpheus H. *Old Bill Williams Mountain Man*. Norman, Oklahoma: University of Oklahoma Press, 1962.

Fifer, Barbara. *Montana Battlefields, 1806-1877: Native Americans and the U.S. Army at War*. Helena, Montana: Farcountry Press, 2005.

Garavaglia, Louis A., and Charles G. Worman. *Firearms of the American West, 1866-1894*. Niwot, Colorado: University Press of Colorado, 1985.

Gilbert, Miles, Leo Remiger, and Sharon Cunningham. *Encyclopedia of Buffalo Hunters and Skinners, Volume 1—A-D*. Union City, Tennessee, 2003.

Gilbert, Miles, Leo Remiger, and Sharon Cunningham. *Encyclopedia of Buffalo Hunters and Skinners, Volume 2—E-K.* Union City, Tennessee, 2006.

Gilbert, Miles. *Getting a Stand.* Union City, Tennessee: Pioneer Press, 2001.

Graham, Colonel W. A. *The Custer Myth: A Source Book of Custeriana.* Mechanicsburg, Pennsylvania: Stackpole Books, 2000.

Gray, John S. *Centennial Campaign: The Sioux War of 1876.* Fort Collins, Colorado: The Old Army Press, 1976.

Gray, John S. *Custer's Last Campaign: Mitch Boyer and the Little Bighorn Reconstructed.* Lincoln, Nebraska: University of Nebraska Press, 1991.

Greene, Jerome A. *Battles and Skirmishes of the Great Sioux War, 1876-1877: The Military View.* Norman, Oklahoma: University of Oklahoma Press, 1993.

Greene, Jerome A. *Lakota and Cheyenne: Indian Views of the Great Sioux War, 1876-1877.* Norman, Oklahoma: University of Oklahoma Press, 1994.

Greene, Jerome A. *Nez Perce Summer 1877: The U.S. Army and Nee-Me-Poo Crisis.* Helena, Montana: Montana Historical Society Press, 2001.

Hamilton, William T. *My Sixty Years on the Plains: Trapping, Trading and Indian Fighting.* New York: Forest and Stream Publishing Company, 1905.

Hammer, Kenneth. *Custer in '76: Walter Camp's Notes on the Custer Fight.* Provo, UT: Brigham Young University, 1976.

Hardorff, Richard G. *Hokahey! A Good Day to Die; The Indian Casualties of the Custer Fight.* London: Bison Publishing, 1999.

Hardorff, Richard G. *Indian Views of the Custer Fight.* Norman, Oklahoma: University of Oklahoma Press, 2005.

Hardorff, Richard G. *Lakota Recollections of the Custer Fight.* Lincoln, Nebraska: University of Nebraska Press, 1997.

Hardorff, Richard G., ed. *On the Little Bighorn with Walter Camp; A Collection of Walter Mason Camp's Letters, Notes and opinions on Custer's Last Fight.* El Segundo, California: Upton & Sons Publishers, 2002.

Hazlett, James C., Edwin Olmstead, and M. Hume Parks. *Field Artillery Weapons of the American Civil War*, rev. ed. Urbana: University of Illinois Press, 1983.

Hedren, Paul L., ed. *The Great Sioux War 1876-77.* Helena, Montana: Montana Historical Society Press, 1991.

Hedren, Paul L. *Traveler's Guide to the Great Sioux War: The Battlefields, Forts and Related Sites of America's Greatest Indian War.* Helena, Montana: Montana Historical Society Press, 1996.

Hidy, Ralph W. et al. *The Great Northern Railway: A History.* Minneapolis, Minnesota: University of Minnesota Press, 2004.

Holmes, Krys. *Montana: Stories of the Land.* Helena, Montana: Montana Historical Society Press, 2008.

Hook, Richard. *U.S. Army Frontier Scouts 1840—1921,* Osprey Elite 91. Oxford, Great Britain: Osprey Publishing, 2003.

Howell, Kenneth Wayne. *The Seventh Star of the Confederacy: Texas during the Civil War.* Denton, Texas: University of North Texas Press, 2009.

An Illustrated History of the Yellowstone Valley. Spokane, Washington: Western Historical Publishing Company, 1907.

Johansen, Bruce E., and Donald A. Grinde Jr. *The Encyclopedia of Native American Biography.* New York: Henry Holt and Company, 1997.

Kappler, Charles J. *Indian Affairs: Laws and Treaties, Volume II, Treaties.* Washington, DC: Government Printing Office, 1904.

Leeson, Michael A., ed. *History of Montana, 1739-1885.* Chicago: Warner, Beers & Company, 1885.

MacLean, French L. *Custer's Best: The Story of Company M, 7th Cavalry at the Little Bighorn.* Atglen, Pennsylvania: Schiffer Publishing, 2011.

Markham, George. *Guns of the Wild West: Firearms of the American Frontier 1849-1917.* London: Arms & Armour Press, 1991.

Marquis, Thomas, ed, and trans. *A Warrior Who Fought Custer.* Minneapolis, MN: The Midwest Company, 1931.

McChristian, Douglas C. *The U.S. Army in the West 1870-1880.* Norman, Oklahoma, University of Oklahoma Press, 1995.

McPherren, Ida. *Imprints on Pioneer Trails.* Boston: Christopher Publishing House, 1950.

Michno, Gregory F. *Encyclopedia of Indian Wars: Western Battles and Skirmishes 1850-1890.* Missoula, Montana: Mountain Press Publishing Company, 2003.

Michno, Gregory F. *Lakota Noon: The Indian Narrative of Custer's Defeat.* Missoula, Montana: Mountain Press Publishing, 2007.

Michno, Gregory. *The Settler's War: The Struggle for the Texas Frontier in the 1860s.* Caldwell, Idaho: Caxton Press, 2011.

Miller, Joachim. *Illustrated History of the State of Montana.* Chicago: The Lewis Publishing Company, 1894.

Monnett, John M. *Where a Hundred Soldiers Were Killed: The Struggle for the Powder River Country in 1866 and the Making of the Fetterman Myth.* Albuquerque, New Mexico: University of New Mexico Press, 2008.

Montana Hyalite Chapter Daughters of the American Revolution, "Old Tombstone Records in Gallatin County, Montana Cemeteries," 1957 as found at http://files.usgwarchives.net/mt/gallatin/cemetery/sunsethills.txt

Nichols, Ronald Hamilton. *In Custer's Shadow: Major Marcus Reno.* Norman, Oklahoma: University of Oklahoma Press, 2000.

Nichols, Ronald Hamilton, ed. *Reno Court of Inquiry Proceedings of a Court of Inquiry in the Case of Major Marcus A. Reno, Concerning His Conduct at the Battle of the Little Big Horn River on June 25-26, 1876.* Hardin, Montana: Custer Battlefield Historical and Museum Association, 2007.

Noyes, Alva Josiah. *In the Land of Chinook; or, the Story of Blaine County.* Helena, Montana: State publishing company, 1917.

Olson, James C. *Red Cloud and the Sioux Problem.* Lincoln, Nebraska: University of Nebraska Press, 1965.

Powell, William H., Lt. Col., US Army, ed. *Officers of the Army and Navy (Volunteer) Who Served in the Civil War.* Philadelphia, Pennsylvania: L.R. Hamersly and Co., 1893.

Prodgers, Jeanette. *The Champion Buffalo Hunter: The Frontier Memoirs of Yellowstone Vic Smith.* Guilford, Connecticut: The Global Pequot Press, 2009.

Progressive Men of the State of Montana, Part 2. Chicago, Illinois: A. W. Bowen and Company, 1901.

Quivey, Addison M. "The Yellowstone Expedition of 1874," *Contributions to the Historical Society of Montana, Volume One.* Helena, Montana: Rocky Mountain Publishing Company, 1876.

Register of Graduates, and Former Cadets of the United States Military Academy, West Point, New York. West Point, New York: Association of Graduates, 2000.

Reid, Whitelaw. *History of Ohio during the War, Her Statesmen, Generals and Soldiers, Volume 1: The History of Ohio during the War and the Lives of Her Generals.* Cincinnati, Ohio: The Robert Clarke Company, 1895.

Rosa, Joseph G. *Guns of the American West.* New York: Crown Publishers, 1985.

Rosen, Reverend Peter. *Pa-Ha-Sa-Pah, or the Black Hills of South Dakota.* St. Louis, Missouri, Nixon-Jones Printing, 1895.

Sanders, James U., ed. *Society of Montana Pioneers, Constitution, Members, and Officers, with Portraits and Maps, Volume 1—Register.* Helena, Montana: Society of Montana Pioneers, 1899.

Sandoz, Mari. *The Buffalo Hunters: The Story of the Hide Men.* Second Edition, Lincoln, Nebraska: University of Nebraska Press, 2008.

Sellers, Frank. *Sharps Firearms.* Maricopa, Arizona: Karen S. Sellers, 2011.

Slatta, Richard W. *The Mythical West: An Encyclopedia of Legend: Lore and Popular Culture.* Santa Barbara, California: ABC-CLIO Inc., 2001.

Smalley, Eugene Virgil. *History of the Northern Pacific Railway.* New York: G. P. Putnam's Sons, 1883.

Smith, Phyllis. *Bozeman and the Gallatin Valley: A History.* Guilford, Connecticut: Twodot Publications, 2002.

Sprague, Donovin Arleigh. *Images of America: Cheyenne River Sioux.* Charleston, South Carolina: Arcadia Publishing, 2003.

Sprague, Donovin Arleigh. *Images of America: Standing Rock Sioux.* Charleston, South Carolina: Arcadia Publishing, 2004.

Stout, Tom, ed. *Montana: Its Story and Biography, Volume 3.* Chicago: The American Historical Society, 1921.

Sunderland, Glenn W. *Lightning at Hoover's Gap*. New York: Thomas Yoseloff, 1969.

Thompson, Francis M. *A Tenderfoot in Montana: Reminiscences of the Gold Rush, the Vigilantes, and the Birth of the Montana Territory*. Helena, Montana: Montana Historical Society, 2004.

Thompson, Neil Baird. *Crazy Horse Called Them Walk-A-Heaps*. Saint Cloud, Minnesota: North Star Press, 1979.

Topping, Eugene Sayre. *The Chronicles of the Yellowstone*. Minneapolis, Minnesota: Ross & Haines, INC., 1968. Eugene S. Topping did not take part in the expedition, but did interview Addison M. Quivey, James Gourley, and others.

Utley, Robert Marshall. *The Lance and the Shield: The Life and Times of Sitting Bull*. New York: The Random House Publishing Group (Ballantine Book,) 1993.

Utley, Robert M. *Lone Star Justice: The First Century of The Texas Rangers*. New York: Oxford University Press, 2002.

Utley, Robert. *Sitting Bull: The Life and Times of an American Patriot*. New York: Holt Paperbacks, 2008.

Van Nuys, Maxwell. *Inkpaduta—The Scarlet Point: Terror of the Dakota Frontier and Secret Hero of the Sioux*. Denver, Colorado: Maxwell Van Nuys, 1998.

Van West, Carroll. *Capitalism on the Frontier: Billings and the Yellowstone Valley in the Nineteenth Century*. Lincoln, Nebraska: University of Nebraska Press, 1993.

Venturino, Mike. *Shooting Buffalo Rifles of the Old West*. Livingston, Montana: MLV Enterprises, 2002.

Vestal, Stanley. *Sitting Bull, Champion of the Sioux: A Biography*. Norman, Oklahoma: University of Oklahoma Press, 1989.

Walker Jr., Dr. L.G. *Dr. Henry R. Porter: The Surgeon Who Survived Little Bighorn*. Jefferson, North Carolina: McFarland & Company, 2008.

Walstrom, Cleve. *Search for the Lost Trail of Crazy Horse*. Crete, Nebraska: Dageforde Publishing, 2003.

Walter, Dave, et al. *Speaking Ill of the Dead: Jerks in Montana History*. Guilford, Connecticut: Morris Book Publishing, 2011.

Walter, John. *The Guns That Won the West: Firearms on the American Frontier, 1848-1898*. London: Greenhill Books, 2006.

Watry, Elizabeth A., and Robert V. Gross. *Livingston*, Images of America Series. Charleston, South Carolina: Arcadia Publishing, 2009.

Weibert, Don L. *Buckskin, Buffalo Robes & Black Powder: Fifty Years in the Old West*. San Jose, California: John L. Bean Publishing, 1997.

Weibert, Don L. *The 1874 Invasion of Montana: A Prelude to the Custer Disaster*. Self-Published: D. L. Weibert, 1993.

Whittlesey, Lee H. *Gateway to Yellowstone: The Raucous Town of Cinnabar on the Montana Frontier*. Guilford, Connecticut: Twodot Publishing, 2015.

Willert, James. *After Little Bighorn: 1876 Campaign Rosters*. La Mirada, California: James Willert, 1985.

Wingerd, Mary Lethert. *North Country: The Making of Minnesota*. Minneapolis, Minnesota: University of Minnesota Press, 2009.

Historical Site Informational Pamphlets

Fort Phil Kearny State Historic Site

Interviews and Discussions

Telephone discussions with Patricia Adkins-Rochette, historian and author of *Bourland in North Texas and Indian Territory during the Civil War: Fort Cobb, Fort Arbuckle & The Wichita Mountains*, 2015.

Telephone discussion with Mr. John Bean, grandson of Jack Bean, July 30, 2013, and August 11, 2013. John was born in March 1923, some four months before his grandfather died. An experienced firearms expert himself, John served as a flight engineer/top turret gunner on a B-25 Mitchell in the 7th Air Force in the Pacific theater. On one mission to bomb Eniwetok, his B-25 was severely damaged by enemy ground machine-gun fire. After dropping their bomb load, the crew nursed the plane back to base, jettisoning machine-guns and other weighty equipment, as one of the two engines was inoperative. The captain told the crew to bail out over the landing field, which two did. John remained with the aircraft, occupying the co-pilot seat. The ensuing belly landing was the "longest ride of my life."

Email discussion with Professor Paul N. Beck, author of *Inkpaduta: Dakota Leader*, August 23, 2013.

Telephone discussions with Steve Florman, great-great-grandson of William Officer, June 2015. Included in these were excerpts from "Happenings and Remembrances of the Officer Family, as Written and Told by Guy C. Officer," September 1964 (Transcribed by Karen Officer Dean, 1971.) Guy Officer, born in 1891, was the son of William Officer.

Telephone discussion with Dr. Richard J. Labowski, September 3, 2013. Dr. Labowski is the current owner of the surviving production and shipment records for the Sharps Rifle Manufacturing Company/Sharps Rifle Company.

Multiple telephone discussions and emails with Dorman Nelson, noted researcher of "Liver-Eatin" Johnson, Los Angeles, California, June-July 2015.

Multiple discussions and emails with Rachel Phillips, Research Coordinator, Gallatin History Museum, Bozeman, Montana, 2014–2015.

Multiple discussions with Wes Pietsch, noted American West gun collector, 2015.

Discussion with Penny Redli, executive director of the Museum of the Beartooths in Columbus, Montana, June 2015.

Multiple discussions with Donovin A. Sprague Hump of Black Hills State University, in Rapid City, South Dakota, June 2015. Donovin is the great-great-grandson of Hump the younger and is also related to Crazy Horse.

Multiple discussions with Mike Parr on the Yates family, March 2016.

Multi-Media Productions

"Fort Laramie Treaty, 1868," Archives of the West, Episode Four (1856 to 1868,) PBS, as found at http://www.pbs.org/weta/thewest/resources/archives/four/

Newspapers and Magazines

"Addison M. Quivey," *The Billings Gazette* (Billings, Montana,) 13 July 1895.

Adler, Dennis, "Top 12 Western Classics," Guns of the Old West, Fall 2014, New York: Harris Publications.

"Another Pioneer Called by Death," *The Livingston Enterprise*, Livingston, Montana, December 6, 1921.

Belkin, M. "Wound Ballistics," *Progress in Surgery*, Issue 16, Basel, Switzerland and New York, 1978.

"Ben Dexter Dead," *Fergus County Argus*, Lewiston, Fergus County, Montana, November 8, 1907.

Benoit, Zach. "YelCo 52: 'Born by the River and killed by the Railroad,'" *Billings Gazette*, September 13, 2014.

"Boot Hill—silent reminder of a rough past," *The Billings Gazette* (Billings, Montana,) 1 July 1973.

Brown, Mabel Nair. "The Tragedy of Milton Lott," *The Ogden Reporter* (Ogden, Iowa,) July 8, 1970.

Bunch, Joey. "Downfall of Colorado's Jack Slade: Bottle did what the outlaw's shotgun could not," *Denver Post*, August 20, 2012.

"Con Smith Dies at Boulder Home; Pioneer of State," *The Helena Independent*, Helena, Montana, June 24, 1925.

"Death of A. M. Quivey," *Avant Courier* (Bozeman, Montana,) 13 July 1895.

"Death of Hugo J. Hoppe," *The Livingston Enterprise*, Livingston, Montana, September 14, 1895.

DeHaas, John N. and Bernice W. "Footlights and Fire Engines," *Montana: The Magazine of Western History*, Volume XVII, Number 4.

"The Eastern Montana Expedition," *Avant Courier* (Bozeman,) March 27, 1874.

"The Expedition!" *Avant Courier*—Extra (Bozeman,) May 1, 1874.

"The Expedition Moving to the Front," *Avant Courier* (Bozeman,) February 6, 1874.

"Expeditions to Yellowstone," *Avant Courier* (Bozeman,) January 9, 1874.

"Exploits of 'Uncle Billy' Hamilton in Yellowstone Country Like Fiction," *Billings Gazette* (Billings, Montana,) June 30, 1927.

Fode, Mark. "Inkpaduta's bloody path in 1856 went through quarries," *The Pipestone County Star*, April 10, 1997.

Foster, John R. "Kendall: Twentieth Century Ghost Town," *Montana; The Magazine of Western History*, Volume XXIV, Number 2.

"From the Expedition!" *Avant Courier* (Bozeman,) May 1, 1874.

"Founder of Famous Stage Station of 'Seventies Recalls Picturesque Characters of Early Days," *Billings Gazette* (Billings, Montana,) June 30, 1927.

"From the Yellowstone Expedition," *Avant Courier* (Bozeman,) February 27, 1874.

"From the Expedition," *Avant Courier* (Bozeman,) March 6, 1874.

Heidenreich, C. Adrian. "The Crow Indian Delegation to Washington, D.C., in 1880," *Montana: The Magazine of Western History*, Volume XXXI, Number 2, Spring 1981.

Heinz, Ralph A. "Montana Sharps," *Man at Arms: The Magazine of Arms Collecting-Investing*, Volume 3, Number 6, November/December 1981, St. Providence, Rhode Island: Mowbray Company.

Hergett, Rachel. "Mixed-race pioneer has place in Bozeman history," *Bozeman Daily Chronicle* (Bozeman, Montana,) 21 February 2010.

Hutchins, James S. "Poison in the Pemmican: The Yellowstone Wagon-Road & Prospecting Expedition of 1874," *Montana: The Magazine of Western History*, Volume 8, Number 3, Summer 1958.

Lincoln, Marga. "History in the Baking: Savor Montana's early recipes with 'A Taste of the Past' presentation," *Independent Record* (Helena, Montana,) March 24, 2013.

"Improvement and Opening of New Roads," *Avant Courier* (Bozeman,) December 12, 1873.

"Improvement of the Yellowstone," *Avant Courier* (Bozeman,) November 21, 1873.

"John Anderson, Who Broke Sitting Bull's Heart," *The Angelica Advocate*, Angelica, New York, 1918, as found at http://fultonhistory.com/ Newspapers%2021/Angelica%20NY%20 Advocate/Angelica%20NY%20Advocate%20 1915-1919/Angelica%20NY%20Advocate%20 1915-1919%20-%200072.pdf

Keith, Elmer. "The 'Big Fifty' Sharps," *The American Rifleman*, Volume 88, Number 6, June 1940, published by the National Rifle Association of America, as found in http://www.americanrifleman. org/article.php?id=14150&cat=3&sub=0&q=1

Lampi, Leona. "Red Lodge: From a Frenetic Past of Crows, Coal and Boom and Bust Emerges a Unique Festival of Diverse Nationality Groups," *Montana: The Magazine of Western History*, Volume XI, Number 3, Summer 1961.

"LOST 'CABIN' GOLD MINE AGAIN LOCATED.; Discovery of the Fabulously Rich Mine Causes a Stampede – Wyoming Town Almost Deserted on Account of the Find," *New York Times*, August 18, 1902.

Marquis, Dr. Thomas B. "Bozeman Men Located Highway, Sought Gold and Fought Indians on Yellowstone in '74," *The Billings Gazette* (Billings, Montana,) February 10, 1935.

McGillycuddy, V. T. "Narrative of the life of Crazy Horse," *Nebraska History Magazine*, Volume 19, Lincoln, Nebraska: Nebraska State Historical Society, 1929.

McLemore, Clyde. "Fort Pease: The First Attempted Settlement in Yellowstone Valley," *The Montana Magazine of History,* Volume 2, Number 1 (January 1952,) Helena, Montana: Montana Historical Society, 1952.

"Meets an Untimely Death," *Billings Gazette*, February 12, 1891.

Moore, Bob. "Buffalo Bill Cody's Cinnabar Cowboys," *The Montana Pioneer*, Livingston, Montana: Montana Pioneer Publishing, March 2008.

"Muggins Taylor First Officer to Lose Life in Maintaining Order," *Billings Gazette* (Billings, Montana,) June 30, 1927.

"Nine Big Horn Survivors Clasp Hands in Bozeman," *The Weekly Courier* (Bozeman, Montana,) August 12, 1914.

O'Malley, M. G. "Thrilling Frontier Experiences in Montana," *Montana Standard*, Butte, Montana, September 7, 1942.

O'Malley, M. G. "Thrilling Frontier Experiences in Montana," Part 2, *Montana Standard*, Butte, Montana, October 4, 1942.

Parker, Richard and Emily Boyd. "The Great Hanging at Gainesville," *New York Times* (Opinion Pages,) October 16, 2012.

Perrottet, Tony. "Little Bighorn Reborn," *Smithsonian Magazine*, April 2005, Washington, D.C.

Peterson, Larry Len, editor, "The Footrace: From the Frontier Adventures of Walter Cooper," *Montana: The Magazine of Western History*, Volume 50, Number 2.

"Pioneer Dies," *The Helena Independent*, Helena, Montana, February 16, 1919.

"Pioneer Succumbs," *The Billings Daily Gazette*, Billings, Montana, May 26, 1908.

"Raymond Brady, Sr.," *Billings Gazette*, June 2, 2010.

"Report of the Executive Committee of the Yellowstone Wagon Road & Prospecting Expedition," *Avant Courier* (Bozeman,) February 6, 1874.

"Report of the Executive Committee of the Yellowstone Wagon Road & Prospecting Expedition," *Avant Courier* (Bozeman,) February 20, 1874.

"Reports of Receipts and Expenditures of Gallatin County, Montana, from March 1, 1873 to March 1, 1874," *Avant Courier* (Bozeman,) March 20, 1874.

Schontzler, Gail. "Bozeman's wild West days captured in diaries of pioneer Peter Koch," *Bozeman Daily Chronicle*, Bozeman, Montana, July 27, 2010.

Schontzler, Gail. "A mix of old and new at Malmborg," *Bozeman Daily Chronicle*, Bozeman, Montana, May 23, 1998.

Schontzler, Gail. "Street names keep Bozeman's colorful history alive," *Bozeman Daily Chronicle*, Bozeman, Montana, October 2, 2011.

Scott, Kim Allen. "The Willson Brothers Come to Montana," *Montana: The Magazine of Western History*, Volume 49, Number 1.

Stewart, Edgar I. "Major Brisbin's Relief of Fort Pease: A prelude to the bloody Little Big Horn Massacre," *Montana: The Magazine of Western History*, Volume VI, Number 3, Summer 1956.

"The Story of a March," *The Northwest Illustrated Monthly Magazine*, St. Paul, Minnesota, Volume VII—No. 8, August 1890.

"Ten Thousand Rounds of Ammunition," *The Montanian* (Virginia City,) January 16, 1874.

"The Yellowstone Expedition," *The Montanian* (Virginia City,) May 7, 1874.

"Uncle Joe Brown, Pioneer Miner and Everybody's Friend, Passes Away," *The Daily Enterprise*, Livingston, Montana, July 5, 1913.

"Yellowstone Expedition," *Avant Courier* (Bozeman,) February 20, 1874.

"Yellowstone Expedition," *Avant Courier* (Bozeman,) March 13, 1874.

"Yellowstone Expedition," *Avant Courier* (Bozeman,) March 20, 1874.

"Yellowstone Expedition," *Avant Courier* (Bozeman,) April 3, 1874.

"Yellowstone Expedition," *Avant Courier* (Bozeman,) April 17, 1874.

"Yellowstone Expedition," *Avant Courier* (Bozeman,) April 24, 1874.

"Yellowstone Expedition," *Avant Courier* (Bozeman,) May 8, 1874.

"Yellowstone Expedition," *Avant Courier* (Bozeman,) May 15, 1874.

"Yellowstone Expedition," *Avant Courier* (Bozeman,) May 22, 1874.

"Yellowstone Expedition," *Avant Courier* (Bozeman,) June 12, 1874.

"Yellowstone Wagon Road," *Avant Courier* (Bozeman,) January 16, 1874.

"Yellowstone Wagon Road and Prospecting Expedition," *Avant Courier* (Bozeman,) January 23, 1874.

Primary Source Documents found on *Ancestry.com*

1850 United States Census for Fulton County, Arkansas.

1850 United States Census for Switzerland County, Indiana.

1850 United States Census for Andrew County, Missouri.

1850 United States Census for Erie County, Pennsylvania.

1850 United States Census for St. Lawrence County, New York.

1860 United States Census for Noble County, Indiana.

1860 United States Census for Switzerland County, Indiana.

1860 United States Census for Scott County, Kentucky.

1860 United States Census for Dakota County, Minnesota.

1860 United States Census for Andrew County, Missouri.

1860 United States Census for Saratoga County, New York.

1860 United States Census for Geauga County, Ohio.

1870 United States Census for Macomb County, Michigan.

1870 United States Census for Deer Lodge County, Montana Territory.

1870 United States Census for Gallatin County, Montana Territory.

1870 United States Census for Jefferson County, Montana Territory.

1870 United States Census for Lewis and Clark County, Montana Territory.

1870 United States Census for Meagher County, Montana Territory.

1870 United States Census for Missoula County, Montana Territory.

1870 United States Census for Humboldt County, Nevada.

1880 United States Census for Pima County, Arizona Territory.

1880 United States Census for Tehama County, California.

1880 United States Census for Lawrence County, Dakota Territory.

1880 United States Census for Kingman County, Iowa.

1880 United States Census for Dawson County, Montana Territory.

1880 United States Census for Deer Lodge County, Montana, Territory.

1880 United States Census for Gallatin County, Montana Territory.

1880 United States Census for Madison County, Montana Territory.

1880 United States Census for Meagher County, Montana Territory.

1880 United States Census for Niagara County, New York.

1880 United States Census for Albany County, Wyoming Territory.

1900 United States Census for Trinity County, California.

1900 United States Census for Beaverhead County, Montana.

1900 United States Census for Fergus County, Montana.

1900 United States Census for Gallatin County, Montana.

1900 United States Census for Helena City, Montana.

1900 United States Census for Lawrence County, South Dakota.

1900 United States Census for Niagara County, New York.

1900 United States Census for Park County, Montana.

1900 United States Census for Silver Bow County, Montana.

1910 United States Census for Deer Lodge County, Montana.

1910 United States Census for Gallatin County, Montana.

1910 United States Census for Madison County, Montana.

1910 United States Census for Silver Bow County, Montana.

1910 United States Census for Spokane County, Washington.

1910 US Census for Portage County, Ohio.

1920 United States Census for Deer Lodge County, Montana.

1920 United States Census for Gallatin County, Montana.

1920 United States Census for Butte County, South Dakota.

1852 California State Census for Placer County.

1855 New York State Census for Saratoga County.

1865 New York State Census for Richmond County.

1875 New York State Census for Niagara County.

1905 New York State Census for Saratoga County.

Interment Form (QMC Form No. 14) for Interment in the Custer Battlefield National Cemetery for BARKLEY, William, dated January 5, 1932, signed by Victor A. Bolsius.

Montana County Marriages, 1865-1950, RICH-ARDSON, Herbert F.; WILLSON, Henry A.

Montana Death Index, 1868-2011, AVERY, Charles E.; BUCHANAN, William; FERGUSON, Enoch D.; GIBSON, George; MCDONALD, Archibald; MCDUFF, William.

California Death Index, 1905-1939, Anderson, John.

US Civil War Pension Index Card, BARKLEY, William; DILLABAUGH, John H.

US Civil War Pension Index Card, CAMERON, William D.

US Army Record of Enlistments, 1798–1914, Volume 1816-1862, A-G, ASHMEAD, Henry.

Helena, Montana, 1879 City Directory.

Websites

Ancestry at www.Ancestry.com

Astonisher.com by Bruce Brown at: http://www.astonisher.com/archives/museum/horn_chips_crazy_horse2.html.

Bourland in North Texas and Indian Territory during the Civil War at: www.bourlandcivilwar.com.

Bushnell Optics at: www.bushnell.com.

Fold3.com by Ancestry

Friends of the Little Bighorn, The Next Generation in the Study of Custer's Last Stand, page Custer's Last Fight: Remembered by Participants at the Tenth Anniversary June 25, 1886 and the Fiftieth Anniversary June 25, 1926 at: http://www.friendslittlebighorn.com/upton50anniversary.htm.

Hecla Consolidated Mining Company, Welcome to Glendale, Montana at: http://www.glendalemontana.com/, and http://glendalemt.com/Biographies/Dillabaugh_John.htm.

John Liver-Eating Johnston at: www.johnlivereatingjohnston.com/home.

Mocavo Genealogy: 1873 Official Register of the United States at: http://www.mocavo.com/Official-Register-of-the-United-States-1873/228899/347.

The original printed version of this document was titled Official Register of the United States of Officers and Agents, Civil, Military, and Naval, in the Service of the United States on the Thirtieth of September 1873.

Montana Cadastral program, Montana State Government at:

http://svc.mt.gov/msl/mtcadastral/.

Montana Vintage Arms at: www.montanavintagearms.com.

National Park Service, The Civil War, Soldiers and Sailors Database at: http://www.nps.gov/civilwar/soldiers-and-sailors-database.htm.

The New Buffalo Soldiers at: http://www.abuffalosoldier.com/slang.htm.

PBS New Perspectives on The West at: http://www.pbs.org/weta/thewest/resources/archives/eight/sbarrest.htm.

C. Sharps Arms Inc. at:

http://csharpsarms.com/famoussharps-article/16/Hanna-and-White.html.

Shiloh Sharps at: www.shilohrifle.com.

Worth County, Missouri, Genealogy and History at: http://www.predinkle.com.

Yellowstone Gateway Museum of Park County, The Bill and Doris Whithorn Collection Online Database at: http://yellowstone.pastperfect-online.com.

Index

1874 Expedition Members

Civil War Army Personalities

Lakota and Northern Cheyenne Warrior Participants in 1874 Fighting

Warriors Not Present in 1874

Montana Territory Personalities